A Practical Guide to Hybrid
Natural Language Processing

Jose Manuel Gomez-Perez • Ronald Denaux •
Andres Garcia-Silva

A Practical Guide to Hybrid Natural Language Processing

Combining Neural Models and
Knowledge Graphs for NLP

 Springer

Jose Manuel Gomez-Perez
Expert System
Madrid, Spain

Ronald Denaux
Expert System
Madrid, Spain

Andres Garcia-Silva
Expert System
Madrid, Spain

ISBN 978-3-030-44832-5   ISBN 978-3-030-44830-1   (eBook)
https://doi.org/10.1007/978-3-030-44830-1

This Springer imprint is published by the registered company Springer Nature Switzerland AG.
The registered company address is: Gewerbestrasse 11, 6330 Cham, Switzerland

To family and friends and all who made this book possible in one way or another.

Foreword

"Don't Read This Book. Use It!" by Ken Barker

For as long as Knowledge-based Language Understanding and Statistical Natural Language Processing have coexisted, we have fought over them. "Statistical NLP is superficial! It is not real understanding. It will never offer more than parlor tricks learned from common patterns in text." But "Knowledge heavy approaches are brittle! They rely on arbitrary, expensive, hand-coded rules that are not flexible enough to deal with the incredible variety found in real-world text. Besides, you can do anything with BERT."

Both of these positions are caricatures, and both contain some truth. But they are barriers to exploring all of the available tools that may be needed *just to get the job done*. By focusing on the limitations of symbolic or data-driven approaches, we risk losing out on the unique advantages each can offer, as well as the even greater power of combining them.

A Practical Guide to Hybrid Natural Language Processing does not belong in either camp. It devotes no space to ancient wars and is not intended for an audience interested in rehashing old arguments. It *is* intended for those coming from a background of Symbolic AI; those who have been following the impressive successes of Statistical and now Neural NLP, but have not yet taken the plunge into embeddings, language models, transformers, and Muppets. The book is also for those statistical NLP practitioners who have struggled against the insatiable appetite of modern techniques for data; those who suspect that adding knowledge might enable learning from fewer examples, if only there were an effective way to incorporate it. More practically, this book is ideal for those who want to build something useful that requires getting at the meaning locked in text and language and who don't want to have to get a Ph.D. in Logic or spend Googles of dollars on GPU time.

The authors have taken care to include thorough treatments of all of the basic components for building hybrid NLP systems that combine the power of knowledge graphs with modern, neural techniques. This is not to say that the book is an encyclopedia of techniques, either data-oriented or symbolic. It is also not a textbook, dragging you through a fixed path of education. The book is divided into three parts: knowledge-based and neural building blocks; hybrid architectures combining both; and real applications. Within the parts, topics are conveniently standalone, allowing quick, easy access to needed information. But the two most valuable properties of the book are that it is practical and that it is up to date. It demonstrates exactly how to create and use contextual representations. It has clear treatments of sense embeddings and knowledge graph embeddings. It explains language models and transformer architectures that use them. It also shows how to evaluate the performance of systems using these. Most usefully, the book takes you from theory to code as painlessly as possible through experiments and exercises on real NLP tasks in real domains with real corpora. It is packed with working code and step-by-step explanations. And it uses Jupyter notebooks with pandas that you can get from GitHub!

My advice is: Don't read this book. Use it! Work through its experiments and exercises. Step through the notebooks and see what happens. Then steal the code and build the NLP system you need.

IBM Research   Ken Barker
Yorktown Heights, NY, USA
February 2020

"Most of the Knowledge in the World Is Encoded Not in Knowledge Graphs but in Natural Language" by Denny Vrandecic

In 2005, Wikipedia was still a young website, and most of the public just started to become aware of it. The Wikipedia community sent out calls for the very first global meet-up of contributors, named Wikimania. Markus Krotzsch and I were both early contributors and have just started as Ph.D. students working on the Semantic Web. We wanted to go to Wikimania and meet those people we knew only online.

We sat down and thought about what kind of idea to submit to Wikimania. The most obvious one was to combine Wikipedia with Semantic Web technologies. But what would that mean?

Wikipedia's power lies in the ease of editing, and in the idea that anyone can contribute to it. It lies in its community, and in the rules and processes the community had set up. The power of the Semantic Web was to publish machine-readable data on the Web and to allow agents to combine the data from many different sources. Our idea was to enable Wikipedia communities to create content that is more machine-readable and can participate in the Semantic Web.

Our talk was set up for the first session on the first day, and we used the talk to start a conversation that would continue for years. The talk led to the creation of Semantic MediaWiki, an extension to the MediaWiki software powering Wikipedia

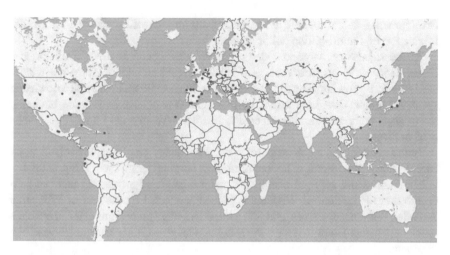

Fig. 1 Map showing the 100 largest cities with a female mayor. Data from Wikidata, Map from Open StreetMaps. Link: https://w.wiki/GbC

and other wikis, and that has found use in numerous places, such as NASA, the Museum of Modern Art, the US Intelligence community, General Electric, and many more. The talk also eventually led to the creation of Wikidata, but it took many years to get there.

In the talk, we proposed a system that would allow us to answer questions using Wikipedia's content. Our example question was: what are the world's largest cities with a female mayor?

Wikipedia, at that point, already had all the relevant data, but it was spread out through many articles. One could, given enough time, comb through the articles of all the largest cities, check who the mayor is, and start keeping a spreadsheet of potential answers, and finally clean it up and produce the end result.

Today, with the availability of Wikidata, we can get answers to that question (see Fig. 1) and many others within seconds. Wikidata is a large knowledge base that anyone can edit and that has, as of early 2020, collected nearly a billion statements about more than 75 million topics of interest.

But, although we finally have a system that allows all of us to ask these questions and get beautiful visualizations as answers, there is still a high barrier towards allowing a wide range of people to actually benefit from this data. It requires writing queries in the query language SPARQL, a rare skill set. Can we do better?

Most of the knowledge in the world is encoded not in knowledge graphs but in natural language. Natural language is also the most powerful user interface we know.

The 2010s saw neural models created through deep learning applied to tasks in natural language processing become hugely popular. Whether generation, summarization, question answering, or translation—undoubtedly the poster child of this development—neural models have turned from an interesting research idea to the foundation of a multi-billion dollar market.

At the same time, large knowledge graphs have become widely available and blossomed. Public projects such as DBpedia, Freebase, and Wikidata are widely used, while a growing number of companies have built their internal knowledge graphs. Foremost Google, whose Knowledge Graph popularized the name, but today many large companies across diverse industries have internal knowledge graphs used in diverse ways.

Both technologies, machine learning and knowledge graphs, have evolved much over the last few years. The opportunities coming from their integration are underexplored and very promising. It is natural language processing that can help ensure that the content of Wikidata is indeed supported by the text of Wikipedia and other referenced sources, and it is natural language processing that can enable a much larger population to access the rich knowledge within a knowledge base like Wikidata.

This is where this book comes into play. Jose, Ronald, and Andres are experts in their fields, with decades of experience shared between them. But, in order to write this book, they had to resolve the hard problems of aligning terminology and how to present the ideas from both sides in a unified framework that is accessible to all kinds of readers. They are generously linked to resources on the Web that let you try out the techniques described in the book. The content of the book has been tested in tutorials and refined over many months.

Natural language is, without any doubt, one of the most important user interface modalities of the future. Whereas we see a growing number of devices that aim to converse with us in natural language, this is only the very beginning of a massive revolution. Natural language interfaces provide extremely powerful and intuitive methods to access the ever-growing capabilities of computer systems. Already today, the services computers could offer are far behind the services that are, in fact, being offered to the user. There is so much more users could do, but we do not know how to build the user interface to these powerful capabilities.

Knowledge graphs provide the most interpretable and efficient way to store heterogeneous knowledge we are aware of today. Knowledge graphs allow for human interpretation and editing capabilities. In a knowledge graph-based system, you can dive in and make a change, and be sure that this change will propagate to the users. In many industries, such as finance or medicine, this is not only a nice to have, but absolutely crucial. And in other industries, such requirements are starting to become increasingly important. Knowledge graphs offer an ease of maintenance and introspection that outmatches many alternatives.

Natural language processing is unlocking knowledge expressed in natural language, which can then be used to update and be checked for consistency regarding a knowledge graph, which in turn can be made available through natural language for querying and answer generation. The two technologies support and enhance each other. This book shows practical ways to combine them and unlock new capabilities to engage and empower users.

Enjoy the book, and use your newly acquired knowledge wisely!

Google Knowledge Graph   Denny Vrandecic
San Francisco, CA, USA
January 2020

Preface

Both neural and knowledge-based approaches to natural language processing have strong and weak points. Neural methods are extremely powerful and consistently claim the top positions of current NLP leaderboards. However, they are also sensitive to challenges like the amount and quality of training data or linking the models to how humans use the language and their understanding of the world. On the other hand, although not entirely free from such challenges, NLP systems based on structured knowledge representations tend to be better suited to address some of them. However, they may require considerable knowledge engineering work in order to continuously curate such structured representations.

The main premise of this book is that data-driven and knowledge-based approaches can complement each other nicely to boost strengths and alleviate weaknesses. Although many advocate for the combined application of both paradigms in NLP and many other areas of Artificial Intelligence, the truth is that until now such combination has been unusual, due to reasons that may include a possible lack of principled approaches and guidelines to accomplish such goal and a shortage of compelling success stories.

On the other hand, AI research, especially in the areas of NLP and knowledge graphs, has reached a level of maturity that permeates all sectors, causing profound societal and business changes. Therefore, this book focuses particularly on the practical side of the topics discussed herein and aims to provide the interested reader with the necessary means to acquire a hands-on understanding about how to combine neural and knowledge-based approaches to NLP, bridging the gap between them.

In general, this book seeks to be of value for anyone interested in the interplay between neural and knowledge-based approaches to NLP. Readers with a background on structured knowledge representations from the Semantic Web, knowledge acquisition, representation, and reasoning communities, and in general those whose main approach to AI is fundamentally based on logic can find in this book a useful and practical guide. Likewise, we expect it to be similarly useful for readers from communities whose main background is in the areas of machine and deep learning, who may be looking for ways to leverage structured knowledge bases to optimize results along the NLP downstream.

Readers from industry and academia in the above-mentioned communities will thus find in this book a practical resource to hybrid NLP. Throughout the book, we show how to leverage complementary representations stemming from the analysis of unstructured text corpora as well as the entities and relations described explicitly in a knowledge graph, integrate such representations, and use the resulting features to effectively solve different NLP tasks in different domains. In these pages, the reader will have access to actual executable code with examples, exercises, and real-world applications in key domains like disinformation analysis and machine reading comprehension of scientific literature.

In writing this book, we did not seek to provide an exhaustive account of current NLP approaches, techniques, and toolkits, either knowledge-based, neural, or based on other forms of machine learning. We consider this is sufficiently well covered in the literature. Instead, we chose to focus on the main building blocks that the reader actually needs to be aware of in order to assimilate and apply the main ideas of this book. Indeed, all the chapters are self-contained and the average reader should not encounter major difficulties in their comprehension. As a result, you have in your hands a compact yet insightful handbook focused on the main challenge of reconciling knowledge-based and neural approaches to NLP. We hope you will enjoy it.

Madrid, Spain   Jose Manuel Gomez-Perez
January 2020   Ronald Denaux
                                                                              Andres Garcia-Silva

Purpose of the Book

This book provides readers with a principled yet practical guide to hybrid approaches to natural language processing involving a combination of neural methods and knowledge graphs. The book addresses a number of questions related to hybrid NLP systems, including:

- How can neural methods extend previously captured knowledge explicitly represented as knowledge graphs in cost-efficient and practical ways and vice versa?
- What are the main building blocks and techniques enabling a hybrid approach to NLP that combines neural and knowledge-based approaches?
- How can neural and structured, knowledge-based representations be seamlessly integrated?
- Can this hybrid approach result in better knowledge graphs and neural representations?

- How can the quality of the resulting hybrid representations be inspected and evaluated?
- What is the impact on the performance of NLP tasks, the processing of other data modalities, like images or diagrams, and their interplay?

To this purpose, the book first introduces the main building blocks and then describes how they can be intertwined, supporting the effective implementation of real-life NLP applications. To illustrate the ideas described in the book, we include a comprehensive set of experiments and exercises involving different algorithms over a selection of domains and corpora in several NLP tasks.

Overview of the Chapters in This Book

We have structured the book in the chapters introduced next.

Chapter 1: Introduction motivates the book and its overall purpose in the current context of the NLP discipline.

Chapter 2: Word, Sense, and Graph Embeddings introduces word, sense/concept, and knowledge graph embeddings as some of the main building blocks towards producing hybrid NLP systems. Different approaches are considered, varying from those learning plain word embeddings, to those learning sense and concept embeddings from corpora and semantic networks, and those which do not use corpora at all, but instead attempt to learn concept embeddings directly from a knowledge graph.

Chapter 3: Understanding Word Embeddings and Language Models focuses on word embeddings and delves in the analysis of the information contained in them, depending on the method and corpora used. Beyond pre-trained static embeddings, the emphasis is placed on neural language models and contextual embeddings.

Chapter 4: Capturing Meaning from Text as Word Embeddings guides the reader through an executable notebook, which focuses on a specific word embedding algorithm like Swivel [164] and its implementation to illustrate how word embeddings can be easily generated from text corpora.

Chapter 5: Capturing Knowledge Graph Embeddings. In a way analogous to the previous chapter, this chapter takes an existing knowledge graph like WordNet to produce graph embeddings using a specific knowledge graph algorithm like HolE. An executable notebook is also provided.

Chapter 6: Building Hybrid Knowledge Representations from Text Corpora and Knowledge Graphs presents **Vecsigrafo** [39], an approach to jointly learn word and concept embeddings from text corpora using knowledge graphs. As opposed to the methods described in the previous chapter, Vecsigrafo not only learns from the knowledge graph but also from the training corpus, with several advantages, as we will see, which are illustrated in an accompanying notebook. In the second half of the chapter, we take a step further and show how to apply transformers and neural language models to generate an analogous representation of Vecsigrafo, called **Transigrafo**. This part of the chapter is also illustrated using a notebook.

Chapter 7: Quality Evaluation discusses several evaluation methods that provide an insight on the quality of the hybrid representations learnt by Vecsigrafo. To this purpose, we will use a notebook that illustrates the different techniques entailed. In this chapter, we also study how such representations compare against lexical and semantic embeddings produced by other algorithms.

Chapter 8: Capturing Lexical, Grammatical, and Semantic Information with Vecsigrafo. Building hybrid systems that leverage both text corpora and a knowledge graph needs to generate embeddings for the items represented in the graph, such as concepts, which are linked to the words and expressions in the corpus singled out through some tokenization strategy. In this chapter and associated notebook, we investigate the impact of different tokenization strategies and how these may impact on the resulting lexical, grammatical, and semantic embeddings in Vecsigrafo.

Chapter 9: Aligning Embedding Spaces and Applications for Knowledge Graphs presents several approaches to align the vector spaces learned from different sources, possibly in different languages. We discuss various applications such as multi-linguality and multi-modality, which we also illustrate in an accompanying notebook. The techniques for vector space alignment are particularly relevant in hybrid settings, as they can provide a basis for knowledge graph interlinking and cross-lingual applications.

Chapter 10: A Hybrid Approach to Fake News and Disinformation Analysis. In this chapter and corresponding notebooks, we start looking at how we can apply hybrid representations in the context of specific NLP tasks and how this improves the performance of such tasks. In particular, we will see how to use and adapt deep learning architectures to take into account hybrid knowledge sources to classify documents which in this case may contain misinformation.

Chapter 11: Jointly Learning Text and Visual Information in the Scientific Domain. In this chapter and its notebook, we motivate the application of hybrid techniques to NLP in the scientific domain. This chapter will guide the reader to implement state-of-the-art techniques that relate both text and visual information, enrich the resulting features with pre-trained knowledge graph embeddings, and use the resulting features in a series of transfer learning tasks, ranging from figure and caption classification to multiple-choice question answering over text and diagram of 6th grade science questions.

Chapter 12: Looking Into the Future of Natural Language Processing provides final thoughts and guidelines on the matter of this book. It also advances some of the future developments in hybrid natural language processing in order to help professionals and researchers configure a path of ongoing training, promising research fields, and areas of industrial application. This chapter includes feedback from experts in areas related to this book, who were asked about their particular vision, foreseeable barriers, and next steps.

Materials

All the examples and exercises proposed in the book are available as executable Jupyter notebooks in our GitHub repository.[1] All the notebooks are ready to be run on Google Colaboratory or, if the reader so prefers, in a local environment. The book also leverages experience and feedback acquired through our tutorial on *Hybrid Techniques for Knowledge-based NLP*,[2] initiated at K-CAP'17[3] and continued in ISWC'18[4] and K-CAP'19.[5] The current version of the tutorial is available online and the reader is encouraged to use it in combination with the book to consolidate the knowledge acquired in the different chapters with executable examples, exercises, and real-world applications.

Relation to Other Books in the Area

The field addressed by this book is tremendously dynamic. Much of the relevant bibliography in critical and related areas like neural language models has erupted in the last months, configuring a thriving field which is taking shape as we write these lines. New and groundbreaking contributions are therefore expected to appear during the preparation of this book that will be studied and incorporated and may even motivate future editions. For this reason, resources like the above-mentioned tutorial on *Hybrid Techniques for Knowledge-based NLP* and others like Graham Neubig et al.'s *Concepts in Neural Networks for NLP*[6] are of particular importance.

This book does not seek to provide an exhaustive survey on previous work in NLP. Although we provide the necessary pointers to the relevant bibliography in each of the areas we discuss, we have purposefully kept it succinct and focused. Related books that will provide the reader with a rich background in relevant areas for this book include the following.

Manning and Schutze's *Foundations of Statistical Natural Language Processing* [114] and Jurafsky and Martin's *Speech and Language Processing* [88] provide excellent coverage for statistic approaches to natural language processing and their applications, as well as introduce how (semi)structured knowledge representations and resources like WordNet and FrameNet [12] can play a role in the NLP pipeline.

More recently, a number of books have covered the field with special emphasis on neural approaches. Eisenstein's *Introduction to Natural Language Processing* [51]

---

[1] https://github.com/hybridnlp/tutorial.

[2] http://hybridnlp.expertsystemlab.com/tutorial.

[3] 9th International Conference on Knowledge Capture (https://www.k-cap2017.org).

[4] 17th International Semantic Web Conference (http://iswc2018.semanticweb.org).

[5] 10th International Conference on Knowledge Capture (http://www.k-cap.org/2019).

[6] https://github.com/neulab/nn4nlp-concepts.

offers a comprehensive and up-to-date survey of the computational methods necessary to understand, generate, and manipulate human language, ranging from classical representations and algorithms to contemporary deep learning approaches. Also of particular interest to acquire a deep and practical understanding of the area is Goldberg's *Neural Network Methods in Natural Language Processing* [67].

We also look at books that pay special attention to the knowledge-based side of the NLP spectrum like Cimiano et al.'s *Ontology-Based Interpretation of Natural Language* [33] and Barrière's *Natural Language Understanding in a Semantic Web Context* [17]. A good overview on the application of distributed representations in knowledge graphs is provided by Nickel et al. in [129].

Relevant books on knowledge graphs include Pan et al.'s *Exploiting Linked Data and Knowledge Graphs in Large Organisations* [135], which addresses the topic of exploiting enterprise linked data with a particular focus on knowledge graph construction and accessibility. Kejriwal's *Domain-Specific Knowledge Graph Construction* [91] also focuses on the actual creation of knowledge graphs. Finally, *Ontological Engineering* [68] by Asuncion Gomez-Perez et al. provides key principles and guidelines for the tasks involved in knowledge engineering.

Acknowledgements

We gratefully acknowledge the European Language Grid-825627 and Co-inform-770302 EU Horizon 2020 projects, as well as previous grants, including DANTE-700367, TRIVALENT-740934, and GRESLADIX-IDI-20160805, whose research challenges related to different areas of natural language processing encouraged us to find solutions based on the combination of knowledge graphs and neural models. We are especially thankful to Flavio Merenda, Cristian Berrio, and Raul Ortega for their technical contributions to this book.

Contents

Part I   Preliminaries and Building Blocks

1   Hybrid Natural Language Processing: An Introduction 3
  1.1   A Brief History of Knowledge Graphs, Embeddings,
        and Language Models 3
  1.2   Combining Knowledge Graphs and Neural Approaches
        for NLP 5

2   Word, Sense, and Graph Embeddings 7
  2.1   Introduction 7
  2.2   Distributed Word Representations 7
  2.3   Word Embeddings 8
  2.4   Sense and Concept Embeddings 10
  2.5   Knowledge Graph Embeddings 11
  2.6   Conclusion 15

3   Understanding Word Embeddings and Language Models 17
  3.1   Introduction 17
  3.2   Language Modeling 18
        3.2.1   Statistical Language Models 18
        3.2.2   Neural Language Models 19
  3.3   Fine-Tuning Pre-trained Language Models for Transfer
        Learning in NLP 19
        3.3.1   ELMo 20
        3.3.2   GPT 20
        3.3.3   BERT 21
  3.4   Fine-Tuning Pre-trained Language Models for Bot Detection 21
        3.4.1   Experiment Results and Discussion 24
        3.4.2   Using the Transformers Library to Fine-Tune BERT 26
  3.5   Conclusion 30

4   Capturing Meaning from Text as Word Embeddings 33
   4.1   Introduction 33
   4.2   Download a Small Text Corpus 34
   4.3   An Algorithm for Learning Word Embeddings (`Swivel`) 34
   4.4   Generate Co-occurrence Matrix Using Swivel `prep` 35
   4.5   Learn Embeddings from Co-occurrence Matrix 36
       4.5.1   Convert `tsv` Files to `bin` File 36
   4.6   Read Stored Binary Embeddings and Inspect Them 37
       4.6.1   Compound Words 38
   4.7   Exercise: Create Word Embeddings from Project Gutenberg 38
       4.7.1   Download and Pre-process the Corpus 38
       4.7.2   Learn Embeddings 39
       4.7.3   Inspect Embeddings 39
   4.8   Conclusion 39

5   Capturing Knowledge Graph Embeddings 41
   5.1   Introduction 41
   5.2   Knowledge Graph Embeddings 42
   5.3   Creating Embeddings for WordNet 43
       5.3.1   Choose Embedding Algorithm: HolE 43
       5.3.2   Convert WordNet KG to the Required Input 45
       5.3.3   Learn the Embeddings 50
       5.3.4   Inspect the Resulting Embeddings 50
   5.4   Exercises 53
       5.4.1   Exercise: Train Embeddings on Your Own KG 53
       5.4.2   Exercise: Inspect WordNet 3.0 Pre-calculated
           Embeddings 53
   5.5   Conclusion 54

Part II   Combining Neural Architectures and Knowledge Graphs

6   Building Hybrid Representations from Text Corpora,
   Knowledge Graphs, and Language Models 57
   6.1   Introduction 57
   6.2   Preliminaries and Notation 58
   6.3   What Is Vecsigrafo and How to Build It 58
   6.4   Implementation 61
   6.5   Training Vecsigrafo 62
       6.5.1   Tokenization and Word-Sense Disambiguation 62
       6.5.2   Vocabulary and Co-occurrence Matrix 65
       6.5.3   Learn Embeddings from Co-occurrence Matrix 69
       6.5.4   Inspect the Embeddings 71
   6.6   Exercise: Explore a Pre-computed Vecsigrafo 73
   6.7   From Vecsigrafo to Transigrafo 75
       6.7.1   Setup 77
       6.7.2   Training Transigrafo 79

	6.7.3	Extend the Coverage of the Knowledge Graph	80
	6.7.4	Evaluating a Transigrafo	81
	6.7.5	Inspect Sense Embeddings in Transigrafo	82
	6.7.6	Exploring the Stability of the Transigrafo Embeddings	84
	6.7.7	Additional Reflections	88
6.8	Conclusion		89

7   Quality Evaluation 91
- 7.1   Introduction 91
- 7.2   Overview of Evaluation Methods 92
  - 7.2.1   Recommended Papers in This Area 93
- 7.3   Practice: Evaluating Word and Concept Embeddings 93
  - 7.3.1   Visual Exploration 94
  - 7.3.2   Intrinsic Evaluation 94
  - 7.3.3   Word Prediction Plots 96
  - 7.3.4   Extrinsic Evaluation 99
- 7.4   Practice 2: Assessing Relational Knowledge Captured by Embeddings 100
  - 7.4.1   Download the embrela Project 101
  - 7.4.2   Download Generated Datasets 101
  - 7.4.3   Load the Embeddings to Be Evaluated 102
  - 7.4.4   Learn the Models 104
  - 7.4.5   Analyzing Model Results 104
  - 7.4.6   Data Pre-processing: Combine and Add Fields 106
  - 7.4.7   Calculate the Range Thresholds and Biased Dataset Detection 107
  - 7.4.8   Finding Statistically Significant Models 108
  - 7.4.9   Conclusion of Assessing Relational Knowledge 111
- 7.5   Case Study: Evaluating and Comparing Vecsigrafo Embeddings 111
  - 7.5.1   Comparative Study 111
  - 7.5.2   Discussion 121
- 7.6   Conclusion 125

8   Capturing Lexical, Grammatical, and Semantic Information with Vecsigrafo 127
- 8.1   Introduction 127
- 8.2   Approach 129
  - 8.2.1   Vecsigrafo: Corpus-Based Word-Concept Embeddings 130
  - 8.2.2   Joint Embedding Space 130
  - 8.2.3   Embeddings Evaluation 131
- 8.3   Evaluation 132
  - 8.3.1   Dataset 132
  - 8.3.2   Word Similarity 133

	8.3.3	Analogical Reasoning	136
	8.3.4	Word Prediction	137
	8.3.5	Classification of Scientific Documents	138
8.4	Discussion		141
8.5	Practice: Classifying Scientific Literature Using Surface Forms		142
	8.5.1	Import the Required Libraries	143
	8.5.2	Download Surface form Embeddings and SciGraph Papers	143
	8.5.3	Read and Prepare the Classification Dataset	143
	8.5.4	Surface form Embeddings	145
	8.5.5	Create the Embeddings Layer	146
	8.5.6	Train a Convolutional Neural Network	147
8.6	Conclusion		148

9   Aligning Embedding Spaces and Applications for Knowledge Graphs **151**
9.1	Introduction		151
9.2	Overview and Possible Applications		152
	9.2.1	Knowledge Graph Completion	153
	9.2.2	Beyond Multi-Linguality: Cross-Modal Embeddings	154
9.3	Embedding Space Alignment Techniques		154
	9.3.1	Linear Alignment	154
	9.3.2	Non-linear Alignment	160
9.4	Exercise: Find Correspondences Between Old and Modern English		160
	9.4.1	Download a Small Text Corpus	160
	9.4.2	Learn the Swivel Embeddings over the Old Shakespeare Corpus	161
	9.4.3	Load Vecsigrafo from UMBC over WordNet	163
	9.4.4	Exercise Conclusion	164
9.5	Conclusion		164

Part III   Applications

10   A Hybrid Approach to Disinformation Analysis **167**
10.1	Introduction		167
10.2	Disinformation Detection		168
	10.2.1	Definition and Background	168
	10.2.2	Technical Approach	170
10.3	Application: Build a Database of Claims		171
	10.3.1	Train a Semantic Claim Encoder	171
	10.3.2	Create a Semantic Index of Embeddings and Explore It	179
	10.3.3	Populate Index with STS-B dev	180
	10.3.4	Create Another Index for a Claims Dataset	181

| | | 10.3.5 | Load Dataset into a Pandas DataFrame | 182 |

10.3.5   Load Dataset into a Pandas DataFrame................... 182
10.3.6   Conclusion of Building a Database of Claims 186
10.4   Application: Fake News and Deceptive Language Detection 187
    10.4.1   Basic Document Classification Using Deep Learning 187
    10.4.2   Using HolE Embeddings 191
    10.4.3   Using Vecsigrafo UMBC WNet Embeddings 193
    10.4.4   Combine HolE and UMBC Embeddings 194
    10.4.5   Discussion and Results 195
10.5   Propagating Disinformation Scores Through a Knowledge
    Graph 198
    10.5.1   Data Commons ClaimReview Knowledge Graph........ 198
    10.5.2   Discredibility Scores Propagation 202
10.6   Conclusion.. 206

**11   Jointly Learning Text and Visual Information in the Scientific
Domain**... 207
11.1   Introduction.. 207
11.2   Figure-Caption Correspondence Model and Architecture.......... 209
11.3   Datasets 211
11.4   Evaluating the Figure-Caption Correspondence Task 212
11.5   Figure-Caption Correspondence vs. Image-Sentence Matching ... 213
11.6   Caption and Figure Classification 215
11.7   Multi-Modal Machine Comprehension for Textbook
    Question Answering.. 216
11.8   Practice with Figure-Caption Correspondence..................... 217
    11.8.1   Preliminary Steps 218
    11.8.2   Figure-Caption Correspondence 219
    11.8.3   Image-Sentence Matching................................. 233
    11.8.4   Caption/Figure Classification 236
    11.8.5   Textbook Question Answering............................ 240
11.9   Conclusion.. 245

12   Looking into the Future of Natural Language Processing 247
12.1   Final Remarks, Thoughts and Vision.............................. 247
12.2   What Is Next? Feedback from the Community 250

References.. 257

Part I
Preliminaries and Building Blocks

Chapter 1
Hybrid Natural Language Processing: An Introduction

Abstract The proliferation of knowledge graphs and recent advances in artificial intelligence have raised great expectations related to the combination of symbolic and data-driven approaches in cognitive tasks. This is particularly the case of knowledge-based approaches to natural language processing as near-human symbolic understanding relies on expressive, structured knowledge representations. Engineered by humans, knowledge graphs are frequently well curated and of high quality, but they can also be labor-intensive, rely on rigid formalisms and sometimes be biased towards the specific viewpoint of their authors. This book aims to provide the reader with means to address limitations like the above by bringing together bottom-up, data-driven models and top-down, structured knowledge graphs. To this purpose, the book explores how to reconcile both views and enrich the resulting representations beyond the possibilities of each individual approach. Throughout this book, we delve into this idea and show how such hybrid approach can be used with great effectiveness in a variety of natural language processing tasks.

1.1 A Brief History of Knowledge Graphs, Embeddings, and Language Models

The history of artificial intelligence can be seen as a quest for the perfect combination of reasoning accuracy and the ability to capture knowledge in machine-actionable formats. Early AI systems developed during the '70s like MYCIN [169] already proved it was possible to effectively emulate human reasoning in tasks like classification or diagnosis through artificial means. However, the acquisition of expert knowledge from humans soon proved to be a challenging task, resulting in what was known ever after as the knowledge acquisition bottleneck [58].

Knowledge acquisition eventually became a modeling activity rather than a task focused on extracting knowledge from the mind of an expert in an attempt to address such challenge and work at the so-called knowledge level [124]. The modeling approach and working at the knowledge level facilitates focusing on what an AI agent knows and what its goals are as an abstraction separate from implementation details. Along the knowledge level path came ontologies, semantic

© Springer Nature Switzerland AG 2020
J. M. Gomez-Perez et al., *A Practical Guide to Hybrid Natural Language Processing*, https://doi.org/10.1007/978-3-030-44830-1_1

networks, and eventually knowledge graphs, which provide rich, expressive, and actionable descriptions of the domain of interest and support logical explanations of reasoning outcomes.

As Chris Welty put it in his foreword to *Exploiting Linked Data and Knowledge Graphs in Large Organizations* [135]: "Knowledge Graphs are Everywhere! Most major IT companies or, more accurately, most major information companies including Bloomberg, NY Times, Google, Microsoft, Facebook, Twitter, and many more, have significant graphs and invested in their curation. Not because any of these graphs is their business, but because using this knowledge helps them in their business." However, knowledge graphs can be costly to produce and scale since a considerable amount of well-trained human labor is needed to curate high-quality knowledge in the required formats. Furthermore, the design decisions made by knowledge engineers can also have an impact in terms of depth, breadth, and focus, which may result in biased and/or brittle knowledge representations, hence requiring continuous supervision. Ambitious research programs in the history of AI, like CYC [101] and Halo [72],[1] invested large amounts of effort to produce highly curated knowledge bases either by knowledge engineers or by subject matter experts, and all of them had to face challenges like the ones mentioned above.

In parallel, the last decade has witnessed a noticeable shift from knowledge-based, human-engineered methods to data-driven and particularly neural methods due to the increasing availability of raw data and more effective architectures, facilitating the training of increasingly performing models. Areas of AI like computer vision soon leveraged the advantages brought about by this new scenario. Also the natural language processing (NLP) community has embraced the trend with remarkably good results.

Relatively recent breakthroughs in the field of distributional semantics and word embeddings [16] have proved particularly successful ways to capture the meaning of words in document corpora as a vector in a dense, low-dimensional space. Much research has been put into the development of more and more effective means to produce word embeddings, ranging from algorithms like word2vec [121], GloVe [138], or fastText [23] to neural language models capable to produce context-specific word representations at a scale never seen before, like ELMo [139], BERT [44], and XLNet [195]. Paraphrasing Welty: "Embeddings are Everywhere!". Among many applications, they have proved to be useful in terms of similarity, analogy, and relatedness, as well as most NLP tasks, including, e.g. classification [96], question answering [95, 137, 162], or machine translation [11, 32, 89, 175].

Certainly, word embeddings and language models are pushing the boundaries of NLP at an unprecedented speed. However, the complexity and size of language models[2] imply that training usually requires large computational resources, often out of reach for most researchers outside of the big corporate laboratories. Additionally,

---

[1] Halo eventually motivated the current project Aristo (https://allenai.org/aristo).

[2] At the time of writing this introduction, BERT, with over 200 million parameters, looks small compared to new neural language models like Salesforce's CTRL [94] (1.6 billion parameters) or

although context-free and context-aware embeddings coming from neural language models are without a doubt a powerful tool in most modern NLP architectures, the truth is that we are still uncertain as to what type of knowledge is captured in them.

Pre-BERT work like [18, 116, 139] already indicated that it may be possible to learn actual meaning exclusively from text through language modeling and other NLP tasks like textual entailment, thus capturing not only lower-level aspects of the text like syntactic information but also exhibiting a certain abstraction capability in the form of context-dependent aspects of word meaning that can be used, e.g. for word-sense disambiguation. More recently, several papers have been published with the objective to shed some light on what is actually learnt by language models. In [84], the authors focus on what BERT learns about the structure of language. They report how BERT seems to capture surface features at the bottom layers, syntactic features in the middle, and semantic features at the top, following a compositional tree-like structure. Others [35] reach similar conclusions and show how BERT attends at linguistic notions of syntax and coreference. In [178], Tenney et al. find that BERT represents the steps of the traditional NLP pipeline in an interpretable and localizable way, and that the regions responsible for each step appear in the expected sequence: POS tagging, parsing, NER, semantic roles, then coreference. However, the knowledge captured in language models is still hard to interpret logically, let alone matched to existing concepts and relations [132], which, on the other hand, happen to be the main information artifacts explicitly represented in a knowledge graph.

1.2 Combining Knowledge Graphs and Neural Approaches for NLP

Many argue [46, 166, 168] that knowledge graphs can enhance both expressivity and reasoning power in machine learning architectures and advocate for a hybrid approach that leverages the best of both worlds. From a practical viewpoint, the advantages are particularly evident, e.g. in situations where there may be a lack of sufficient training data. For example, text data can be augmented using a knowledge graph by expanding the corpus based on hypernymy, synonymy, and other relations represented explicitly in the graph.

Neural-symbolic integration [10], as a field of research, addresses fundamental problems related to building a technical bridge between both paradigms in AI. Recently, this discussion has rekindled in the context of the Semantic Web [78]. In the area of NLP, a similar discussion is also gaining traction. Among the benefits hybrid approaches that combine neural and knowledge-based methods can entail, models that learn to represent textual and knowledge base entities like relations in

---

Google's Text-to-Text Transfer Transformer (T5) [149], which can exceed 11 billion parameters in its largest configuration.

the same continuous latent space for tasks like knowledge base completion have shown to perform joint inferences involving text and knowledge bases with high accuracy [151]. Others [180] follow up to capture the compositional structure of textual relations and jointly optimize entity, knowledge base, and textual relation representations. More generally, knowledge graphs can contribute to train more expressive NLP models that are able to learn the meaning of words by linking them to explicitly represented concepts [29, 112] in a knowledge graph and, in addition, jointly learning the representations of both words and concepts in a single embedding space [39].

Focused on the pragmatics of language, [6, 20] another line of research argues that effectively capturing meaning requires not only taking into account the form of the text but also other aspects like the particular context in which such form is used or the intent and cognitive state of the speaker, suggesting that the text needs to be enriched with additional information in order to actually convey the required meaning. Accordingly, for NLP to scale beyond partial, task-specific solutions, it must be informed by what is known about how humans use the language and their understanding of the world.

General-purpose knowledge graphs [7, 183] in combination with domain-specific structured resources, as well as lexical databases like WordNet [59], which group words based on their semantics and define relations between such concepts, seem well suited to such purpose, too. Other resources like ConceptNet [173] or ATOMIC [156], focused on modeling commonsense, have shown that it is actually possible to capture human understanding in knowledge graphs and train neural models based on such graphs that exhibit commonsense reasoning capabilities in NLP tasks.

In this book we take a step further in the combination of knowledge graphs and neural methods for NLP. Doing so requires that we address a number of questions. Such questions include the following: (1) how can neural methods extend previously captured knowledge explicitly represented as knowledge graphs in cost-efficient and practical ways and vice versa; (2) what are the main building blocks and techniques enabling such hybrid approach to NLP; (3) how can knowledge-based and neural representations be seamlessly integrated; (4) how can the quality of the resulting hybrid representations be inspected and evaluated; (5) how can a hybrid approach result in higher quality structured and neural representations compared to the individual scenario; and (6) how does this impact on the performance of NLP tasks, as well as the processing and interplay with other data modalities, like visual data, in tasks related to machine comprehension. Next, we try to provide answers to these questions.

Chapter 2
Word, Sense, and Graph Embeddings

Abstract Distributed word representations in the form of dense vectors, known as word embeddings, are the basic building blocks for machine-learning based natural language processing. Such embeddings play an important role in tasks such as part-of-speech tagging, chunking, named entity recognition, and semantic role labeling, as well as downstream tasks including sentiment analysis and more in general text classification. However, early word embeddings were static context-independent representations that fail to capture multiple meanings for polysemous words. This chapter presents an overview of such traditional word embeddings, but also of alternative approaches that have been proposed to produce sense and concept embeddings using disambiguated corpora or directly from knowledge graphs. As a result, this chapter serves as a conceptual framework for the rest of book.

2.1 Introduction

As discussed in the previous chapter, one of the main questions addressed by this book deals with how to represent in a shared vector space both words and their meaning and how doing this can be beneficial in NLP. In this chapter, we first describe the origins of word embeddings as *distributed word representations* in Sect. 2.2. Then, in Sect. 2.3, we describe a variety of methods that have been proposed to learn word embeddings and shortly describe the type of knowledge they seem to capture (and where they have shortcomings) and how we evaluate such embeddings. We then move on to describing, in a similar manner, sense and concept embeddings in Sect. 2.4 derived from text. Finally, we describe a final type of embeddings derived from knowledge graphs in Sect. 2.5.

2.2 Distributed Word Representations

To inject text in machine learning approaches, it is necessary to represent it in a numerical format. One alternative is to use one-hot encoding where vectors have as many dimensions as the number of words in the vocabulary, and each word

© Springer Nature Switzerland AG 2020
J. M. Gomez-Perez et al., *A Practical Guide to Hybrid Natural Language Processing*, https://doi.org/10.1007/978-3-030-44830-1_2

is represented as vector with a one in the dimension corresponding to the word in the vocabulary. As a result, for a text the one-hot encoding results on a large sparse matrix that can be challenging to fit in memory. Another widely used text representation is the bag-of-words typically used in information retrieval processes. Bag-of-words representations work at the document level and, similarly to one-hot encoding, the number of dimensions in the vector is the number of words in the vocabulary. In the bag-of-words model, each document is represented by a vector with values different to zero in the dimensions corresponding to the document words in the vector. TF–IDF is a widely used weighting scheme to identify the importance of words in documents according to their frequency in the same document and also in the overall document collection. However, in addition to the highly multidimensional vectors used in one-hot encoding and bag-of-words that can make these representations challenging to process in terms of computational power and memory, the main drawback is that they fail to represent word meanings. They only provide representations based on the presence and absence of words in one-hot encoding, or the frequency at the document and collection level in the bag-of-word model.

Distributed word representations, on the other hand, are based on the distributional hypothesis where words that co-occur in similar context are considered to have similar (or related) meaning. Word embedding algorithms yield dense vectors so that words with similar distributional context appear in the same region in the embedding space [164].

2.3 Word Embeddings

Learning word embeddings[1] has a relatively long history [16], with earlier works focused on deriving embeddings from co-occurrence matrices and more recent work focusing on training models to predict words based on their context [15]. Both approaches are roughly equivalent as long as design choices and hyperparameter optimization are taken into account [103].

Most of the recent work in this area focused on learning embeddings for individual words based on a large corpus and was triggered by the word2vec algorithm proposed in [121] which provided an efficient way to learn word embeddings by predicting words based on their context words[2] and using negative sampling. More recent improvements on this family of algorithms [118] also take into account (1) subword information by learning embeddings for three to six character n-grams, (2) multi-words by pre-processing the corpus and combining n-grams of words with high mutual information like "New_York_City," and (3) learning a weighting scheme (rather than predefining it) to give more weight to context words depending

---

[1] Also called the vector space model in the literature.

[2] Or vice versa, respectively, called continuous bag-of-words (cbow) and skip-gram architectures.

on their relative position to the center word.[3] These advances are available via the fastText implementation and pre-trained embeddings.

Algorithms based on word co-occurrences are also available. GloVe [138] and Swivel [164] are two algorithms which learn embeddings directly from a sparse co-occurrence matrix that can be derived from a corpus; they do this by calculating relational probabilities between words based on their co-occurrence and total counts in the corpus.

These approaches have been shown to learn lexical and semantic relations. However, since they stay at the level of words, they suffer from issues regarding word ambiguity. And since most words are polysemic, the learned embeddings must either try to capture the meaning of the different senses or encode only the meaning of the most frequent sense. In the opposite direction, the resulting embedding space only provides an embedding for each word, which makes it difficult to derive an embedding for the concept based on the various words which can be used to refer to that concept.

Vecsigrafo, which will be described in detail in Chap. 6 provides extensions that can be applied to both word2vec style algorithms and to co-occurrence algorithms. In this book, we focus on the former and show how such extensions can be applied to Swivel. We pick Swivel for ease of implementation, which has proved very useful for illustration purposes in a practical handbook like this. However, applying the Vecsigrafo approach to GloVe and the standard word2vec implementations should be straightforward. Applying it to other approaches like fastText is a priori more complicated, especially when taking into account subword information, since words can be subdivided into character n-grams, but concepts cannot.

Another way that has been proposed recently to deal with problems like polysemy of word embeddings is to use language models to learn *contextual embeddings*. In such cases, the corpus is used to train a model which can be used to compute embeddings for words based on a specific context like a sentence or a paragraph. The main difference is that words do not have a unique embedding; instead the embedding of the word depends on the words surrounding it. In Chap. 3 we will explore this type of word embeddings, including current popular language modeling approaches such as ELMo [107], GPT [146], and BERT [44].

Word embeddings are evaluated using intrinsic methods [158] that assess whether the embedding space actually encodes the distributional context of words, and extrinsic methods where they are evaluated according to the performance of a downstream task. Analogical reasoning [121] and word similarity [150] are often used as intrinsic evaluation methods. The analogy task[4] relies on words relations of the form a:a* :: b:b* (i.e., a is to a* as b is to b*) and the goal is try to predict b* given the other variables by operating on the corresponding word vectors. Word

---

[3] Sometimes also called "target" or "focus" word in the literature.

[4] https://aclweb.org/aclwiki/Analogy_(State_of_the_art).

similarity,[5] on the other hand, attempts to match a human score of relatedness between two words with an embedding similarity measure.

2.4 Sense and Concept Embeddings

A few approaches have been proposed to produce sense and concept embeddings from corpora. One approach to resolve this is to generate *sense embeddings* [82], whereby the corpus is disambiguated using Babelfy and then word2vec is applied over the disambiguated version of the corpus. Since plain word2vec is applied, only vectors for senses are generated. Jointly learning both words and senses was proposed by Chen et al. [31] and Rothe et al. [153] via multi-step approaches where the system first learns word embeddings, then applies disambiguation based on WordNet and then learns the joint embeddings. While this addresses ambiguity of individual words, the resulting embeddings focus on synonymous word-sense pairs,[6] rather than on knowledge graph concepts.

Another approach for learning embeddings for concepts based on a corpus without requiring word-sense disambiguation is NASARI [29], which uses lexical specificity to learn concept embeddings from Wikipedia subcorpora. These embeddings have as their dimensions the lexical specificity of words in the subcorpus, hence they are sparse and harder to apply than low-dimensional embeddings such as those produced by word2vec. For this reason, NASARI also proposes to generate "embedded vectors" which are weighted averaged vectors from a conventional word2vec embedding space. This approach only works for Wikipedia and BabelNet, since you need a way to create a subcorpus that is relevant to entities in the knowledge base.

Finally, SW2V (Senses and Words to Vectors) [112] proposes a lightweight word-disambiguation algorithm and extends the continuous bag-of-words architecture of word2vec to take into account both words and senses. Vecsigrafo adopts a similar approach, leveraging various differences, including the use of an industry-grade disambiguator, a learning algorithm implemented as a variation of correlation-based algorithms, and considering the distance of context words and concepts to the center word. In terms of evaluation, Mancini et al. [112] report results for 2 word similarity datasets while Vecsigrafo is substantiated by an extensive analysis on 14 datasets and different corpus sizes. Vecsigrafo also takes into account the inter-agreement between different vector spaces, as a measure of how similar two vector spaces are based on the predicted distances between a set of word pairs, in order to assess the quality of the resulting embeddings.

---

[5] https://aclweb.org/aclwiki/Similarity_(State_of_the_art).

[6] E.g. word-sense pairs $apple_2^N$ and $Malus\_pumila_1^N$ have separate embeddings, but the concept for *apple tree* they represent has no embedding.

2.5 Knowledge Graph Embeddings

Knowledge graphs have been useful to solve a wide variety of natural language processing tasks such as semantic parsing, named entity disambiguation, information extraction, and question answering among others. A knowledge graph is a multi-relational graph that includes entities (nodes) and a set of relation types (edges). Several approaches have been proposed to create concept embeddings directly from these representations [129, 188].

Let $\mathbb{E}$ be a set of entities and $\mathbb{R}$ a set of relations, a *triple* of the form h, r, t (*head, relation, tail*) denotes a *fact*, such that $h, t \in \mathbb{E}$ and $r \in \mathbb{R}$. Facts are stored in a knowledge base as a collection of triples $\mathbb{D}+ = \{(h, r, t)\}$. Embeddings allow to translate these symbolic representations in a format that simplify the manipulation while preserving the inherent structure. Usually, knowledge graphs adhere to some deterministic rules, e.g. constraints or transitivity. However, there are also some latent features that reflect inner statistical properties, such as the tendency of some entities to be related by similar characteristics (*homophily*) or entities that can be divided into different groups (*block structure*). These latent features which may emerge through the application of statistical relational learning techniques [129].

Generally, in a typical knowledge graph embeddings model, entities are represented by vectors in a continuous vector space and relations are taken as operations in the same space and can be represented by vectors, matrices, or tensors among others. Many algorithms that try to learn these representations have been proposed. Since the knowledge graphs are typically incomplete, one of the main applications of such concept embeddings is usually graph completion. Knowledge graph completion (KGC) has been proposed to improve knowledge graphs by filling in its missing connections.

Several algorithms have been implemented to tackle this task [125]. The general approach is the following: given a triple (h, r, t), these models assign a function $f(h, r, t)$ of its plausibility. The aim of this learning process is to choose a function such that the score of a correct triple will be higher than the score of an incorrect one, usually a corrupted triple.

A family of graph embedding algorithms is the *translational models* that uses distance-based scoring functions. These models basically use vector translations to represent the relations. One of the most representative algorithms in this group is the TransE model [25], inspired by the word2vec skipgram. This model represents both entities and relations as vectors in the same space. A relation r here is presented as a translation in the embedding space such that $h + r \approx t$ or $t + r \approx h$ when (h, r, t) holds. Since TransE presents some disadvantages in dealing with relations between more than two entities (e.g., 1-to-N, N-to-1, or N-to-N), some model improvements have been proposed. TransH [190] basically uses vector projections to represent relations. TransR [106] uses projections and represents the relations in a separate vector space. TransD [54] simplifies TransR assigning two vectors for both entities and relations and avoids matrix-vector multiplication operations. TransM [57] that assigns different weights for each triple based on their relational mapping property, or rather the different number of heads and tails. Finally, the most recent and efficient translational models are TorusE [48] that solve a TransE regularization problem, TranSparse [30] that uses adaptive sparse matrices, and TranSparse-DT [85] that is an extension of TranSparse with a dynamic translation.

Another group is formed of *bi-linear models* which employs bi-linear scoring functions to capture the latent semantics of entity vectors. RESCAL [131] is the first bi-linear algorithm implemented and it represents each entity as a vector and each relation as a matrix which models pairwise interactions between latent factors. DISTMULT [193] is a RESCAL simplification in which the relation matrix is substituted with a diagonal matrix, such that the score function reduces the number of parameters per relation. SimplE [90] allows learning two different embeddings for each entity when encountered either as head or tail. An extension of DISTMULT is ComplEx [181], where the embeddings are represented as complex values to better model asymmetric relations, h, r, t values lie in a complex space and the scoring function is not symmetric. ComplEx-N3 [99] extends ComplEx with weighted nuclear 3-norm, and RotatE [174] represents entities as complex vectors and relations as rotations from the source entity to the target entity in a complex vector space.

There is also a wide variety of algorithms implemented using neural network architectures. Models that implement recurrent neural networks to learn relationships are IRN [165] and PTransE-RNN [105]. A model inspired by holographic models of associative memory is HolE [130] (*holographic embeddings*). These models develop a memory system inspired by holography and use convolutions and correlations to store and retrieve information [61]. HolE tries to combine the expressive power of tensor product, e.g. RESCAL, and the lightness and simplicity of TransE. It is a compositional model that uses circular correlation of vectors to represent pairs of entities and takes into account asymmetrical relations. The SME [24] (*semantic matching energy*) algorithm represents both entities and relations using vectors, modeling the relation types and the entity types in the same way. Then, a relation is combined respectively with its head and its tail. Finally, the dot product of these combinations returns the score of a fact. The NTN model [171] (*neural tensor network*) replaces a standard linear layer with a bi-linear tensor layer able to relate entity vectors. A scored function computes how likely a relation between two entities is. A special case of NTN is the SLM (single-layer model) that connects the entity vectors implicitly through the non-linearity of a standard, single-layer neural network when tensor is set to 0. ProjE [167] is a two-layer neural network formed by a combined layer and a projection layer. It is a simplified version of NTN in which combination operators as diagonal matrices allow to combine an entity embedding matrix with a relation embedding matrix. Given an entity embeddings and a relation embeddings, the output of this model is a candidate-entity matrix that returns top-ranked candidates to complete the triple.

There are also some models based on convolutional neural networks. ConvE [43] is a neural link prediction model that applies convolution operations over 2D shaped embeddings in order to extract more feature interactions. ConvKB [126], instead, can be viewed as an extension of TransE to further model global relationships among same dimensional entries of the entity and relation embeddings. Each triple in this model is represented as a 3-column matrix fed to a convolution layer where multiple filters are operated to generate different feature maps. Conv-TransE [163] and CapsE [128] are extensions of ConvE and ConvKB, respectively. The first one is designed to take into account also translational characteristics between entities and relations, the latter adds a capsule network layer on top of the convolution layer.

Several recent studies have shown that enriching the triple knowledge with additional information present in the graph can improve the strength of models. Relation paths between entities and neighborhood information are two examples. The first refers to a sequence of linked relations and the second refers to model an entity as a relation-specific mixture of its neighborhood in the graph. Relation paths can improve the performances of models such as TransE and SME [110]. Neighborhood information has been also used in TransENMM [127] to improve TransE and in R-GCN [157] to deal with the highly multi-relational data in which a DISTMULT decoder takes an R-GCN encoder input to produce a score for every potential edge in the graph.

Research that try to adapt language models to knowledge graph embeddings have been presented in RDF2Vec [152] and KG-BERT [196]. Language models are probabilistic models able to predict a sequence of words in a given language and try to encode both grammatical and semantic information. In RDF2Vec, the algorithm transforms the graph data into sequences of entities in order to consider them as sentences. To do that, the graph is divided into subgraphs using different techniques. In the end, these sentences are used to train the neural language model to represent each entity in the RDF graph as a vector of numerical values in a latent feature space. The language model used in this research is word2vec. Instead, KG-BERT uses the BERT language model to represent information, both entities and relations as their name or description textual sequences. Therefore, this model is able to take into account also extra textual information in addition to the one encoded by triples. This algorithm turns the knowledge graph completion into a sequence classification problem.

Among the most recent models in this research field can be mentioned CrossE [199], GRank [49], and TuckER [14]. For each entity and relation, CrossE creates a *general embeddings* that stores high-level properties and multiple *interaction embeddings*. These embeddings are derived from an interaction matrix which encodes specific properties and information about crossover interactions, or rather, bidirectional effects between entities and relations. To overcome the non-interpretability of how knowledge graph embeddings encode information, GRank proposes a different approach that utilizes graph patterns. This model constructs an entity ranking system for each graph pattern and then evaluates them using a ranking measure. Instead, TuckER is a linear model based on Tucker decomposition of the binary tensor representation of knowledge graph triples. This algorithm models entities and relations into two different matrices.

Although these approaches are really interesting, all have the same drawback: they encode the knowledge (including biases) explicitly contained in the source knowledge graph, which is typically already a condensed and filtered version of the real-world data. Even large knowledge graphs only provide a fraction of the data that can be gleaned from raw datasets such as Wikipedia and other web-based text corpora, i.e. these embeddings cannot learn from raw data as it appears in real-world documents. Approaches like KnowBert [140] and Vecsigrafo [39], on the other hand, combine corpora and knowledge graphs, showing evidence of improved perplexity, ability to recall facts and downstream performance on relationship extraction, entity typing, and word-sense disambiguation.

Tables 2.1 and 2.2 report the results of the most popular KGE models on the widespread datasets used in the scientific community.

Table 2.1 KGE models benchmarking (FB15K and WN18 [25])

Model	Architecture	Benchmarks					
		FB15K			WN18		
		MR	@10	MMR	MR	@10	MMR
SME [110]	Neural network	154	40.8	–	533	74.1	–
TransH [190]	Translation-based	87	64.4	–	303	86.7	–
TransR [106]	Translation-based	77	68.7	–	225	92.0	–
TransD [54]	Translation-based	91	77.3	–	212	92.2	–
TranSparse [30]	Translation-based	82	79.5	–	211	93.2	–
TranSparse-DT [85]	Translation-based	79	80.2	–	221	94.3	–
NTN [171]	Neural network	–	41.4	0.250	–	66.1	0.530
RESCAL [131]	Bi-linear	–	58.7	0.354	–	92.8	0.890
TransE [25]	Translation-based	–	74.9	0.463	–	94.3	0.495
HolE [130]	HAM (NN)	–	73.9	0.524	–	94.9	0.938
ComplEx [181]	Bi-linear	–	84.0	0.692	–	94.7	0.941
SimplE [90]	Bi-linear	–	83.8	0.727	–	94.7	0.942
TorusE [48]	Translation-based	–	83.2	0.733	–	95.4	0.947
DISTMULT [193]	Bi-linear	42	89.3	0.798	655	94.6	0.797
ConvE [43]	Convolutional-NN	64	87.3	0.745	504	95.5	0.942
RotatE [174]	Bi-linear	40	88.4	0.797	309	95.9	0.949
ComplEx-N3 [99]	Bi-linear	–	91.0	0.860	–	96.0	0.950
IRN [165]	Neural network	38	92.7	-	249	95.3	-
ProjE [167]	Neural network	34	88.4	–	–	–	–
PTransE-RNN [105]	Recurrent-NN	92	82.2	–	–	–	–
TransM [57]	Translation-based	93	–	–	280	–	–
R-GCN [157]	Convolutional-NN	–	84.2	0.696	–	96.4	0.819
CrossE [199]	ML-based	–	87.5	0.728	–	95.0	0.830
GRank [49]	ML-based	–	89.1	0.842	–	95.8	0.950
TuckER [14]	ML-based	–	89.2	0.795	–	95.8	0.953

Table 2.2 KGE models benchmarking (FB15K-237 [180] and WN18RR [43])

Model	Architecture	Benchmarks					
		FB15K-237			WN18RR		
		MR	@10	MMR	MR	@10	MMR
DISTMULT [193]	Bi-linear	–	41.9	0.241	–	49.0	0.430
ComplEx [181]	Bi-linear	–	42.8	0.247	–	51.0	0.440
ConvE [43]	Convolutional-NN	–	50.1	0.325	–	50.2	0.430
RotatE [174]	Bi-linear	–	48.0	0.297	–	–	–
R-GCN [157]	Convolutional-NN	–	–	–	–	41.7	0.248
Conv-TransE [163]	Convolutional-NN	–	51.0	0.330	–	52.0	0.460
ConvKB [126]	Convolutional-NN	257	51.7	0.396	2554	52.5	0.248
CapsE [128]	Convolutional-NN	303	59.3	0.523	719	56.0	0.415
CrossE [199]	ML-based	–	47.4	0.299	–	–	–
GRank [49]	ML-based	–	48.9	0.322	–	53.9	0.470
KG-BERT [196]	Transformer	153	42.0	–	97	52.4	–
TuckER [14]	ML-based	–	54.4	0.358	–	52.6	0.470

2.6 Conclusion

This chapter provided an overview of word embeddings as well as alternative embeddings to represent senses and concepts. We saw the origins of word embeddings as distributed representations and explored a wide variety of algorithms to calculate such embeddings, each of them with their own trade-offs. We also saw that embeddings seem to capture some lexical and even semantic information based on a range of evaluation approaches. After reading this chapter you should have a broad idea of the history of word (and concept) embeddings and interested readers can follow references to scientific papers describing embedding learning algorithms and evaluations. The gained basic understanding of these concepts will be useful to understand the following chapters, where we will look into each of the embedding types in much more detail and will gain practical experience on learning embeddings, as well as evaluating and applying them in NLP tasks.

Chapter 3
Understanding Word Embeddings and Language Models

Abstract Early word embeddings algorithms like word2vec and GloVe generate static distributional representations for words regardless of the context and the sense in which the word is used in a given sentence, offering poor modeling of ambiguous words and lacking coverage for out-of-vocabulary words. Hence a new wave of algorithms based on training language models such as Open AI GPT and BERT has been proposed to generate contextual word embeddings that use as input word constituents allowing them to generate representations for out-of-vocabulary words by combining the word pieces. Recently, fine-tuning pre-trained language models that have been trained on large corpora have constantly advanced the state of the art for many NLP tasks.

3.1 Introduction

The interest on word embeddings was significantly sparkled by the word2vec algorithm proposed in [117], which provided an efficient way to learn word embeddings from large corpora based on word context and negative sampling and continues to date. Originally proposed in [16], much research has been put into the development of increasingly effective means to produce word embeddings, resulting in algorithms like GloVe [138], Swivel [164], or fastText [23]. One important drawback of this type of representations is related to out-of-vocabulary (OOV) words, i.e. words that were not in the training corpus and therefore do not have an associated embedding. Usually, approaches like fastText address the OOV problem by falling back to character-based representations, which can be combined to learn embeddings for OOV words. Another important drawback is that these approaches generate static, context-independent embeddings. That is, a word embedding is always the same regardless of the sentence where the word appears, e.g. "jaguar" would have the same embedding either as an animal or as a car brand. Plus, they ignore multi-word expressions, grammatical, and word-sense information, which may be useful, e.g. to deal with polysemy and homonymy.

To overcome these limitations a new generation of algorithms was proposed, including among many other systems like ELMo [139], ULMFiT [81], Open AI

© Springer Nature Switzerland AG 2020

J. M. Gomez-Perez et al., *A Practical Guide to Hybrid Natural Language Processing*, https://doi.org/10.1007/978-3-030-44830-1_3

GPT [146], or BERT [44]. Such approaches generate contextual word embeddings by relying on word constituents at different degrees of granularity and using a language model as learning objective. Since their emergence, language models have constantly improved the state of the art in most NLP benchmarks. In this chapter we characterize the main approaches to generate contextual word embeddings through neural language models. In doing so, we will also describe how language models have generalized the use of transfer learning in natural language processing.

3.2   Language Modeling

A language model is a probabilistic model that predicts how likely a sequence of words is to appear in a given language. A successful language model estimates the distribution over word sequences, encoding not only the grammatical structure, but also the knowledge that the training corpora may contain [87]. In fact, grammatically correct sentences can have a low probability if they are very unlikely in the corpus. For example, a language model that assigns a higher probability to the sequence "fast car" than to "rapid car" can be of help in machine translation.

Language models have been used in speech recognition [119], machine translation [182], and more recently in a variety of NLP tasks such as text classification, question answering, or named entity recognition [44, 81, 146, 147]. Nowadays, language models are pushing the state of the art in several tasks [149] in the General Language Understanding Evaluation, GLUE [186] and the extended version super GLUE [185].

Next, we go through the definition of the main types of language models discussed in the bibliography: statistical language models and neural language models.

3.2.1   Statistical Language Models

A statistical model of language uses the chain rule to calculate joint probabilities over word sequences:

$$p(x_1, \ldots, x_n) = \Pi_{i=1}^{n} p(x_i | x_1, \ldots, x_{i-1}) \tag{3.1}$$

Nevertheless, modeling joint distributions of discrete random variables such as words in sentences is affected by the curse of dimensionality [21]. For example, to calculate the joint distributions of three consecutive words using a vocabulary of size 100,000 there are around $100,000^3$ free parameters. To simplify the calculation of the joint probability the Markov assumption is used limiting the conditional probabilities on a window of n previous words:

$$p(x_1, \ldots, x_n) \approx \Pi_{i=1}^{n} p(x_i | x_{i-k}, \ldots, x_{i-1}) \tag{3.2}$$

Statistical language model implementations calculate Eq. (3.2) using counting methods based on n-grams and smoothing techniques to avoid zero conditional probabilities on n-grams not represented in the corpus.

3.2.2   Neural Language Models

Learning a neural language model [21] is an unsupervised task where the model is trained to predict the next word in a sequence given some previous words, i.e. the model calculates the probability of an each word in the vocabulary of being the next word in the sequence. Neural language models have been implemented as a feed-forward network [21] and LSTM architectures in [81, ULMFiT] and [139, ELMo]. Nevertheless, recurrent networks, including LSTMs, are inherently sequential, which hampers parallelization on training data, a desired feature at longer sequence lengths as memory constraints limit batching across examples [182]. Thus, LSTMs were replaced in [146, Open AI GPT] and [44, BERT] by transformer architectures [182], which are not recurrent and rely on a self-attention mechanism to extract global dependencies between input and output sequences.

Neural language models are usually learnt from high quality, grammatically correct and curated text corpora, such as Wikipedia (ULMFiT), BookCorpus (Open AI GPT), a combination of Wikipedia and BookCorpus (BERT) or News (ELMo). To overcome the OOV problem these approaches use different representations based on characters (ELMo), byte-pair encoding [160] (GPT), and word pieces [159] (BERT).

3.3   Fine-Tuning Pre-trained Language Models for Transfer Learning in NLP

The main purpose of using transfer learning [136] is to avoid building task-specific models from scratch by leveraging knowledge previously acquired by training another task. While word embeddings are learnt from large corpora, their use in neural models to solve specific tasks is limited to the input layer. So, in practice a task-specific neural model is built almost from scratch since the rest of model parameters, which are typically initialized at random, need to be optimized for the task at hand, requiring large amounts of data to produce a high performance model.

A step forward towards transfer learning in NLP were ELMo's contextual representations [139], which can be fine-tuned against domain data as a result of adjusting a linear combination of the internal representations of the model. However, the need for specific architectures to solve different tasks still remains. Recent work based on transformers to learn language models [44, 146] has shown evidence that transferring internal self-attention blocks along with shallow feed-forward networks is sufficient to advance the state of the art in different evaluation tasks, showing task-specific architectures are no longer necessary.

The amount of neural language models currently available has exploded in the last months, with a large and varied number of options. Here, we provide an overview on ELMo, GPT, and BERT, which marked especially significant milestones in the history of language models and their implications for NLP.

3.3.1   ELMo

ELMo [139] (embeddings from language models) learns contextual word embeddings as a function of the entire input sentence. Contextual embeddings allow dealing with, e.g. word polysemy, a feature that traditional word embedding approaches did not support. ELMo trains a 2-layer BiLSTM with character convolutions to learn a bidirectional language model from a large text corpus. Then, deep contextualized word embeddings are generated as a linear function of the BiLSTM hidden states.

The bidirectional language model is actually two language models: one forward language model to process the input sentence and predict the next word and one backward language model that runs the input sequence in reverse, predicting the previous token given the future tokens.

ELMo embeddings can be used in a downstream model by collapsing all the internal layers into a single vector. It is also possible to fine-tune the model in a downstream task, computing a task-specific weighing of all the internal layers.

3.3.2   GPT

The Generative Pre-trained Transformer (GPT) [146], as well as its sequel GPT-2, trained on even larger corpora, is a neural language model that can be fine-tuned for a specific task by applying task-dependent transformations to the input, requiring minimal changes to the model architecture. GPT is first pre-trained in an unsupervised stage to learn a language model on a large corpus of text using a multi-layer transformer decoder [107]. Then, in a supervised stage, the model is fine-tuned to adjust the parameters to the target task. GPT processes the text sequences from left to right and hence each token can only attend to previous tokens in the self-attention layer. Fine-tuning GPT for different evaluation tasks achieves better results than using task-specific architectures, showing that the latter are no longer required.

During supervised fine-tuning a linear layer is added on top of the transformer to learn a classifier. Thus, the task dataset is assumed to be a sequence of input tokens along with a label. The only new parameters are the linear layer parameters, while the transformer parameters are just adjusted. For tasks other than text classification, the input is transformed into an ordered sequence that the pre-trained model can process.

The authors choose a transformer architecture following up on its successful use in a variety of NLP tasks, such as machine translation and document generation. Another interesting property of transformer architectures is their structured memory, which allows handling long-term dependencies in text, a problematic issue for recurrent networks like LSTMs. In addition, transformers support parallel processing since they are not sequential models like recurrent networks. To learn the language model, GPT uses a multi-layer transformer decoder that applies multi-headed self-attention over the input tokens plus position-wise feed-forward layers to produce an output distribution over target tokens.

3.3.3   BERT

BERT [44] (bidirectional encoder representations from transformers) is a neural language model that similarly to GPT can be fine-tuned for a task without requiring task-specific architectures. Nevertheless, the approach followed in BERT is different in the way the input text is processed, the neural architecture itself, and the learning objectives used to pre-train the model. One of the drawbacks of previous language models is that they are unidirectional, limiting the processing of text to just one direction, typically from left to right. BERT is designed to learn deep bidirectional representations by jointly conditioning on left and right context in all layers.

To learn the bidirectional representations BERT uses a masked language model objective where some of the input tokens are randomly masked, and the objective is to predict the original vocabulary id of the masked word relying only on its context. The masked language model allows to process jointly the left and right context. BERT also has a next sentence prediction learning objective that enables the model to support tasks dealing with sentence pairs.

The BERT model architecture is a multi-layer bidirectional transformer encoder. The input representation supports a single sentence or sentence pairs, e.g. sentences in an entailment task. BERT uses word-piece embeddings [159] with a 30K token vocabulary. The first token of every sequence is special token [CLS], which stands for classification. The final embedding corresponding to the CLS token is used as the sentence representation for a classification task. Sentence pairs are concatenated in a single sentence using the special token [SEP] as separator. In addition, a learned embedding is added to each token indicating the sentence it belongs. Thus, the token representations are the addition of the token, sentence, and position embeddings.

3.4   Fine-Tuning Pre-trained Language Models for Bot Detection

In [63] we presented an experimental study on the use of word embeddings as input of CNN architectures and BiLSTMs to tackle the bot detection task and compared these results with fine-tuning pre-trained language models. Detecting bots can be addressed as a binary classification task, provided we focus only in Twitter text content, regardless of other features that might be drawn from, e.g. the social network of an account, user metadata, network features based on follower and followee relations, and tweet and retweet activity.

Dataset

To generate a dataset of tweets produced by bots or humans we rely on an existing dataset of bot and human accounts produced by Gilani et al. [65]. We create a balanced dataset containing tweets labeled as bot or human according to the account label. In total our dataset comprises 500,000 tweets where 279,495 tweets were created by 1208 human accounts, and 220,505 tweets were tweeted from 722 bot accounts. In addition, we generate another version of the dataset after pre-processing the dataset using a script[1] released by the GloVe team. This script replaces, e.g. URLs, numbers, user mentions, hashtags, and some ASCII emoticons with the corresponding tags.

An analysis of the dataset shows that bots tend to be more prolific than humans since they average 305 tweets per account, which contrasts with the human average, 231. In addition, bots tend to use more URLs (0.8313) per tweet and hashtags (0.4745) than humans (0.5781 and 0.2887, respectively). This shows that bots aim at maximizing visibility (hashtags) and to redirect traffic to other sources (URLs). Finally, we found that bots tend to display more egoistic behavior than humans since they mention other users in their tweets (0.4371 user mentions per tweet) less frequently than humans (0.5781 user mentions per tweet).

Embeddings

To train the classifiers we use a mix of pre-trained embeddings, contextualized embeddings and also allow the neural networks to adjust the embeddings during the learning process.

Pre-trained Embeddings

We use pre-trained embeddings to train the classifiers rather than doing it from scratch. We use pre-trained embeddings learned from Twitter itself, urban dictionary definitions to accommodate the informal vocabulary often used in the social network, and Common Crawl as a general source of information:

- glove.twitter[2] : 200 dimension embeddings generated from Twitter (27B tokens, 1.2M vocabulary) using GloVe [138].
- word2vec.urban[3] : 100 dimension embeddings generated from Urban Dictionary definitions (568K vocabulary) using word2vec [117].
- fastText.crawl[4] : 300 dimension embeddings generated from Common Crawl (600B tokens, 1.9M vocabulary) using fastText [118].

---

[1] https://nlp.stanford.edu/projects/glove/pre-process-twitter.rb.

[2] https://nlp.stanford.edu/projects/glove/.

[3] https://data.world/jaredfern/urban-dictionary-embedding.

[4] https://fasttext.cc/docs/en/english-vectors.html.

Contextualized Embeddings
In addition to static pre-trained embeddings we use dynamically generated embeddings using ELMo. ELMo embeddings were generated from our dataset; however, none of the trainable parameters, i.e. linear combination weights, was modified in the process. Due to the high dimensionality of such embeddings (dim=1024) and to prevent memory errors, we reduced the sequence size used in the classifiers to 50.

Learned and Pre-trained Embeddings
Another option to improve the classifiers is to allow the neural architecture to adjust dynamically the embeddings or part of them in the learning process. To do so, we generate 300 dimension embeddings initialized randomly and set them as trainable. In addition, we concatenate these random and trainable embeddings to the pre-trained and ELMo embeddings, which were not modified in the learning process. In this round of experiments we always use pre-processing since in the previous sections this option always improved the results.

Task-Specific Neural Architectures
We train text binary classifiers using convolutional neural networks and bidirectional long short-term memory networks.

Convolutional Neural Network
For the bot detection task we use convolutional neural networks (CNNs) inspired by Kim's work [96], who showed how this architecture achieved good performance in several sentence classification tasks, and other reports like [197] with equally good results in NLP tasks. Our architecture uses 3 convolutional layers and a fully connected layer. Each convolutional layer has 128 filters of size 5, ReLu was used as activation function and max-pooling was applied in each layer. The fully connected layer uses softmax as activation function to predict the probability of each message being written by a bot or a human. All the experiments reported henceforth use a vocabulary size of 20K tokens, sequence size 200, learning rate 0.001, 5 epochs, 128 batch size, static embeddings unless otherwise stated, and 10-fold cross-validation.

First we train the CNN classifier on our dataset using pre-trained embeddings and compare them with randomly generated embeddings. In addition, we pre-process our dataset using the same pre-processing script[5] that was applied when learning the GloVe Twitter embeddings.

Bidirectional Long Short-Term Memory Networks
In addition to CNN we test long short-term memory (LSTM) networks, [79], a neural architecture that is also often used in NLP tasks [197]. LSTM networks are sequential networks that are able to learn long-term dependencies. In our experiments we use a bidirectional LSTM that processes the sequence of text forward and backward to learn the model. The architecture of the BiLSTM comprises an embedding layer, the BiLSTM layer with 50 processing cells, and a fully connected layer that uses softmax as activation function to predict the probability of each

---

[5] https://nlp.stanford.edu/projects/glove/pre-process-twitter.rb.

message being written by a bot or a human. The rest of hyperparameters are set with the same values that we use for the CNN experiments.

Pre-trained Language Models

We fine-tuned the following language models to carry out the bot detection classification task: ULMFit,[6] Open AI GPT,[7] BERT.[8] In all cases we use the default hyperparameters:

- BERT base: 3 epochs, batch size of 32, and a learning rate of 2e−5
- Open AI GPT: 3 epochs, batch size of 8, and a learning rate of 6.25e−5
- ULMFiT: 2 epochs for the language model fine-tuning and 3 epochs for the classifier, batch size of 32, and a variable learning rate.

At the end of this chapter we present a Jupyter notebook where we fine-tune BERT for the bot detection task.

3.4.1 Experiment Results and Discussion

Evaluation results, presented in the figure below (Fig. 3.1), show that fine-tuning language models yields overall better results than training specific neural architectures that are fed with mixture of: (1) pre-trained contextualized word embeddings (ELMo), (2) pre-trained context-independent word embeddings learnt from Common Crawl (fastText), Twitter (GloVe), and urban dictionary (word2vec), plus embeddings optimized by the neural network in the learning process.

Fine-tuning GPT on the non-pre-processed dataset learnt the best classifier in terms of f-measure followed by BERT. For these two approaches, the pre-processed dataset learnt classifiers with a lower f-score, although overall these classifiers were better than all the other tested approaches. ULMFit [81], another pre-trained language model approach, learnt the best classifier after GPT and BERT, after pre-processing the dataset.

Next in the ranking appears a BiLSTM classifier learnt from the pre-processed dataset that uses a concatenation of dynamically adjusted embeddings in the training process plus contextualized embeddings generated by ELMo. Another version of this classifier using in addition fastText embeddings from Common Crawl performed slightly worse. The performance of CNN-based classifiers was lower, in general. Similarly to BiLSTMs, the best classifier was learnt from trainable embeddings and ELMo embeddings. Adding other pre-trained embeddings did not improve performance. In general, pre-trained embeddings and their combinations produced the least performing classifiers. Performance improves when pre-trained

---

[6]https://docs.fast.ai/text.html#Fine-tuning-a-language-model.

[7]https://github.com/tingkai-zhang/pytorch-openai-transformer_clas.

[8]https://github.com/google-research/bert#fine-tuning-with-bert.

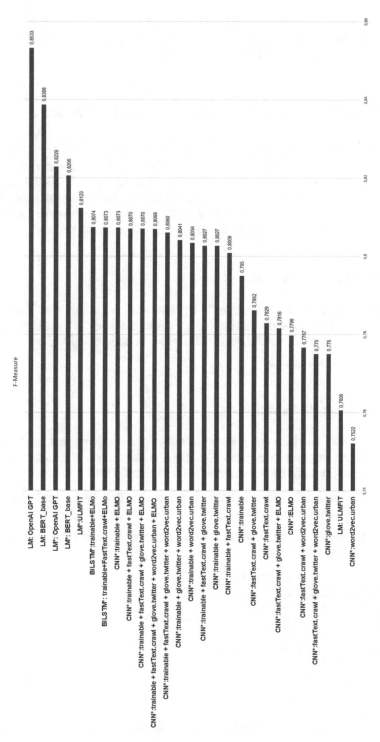

Fig. 3.1 Experiment results of the bot detection classification task. Metric reported *F*-measure. The asterisk in the classifier shows that the pre-processed version of the dataset was used to learn or fine-tune the classifiers. LM stands for language model

embeddings are used jointly with trainable embeddings or contextualized word embeddings. The next section illustrates a practical way to fine-tune one of these language models, in this case BERT, using available libraries.

3.4.2 Using the Transformers Library to Fine-Tune BERT

Fine-tuning BERT requires to incorporate just one additional output layer. So, a minimal number of parameters need to be learned from scratch. To fine-tune BERT for a sequence classification task the transformer output for the CLS token is used as the sequence representation and connected to a one layer feed-forward network that predicts the classification labels. All the BERT parameters and the FF network are fine-tuned jointly to maximize the log probability of the correct label.

3.4.2.1 The Transformers Library

We use transformers from Huggingface.[9] The library, interoperable with Tensor-Flow and PyTorch, provides over 32 pre-trained language models in more than 100 languages including BERT, GPT-2, RoBERTa, XLM, DistilBert, and XLNet.

```
In [1]: !pip install transformers
```

3.4.2.2 Download the Dataset

In the notebook we provide a complete version of the dataset (large) and a reduced one (small) to be able to run the notebook within the time frame, since fine-tuning BERT on the large version takes more than 5 h on a regular GPU.

- Large: 500K train and 100K test labeled tweets at ./09_BERT/Large_Dataset/
- Small: 1K train and 100 test labeled tweets at ./09_BERT/Small_Dataset/

Let us download the datasets and the models from Google Drive and then decompress the file.

```
In [16]: !wget --load-cookies /tmp/cookies.txt
"https://docs.google.com/uc?export=download&confirm=$(
wget --quiet --save-cookies /tmp/cookies.txt
--keep-session-cookies --no-check-certificate
'https://docs.google.com/uc?export=download&id=12Hn0uGUHLjR2VDAV
-uWysBMJmaUjHasA' -O- | sed -rn
's/.*confirm=([0-9A-Za-z_]+).*/\1\n/p')
&id=12Hn0uGUHLjR2VDAV-uWysBMJmaUjHasA" -O BERT.tar
&& rm -rf /tmp/cookies.txt
```

---

[9]Huggingface transformers library: https://github.com/huggingface/transformers.

The environment variable DATA_DIR holds the path to the dataset that is going to be used on the rest of the notebook. The reader can choose the large or small version.

```
In [20]: %env DATA_DIR=./09_BERT/Small_Dataset/

#Uncomment this line to use the large version
#%env DATA_DIR=./09_BERT/Large_Dataset/
```

The dataset is in the tsv format expected by transformer library. We can use the panda library to load the data and visualize an excerpt of the dataset:

```
In [21]: import os
import pandas as pd

test = pd.read_csv(os.environ["DATA_DIR"] + "dev.tsv", header=None, sep = '\t')
data = pd.DataFrame(test)
data.columns = ["index", "label", "mark", "tweet"]
%data

Out[21]: index  label mark tweet
         0      0     1    a  Now Playing: Dick...
         1      1     0    a  Not only are you co...
         2      2     1    a  Follow @iAmMySign !...
         3      3     0    a  These strawberry sa...
         4      4     0    a  Do These Two Lines ...
         ..     ...   ...  ...          ...
         95     95    0    a  I'm sorry you hurt ...
         96     96    1    a  #HometimeReading: ...
         97     97    1    a  Miss_5_Thousand :...
         98     98    0    a  A bunch of associat...
         99     99    1    a    Chokehold - Under

         [100 rows x 4 columns]
```

3.4.2.3 BERT Tokenization

Recent neural languages models use subword representations. ELMO relies on characters, Open AI GPT on byte-pair encoding, and BERT on the word pieces algorithms. These **subword representations are combined when unseen words during training need to be processed, hence avoiding the OOV problem**.

BERT uses a 30k WordPieces vocabulary. Let us move on and see how the BERT Tokenizer works

```
In [6]: from transformers import *

tokenizer = BertTokenizer.from_pre-trained('bert-base-uncased')
text = input("Enter a word or a sentence: ")
print(tokenizer.tokenize(text))
print(tokenizer.encode(text))

Out[6]: Enter a word or a sentence:
Recent neural languages models use subword representations.
['recent', 'neural', 'languages', 'models', 'use', 'sub',
'##word', 'representations', '.']
[3522, 15756, 4155, 4275, 2224, 4942, 18351, 15066, 1012]
```

3.4.2.4   Fine-Tuning the Model

Running the following script, it is possible to fine-tune the model and evaluate the model. During evaluation, the classification of the tweets on the test set is saved in "predictions.txt," which we will use later.

The most relevant parameters of the script are:

- model type: the model that we are going to use, in this case BERT.
- model name or path: the name of the model or path storing a specific model.
- task name: the task that we want to perform, in this case CoLA because we want to do classification.
- output dir: the directory in which it stores the fine-tuned model.

The reader can try to change the parameters and see how it affects performance. This process is slow even though we reduced the size of the dataset. The expected duration in its current configuration is around 1 min.

```
In [9]: !python /content/gdrive/My\ Drive/09_BERT/run_glue.py \
           --model_type bert \
           --model_name_or_path bert-base-uncased \
           --task_name CoLA \
           --do_train \
           --do_eval \
           --do_lower_case \
           --data_dir "$DATA_DIR" \
           --max_seq_length 128 \
           --per_gpu_eval_batch_size=8    \
           --per_gpu_train_batch_size=8   \
           --learning_rate 2e-5 \
           --num_train_epochs 1.0 \
           --save_steps 62500 \
           --overwrite_output_dir \
           --output_dir  ./Bert_Classifier/
```

The binary classifier is evaluated using the MCC score. This score measures how accurately the algorithm performs on both positive and negative predictions. MCC values range from -1 to 1 being 0 the random case, -1 the worst value, and $+1$ the best value. With the small dataset the expected MCC is 0.24. On the other hand, if trained on the larger dataset, MCC will increase to around 0.70.

3.4.2.5   Other Evaluation Metrics

Let us compute the traditional evaluation metrics (accuracy, precision, recall, and f-measure) of our fine-tuned model to see how it performs on the test set.

```
In [10]: import numpy as np
from sklearn.metrics import classification_report
from sklearn.metrics import accuracy_score
from sklearn.metrics import matthews_corrcoef

preds = np.loadtxt("./Bert_Classifier/predictions.txt")
test = pd.read_csv(os.environ["DATA_DIR"] + "dev.tsv",
          header=None, sep = '\t')

print(classification_report(np.asarray(test[1]), preds))
print("Accuracy: ", accuracy_score(np.asarray(test[1]), preds))
print("MCC: ", matthews_corrcoef(test[1], preds))

Out[10]:
              precision    recall  f1-score   support

           0       0.63      0.70      0.67        54
           1       0.60      0.52      0.56        46

    accuracy                           0.62       100
   macro avg       0.62      0.61      0.61       100
weighted avg       0.62      0.62      0.62       100

Accuracy:  0.62
MCC:  0.22935415401872886
```

The reader should see an accuracy of 62% and an f1-score of 62% which is a good result considering the size of the dataset used in the notebook. The full model fine-tuned against the complete dataset produces the following metrics:

```
- Accuracy = 0.85
- Recall = 0.85
- Precision = 0.86
- Recall = 0.85
```

3.4.2.6 Model Inference

We use some random examples from the test set and use the model to predict whether the tweet was generated by a bot or not.

```
In [11]: # Let's use some tweets from the test dataset
os.mkdir("./Test_Dataset/")

test_evaluate = test[:4]
print(test_evaluate)
test_evaluate.to_csv("./Test_Dataset/dev.tsv", sep='\t',
              index=False, header=False)

Out[11]:
   0  1  2                                                  3
0  0  1  a  Now Playing:Dick Curless - Evil Hearted Me ...
1  1  0  a  Not only are you comfortably swaddled in secur...
2  2  1  a  Follow @iAmMySign !!!  Follow @iAmMySign our o...
3  3  0  a  These strawberry sandwich cookies are so easy ...
```

To perform inference with the larger model we provide an already trained version. Change the argument in model_name_or path from Bert_Classifier_small to Bert_Classifier_Large

```
In [12]: %env MODEL_PATH=./Bert_Classifier/

         #Uncomment to use the large mode
         #%env MODEL_PATH=./09_BERT/Bert_Classifier_Large/

         !python /content/gdrive/My\ Drive/09_BERT/run_glue.py \
         --model_type bert \
         --model_name_or_path "$MODEL_PATH" \
         --task_name CoLA \
         --do_eval \
         --do_lower_case \
         --data_dir ./Test_Dataset/ \
         --max_seq_length 128 \
         --per_gpu_eval_batch_size=8    \
         --per_gpu_train_batch_size=8   \
         --learning_rate 2e-5 \
         --num_train_epochs 1.0 \
         --save_steps 62500 \
         --output_dir  "$MODEL_PATH"

Out[12]:
...
./Test_Dataset/cached_dev_Bert_Classifier_Large_128_cola
... - INFO - __main__ -    ***** Running evaluation *****
... - INFO - __main__ -       Num examples = 4
... - INFO - __main__ -       Batch size = 8
Evaluating: 100% 1/1 [00:00<00:00, 11.38it/s]
... - INFO - __main__ -    ***** Eval results *****
... - INFO - __main__ -       mcc = 1.0
```

Check if the model has correctly classified the examples:

```
In [14]: import os

         results = np.loadtxt(os.environ['MODEL_PATH'] +
                              "predictions.txt")
         for i,t in enumerate(test_evaluate[3]):
         print(t + " --> ", "BOT" if results[i]> 0.5
                             else "NOT BOT")

Out[12]:
Now Playing:  Dick Curless - Evil Hearted ...-->  BOT
Not only are you comfortably swaddled in ... -->  NOT BOT
Follow @iAmMySign !!!  Follow @iAmMySign ... -->  BOT
These strawberry sandwich cookies are so ... -->  NOT BOT
```

3.5   Conclusion

In this chapter we have seen that neural language models trained on large corpora have overcome traditional pre-trained word embeddings in NLP tasks. Language models introduce a major shift in the way that word embeddings are used in neural networks. Before them, pre-trained embeddings were used at the input of task-specific models that were trained from scratch, requiring a large amount of labeled data to achieve good learning results.Language models on the other hand only require to adjust their internal representations through fine-tuning. The main benefit is that the amount of data necessary to fine-tune the language model for a specific task is considerably smaller compared to training a task model from scratch. In the remainder of this book we will leverage this observation, drilling down on the application of language models in combination with structured knowledge graphs across different NLP tasks. In Chap. 6 we will use language models to derive concept-level embeddings from an annotated corpus and the WordNet graph. In a different scenario, Chap. 10 will illustrate how to apply language models to semantically compare sentences as part of a semantic search engine for fact-checked claims and build a knowledge graph with them.

Chapter 4
Capturing Meaning from Text as Word Embeddings

Abstract This chapter provides a hands-on guide to learn word embeddings from text corpora. To this purpose we choose Swivel, whose extension is the basis for the Vecsigrafo algorithm, which will be described in Chap. 6. As introduced in Chap. 2, word embedding algorithms like Swivel are not contextual, i.e. they do not provide different representations for the different meanings a polysemous word may have. As we will see in the subsequent chapters of the book, this can be addressed in a variety of ways. For the purpose of this chapter, we focus on a basic way to represent words using embeddings.

4.1 Introduction

In Chap. 2 we introduced the main approaches and algorithms to generate word embeddings. In this chapter we illustrate how to generate word embeddings from a text corpus using a specific algorithm and its implementation: Swivel [164]. In particular, we reuse the Swivel implementation included in the TensorFlow models repository[1] with some small modifications. The complete executable notebook corresponding to this chapter is also available online.[2]

In this chapter we: (1) provide executable code samples to download a sample corpus that will be the basis for learning the embeddings; (2) describe the Swivel algorithm; (3) generate the co-occurrence matrix for the sample corpus, which is the first step in Swivel; (4) learn the embeddings based on the co-occurrence matrix; and (5) read and inspect the learned embeddings. We finally also leave an exercise for the reader to learn embeddings from a slightly larger corpus.

---

[1]https://github.com/tensorflow/models/tree/master/research/swivel.

[2]https://colab.research.google.com/github/hybridnlp/tutorial/blob/master/01_capturing_word_embeddings.ipynb.

© Springer Nature Switzerland AG 2020

J. M. Gomez-Perez et al., *A Practical Guide to Hybrid Natural Language Processing*, https://doi.org/10.1007/978-3-030-44830-1_4

4.2 Download a Small Text Corpus

First, let us download a corpus into our environment. We will use a small sample of the UMBC corpus that has been pre-tokenized and that we have included as part of our GitHub[3] repository. First, we will clone the repository so we have access to it from this environment.

```
In [ ]: %ls
```

```
In [ ]: !git clone https://github.com/hybridnlp/tutorial.git
```

The dataset comes as a zip file, so we unzip it by executing the following cell. We also define a variable pointing to the corpus file:

```
In [ ]: !unzip tutorial/datasamples/umbc_t_5K.zip -d \
    tutorial/datasamples/
        input_corpus='tutorial/datasamples/umbc_t_5K'
```

The reader can inspect the file using the %less command to print the whole input file at the bottom of the screen. It will be quicker to just print a few lines:

```
In [ ]: #%less {input_corpus}
        !head -n1 {input_corpus}
```

This should produce an output similar to:

```
Out [ ]: the mayan image collection was contributed by oberlin
    college faculty and library staff . professor linda grimm ,
    associate professor of anthropology and project coordinator
    at oberlin , explained the educational goals for this
    online project .
```

The output above shows that the input text has already been pre-processed. All the words have been converted to lowercase (this will avoid having two separate words for *The* and *the*) and punctuation marks have been separated from words. This will avoid failed tokenizations like "words" such as "staff." or "grimm," in the example above, which would otherwise add to our vocabulary.

4.3 An Algorithm for Learning Word Embeddings (`Swivel`)

Now that we have a corpus, we need an (implementation of an) algorithm for learning embeddings. There are various libraries and implementations for this:

- **word2vec**,[4] the system proposed by Mikolov that introduced many of the techniques now commonly used for learning word embeddings. It directly generates word embeddings from the text corpus by using a sliding window and trying to predict a target word based on neighboring context words.

---

[3]https://github.com/hybridnlp/tutorial.
[4]https://pypi.org/project/word2vec.

- **GloVe**[5] an alternative algorithm by Pennington, Socher, and Manning. It splits the process into two steps: (1) Calculating a word–word co-occurrence matrix and (2) learning embeddings from this matrix.
- **fastText**[6] is a more recent algorithm by Mikolov et al. (now at Facebook) that extends the original word2vec algorithm in various ways. Among others, this algorithm takes into account subword information.

In this notebook we will be using Swivel, an algorithm similar to GloVe, which makes it easier to extend to include both words and concepts (which we will do in Chap. 6). As with GloVe, Swivel first extracts a word–word co-occurrence matrix from a text corpus and then uses this matrix to learn the embeddings.

The official Swivel implementation has a few issues when running on Colaboratory; hence, we have included a slightly modified version, which can be found in our GitHub repository.

```
In [ ]: %ls tutorial/scripts/swivel/
```

4.4   Generate Co-occurrence Matrix Using Swivel `prep`

We call Swivel's `prep` command to calculate the word co-occurrence matrix. We use the `%run` magic command, which runs the named Python file as a program, allowing us to pass parameters as if using a command-line terminal.

We set the `shard_size` to 512 since the corpus is quite small. For larger corpora we could use the standard value of 4096.

```
In [ ]: coocs_path = 'umbc/coocs/t_5K/'
        shard_size = 512
        !python tutorial/scripts/swivel/prep.py \
          --input="tutorial/datasamples/umbc_t_5K" \
          --output_dir="umbc/coocs/t_5K/" \
          --shard_size=512
```

The expected output is:

```
... tensorflow parameters ...
vocabulary contains 5120 tokens

writing shard 100/100
done!
```

We see that first, the algorithm determined the vocabulary V, this is the list of words for which an embedding will be generated. Since the corpus is fairly small, so is the vocabulary, which consists of only about 5K words (large corpora can result in vocabularies with millions of words).

The co-occurrence matrix is a sparse matrix of $|V| \times |V|$ elements. Swivel uses shards to create submatrices of $|S| \times |S|$, where S is the shard-size specified above. In this case, we have 100 submatrices.

---

[5]https://github.com/stanfordnlp/GloVe.
[6]https://fasttext.cc.

All this information is stored in the output folder we specified above. It consists of 100 files, one per shard/submatrix and a few additional files:

```
In [ ]: %ls {coocs_path} | head -n 10
```

The `prep` step does the following: (a) it uses a basic, white space, tokenization to get sequences of tokens, (b) in a first pass through the corpus, it counts all tokens and keeps only those that have a minimum frequency (5) in the corpus. Then it keeps a multiple of the `shard_size` of that. The tokens that are kept form the vocabulary with size $v = |V|$. (c) On a second pass through the corpus, it uses a sliding window to count co-occurrences between the focus token and the context tokens (similar to `word2vec`). The result is a sparse co-occurrence matrix of size $v \times v$. For easier storage and manipulation, Swivel uses *sharding* to split the co-occurrence matrix into submatrices of size $s \times s$, where s is the `shard_size`. The sharded co-occurrence submatrices are stored as protobuf[7] files.

4.5   Learn Embeddings from Co-occurrence Matrix

With the sharded co-occurrence matrix it is now possible to learn embeddings. The input is the folder with the co-occurrence matrix (protobuf files with the sparse matrix). - `submatrix_` rows and `submatrix_` columns need to be the same size as the `shard_size` used in the `prep` step.

```
In [ ]: vec_path = 'umbc/vec/t_5K/'
        !python tutorial/scripts/swivel/swivel.py \
            --input_base_path={coocs_path} \
            --output_base_path={vec_path} \
            --num_epochs=40 --dim=150 \
            --submatrix_rows={shard_size} \
            --submatrix_cols={shard_size}
```

This should take a few minutes, depending on the machine. The result is a list of files in the specified output folder, including checkpoints of the model and `tsv` files for the column and row embeddings.

```
In [ ]: %ls {vec_path}
```

One thing missing from the output folder is a file with just the vocabulary, which we will need later on. We copy this file from the folder with the co-occurrence matrix.

```
In [ ]: %cp {coocs_path}/row_vocab.txt {vec_path}vocab.txt
```

4.5.1   Convert tsv Files to bin File

The `tsv` files are easy to inspect, but they take too much space and they are slow to load since we need to convert the different values to floats and pack them as vectors.

---

[7]https://developers.google.com/protocol-buffers/.

Swivel offers a utility to convert the `tsv` files into a `binary` format. At the same time it combines the column and row embeddings into a single space (it simply adds the two vectors for each word in the vocabulary).

```
In [ ]: !python tutorial/scripts/swivel/text2bin.py \
               --vocab={vec_path}vocab.txt \
               --output={vec_path}vecs.bin \
               {vec_path}row_embedding.tsv \
               {vec_path}col_embedding.tsv
```

This adds the `vocab.txt` and `vecs.bin` to the folder with the vectors, which the reader can verify using the following command:

```
In [ ]: %ls -lah {vec_path}
```

4.6 Read Stored Binary Embeddings and Inspect Them

Swivel provides the `vecs` library which implements the basic `Vecs` class. It accepts a `vocab_file` and a file for the binary serialization of the vectors (`vecs.bin`).

```
In [ ]: from tutorial.scripts.swivel import vecs
```

...and we can load existing vectors. We assume the reader managed to generate the embeddings by following the tutorial up to now. Note that, due to random initialization of weight during the training step, results may be different from the ones presented below.

```
In [ ]:
    #uncomment next lines if you did not manage to train embedding above
    #!tar -xzf tutorial/datasamples/umbc_swivel_vec_t_5K.tar.gz -C /
    #vec_path = umbc/vec/t_5K/
    vectors = vecs.Vecs(vec_path + 'vocab.txt',
                        vec_path + 'vecs.bin')
```

We have extended the standard implementation of `swivel.vecs.Vecs` to include a method `k_neighbors`. It accepts a string with the word and an optional k parameter that defaults to 10. It returns a list of Python dictionaries with fields: * `word`: a word in the vocabulary that is near the input word and * `cosim`: the cosine similarity between the input word and the near word. It is easier to display the results as a `pandas` table:

```
In [ ]: import pandas as pd
        pd.DataFrame(vectors.k_neighbors('california'))

In [ ]: pd.DataFrame(vectors.k_neighbors('knowledge'))

In [ ]: pd.DataFrame(vectors.k_neighbors('semantic'))

In [ ]: pd.DataFrame(vectors.k_neighbors('conference'))
```

The cells above should display results similar to those in Table 4.1 (for words *california* and *conference*).

Table 4.1 K-nearest neighbors for *california* and *conference*

cosim	Word	cosim	Word
1.000	california	1.0000	conference
0.5060	university	0.4320	international
0.4239	berkeley	0.4063	secretariat
0.4103	barbara	0.3857	jcdl
0.3941	santa	0.3798	annual
0.3899	southern	0.3708	conferences
0.3673	uc	0.3705	forum
0.3542	johns	0.3629	presentations
0.3396	indiana	0.3601	workshop
0.3388	melvy	0.3580	...

4.6.1 Compound Words

Note that the vocabulary only has single-word expressions, i.e. compound words are not present:

```
In [ ]: pd.DataFrame(vectors.k_neighbors('semantic web'))
```

A common way to work around this issue is to use the average vector of the two individual words (of course this only works if both words are in the vocabulary):

```
In [ ]: semantic_vec = vectors.lookup('semantic')
        web_vec = vectors.lookup('web')
        semweb_vec = (semantic_vec + web_vec)/2
        pd.DataFrame(vectors.k_neighbors(semweb_vec))
```

4.7 Exercise: Create Word Embeddings from Project Gutenberg

4.7.1 Download and Pre-process the Corpus

The reader can try generating new embeddings using a small `Gutenberg` corpus that is provided as part of the NLTK library. It consists of a few public-domain works published as part of the Project Gutenberg.[8]

First, we download the dataset into our environment:

```
In [ ]: import os
        import nltk
        nltk.download('gutenberg')
        %ls '/root/nltk_data/corpora/gutenberg/'
```

---

[8]https://www.gutenberg.org.

As can be seen, the corpus consists of various books, one per file. Most word2vec implementations require to pass a corpus as a single text file. We can issue a few commands to do this by concatenating all the txt files in the folder into a single all.txt file, which we will use later on.

A couple of the files are encoded using iso-8859-1 or binary encodings, which will cause trouble later on, so we rename them to avoid including them into our corpus.

```
In [ ]: %cd /root/nltk_data/corpora/gutenberg/
        # avoid including books with incorrect encoding
        !mv chesterton-ball.txt chesterton-ball.badenc-txt
        !mv milton-paradise.txt milton-paradise.badenc-txt
        !mv shakespeare-caesar.txt shakespeare-caesar.badenc-txt
        # now concatenate all other files into 'all.txt'
        !cat *.txt >> all.txt
        # print result
        %ls -lah '/root/nltk_data/corpora/gutenberg/all.txt'
        # go back to standard folder
        %%cd /content/
```

The full dataset is about 11MB.

4.7.2   Learn Embeddings

Run the steps described above to generate embeddings for the Gutenberg dataset.

4.7.3   Inspect Embeddings

Use methods similar to the ones shown above to get a feeling for whether the generated embeddings have captured interesting relations between words.

4.8   Conclusion

If you followed the instructions in this chapter (or executed the accompanying notebook) you should be able to apply Swivel to learn word embeddings from any text corpus. You should also be now able to load the embeddings and explore the learned vector space. Based on the explorations described in this paper you will have seen that the learned embeddings seem to have captured some semantic similarity notions for the words. In the following chapters you will see how to learn embeddings from knowledge graphs as well as how to modify Swivel to learn not only word embeddings, but also embeddings for the concepts associated with individual words. In Chap. 7 you will also learn more principled ways to measure how good the learned embeddings are.

Chapter 5
Capturing Knowledge Graph Embeddings

Abstract In this chapter we focus on knowledge graph embeddings, an approach to produce embeddings for concepts and names that are the main nodes in knowledge graphs, as well as the relations between them. The resulting embeddings aim to capture the knowledge encoded in the structure of the graph, in terms of how nodes are related to one another. This technique allows translating the symbolic representation of graphs in a format that simplifies manipulation without altering the inherent structure of the graph. Several algorithms to create knowledge graph embeddings have been proposed. In this chapter we will give a brief overview of the most important models and the libraries and tools that implement them. Lastly, we select one of such approaches (HolE) and provide practical guidance to learn embeddings based on WordNet.

5.1 Introduction

While Chap. 2 gave a thorough overview of the different families of knowledge graph embedding algorithms, here we focus on providing a hands-on tutorial that will allow the reader to learn more about what knowledge graph embeddings are in practice and how to apply a concrete approach to learn such embeddings. We start by quickly reviewing some of the most popular algorithms and libraries that implement them. Then, in Sect. 5.3 we use an implementation of HolE to learn embeddings for WordNet. This chapter includes detailed steps to help you understand the process of transforming the WordNet graph structure into the structure required by HolE (and many other KG embedding algorithms). In this chapter we also propose some exercises that will allow the reader to gain further experience with deriving KG embeddings from other well-known knowledge graphs.

© Springer Nature Switzerland AG 2020
J. M. Gomez-Perez et al., *A Practical Guide to Hybrid Natural Language Processing*, https://doi.org/10.1007/978-3-030-44830-1_5

5.2   Knowledge Graph Embeddings

Word embeddings aim at capturing the meaning of words based on very large corpora; however, there are decades of experience and approaches that have tried to capture this meaning by structuring knowledge into semantic nets, ontologies, and graphs. Table 5.1 provides a high-level overview of how neural and symbolic approaches address such challenges.

Table 5.1 Capturing different dimensions of meaning through neural and symbolic approaches

Dimension	Neural	Symbolic
Representation	Vectors	Symbols (URIs)
Input	Large corpora	Human editors (knowledge engineers)
Interpretability	Linked to model and data splits	Requires understanding of the schema
Alignability	Parallel (annotated) corpora	Heuristics and manual
Compositionality	Combine vectors	Merge graphs
Extensibility	Fixed vocabulary, word pieces	Node interlinking
Certainty	Probability distribution	Exact
Debugability	*fix* training data	Edit graph

In recent years, many new approaches have been proposed to derive neural representations for existing knowledge graphs. Think of this as trying to capture the knowledge encoded in the KG to make it easier to use this in deep learning models.

- TransE tries to assign an embedding to nodes and relations, so that $h + r$ is close to t, where h and t are nodes in the graph and r is an edge. In the RDF world, this is simply an RDF triple, where h is the subject, r is the property, and t is the object of the triple.
- **HolE** is a variant of TransE, but uses a different operator (circular correlation) to represent pairs of entities.
- **RDF2Vec** applies word2vec to random walks on an RDF graph (essentially paths or sequences of nodes in the graph).
- **Graph convolutions** apply convolutional operations on graphs to learn the embeddings.
- **Neural message passing** merges two strands of research on KG embeddings: recurrent and convolutional approaches.

For additional information, Nickel et al. [129] compile a collection of relational machine learning for knowledge graphs, while Nguyen [125] provides an overview on embedding models of entities and relations for knowledge base completion.

There are several useful libraries that allow training many of the existing KGE algorithms. Next, we enumerate some of the most popular ones in Python:

- **Pykg2vec**[1] is one of the most complete, it is written on top of TensorFlow[2] and allows to train a wide variety of models such as NTN, TransE, RESCAL, ProjE, ConvE, ComplEx, DISTMULT, TuckER.
- **PBG**[3] (*PyTorch Big Graph*) is written on top of PyTorch[4] and it is designed to scale very big knowledge graphs exploiting also distributed environments. This library is very efficient, achieves great embeddings quality, and requires less time to train. Some of the algorithms implemented are TransE, RESCAL, DISTMULT, and ComplEx.
- **Dgl**[5] (*Deep Graph Library*), instead, allows to train graph neural networks including graph convolution networks such as GCN and R-GCN. It is written on top of PyTorch and MXNet.[6]
- Lastly, **AmpliGraph**[7] is also a very used library written on top of TensorFlow.

5.3 Creating Embeddings for WordNet

In this section, we go through the steps of generating word and concept embeddings using WordNet, a lexico-semantic knowledge graph.

1. Choose (or implement) a KG embedding algorithm.
2. Convert the KG into format required by the KG embedding algorithm.
3. Train the model.
4. Evaluate/inspect results.

5.3.1 Choose Embedding Algorithm: HolE

In this case, we will use an existing implementation[8] of the HolE algorithm available on GitHub.

---

[1] https://github.com/Sujit-O/pykg2vec.

[2] https://github.com/tensorflow/tensorflow.

[3] https://github.com/facebookresearch/PyTorch-BigGraph.

[4] https://github.com/pytorch/pytorch.

[5] https://github.com/dmlc/dgl.

[6] https://github.com/apache/incubator-mxnet.

[7] https://github.com/Accenture/AmpliGraph.

[8] https://github.com/mnick/holographic-embeddings.

5.3.1.1   Install `scikit-kge`

The `holographic-embeddings` repo is actually just a wrapper around `scikit-kge` or SKGE,[9] a library that implements a few KG embedding algorithms. First, we need to install `scikit-kge` as a library in our environment. Execute the following cells to clone the repository and install the library:

```
In [ ]: # make sure we are in the right folder to perform the git clone
        %cd /content/
        !git clone https://github.com/hybridNLP2018/scikit-kge

In [ ]: %cd scikit-kge
        # install a dependency of scikit-kge on the environment,
        #   needed to correclty build scikit-kge
        !pip install nose
        # now build a source distribution for the project
        !python setup.py sdist
```

Executing the previous cell should produce a lot of output as the project is built. Towards the end you should see something like:

```
Writing scikit-kge-0.1/setup.cfg
creating dist
Creating tar archive
```

This should have created a `tar.gz` file in the `dist` subfolder:

```
In [ ]: !ls dist/
```

which we can install on the local environment by using `pip`, the Python package manager.

```
In [ ]: !pip install dist/scikit-kge-0.1.tar.gz
        %cd /content
```

5.3.1.2   Install and Inspect `holographic_embeddings`

Now that `skge` is installed on this environment, we are ready to clone the holographic-embeddings repository, which will enable us to train `HolE` embeddings.

```
In [ ]: # let's go back to the main \content folder and clone the holE repo
        %cd /content/
        !git clone https://github.com/mnick/holographic-embeddings
```

If you want, you can browse the contents of this repo on GitHub or execute the following to see how you can start training embeddings for the wn18 knowledge graph, a WordNet 3.0 subset in which are filtered out the synsets appearing in less than 15 triplets and relation types appearing in less than 5000 triplets [24]. In the following sections we will go into more detail about how to train embeddings, so there is no need to actually execute this training just yet.

```
In [ ]: %less holographic-embeddings/run_hole_wn18.sh
```

---

[9]https://github.com/mnick/scikit-kge.

You should see a section on the bottom of the screen with the contents of the `run_hole_wn18.sh` file. The main execution is:

```
python kg/run_hole.py --fin data/wn18.bin
       --test-all 50 --nb 100 --me 500
       --margin 0.2 --lr 0.1 --ncomp 150
```

which is just executing the `kg/run_hole.py` script on the input data `data/wn18.bin` and passing various arguments to control how to train and produce the embeddings:

- me: states the number of epochs to train for (i.e., number of times to go through the input dataset)
- ncomp: specifies the dimension of the embeddings, each embedding will be a vector of 150 dimensions
- nb: number of batches
- test-all: specifies how often to run validation of the intermediate embeddings. In this case, every 50 epochs.

5.3.2   Convert WordNet KG to the Required Input

5.3.2.1   KG Input Format Required by SKGE

SKGE requires a graph to be represented as a serialized Python dictionary with the following structure:

- `relations`: a list of relation names (the named edges in the graph).
- `entities`: a list of entity names (the nodes in the graph).
- `train_subs`: a list of triples of the form `(head_id, tail_id, rel_id)`, where `head_id` and `tail_id` refer to the index in the `entities` list and `rel_id` refers to the index in the `relations` list. This is the list of triples that will be used to train the embeddings.
- `valid_subs`: a list of triples of the same form as `train_subs`. These are used to validate the embeddings during training (and thus to tune hyperparameters).
- `test_subs`: a list of triples of the same form as `test_subs`. These are used to test the learned embeddings.

The `holographic-embeddings` GitHub repo comes with the example input file `data/wn18.bin`. In the following executable cell, we show how to read and inspect data:

```
In [ ]: import pickle
        import os

        with open('holographic-embeddings/data/wn18.bin', 'rb') as fin:
            wn18_data = pickle.load(fin)

        for k in wn18_data:
            print(k, type(wn18_data[k]), len(wn18_data[k]), wn18_data[k][-3:])
```

The expected output should be similar to:

```
relations 18 ['_synset_domain_region_of', '_verb_group', '_similar_to']
train_subs 141442 [(5395, 37068, 9), (5439, 35322, 11), (28914, 1188, 10)]
entities 40943 ['01164618', '02371344', '03788703']
test_subs 5000 [(17206, 33576, 0), (1179, 11861, 0), (30287, 1443, 1)]
valid_subs 5000 [(351, 25434, 0), (3951, 2114, 7), (756, 14490, 0)]
```

This shows that WordNet wn18 has been represented as a graph of 40943 nodes (which we assume correspond to the synsets) interlinked using 18 relation types. The full set of relations has been split into 141K triples for training and 5K triples each for testing and validation.

5.3.2.2 Converting WordNet 3.0 into the Required Input Format from Scratch

It will be useful to have experience converting your KG into the required input format. Hence, rather than simply reusing the `wn18.bin` input file, we will generate our own directly from the NLTK WordNet API.[10]

First we need to download WordNet:

```
In [ ]: import nltk
        nltk.download('wordnet')
```

Explore the WordNet API

Now that we have the KG, we can use the WordNet API to explore the graph. Refer to the how-to document for a more in-depth overview, here we only show a few methods that will be needed to generate our input file.

```
In [ ]: from nltk.corpus import wordnet as wn
```

The main nodes in WordNet are called synsets (synonym sets). These correspond roughly to *concepts*. You can find all the synsets related to a word like this:

```
In [ ]: wn.synsets('dog')
```

The output from the cell above shows how synsets are identified by the NLTK WordNet API. They have the following form:

`<main-lemma>.<POS-code>.<sense-number>`.

As far as we are aware, this is a format chosen by the implementors of the NLTK WordNet API and other APIs may choose diverging ways to refer to synsets. You can get a list of all the synsets as follows (we only show the first 5):

```
In [ ]: for synset in list(wn.all_synsets())[:5]:
            print(synset.name())
```

Similarly, you can also get a list of all the lemma names (again we only show 5):

---

[10]See how-to at: http://www.nltk.org/howto/wordnet.html.

```
In [ ]: for lemma in list(wn.all_lemma_names())[5000:5005]:
            print(lemma)
```

For a given synset, you can find related synsets or lemmas, by calling the functions for each relation type. Below we provide a couple of examples for the first sense of adjective *adaxial*. In the first example, we see that this synset belongs to topic domain biology.n.01, which is again a synset. In the second example, we see that it has two lemmas, which are relative to the synset. In the third example, we retrieve the lemmas in a form that are not relative to the synset, which is the one we will use later on.

```
In [ ]: wn.synset('adaxial.a.01').topic_domains()
```

```
In [ ]: wn.synset('adaxial.a.01').lemmas()
```

```
In [ ]: wn.synset('adaxial.a.01').lemma_names()
```

Entities and Relations to Include

The main nodes in WordNet are the synsets; however, lemmas can also be considered to be nodes in the graph. Hence, you need to decide which nodes to include. Since we are interested in capturing as much information as can be provided by WordNet, we will include both synsets and lemmas.

WordNet defines a large number of relations between synsets and lemmas. Again, you can decide to include all or just some of these. One particularity of WordNet is that many relations are defined twice: e.g. hypernym and hyponym are the exact same relation, but in reverse order. Since this is not really providing additional information, we only include such relations once. The following cell defines all the relations we will be taking into account. We represent these as Python dictionaries, where the keys are the name of the relation and the values are functions that accept a head entity and produce a list of tail entities for that specific relation:

```
In [ ]: syn_relations = {
            'hyponym': lambda syn: syn.hyponyms(),
            'instance_hyponym': lambda syn: syn.instance_hyponyms(),
            'member_meronym': lambda syn: syn.member_meronyms(),
            'has_part': lambda syn: syn.part_meronyms(),
            'topic_domain': lambda syn: syn.topic_domains(),
            'usage_domain': lambda syn: syn.usage_domains(),
            '_member_of_domain_region': lambda syn: syn.region_domains(),
            'attribute': lambda syn: syn.attributes(),
            'entailment': lambda syn: syn.entailments(),
            'cause': lambda syn: syn.causes(),
            'also_see': lambda syn: syn.also_sees(),
            'verb_group': lambda syn: syn.verb_groups(),
            'similar_to': lambda syn: syn.similar_tos()
        }
        lem_relations = {
            'antonym': lambda lem: lem.antonyms(),
            'derivationally_related_form':
                lambda lem: lem.derivationally_related_forms(),
            'pertainym': lambda lem: lem.pertainyms()
        }

        syn2lem_relations = {
            'lemma': lambda syn: syn.lemma_names()
        }
```

Triple Generation

We are now ready to generate triples by using the WordNet API. Recall that skge
requires triples of the form (head_id, tail_id, rel_id); hence, we will
need to have some way of mapping entity (synset and lemma) names and relations
types to unique ids. We therefore assume we will have an entity_id_map and
a rel_id_map, which will map the entity name (or relation type) to an id. The
following two cells implement functions which will iterate through the synsets and
relations to generate the triples:

```
In [ ]: def generate_syn_triples(entity_id_map, rel_id_map):
          result = []
          for synset in list(wn.all_synsets()):
            h_id = entity_id_map.get(synset.name())
            if h_id is None:
              print('No entity id for ', synset)
              continue
            for synrel, srfn in syn_relations.items():
              r_id = rel_id_map.get(synrel)
              if r_id is None:
                print('No rel id for', synrel)
                continue
              for obj in srfn(synset):
                t_id = entity_id_map.get(obj.name())
                if t_id is None:
                  print('No entity id for object', obj)
                  continue
                result.append((h_id, t_id, r_id))

            for rel, fn in syn2lem_relations.items():
              r_id = rel_id_map.get(rel)
              if r_id is None:
                print('No rel id for', rel)
                continue
              for obj in fn(synset):
                lem = obj.lower()
                t_id = entity_id_map.get(lem)
                if t_id is None:
                  print('No entity id for object', obj, 'lowercased:', lem)
                  continue
                result.append((h_id, t_id, r_id))
          return result

In [ ]: def generate_lem_triples(entity_id_map, rel_id_map):
          result = []
          for lemma in list(wn.all_lemma_names()):
            h_id = entity_id_map.get(lemma)
            if h_id is None:
              print('No entity id for lemma', lemma)
              continue
            _lems = wn.lemmas(lemma)
            for lemrel, lrfn in lem_relations.items():
              r_id = rel_id_map.get(lemrel)
              if r_id is None:
                print('No rel id for ', lemrel)
                continue
              for _lem in _lems:
                for obj in lrfn(_lem):
                  t_id = entity_id_map.get(obj.name().lower())
                  if t_id is None:
                    print('No entity id for obj lemma', obj, obj.name())
                    continue
                  result.append((h_id, t_id, r_id))
          return result
```

Putting It All Together

Now that we have methods for generating lists of triples, we can generate the input dictionary and serialize it. We need to:

1. create our lists of entities and relations,
2. derive a map from entity and relation names to ids,
3. generate the triples,
4. split the triples into training, validation, and test subsets, and
5. write the Python dict to a serialized file.

We implement this in the following method:

```
In [ ]: import random # for shuffling list of triples

        def wnet30_holE_bin(out):
            """Creates a skge-compatible bin file for training
            HolE embeddings based on WordNet 3.0"""
            synsets = [synset.name() for synset in wn.all_synsets()]
            lemmas = [lemma for lemma in wn.all_lemma_names()]
            entities = list(synsets + list(set(lemmas)))
            print('Found %s synsets, %s lemmas, hence %s entities' %
              (len(synsets), len(lemmas), len(entities)))
            entity_id_map = {ent_name: id for id, ent_name in enumerate(entities)}
            n_entity = len(entity_id_map)

            print("N_ENTITY: %d" % n_entity)

            relations = list( list(syn_relations.keys()) + list(lem_relations.keys()) + \
            list(syn2lem_relations.keys()))
            relation_id_map = {rel_name: id for id, rel_name in enumerate(relations)}
            n_rel = len(relation_id_map)

            print("N_REL: %d" % n_rel)
            print('relations', relation_id_map)

            syn_triples = generate_syn_triples(entity_id_map, relation_id_map)
            print("Syn2syn relations", len(syn_triples))
            lem_triples = generate_lem_triples(entity_id_map, relation_id_map)
            print("Lem2lem relations", len(lem_triples))
            all_triples = syn_triples + lem_triples
            print("All triples", len(all_triples))
            random.shuffle(all_triples)

            test_triple = all_triples[:500]
            valid_triple = all_triples[500:1000]
            train_triple = all_triples[1000:]

            to_pickle = {
                "entities": entities,
                "relations": relations,
                "train_subs": train_triple,
                "test_subs": test_triple,
                "valid_subs": valid_triple
            }

            with open(out, 'wb') as handle:
              pickle.dump(to_pickle, handle, protocol=pickle.HIGHEST_PROTOCOL)

            print("wrote to %s" % out)
```

Generate `wn30.bin`

Now we are ready to generate the `wn30.bin` file which we can feed to the `HolE` algorithm implementation.

```
In [ ]: out_bin='/content/holographic-embeddings/data/wn30.bin'
        wnet30_holE_bin(out_bin)
```

Notice that the resulting dataset now contains 265K entities, compared to 41K in wn18 (to be fair, only 118K of the entities are synsets).

5.3.3   Learn the Embeddings

Now, we will use our WordNet 3.0 dataset to learn embeddings for both synsets and lemmas. Since this is fairly slow, we only train for 2 epochs, which can take up to 10 min. (In the exercises at the end of this chapter, we provide a link to download pre-computed embeddings which have been trained for 500 epochs.)

```
In [ ]: wn30_holE_out='/content/wn30_holE_2e.bin'
        holE_dim=150
        num_epochs=2
        !python /content/holographic-embeddings/kg/run_hole.py \
          --fin {out_bin} --fout {wn30_holE_out} \
          --nb 100 --me {num_epochs} --margin 0.2 --lr 0.1 --ncomp {holE_dim}
```

The output should look similar to:

```
INFO:EX-KG:Fitting model HolE with trainer PairwiseStochasticTrainer and parameters
  Namespace(afs='sigmoid', fin='/content/holographic-embeddings/data/wn30.bin',
  fout='/content/wn30_holE_2e.bin', init='nunif', lr=0.1, margin=0.2,
  me=2, mode='rank', nb=100, ncomp=150, ne=1, no_pairwise=False,
  rparam=0, sampler='random-mode', test_all=10)
INFO:EX-KG:[  1] time = 120s, violations = 773683
INFO:EX-KG:[  2] time = 73s, violations = 334894
INFO:EX-KG:[  2] time = 73s, violations = 334894
INFO:EX-KG:[  2] VALID: MRR = 0.11/0.12, Mean Rank = 90012.28/90006.14, \
  Hits@10 = 15.02/15.12
DEBUG:EX-KG:FMRR valid = 0.122450, best = -1.000000
INFO:EX-KG:[  2] TEST: MRR = 0.11/0.12, Mean Rank = 95344.42/95335.96, \
  Hits@10 = 15.74/15.74
```

5.3.4   Inspect the Resulting Embeddings

Now that we have trained the model, we can retrieve the embeddings for the entities and inspect them.

5.3.4.1   `skge` Output File Format

The output file is again a pickled serialization of a Python dictionary. It contains the `model` itself and results for the test and validation runs as well as execution times.

```
In [ ]: with open(wn30_holE_out, 'rb') as fin:
            hole_model = pickle.load(fin)
        print(type(hole_model), len(hole_model))
        for k in hole_model:
            print(k, type(hole_model[k]))
```

We are interested in the model itself, which is an instance of a skge.hole. HolE class and has various parameters. The entity embeddings are stored in parameter E, which is essentially a matrix of $n_e \times d$, where n_e is the number of entities and d is the dimension of each vector.

```
In [ ]: model = hole_model['model']
        E = model.params['E']
        print(type(E), E.shape)
```

5.3.4.2   Converting Embeddings to a More Manageable Format

Unfortunately, skge does not provide methods for exploring the embedding space (KG embedding libraries are more geared towards prediction of relations). Therefore, we will convert the embeddings into an easier to explore format. We first convert them into a pair of files for the vectors and the vocabulary and we will then use the swivel library to explore the results.

First, we read the list of entities, which will be our vocabulary, i.e. the names of synsets and lemmas for which we have embeddings.

```
In [ ]: with open('/content/holographic-embeddings/data/wn30.bin', 'rb') as fin:
            wn30_data = pickle.load(fin)
        entities = wn30_data['entities']
        len(entities)
```

Next, we generate a vocab file and a tsv file where each line contains the word and a list of d numbers.

```
In [ ]: vec_file = '/content/wn30_holE_2e.tsv'
        vocab_file = '/content/wn30_holE_2e.vocab.txt'

        with open(vocab_file, 'w', encoding='utf_8') as f:
          for i, w in enumerate(entities):
            word = w.strip()
            print(word, file=f)

        with open(vec_file, 'w', encoding='utf_8') as f:
          for i, w in enumerate(entities):
            word = w.strip()
            embedding = E[i]
            print('\t'.join([word] + [str(x) for x in embedding]), file=f)
        !wc -l {vec_file}
```

Now that we have these files, we can use swivel, which we used in the first notebook to inspect the embeddings. First, download the tutorial materials and swivel if necessary, although you may already have it on your environment if you previously executed the first notebook of this tutorial.

```
In [ ]: %cd /content
        !git clone https://github.com/HybridNLP2018/tutorial
```

Use the `swivel/text2bin` script to convert the `tsv` embeddings into `swivel`'s binary format.

```
In [ ]: vecbin = '/content/wn30_holE_2e.tsv.bin'
        !python /content/tutorial/scripts/swivel/text2bin.py \
            --vocab={vocab_file} \
            --output={vecbin} {vec_file}
```

Next, we can load the vectors using `swivel`'s `Vecs` class, which provides easy inspection of neighbors.

```
In [ ]: from tutorial.scripts.swivel import vecs
        vectors = vecs.Vecs(vocab_file, vecbin)
```

Inspect a few example lemmas and synsets:

```
In [ ]: import pandas as pd
        pd.DataFrame(vectors.k_neighbors('california'))
```

```
In [ ]: wn.synsets('california')
```

```
In [ ]: pd.DataFrame(vectors.k_neighbors('california.n.01'))
```

```
In [ ]: pd.DataFrame(vectors.k_neighbors('conference'))
```

```
In [ ]: pd.DataFrame(vectors.k_neighbors('semantic'))
```

```
In [ ]: pd.DataFrame(vectors.k_neighbors('semantic.a.01'))
```

As you can see, the embeddings do not look very good at the moment. In part this is due to the fact we only trained the model for 2 epochs. We have pre-calculated a set of HolE embeddings for 500 epochs, which you can download and inspect as part of an optional exercise below. Results for these are much better:

cosine sim	Entity
1.0000	lem_california
0.4676	lem_golden_state
0.4327	lem_ca
0.4004	lem_californian
0.3838	lem_calif.
0.3500	lem_fade
0.3419	lem_keystone_state
0.3375	wn31_antilles.n.01
0.3356	wn31_austronesia.n.01
0.3340	wn31_overbalance.v.02

For the synset corresponding to *california*, we also see "sensible" results:

cosine sim	Entity
1.0000	wn31_california.n.01
0.4909	wn31_nevada.n.01
0.4673	wn31_arizona.n.01

cosine sim	Entity
0.4593	wn31_tennessee.n.01
0.4587	wn31_new_hampshire.n.01
0.4555	wn31_sierra_nevada.n.02
0.4073	wn31_georgia.n.01
0.4048	wn31_west_virginia.n.01
0.3991	wn31_north_carolina.n.01
0.3977	wn31_virginia.n.01

One thing to notice here is that all of the top 10 closely related entities for california.n.01 are also synsets. Similarly for lemma california, the most closely related entities are also lemmas, although some synsets also made it into the top 10 neighbors. This may indicate a tendency of HolE to keep lemmas close to other lemmas and synsets close to other synsets. In general, choices about how nodes in the KG are related will affect how their embeddings are interrelated.

5.4 Exercises

In this notebook we provided an overview of recent knowledge graph embedding approaches and showed how to use existing implementations to generate word and concept embeddings for WordNet 3.0.

5.4.1 Exercise: Train Embeddings on Your Own KG

If you have a KG of your own, you can adapt the code shown above to generate a graph representation as expected by skge and you can train your embeddings in this way. Popular KGs are Freebase and DBpedia.

5.4.2 Exercise: Inspect WordNet 3.0 Pre-calculated Embeddings

We have used code similar to the one shown above to train embeddings for 500 epochs using HolE. You can execute the following cells to download and explore these embeddings. The embeddings are about 142MB, so downloading them may take a few minutes.

```
In [ ]: !mkdir /content/vec/
        %cd /content/vec/
        !wget https://zenodo.org/record/1446214/files/wn-en-3.0-HolE-500e-150d.tar.gz
        !tar -xzf wn-en-3.0-HolE-500e-150d.tar.gz

In [ ]: %ls /content/vec
```

The downloaded tar contains a `tsv.bin` and a `vocab` file like the one we created above. We can use it to load the vectors using `swivel`'s `Vecs`:

```
In [ ]: vocab_file = '/content/vec/wn-en-3.1-HolE-500e.vocab.txt'
        vecbin = '/content/vec/wn-en-3.1-HolE-500e.tsv.bin'
        wnHolE = vecs.Vecs(vocab_file, vecbin)
```

Now you are ready to start exploring. The only thing to notice is that we have added a prefix to `lem_` to all lemmas and `wn31_` to all synsets, as shown in the following examples:

```
In [ ]: pd.DataFrame(wnHolE.k_neighbors('lem_california'))
```

```
In [ ]: pd.DataFrame(wnHolE.k_neighbors('wn31_california.n.01'))
```

5.5 Conclusion

If you followed the instructions in this chapter, you will have trained a model with concept and word embeddings derived from WordNet, a well-known knowledge graph that encodes knowledge about words and their senses. You will also have learned about the pre-processing needed to select which parts of the KG you want to use to train embeddings, as well as how to export the graph into a format that most KG embedding algorithms expect. Finally, you will have explored the learned embeddings and briefly seen how they compare to word embeddings learned from text corpora in the previous chapter. The main advantage of KG embeddings is that they already encode knowledge about the desired conceptual level. On the other hand, the main issue with KG embeddings is that you need a KG to be available for your domain of choice. In the next chapter we see that it is also possible to learn concept embeddings without a KG, by modifying how word embeddings are learned from text.

Part II
Combining Neural Architectures and Knowledge Graphs

Chapter 6
Building Hybrid Representations from Text Corpora, Knowledge Graphs, and Language Models

Abstract In the previous chapter we saw how knowledge graph embedding algorithms can capture structured knowledge about concepts and relations in a graph as embeddings in a vector space, which then can be used in downstream tasks. However, this type of approaches can only capture the knowledge that is explicitly represented in the graph, hence lacking in recall and domain coverage. In this chapter, we focus on algorithms that address this limitation through the combination of information from both unstructured text corpora and structured knowledge graphs. The first approach is Vecsigrafo, which produces corpus-based word, lemma, and concept embeddings from large disambiguated corpora. Vecsigrafo jointly learns word, lemma, and concepts embeddings, bringing together textual and symbolic knowledge representations in a single, unified formalism for use in neural natural language processing architectures. The second and more recent approach is called Transigrafo, which adopts recent Transformer-based language models to derive concept-level contextual embeddings, providing state-of-the-art performance in word-sense disambiguation with reduced complexity.

6.1 Introduction

In the previous chapters we saw models which were capable of learning word embeddings from text or learning concept embeddings from knowledge graphs. In this chapter we look at hybrid approaches that aim to merge the best of both worlds. In the first half of the chapter we introduce and provide hands-on experience with Vecsigrafo, an extension of the Swivel algorithm to learn word and concept embeddings based on a disambiguated text corpus. We start by introducing the required terminology and notation in Sect. 6.2. Then we provide a conceptual intuition about how Vecsigrafo works and continue with a formal definition of the algorithm. We also describe how Vecsigrafo is implemented (Sect. 6.4) and provide practical Sects. 6.5 and 6.6 to learn embeddings from a sample corpus and explore the results. In the second half of this chapter, in Sect. 6.7, we take a step further and show how to apply transformers and neural language models to generate an analogous representation of Vecsigrafo, called Transigrafo.

© Springer Nature Switzerland AG 2020

J. M. Gomez-Perez et al., *A Practical Guide to Hybrid Natural Language Processing*, https://doi.org/10.1007/978-3-030-44830-1_6

6.2   Preliminaries and Notation

Let T be the set of *tokens* that can occur in text after some tokenization is applied; this means tokens may include words ("running"), punctuation marks (";"), multi-word expressions ("United States of America"), or combinations of words with punctuation marks ("However,", "–"). Let L be the set of *lemmas*: base forms of words (i.e., without morphological or conjugational variations). Note that $L \subset T$.[1]

We also use the term **lexical entry**—or simply **word**—to refer to a token or a lemma. Let C be the set of concept identifiers in some knowledge graph, we use the term **semantic entry**—or simply **concept**—to refer to elements in C.

Let $V \subset T \cup C$ be the set of lexical and semantic entries for which we want to derive embeddings, also called the **vocabulary**. A corpus is a sequence of tokens $t_i \in T$; we follow and extend the definition of **context** around a token (used in, e.g., word2vec, GloVe, and Swivel) as a W-sized sliding window over the sequence of tokens. Therefore we say that tokens $t^{i-W}, \dots, t^{i-1}, t^{i+1}, \dots, t^{i+W}$ are in the context of center token t^i in the context at position i in the corpus.

Each context can be represented as a collection of center-context pairs of the form (t_i, t_j), where $t_i \in T$ and $t_j \in T$. We extend this to take into account lemmas and concepts: let D be the collection of center-context entry pairs (x_i, x_j) observed in a corpus, where $x_i \in V$ and $x_j \in V$.[2] We use notation $\#(x_i, x_j)$ to refer to the number of times the center entry x_i co-occurred with context entry x_j in D. We also define $p(x_i, x_j)$ as the set of positions in the corpus where x_i is the center word and x_j is a context word. Similarly $\#(x)$ is the number of times entry x occurred in D as a center word.

Finally, let d be the dimension of the vector space, so that for each entry x in V has two corresponding vectors $\mathbf{x}_C$ and $\mathbf{x}_F \in \mathbb{R}^d$, which correspond to the vector representation of x as a context or as a center entry, respectively.

6.3   What Is Vecsigrafo and How to Build It

So as to build models that use both bottom-up (corpus-based) embeddings and top-down structured knowledge (in a graph), we generate embeddings that share the same vocabulary as the knowledge graphs. This means generating embeddings for knowledge items represented in the knowledge graph such as concepts and surface forms (words and expressions) associated with the concepts in it. In RDF, this would typically mean values for `rdfs:label` properties, or words and expressions

---

[1] We assume lemmatization correctly strips away punctuation marks (e.g., lemma of "However," is "however" and lemma of "Dr." is "Dr.").

[2] In principle, we could define two vocabularies, one for the center entries and another for the context entries; however, in this paper we assume both vocabularies are equal; hence, we do not make a distinction.

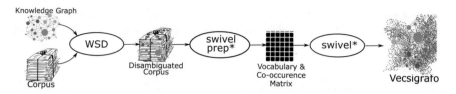

Fig. 6.1 Process for Vecsigrafo generation from a text corpus

encoded as `ontolex:LexicalEntry` instances using the lexicon model for ontologies.[3]

The overall process for learning joint word and concept embeddings in what we call a Vecsigrafo [39] (derived from the term Sensigrafo, Expert System's knowledge graph[4]) is depicted in Fig. 6.1. We start with a text corpus on which we apply tokenization and word-sense disambiguation (WSD). Tokenization on its own results in a sequence of tokens. WSD further results in a *disambiguated corpus*, an enriched form of the sequence of tokens, whereby there are additional sequences aligned to the initial sequence of tokens. In this work we use the following additional sequences: lemmas, concepts, and grammar types. The grammar type assigns a part-of-speech identifier to each token (e.g., article, adjective, adverb, noun, proper noun, punctuation mark); we use these for filtering, but not for generating embeddings. Since some tokens may have no associated lemma or concept, we pad these sequences with $\varnothing_L$ and $\varnothing_C$, which are never included in the vocabulary V.

The disambiguated corpus can optionally be modified or **filtered** in different ways. In our evaluation, we experiment with a filter whereby we (1) remove elements from the sequences if they have grammar type `article, punctuation mark`, or `auxiliary verbs` and (2) generalize tokens with grammar type `entity` or `person proper noun`, which replaces the original token with special tokens `grammar#ENT` and `grammar#NPH`, respectively. The intuition behind this filter is that it produces sequences where each element is more semantically meaningful, since articles, punctuation marks, and auxiliary verbs are binding words which should not contribute much meaning to their co-occurring words. Similarly, in many cases, we are not interested in deriving embeddings for entities (names of people, places, or organizations); furthermore, many entity names may only occur a few times in a corpus and may refer to different real-world individuals.

To generate embeddings for both semantic and lexical entries, we iterate through the disambiguated corpus to decide on a vocabulary V and calculate a representation of D called a co-occurrence matrix M, which is a $|V| \times |V|$ matrix, where each element $x_{ij} = \#(x_i, x_j)$. We follow word2vec, GloVe, and Swivel in using a *dynamic*

---

[3]https://www.w3.org/2016/05/ontolex.

[4]Sensigrafo, Expert System's knowledge graph: https://www.expertsystem.com/products/cogito-cognitive-technology/semantic-technology/knowledge-graph.

context window [103], whereby co-occurrence counts are weighted according to the distance between the center and the context entry using the harmonic function. More formally, we use

$$\#_\delta(x_i, x_j) = \Sigma_{c \in p(x_i, x_j)} \frac{W - \delta_c(x_i, x_j) + 1}{W} \tag{6.1}$$

where $\delta_c(x_i, x_j)$ is the distance, in token positions, between the center entry x_i and the context entry x_j in a particular context at position c in the corpus. W is the window size as presented in Sect. 6.2.

In standard word embedding algorithms, there is only one sequence of tokens; hence $1 <= \delta_c(x_i, x_j) <= W$. In our case we have three aligned sequences: tokens, lemmas, and concepts. Hence $\delta(x_i, x_j)$ may also be 0, e.g. when x_i is a lemma and x_j is its disambiguated concept. Hence, in this work, we use a slightly modified version:

$$\delta'_c(x_i, x_j) = \begin{cases} \delta_c(x_i, x_j) & \text{if } \delta_c(x_i, x_j) > 0 \\ 1 & \text{if } \delta_c(x_i, x_j) = 0 \end{cases} \tag{6.2}$$

This gives us $\#_{\delta'}(x_i x_j)$ and, based on the co-occurrence matrix M we thus apply the training phase of a slightly modified version of the Swivel algorithm to learn the embeddings for the vocabulary. The original Swivel loss function is given by

$$\mathcal{L}_S = \begin{cases} \mathcal{L}_1 & \text{if } \#(x_i, x_j) > 0 \\ \mathcal{L}_0 & \text{if } \#(x_i, x_j) = 0, \text{ where} \end{cases}$$

$$\mathcal{L}_1 = \frac{1}{2}\#(x_i, x_j)^{1/2}(\mathbf{x_i}^\top \mathbf{x_j} - \log \frac{\#(x_i, x_j)|D|}{\#(x_i)\#(x_j)})$$

$$\mathcal{L}_0 = \log[1 + \exp(\mathbf{x_i}^\top \mathbf{x_j} - \log \frac{|D|}{\#(x_i)\#(x_j)})]$$

Our modifications include: using $\#_{\delta'}(x_i, x_j)$ instead of the default definition and the addition of a vector regularization term as suggested by Duong et al. [47] (equation 3) which aims to reduce the distance between the column and row (i.e., center and context) vectors for all vocabulary elements, i.e.

$$\mathcal{L} = \mathcal{L}_S + \gamma \sum_{x \in V} \|\mathbf{x}_F - \mathbf{x}_C\|_2^2 \tag{6.3}$$

Such modification is useful for our purposes, since the row and column vocabularies are the same; while in the general case, usually the sum or the average of both vectors would be used to produce the final embeddings.

6.4   Implementation

Although any knowledge graph, natural language processing toolkit, and WSD algorithm can be used to build a Vecsigrafo, our original implementation used Expert System's proprietary Cogito[5] pipeline to *tokenize and disambiguate* the corpora. Cogito is based on a knowledge graph called **Sensigrafo**, which is similar to WordNet, but larger and tightly coupled to the Cogito disambiguator (i.e., the disambiguator uses intricate heuristic rules based on lexical, domain, and semantic rules to do its job). Sensigrafo contains about 400K lemmas and 300K concepts (called *syncons* in Sensigrafo) interlinked via 61 relation types, which render almost 3M links. Sensigrafo also provides a *glossa*—a human readable textual definition— for each concept, which is only intended for facilitating the inspection and curation of the knowledge graph.

As part of the work that led to the creation of the first Vecsigrafo, we studied the effect of applying alternative disambiguation algorithms[6] and compared them with Cogito. We implemented three disambiguation methods: (1) the shallow connectivity disambiguation (scd) algorithm introduced by [112], which essentially chooses the candidate concepts that are better connected to other candidate concepts according to the underlying knowledge graph; (2) the most frequent disambiguation (mostfreqd), which chooses the most frequent concept associated with each lemma encountered in the corpus; and (3) the random concept candidate disambiguation (rndd), which selects a random concept for each lemma encountered in the corpus. Note that rndd is not completely random, it still assigns a plausible concept to each lemma, since the choice is made out of the set of all concepts associated with the lemma.

To implement our approach, we also extended the matrix construction phase of the Swivel [164] algorithm[7] to generate a co-occurrence matrix which can include both lexical and semantic entries as part of the vocabulary. Table 6.1 provides an example of different tokenizations and disambiguations for a context window derived from the same original text. To get a feeling for concepts and the effect of different disambiguators, notice that Cogito assigns concept #82073 (with glossa *appropriate for a condition or occasion* and synonyms *suitable, right*) to "proper," while scd and mostfreqd have assigned concept #91937 (with glossa *marked by suitability or rightness or appropriateness* and synonyms *kosher*). The rndd disambiguation has assigned an incorrect concept #189906 from mathematics (with glossa *distinguished from a weaker relation by excluding. . .*).

Table 6.1 also introduces notation we will use throughout the remainder of the book to identify embedding variations. We will use t to refer to plain text tokens and assume Cogito-based tokenization, if a different tokenization is meant, we will add a suffix like in the table to show that Swivel tokenization has been used. Similarly, we

---

[5]More about Cogito at: https://www.expertsystem.com/products/cogito-cognitive-technology.

[6]See [123] for a comprehensive survey on the topic.

[7]As implemented in https://github.com/tensorflow/models/tree/master/research/swivel.

Table 6.1 Example tokenizations for the first window of size $W = 3$ for sentence: "With regard to enforcement, proper agreements must also be concluded with the Eastern European countries…"

Context	t^{i-3}	t^{i-2}	t^{i-1}	t^i	t^{i+1}	t^{i+2}	t^{i+3}	
t_{swivel}	With	regard	to	enforcement,	proper	agreements	must	also
t	With regard to enforcement	,	proper	agreements	must	also	be	
l	With regard to enforcement	∅	proper	agreement	must	also	be	
s	en#216081	en#4652	∅	en#82073	en#191513	∅	en#192047	∅
g	PRE	NOU	PNT	ADJ	NOU	AUX	ADV	AUX
$s_{mostfreqd}$	en#216081	en#4652	∅	en#91937	en#191513	en#77903	en#191320	en#77408
s_{scd}	en#216081	en#4652	∅	en#91937	en#191513	en#239961	en#191320	en#134549
s_{rndd}	en#216081	en#4652	∅	en#189906	en#191513	en#101756782	en#191320	en#77445
t_f	With regard to enforcement	proper	agreements	also	concluded	eastern	european	
l_f	With regard to enforcement	proper	agreement	also	conclude	eastern	European	
s_f	en#216081	en#4652	en#82073	en#191513	en#192047	en#150286	en#85866	en#98025
g_f	PRE	NOU	ADJ	NOU	ADV	VERB	ADJ	ADJ

First we show standard Swivel tokenization, next we show the standard Cogito tokenization with sequences for plain text, lemmas, syncons, and grammar type; next we show alternative disambiguation syncons for the same tokenization. Finally, we show cogito tokenization after applying filtering

use l to refer to lemmas and s to refer to concept identifiers (we assume syncons since most of our experiments use Sensigrafo, although in some cases this may refer to other concept identifiers in other knowledge graphs such as BabelNet). As described above, the source sequences may be combined, which in this paper means combinations ts or ls. Finally we use suffix _f to show that the original sequence was filtered based on grammar type information as described above.

6.5 Training Vecsigrafo

We use a transcribed Jupyter notebook to illustrate with real code snippets how to actually generate a Vecsigrafo based on a subset of the UMBC corpus.[8] The notebook, which follows the procedure described in Sect. 6.3 and depicted in Fig. 6.1, is available and executable online.[9] In addition to finalizing this section, we encourage the reader to run the live notebook and do the exercises it includes in order to better understand what we discussed in the following lines:

6.5.1 Tokenization and Word-Sense Disambiguation

As described in Sect. 6.4, the main difference with standard Swivel is that we use word-sense disambiguation as a pre-processing step to identify the lemmas and

---

[8]https://ebiquity.umbc.edu/resource/html/id/351/UMBC-webbase-corpus.

[9]https://colab.research.google.com/github/hybridnlp/tutorial/blob/master/03_vecsigrafo.ipynb.

concepts entailed in the text, while Swivel simply uses white-space tokenization. Therefore, each "token" in the resulting sequences is composed of a lemma and an optional concept identifier.

6.5.1.1 Disambiguators

Since we apply WSD, we need to select some disambiguation strategy. Unfortunately, the number of freely available, open-source high-performance disambiguators available is very limited. Indeed, at Expert System we have our own disambiguator,[10] which assigns **syncon**s to lemmas in the text.

Since Expert System's disambiguator and semantic knowledge graph are proprietary, in this notebook we use WordNet as our knowledge graph. Also, we have implemented a lightweight disambiguation strategy, proposed by Macini et al. [112], allowing us to produce disambiguated corpora based on WordNet 3.1.

To be able to inspect the disambiguated corpus, let us first make sure we have access to WordNet in our environment by executing the following cell:

```
In [ ]: import nltk
        nltk.download('wordnet')
        from nltk.corpus import wordnet as wn
        wn.synset('Maya.n.02')
```

6.5.1.2 Tokenizations

When applying a disambiguator, the tokens are no longer (groups of) words. Each token can contain different types of information. We generally keep the following token information:

- t: text, the original text (possibly normalized, i.e., lowercased).
- l: lemma, the lemma form of the word, without morphological or conjugational information.
- g: grammar: the grammar type.
- s: syncon (or synset in the case of WordNet) identifier.

6.5.1.3 Example WordNet

Our GitHub repository[11] includes a subset of a disambiguated tokenization for the UMBC corpus that contains the first 5000 lines of the corpus (the full corpus has about 40 million lines) with the purpose to illustrate the necessary steps to generate

---

[10]https://www.expertsystem.com/products/cogito-cognitive-technology/semantic-technology/disambiguation.

[11]https://github.com/hybridnlp/tutorial.

the Vecsigrafo embeddings. Execute the following cell to clone the repository, unzip the sample corpus, and print its first line:

```
In [ ]: %cd /content/
        !git clone https://github.com/hybridnlp/tutorial.git
        %cd /content/tutorial/datasamples/
        !unzip umbc_tlgs_wnscd_5K.zip
        toked_corpus = '/content/tutorial/datasamples/umbc_tlgs_wnscd_5K'
        !head -n1 {toked_corpus}
        %cd /content/
```

You should see, among others, the first line in the corpus, starting with:

```
the%7CGT_ART mayan%7Clem_Mayan%7CGT_ADJ%7Cwn31_Maya.n.03
image%7Clem_image%7CGT_NOU%7Cwn31_effigy.n.01
```

The previous line shows the format we are using to represent the tokenized corpus. We use white space to separate the tokens and have URL-encoded each token to avoid mixing up tokens. Since this format is hard to read, we provide a library to inspect the lines in an easy manner. Execute the following cell to display the first line in the corpus as a table, as shown below:

```
In [ ]: %cd /content/
        import tutorial.scripts.wntoken as wntoken
        import pandas

        # open the file and produce a list of python dictionaries describing the tokens
        corpus_tokens = wntoken.open_as_token_dicts(toked_corpus, max_lines=1)
        # convert the tokens into a pandas DataFrame to display in table form
        pandas.DataFrame(corpus_tokens, columns=['line', 't', 'l', 'g', 's', 'glossa'])
```

```
Out[4]:
    line    t        l        g      s            glossa
    0    1   the      None     ART    None         None
    1    1   mayan    Mayan    ADJ    Maya.n.03    None
    2    1   image    image    NOU    effigy.n.01  representation of a person
    3    1   was      be       AUX    be.v.01      have the quality of being
    4    1   donated  donate   VER    donate.v.01  give to charity or good cause
    5    1   by       by       PRE    aside.r.06   in reserve
    6    1   oberlin  Oberlin  NPR    None         None
            college College
    7    1   faculty  faculty  NOU    staff.n.03   teachers and administrators
    ...
    [77 rows x 6 columns]
```

6.5.1.4   Cogito Example Tokenization

As a second example, if we analyze the original sentence (see below), Cogito produces the output shown in Fig. 6.2.

```
"EXPERIMENTAL STUDY  We conducted an empirical evaluation to assess the
effectiveness"
```

We filter some of the words and only keep the lemmas and the syncon ids and encode them into the next sequence of disambiguated tokens:

```
en#86052|experimental en#2686|study en#76710|conduct en#86047|
empirical en#3546|evaluation en#68903|assess en#25094|effectiveness
```

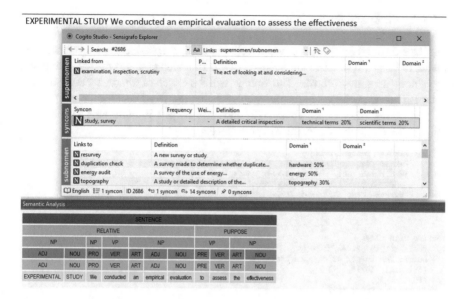

Fig. 6.2 Semantic analysis produced by Cogito on a sample sentence

6.5.2 Vocabulary and Co-occurrence Matrix

Next, we need to count the co-occurrences in the disambiguated corpus. We can either:

- Use **standard Swivel prep**: In this case, each ||| tuple will be treated as a separate token. For the example sentence from UMBC, presented above, we would then get that `mayan|lem_Mayan|GT_ADJ|wn31_Maya.n.03` has a co-occurrence count of 1 with `image|lem_image|GT_NOU|wn31_effigy.n.01`. This would result in a very large vocabulary.
- Use **joint-subtoken prep**: In this case, you can specify which individual subtoken information you want to take into account. In this notebook we will use **ls** information; hence, each synset and each lemma are treated as separate entities in the vocabulary and will be represented with different embeddings. For the example sentence we would get that `lem_Mayan` has a co-occurrence count of 1 with `wn31_Maya.n.03`, `lem_image` and `wn31_effigy.n.01`.

```
In [ ]: import os
        import numpy as np
```

6.5.2.1   Standard Swivel Prep

For the **standard Swivel prep**, we can simply call `prep` using the `!python` command. In this case we have the `toked_corpus` which contains the disambiguated sequences as shown above. The output will be a set of sharded co-occurrence submatrices as explained in the notebook for creating word vectors.

We set the `shard_size` to 512 since the corpus is quite small. For larger corpora we could use the standard value of 4096.

```
In [6]:  !mkdir /content/umbc/
         !mkdir /content/umbc/coocs
         !mkdir /content/umbc/coocs/tlgs_wnscd_5k_standard
         coocs_path = '/content/umbc/coocs/tlgs_wnscd_5k_standard/'
         !python tutorial/scripts/swivel/prep.py
         --input={toked_corpus} --output_dir={coocs_path} --shard_size=512
```

```
running with flags
tutorial/scripts/swivel/prep.py:
  --bufsz: The number of co-occurrences to buffer
    (default: '16777216')
    (an integer)
  --input: The input text.
    (default: '')
  --max_vocab: The maximum vocabulary size
    (default: '1048576')
    (an integer)
  --min_count: The minimum number of times a word should occur to be included in
    the vocabulary
    (default: '5')
    (an integer)
  --output_dir: Output directory for Swivel data
    (default: '/tmp/swivel_data')
  --shard_size: The size for each shard
    (default: '4096')
    (an integer)
  --vocab: Vocabulary to use instead of generating one
    (default: '')
  --window_size: The window size
    (default: '10')
    (an integer)
...

vocabulary contains 8192 tokens

writing shard 256/256
Wrote vocab and sum files to /content/umbc/coocs/tlgs_wnscd_5k_standard/
Wrote vocab and sum files to /content/umbc/coocs/tlgs_wnscd_5k_standard/
done!
```

```
In [7]: !head -n15  /content/umbc/coocs/tlgs_wnscd_5k_standard/row_vocab.txt
the%7CGT_ART
%2C%7CGT_PNT
.%7CGT_PNT
of%7CGT_PRE
and%7CGT_CON
to%7CGT_PRE
a%7CGT_ART
in%7CGT_PRE
for%7CGT_PRE
%22%7CGT_PNT
is%7Clem_be%7CGT_VER%7Cwn31_be.v.01
with%7CGT_PRE
%29%7CGT_PNT
%28%7CGT_PNT
on%7Clem_on%7CGT_PRE
```

As the cells above show, applying standard prep results in a vocabulary of over 8K "tokens"; however, each token is still represented as a URL-encoded combination of the plain text, lemma, grammar type, and synset (when available).

6.5.2.2 Joint-subtoken Prep

For the **joint-subtoken prep** step, next we describe the steps that need to be executed to implement a similar pipeline. Note that we use a Java implementation that is not open-source yet, as it is still tied to proprietary code. Currently we are working on refactoring the code so that Cogito subtokens are just a special case. Until then, in our GitHub repository we provide pre-computed co-occurrence files.

First, we ran our implementation of subtoken prep on the corpus. Please note:

- We are only including lemma and synset information, i.e., we are not including plain text and grammar information.
- Furthermore, we are filtering the corpus by: (1) removing any tokens related to punctuation marks (PNT), auxiliary verbs (AUX), and articles (ART), since we think these do not contribute much to the semantics of words; (2) replacing tokens with grammar types ENT (entities) and NPH (proper names) with generic variants grammar#ENT and grammar#NPH, respectively.

The rationale of the second point is that, depending on the input corpus, names of people or organizations may appear a few times, but may be filtered out if they do not appear enough times. This ensures such tokens are kept in the vocabulary and contribute to the embeddings of words nearby. The main disadvantage is that we will not have some proper names in our final vocabulary.

```
java $JAVA_OPTIONS net.expertsystem.word2vec.swivel.SubtokPrep
  --input C:/hybridnlp/tutorial/datasamples/umbc_tlgs_wnscd_5K
  --output_dir C:/corpora/umbc/coocs/tlgs_wnscd_5K_ls_f/
  --expected_seq_encoding TLGS_WN
  --sub_tokens
  --output_subtokens "LEMMA,SYNSET"
  --remove_tokens_with_grammar_types "PNT,AUX,ART"
  --generalise_tokens_with_grammar_types "ENT,NPH"
  --shard_size 512
```

The output log looked as follows:

```
INFO  net.expertsystem.word2vec.swivel.SubtokPrep
- expected_seq_encoding set to 'TLGS_WN'
INFO  net.expertsystem.word2vec.swivel.SubtokPrep
- remove_tokens_with_grammar_types set to PNT,AUX,ART
INFO  net.expertsystem.word2vec.swivel.SubtokPrep
- generalise_tokens_with_grammar_types set to ENT,NPH
INFO  net.expertsystem.word2vec.swivel.SubtokPrep
- Creating vocab for hybridnlp/tutorial/datasamples/umbc_tlgs_wnscd_5K
INFO  net.expertsystem.word2vec.swivel.SubtokPrep
- read 5000 lines from hybridnlp/tutorial/datasamples/umbc_tlgs_wnscd_5K
INFO  net.expertsystem.word2vec.swivel.SubtokPrep
- filtered 166152 tokens from a total of 427796 (38,839%)
- generalised 1899 tokens from a total of 427796 (0,444%)
- full vocab size 21321
INFO  net.expertsystem.word2vec.swivel.SubtokPrep
- Vocabulary contains 5632 tokens (21321 full count, 5913 appear > 5 times)
INFO  net.expertsystem.word2vec.swivel.SubtokPrep
- Flushing 1279235 co-occ pairs
INFO  net.expertsystem.word2vec.swivel.SubtokPrep
- Wrote 121 tmpShards to disk
```

We have included the output of this process as part of the GitHub repository. Next, we unzip this folder to inspect the results:

```
In [8]: !unzip /content/tutorial/datasamples/precomp-coocs-tlgs_wnscd_5K_ls_f.zip
        -d /content/umbc/coocs/ precomp_coocs_path = \
        '/content/umbc/coocs/tlgs_wnscd_5K_ls_f'

Archive:  /content/tutorial/datasamples/precomp-coocs-tlgs_wnscd_5K_ls_f.zip
   creating: /content/umbc/coocs/tlgs_wnscd_5K_ls_f/
 inflating: /content/umbc/coocs/tlgs_wnscd_5K_ls_f/col_sums.txt
 inflating: /content/umbc/coocs/tlgs_wnscd_5K_ls_f/col_vocab.txt
 inflating: /content/umbc/coocs/tlgs_wnscd_5K_ls_f/init_vocab.txt
 inflating: /content/umbc/coocs/tlgs_wnscd_5K_ls_f/row_sums.txt
 inflating: /content/umbc/coocs/tlgs_wnscd_5K_ls_f/row_vocab.txt
 inflating: /content/umbc/coocs/tlgs_wnscd_5K_ls_f/shard-000-000.pb
 inflating: /content/umbc/coocs/tlgs_wnscd_5K_ls_f/shard-000-001.pb
 inflating: /content/umbc/coocs/tlgs_wnscd_5K_ls_f/shard-000-002.pb
   ...
```

The previous cell extracts the pre-computed co-occurrence shards and defines a variable `precomp_coocs_path` that points to the folder where these shards are stored.

Next, we print the first 10 elements of the vocabulary to see the format that we are using to represent the lemmas and synsets:

```
In [9]: !head -n10 {precomp_coocs_path}/row_vocab.txt

lem_be
wn31_be.v.01
lem_that
lem_this
lem_on
lem_by
lem_information
lem_as
lem_use
lem_from
```

As the output above shows, the vocabulary we get with subtoken prep is smaller (5.6K elements instead of over 8K) and it contains individual lemmas and synsets (it also contains *special* elements grammar#ENT and grammar#NPH, as described above). **More importantly**, the co-occurrence counts take into account the fact that certain lemmas co-occur more frequently with certain other lemmas and synsets, which should be taken into account when learning embedding representations.

6.5.3 Learn Embeddings from Co-occurrence Matrix

With the sharded co-occurrence matrices created in the previous section it is now possible to learn embeddings by calling the `swivel.py` script. This launches a TensorFlow application based on various parameters (most of which are self-explanatory):

- `input_base_path`: The folder with the co-occurrence matrix (protobuf files with the sparse matrix) generated above.
- `submatrix_rows` and `submatrix_columns` need to be the same size as the `shard_size` used in the `prep` step.
- `num_epochs`: The number of times to go through the input data (all the co-occurrences in the shards). We have found that for large corpora, the learning algorithm converges after a few epochs, while for smaller corpora you need a larger number of epochs.

Execute the following cell to generate embeddings for the pre-computed co-occurrences:

```
In [10]: vec_path = '/content/umbc/vec/tlgs_wnscd_5k_ls_f'
         !python /content/tutorial/scripts/swivel/swivel.py \
             --input_base_path={precomp_coocs_path} \
             --output_base_path={vec_path} \
             --num_epochs=40 --dim=150 \
             --submatrix_rows=512 --submatrix_cols=512

INFO:tensorflow:local_step=10 global_step=10 loss=79.3, 0.2% complete
I0926 15:14:24.026667 139968712865664 swivel.py:513]
local_step=10 global_step=10 loss=79.3, 0.2% complete
INFO:tensorflow:local_step=20 global_step=20 loss=78.0, 0.4% complete
I0926 15:14:24.106195 139968712865664 swivel.py:513]
local_step=20 global_step=20 loss=78.0, 0.4% complete
INFO:tensorflow:local_step=30 global_step=30 loss=75.5, 0.6% complete
I0926 15:14:24.184316 139968712865664 swivel.py:513]
local_step=30 global_step=30 loss=75.5, 0.6% complete
INFO:tensorflow:local_step=40 global_step=40 loss=154.8, 0.8% complete
I0926 15:14:24.271500 139968712865664 swivel.py:513]
local_step=40 global_step=40 loss=154.8, 0.8% complete
INFO:tensorflow:local_step=50 global_step=50 loss=69.2, 1.0% complete
I0926 15:14:24.345748 139968712865664 swivel.py:513]
local_step=50 global_step=50 loss=69.2, 1.0% complete
INFO:tensorflow:local_step=60 global_step=60 loss=76.4, 1.2% complete
I0926 15:14:24.417270 139968712865664 swivel.py:513]
local_step=60 global_step=60 loss=76.4, 1.2% complete
...
```

This will take a few minutes, depending on your machine. The result is a list of files in the specified output folder, including:

- The TensorFlow graph, which defines the architecture of the model being trained.

- Checkpoints of the model (intermediate snapshots of the weights).
- tsv files for the final state of the column and row embeddings.

```
In [11]: %ls {vec_path}

checkpoint
col_embedding.tsv
events.out.tfevents.1569510861.dc66177fa300
graph.pbtxt
model.ckpt-0.data-00000-of-00001
model.ckpt-0.index
model.ckpt-0.meta
model.ckpt-4840.data-00000-of-00001
model.ckpt-4840.index
model.ckpt-4840.meta
row_embedding.tsv
```

6.5.3.1 Convert tsv Files to bin File

As we have seen in previous notebooks, the tsv files are easy to inspect, but they take too much space and they are slow to load since we need to convert the different values to floats and pack them as vectors. Swivel offers a utility to convert the tsv files into a binary format. At the same time, it combines the column and row embeddings into a single space, simply adding the two vectors for each word in the vocabulary.

```
In [12]: !python /content/tutorial/scripts/swivel/text2bin.py \
              --vocab={precomp_coocs_path}/row_vocab.txt \
              --output={vec_path}/vecs.bin \
              {vec_path}/row_embedding.tsv \
              {vec_path}/col_embedding.tsv

executing text2bin.
merging files ['/content/umbc/vec/tlgs_wnscd_5k_ls_f/row_embedding.tsv',
              '/content/umbc/vec/tlgs_wnscd_5k_ls_f/col_embedding.tsv']
into output bin.
```

This adds the vocab.txt and vecs.bin to the folder with the vectors:

```
In [13]: %ls {vec_path}

checkpoint
col_embedding.tsv
events.out.tfevents.1569510861.dc66177fa300
graph.pbtxt
model.ckpt-0.data-00000-of-00001
model.ckpt-0.index
model.ckpt-0.meta
model.ckpt-4840.data-00000-of-00001
model.ckpt-4840.index
model.ckpt-4840.meta
row_embedding.tsv
vecs.bin
```

6.5.4 Inspect the Embeddings

As in previous notebooks, we can now use Swivel to inspect the vectors using the Vecs class. It accepts a `vocab_file` and a file for the binary serialization of the vectors (`vecs.bin`).

```
In [ ]: from tutorial.scripts.swivel import vecs
```

Now we can load existing vectors. In this example we load some pre-computed embeddings, but feel free to use the embeddings you computed by following the steps above. Note however that due to random initialization of weight during the training step your results may differ.

```
In [15]: vectors = vecs.Vecs(precomp_coocs_path + '/row_vocab.txt',
                   vec_path + '/vecs.bin')

Opening vector with expected size 5632 from file:
    /content/umbc/coocs/tlgs_wnscd_5K_ls_f/row_vocab.txt
vocab size 5632 (unique 5632)
read rows
```

Next, let us define a basic method for printing the k-nearest neighbors for a given word and use such method on a few lemmas and synsets in the vocabulary:

```
In [16]: import pandas as pd
         pd.DataFrame(vectors.k_neighbors('lem_California'))
```

```
Out[16]:       cosim                    word
         0  1.000000            lem_California
         1  0.570745  lem_University of California
         2  0.337390         wn31_assign.v.02
         3  0.330571         wn31_engage.v.07
         4  0.322535       wn31_recognize.v.08
         5  0.312997             lem_comprise
         6  0.308644           lem_deployment
         7  0.289010      lem_natural resources
         8  0.285247          wn31_order.v.01
         9  0.282973  wn31_representation.n.04
```

```
In [17]: pd.DataFrame(vectors.k_neighbors('lem_semantic'))
```

```
Out[17]:       cosim               word
         0  1.000000       lem_semantic
         1  0.348555  wn31_exemplify.v.01
         2  0.341621  wn31_similarity.n.01
         3  0.336341         lem_object
         4  0.326920     lem_hierarchical
         5  0.325940     lem_distinction
         6  0.318285    lem_relationship
         7  0.316533        lem_elusive
         8  0.314209   lem_heterogeneity
         9  0.311853      lem_procedural
```

```
In [18]: pd.DataFrame(vectors.k_neighbors('lem_conference'))
```

```
Out[18]:       cosim               word
         0  1.000000      lem_conference
         1  0.648084  wn31_conference.n.01
         2  0.523156  wn31_conference.n.03
         3  0.504673     lem_proceedings
         4  0.464521    wn31_session.n.01
         5  0.391413        lem_session
```

```
          6  0.382983              lem_seminar
          7  0.379104              lem_workshop
          8  0.365104              lem_meeting
          9  0.362927              lem_annual

In [19]: pd.DataFrame(vectors.k_neighbors('wn31_conference.n.01'))

Out[19]:       cosim                    word
          0  1.000000     wn31_conference.n.01
          1  0.648084          lem_conference
          2  0.494678        wn31_seminar.n.01
          3  0.453380        wn31_meeting.n.01
          4  0.405092             lem_seminar
          5  0.397628             wn31_at.n.02
          6  0.393092       wn31_workshop.n.01
          7  0.367346          lem_proceedings
          8  0.363903   wn31_practitioner.n.01
          9  0.359585      wn31_external.a.03
```

Note that using the Vecsigrafo approach gets us very different results than when using standard Swivel. The results now include concepts (synsets), besides just words. Without further information, this makes interpreting the results harder since we now only have the concept identifier. However, we can search for these concepts in the underlying knowledge graph (WordNet in this case) to explore the semantic network and get further information.

Of course, the results produced in this example may not be very good since these have been derived from a very small corpus (5K lines from UMBC). In the exercise below, we encourage you to download and inspect pre-computed embeddings based on the full UMBC corpus.

```
In [20]: pd.DataFrame(vectors.k_neighbors('lem_semantic web'))

Out[20]:       cosim                            word
          0  1.000000               lem_semantic web
          1  0.464729          wn31_technology.n.01
          2  0.392353          lem_machine learning
          3  0.384410                 lem_technology
          4  0.361726  lem_natural language processing
          5  0.346679                     lem_mature
          6  0.341555             lem_incorporation
          7  0.334495                 lem_emergence
          8  0.324496        wn31_engineering.n.02
          9  0.320252             lem_educationally

In [21]: pd.DataFrame(vectors.k_neighbors('lem_ontology'))

Out[21]:       cosim             word
          0  1.000000     lem_ontology
          1  0.389556  wn31_center.n.01
          2  0.300476           lem_eye
          3  0.294903   lem_distinction
          4  0.288841           lem_rdf
          5  0.283265       lem_mapping
          6  0.279728         lem_joint
          7  0.278996          lem_edge
          8  0.278543         lem_truly
          9  0.272837        lem_extend
```

6.6   Exercise: Explore a Pre-computed Vecsigrafo

In Sect. 6.5 we generated a Vecsigrafo based on a disambiguated corpus. The resulting embedding space combines concept identifiers and lemmas. We have seen that the resulting vector space:

- May be harder to inspect due to the potentially opaque concept identifier.
- Is clearly different than standard Swivel embeddings.

Hence, the question is: are the resulting embeddings *better*? To get an answer, in Chap. 8, we will look at **evaluation methods for embeddings**.

We also provide pre-computed Vecsigrafo embeddings for the full UMBC corpus. The provided `tar.gz` file is about 1.1GB; hence, downloading it may take several minutes.

```
In [22]:
full_precomp_url =
'https://zenodo.org/record/1446214/files/
vecsigrafo_umbc_tlgs_ls_f_6e_160d_row_embedding.tar.gz'
full_precomp_targz =
'/content/umbc/vec/tlgs_wnscd_ls_f_6e_160d_row_embedding.tar.gz'
!wget {full_precomp_url} -O {full_precomp_targz}

--2019-09-26 15:16:16--
https://zenodo.org/record/1446214/files/
     vecsigrafo_umbc_tlgs_ls_f_6e_160d_row_embedding.tar.gz
Resolving zenodo.org (zenodo.org)... 188.184.65.20
Connecting to zenodo.org (zenodo.org)|188.184.65.20|:443... connected.
HTTP request sent, awaiting response... 200 OK
Length: 1166454112 (1.1G) [application/octet-stream]
Saving to: '/content/umbc/vec/tlgs_wnscd_ls_f_6e_160d_row_embedding.tar.gz'

/content/umbc/vec/t 100%[===================>]   1.09G  10.8MB/s    in 1m 50s

2019-09-26 15:18:09 (10.1 MB/s) -
'/content/umbc/vec/tlgs_wnscd_ls_f_6e_160d_row_embedding.tar.gz'
saved [1166454112/1166454112]
```

Next, we unpack the vectors:

```
In [ ]: !tar -xzf {full_precomp_targz} -C /content/umbc/vec/
        full_precomp_vec_path = '/content/umbc/vec/vecsi_tlgs_wnscd_ls_f_6e_160d'

In [25]: %ls /content/umbc/vec/vecsi_tlgs_wnscd_ls_f_6e_160d/

   row_embedding.tsv
```

The data only includes the `tsv` version of the vectors, so we need to convert these to the binary format that Swivel uses. And for that, we also need a `vocab.txt` file, which we can derive from the tsv as follows:

```
In [ ]: with open(full_precomp_vec_path + '/vocab.txt', 'w',
               encoding='utf_8') as f:
          with open(full_precomp_vec_path + '/row_embedding.tsv', 'r',
                 encoding='utf_8') as vec_lines:
            vocab = [line.split('\t')[0].strip() for line in vec_lines]
            for word in vocab:
              print(word, file=f)
```

Next, let us inspect the vocabulary:

```
In [27]: !wc -1 {full_precomp_vec_path}/vocab.txt

1499136 /content/umbc/vec/vecsi_tlgs_wnscd_ls_f_6e_160d/vocab.txt

In [28]: !grep 'wn31_' {full_precomp_vec_path}/vocab.txt | wc -l

56407

In [29]: !grep 'lem_' {full_precomp_vec_path}/vocab.txt | wc -l

1442727
```

As we can see, the embeddings have a vocabulary of just under 1.5M entries, 56K of which are synsets and most of the rest are lemmas. Next, we convert the tsv into Swivel's binary format. This can take a couple of minutes.

```
In [30]: !python /content/tutorial/scripts/swivel/text2bin.py \
              --vocab={full_precomp_vec_path}/vocab.txt \
              --output={full_precomp_vec_path}/vecs.bin \
              {full_precomp_vec_path}/row_embedding.tsv

executing text2bin
merging files
    ['/content/umbc/vec/vecsi_tlgs_wnscd_ls_f_6e_160d/row_embedding.tsv']
into output bin
```

Now, we are ready to load the vectors.

```
In [31]: vecsi_wn_umbc = vecs.Vecs(full_precomp_vec_path + '/vocab.txt',
                  full_precomp_vec_path + '/vecs.bin')

Opening vector with expected size 1499136 from file
    /content/umbc/vec/vecsi_tlgs_wnscd_ls_f_6e_160d/vocab.txt
vocab size 1499136 (unique 1499125)
read rows

In [32]: pd.DataFrame(vecsi_wn_umbc.k_neighbors('lem_California'))

Out[32]:      cosim                        word
         0  1.000000              lem_California
         1  0.630092            lem_Central Valley
         2  0.595864  lem_University of California
         3  0.554219       lem_Southern California
         4  0.525430              lem_Santa Cruz
         5  0.524089            lem_Astro Aerospace
         6  0.516835          lem_San Francisco Bay
         7  0.509182          lem_San Diego County
         8  0.507356            lem_Santa Barbara
         9  0.506900              lem_Santa Rosa

In [33]: pd.DataFrame(vecsi_wn_umbc.k_neighbors('lem_semantic'))

Out[33]:      cosim              word
         0  1.000000      lem_semantic
         1  0.629694     lem_semantics
         2  0.567266       lem_lexical
         3  0.537733         lem_logic
         4  0.528353      lem_data model
         5  0.528306    lem_semantic web
         6  0.519358        lem_schema
         7  0.510043  wn31_lexical.a.01
         8  0.509647        lem_syntax
         9  0.502321           lem_xml
```

```
In [34]: pd.DataFrame(vecsi_wn_umbc.k_neighbors('lem_conference'))

Out[34]:       cosim                word
         0   1.000000        lem_conference
         1   0.685512   wn31_conference.n.03
         2   0.680377   wn31_conference.n.01
         3   0.622037      wn31_meeting.n.02
         4   0.620641      wn31_meeting.n.01
         5   0.616911           lem_meeting
         6   0.610723      wn31_session.n.01
         7   0.600658       wn31_seance.n.01
         8   0.587808  lem_plenary session
         9   0.587305          lem_symposium
```

```
In [35]: print(wn.synset('conference.n.01').definition())
         pd.DataFrame(vecsi_wn_umbc.k_neighbors('wn31_conference.n.01'))
```

A prearranged meeting for consultation or exchange of information or discussion,
especially one with a formal agenda.

```
Out[35]:       cosim                word
         0   1.000000   wn31_conference.n.01
         1   0.680377        lem_conference
         2   0.656847   wn31_conference.n.03
         3   0.652518       wn31_seance.n.01
         4   0.633268      wn31_seminar.n.01
         5   0.618963    wn31_confluence.n.01
         6   0.611476      wn31_meeting.n.01
         7   0.595094           lem_seminar
         8   0.591273    wn31_symposium.n.01
         9   0.583282        wn31_forum.n.01
```

```
In [36]: print(wn.synset('conference.n.03').definition())
         pd.DataFrame(vecsi_wn_umbc.k_neighbors('wn31_conference.n.03'))
```

A discussion among participants who have an agreed (serious) topic.

```
Out[36]:       cosim                word
         0   1.000000   wn31_conference.n.03
         1   0.685512        lem_conference
         2   0.679651       wn31_seance.n.01
         3   0.656847   wn31_conference.n.01
         4   0.652746      wn31_session.n.01
         5   0.616685          lem_symposium
         6   0.598573    wn31_symposium.n.01
         7   0.598052      wn31_meeting.n.02
         8   0.575875          lem_workshop
         9   0.565252      wn31_meeting.n.01
```

6.7   From Vecsigrafo to Transigrafo

As introduced in Chap. 3, the advantages of neural language models to produce
a model of human language and generate contextual embeddings over traditional
approaches learning static embeddings have been amply demonstrated. Indeed,
language models and their impact on the NLP pipeline are currently subject of
deeper study [35, 84, 178]. In this section, we take a step in this direction and show
how to produce corpus-based knowledge graph embeddings based on transformers
and neural language models, while previously we showed how to train Vecsigrafo
using an extended version of a static word embedding algorithm like Swivel.
Henceforth, we will refer to such Transformer-based model as **Transigrafo**.

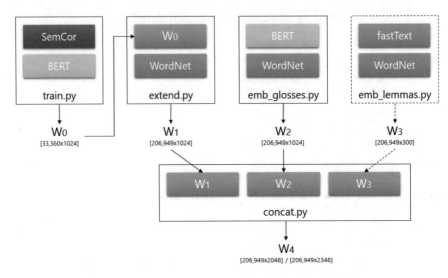

Fig. 6.3 Pipeline of the Language Modeling Makes Sense Algorithm (LMMS)

Our approach is an extension of the algorithm *Language Modeling Makes Sense* (LMMS), presented by Loureiro and Jorge in [109], which uses contextual embeddings for word-sense disambiguation (WSD) exploiting the WordNet graph structure. In this case we do not focus on jointly learning word, lemma, and concept (sense) embeddings as we did in Vecisgrafo. Plus, instead of learning concept embeddings by previously disambiguating the corpus, we will leverage a pre-trained language model like BERT and its ability to produce contextual embeddings for out-of-vocabulary words or, in this case, senses. Future work will require a side-by-side evaluation of the embeddings learnt by Vecsigrafo, Transigrafo, and mixed approaches to better understand the pros and cons of each method.

As shown by the authors of the LMMS algorithm, contextual embeddings produced by pre-trained neural language models like BERT can be used to achieve unprecedented gains in word-sense disambiguation (WSD) tasks. The approach focuses on creating sense-level embeddings with full-coverage of lexico-semantic knowledge graphs like WordNet or Sensigrafo, and without recourse to explicit knowledge of sense distributions or task-specific modeling. Simple methods like nearest neighbors (k-NN) can then be used to leverage the resulting representations in WSD, consistently surpassing the performance of previous systems based on powerful neural sequencing models.

Figure 6.3 shows the complete pipeline of the LMMS algorithm. Here, we will focus on the first two phases, training and extension, to: (1) obtain contextual embeddings for each sense in the SemCor corpus,[12] (2) leverage the hierarchical structure of the graph (from sense to synset, hypernym, and lexname) in order to

---

[12]SemCor is manually disambiguated against the WordNet knowledge graph. Other lexico-semantic graphs like Sensigrafo are equally valid, as long as the corpus is also disambiguated

extend the coverage provided by such embeddings to the senses in the graph that do not appear in SemCor, and (3) evaluate the resulting sense embeddings. Subsequent stages of the LMMS algorithm focus on leveraging WordNet glosses and lemma information to optimize the quality of the resulting sense embeddings.

We also introduce some extensions to the original LMMS algorithm, which are useful to produce a Transigrafo. Such extensions include the following:

- We added a **transformers back-end** based on the Hugging Face transformers library[13] in order to enable experimentation with other transformer architectures in addition to BERT, such as XLNet, XLM, and RoBERTa. Besides the obvious model-independence advantage this represents, this also allows optimizing training performance, i.e. padding sequences to BERT-style 512 word-piece tokens when a different model is being used in the back-end is no longer required.
- We implemented **SentenceEncoder**, a generalization of bert-as-service that encodes services using the transformers back-end. SentenceEncoder allows extracting various types of embeddings from a single execution of a batch of sequences.
- We adopt a **rolling cosine similarity** measure during training in order to monitor how the embeddings representing each sense converge to their optimal representation.

Next, we go through the sequence of steps necessary to produce a Transigrafo and the actual code implementing each step. The complete notebook is available and executable online.[14]

6.7.1 Setup

First, we clone the LMMS GitHub repository and change the current directory to LMMS.

```
In [ ]: !git clone https://github.com/hybridnlp/LMMS
        %cd /content/LMMS

Cloning into 'LMMS'...
remote: Enumerating objects: 58, done.
remote: Counting objects: 100% (58/58), done.
remote: Compressing objects: 100% (45/45), done.
remote: Total 202 (delta 32), reused 25 (delta 13), pack-reused 144
Receiving objects: 100% (202/202), 171.80 KiB | 945.00 KiB/s, done.
Resolving deltas: 100% (95/95), done.
/content/LMMS
```

---

against them. General-purpose graphs like DBpedia or domain-specific ones could also be used by minimally adapting the algorithm.

[13] https://github.com/huggingface/transformers.

[14] https://colab.research.google.com/github/hybridnlp/tutorial/blob/master/03a_LMMS_Transigrafo.ipynb.

Then, we import and download the nltk interface for WordNet and install the transformers library, needed to execute the LMMS scripts.

```
In [ ]: import nltk
        nltk.download("wordnet")
        !pip install transformers

[nltk_data] Downloading package wordnet to /root/nltk_data...
[nltk_data]   Unzipping corpora/wordnet.zip.
Collecting transformers==2.1.1
[...]
Successfully built sacremoses
Installing collected packages: regex, sentencepiece, sacremoses, transformers
Successfully installed regex-2019.11.1 sacremoses-0.0.35 sentencepiece-0.1.83 transformers-2.1.1
```

We use a semantically annotated English corpus: SemCor.[15] The semantic analysis was done manually with WordNet 1.6 senses (SemCor version 1.6) and later automatically mapped to WordNet 3.0 (SemCor version 3.0). The SemCor corpus consists of 352 texts from the Brown corpus.[16]

Next, we download and unzip the SemCor corpus.

```
In [ ]: !mkdir external/wsd_eval
        %cd external/wsd_eval
        !wget http://lcl.uniroma1.it/wsdeval/data/WSD_Evaluation_Framework.zip
        !unzip WSD_Evaluation_Framework
        %cd /content/LMMS/

/content/LMMS/external/wsd_eval
--  http://lcl.uniroma1.it/wsdeval/data/WSD_Evaluation_Framework.zip
Resolving lcl.uniroma1.it (lcl.uniroma1.it)... 151.100.179.52
Connecting to lcl.uniroma1.it (lcl.uniroma1.it)|151.100.179.52|:80... connected.
HTTP request sent, awaiting response... 200 OK
Length: 165655083 (158M) [application/zip]
Saving to: 'WSD_Evaluation_Framework.zip'

WSD_Evaluation_Fram 100%[===================>] 157.98M  11.2MB/s    in 14s

 (11.1 MB/s) - 'WSD_Evaluation_Framework.zip' saved [165655083/165655083]

Archive:  WSD_Evaluation_Framework.zip
   creating: WSD_Evaluation_Framework/
   creating: WSD_Evaluation_Framework/Data_Validation/
  inflating: WSD_Evaluation_Framework/Data_Validation/README
  inflating: WSD_Evaluation_Framework/Data_Validation/ValidateGold.java
  inflating: WSD_Evaluation_Framework/Data_Validation/ValidateXML.java
  inflating: WSD_Evaluation_Framework/Data_Validation/candidatesWN30.txt
   creating: WSD_Evaluation_Framework/Data_Validation/lib/
  inflating: WSD_Evaluation_Framework/Data_Validation/lib/commons-lang-2.6.jar
   creating: WSD_Evaluation_Framework/Data_Validation/sample-dataset/
  inflating: WSD_Evaluation_Framework/Data_Validation/sample-dataset/semeval2015.data.xml
  inflating: WSD_Evaluation_Framework/Data_Validation/sample-dataset/semeval2015.gold.key.txt
  inflating: WSD_Evaluation_Framework/Data_Validation/schema.xsd
  inflating: WSD_Evaluation_Framework/EACL17_WSD_EvaluationFramework.pdf
  [...]
  inflating: WSD_Evaluation_Framework/Training_Corpora/SemCor/semcor.gold.key.txt
/content/LMMS
```

---

[15]https://www.sketchengine.eu/semcor-annotated-corpus.

[16]https://www.sketchengine.eu/brown-corpus.

6.7.2   Training Transigrafo

We use a transformers back-end[17] to train the model with the SemCor corpus. After training, we will have the following files in the output folder:

- **semcor.4-8.vecs.txt** contains the embedding learnt for each sense.
- **semcor.4-8.counts.txt** keeps track, for each sense, of its frequency in the training corpus.
- **semcor.4-8.rolling_cosims.txt** records for each sense the sequence of cosine similarity values between the current average and the one resulting from also considering the next occurrence in the training corpus.
- **lmms_config.json** keeps a record of the parameters used during training.

```
In [ ]: %%time
!python train.py -dataset semcor -backend transformers -out_path data/vectors/semcor.txt
                 -min_seq_len 4 -max_seq_len 8

08-Nov-19 12:22:19 - INFO - Creating TransformerSentenceEncoder
[...]
08-Nov-19 12:22:21 - INFO - Model config {
  "attention_probs_dropout_prob": 0.1,
  "directionality": "bidi",
  "finetuning_task": null,
  "hidden_act": "gelu",
  "hidden_dropout_prob": 0.1,
  "hidden_size": 1024,
  "initializer_range": 0.02,
  "intermediate_size": 4096,
  "layer_norm_eps": 1e-12,
  "max_position_embeddings": 512,
  "num_attention_heads": 16,
  "num_hidden_layers": 24,
  "num_labels": 2,
  "output_attentions": false,
  "output_hidden_states": true,
  "output_past": true,
  "pooler_fc_size": 768,
  "pooler_num_attention_heads": 12,
  "pooler_num_fc_layers": 3,
  "pooler_size_per_head": 128,
  "pooler_type": "first_token_transform",
  "pruned_heads": {},
  "torchscript": false,
  "type_vocab_size": 2,
  "use_bfloat16": false,
  "vocab_size": 28996
}
[...]
08-Nov-19 12:23:24 - INFO - Created TransformerSentenceEncoder
config {'model_name_or_path': 'bert-large-cased', 'model_arch': 'BERT', 'min_seq_len': 4,
       'max_seq_len': 8, 'pooling_strategy': 'NONE', 'pooling_layer': [-4, -3, -2, -1],
       'tok_merge_strategy': 'mean', 'sent_special_tokens': [{'index': 0, 'tok_id': 101,
       'tok': '[CLS]'}, {'index': -1, 'tok_id': 102, 'tok': '[SEP]'}], 'tok_dim': 1024}
08-Nov-19 12:25:26 - INFO - 84.442 sents/sec - 10300 sents, 8507 senses
08-Nov-19 12:25:26 - INFO - Processing remaining batch [3, 16) with 18 < 32 elts
08-Nov-19 12:25:26 - INFO - #sents: 10322 of 37175, 84.141 sents/sec
08-Nov-19 12:25:26 - INFO - Writing Sense Vectors ...
08-Nov-19 12:25:37 - INFO - Written data/vectors/semcor..4-8.vecs.txt
```

---

[17]The *BERT as a service* alternative is not possible in Google Colaboratory, used throughout this book as an executable platform for our notebooks.

```
08-Nov-19 12:25:37 - INFO - Writing Sense counts ...
08-Nov-19 12:25:37 - INFO - Written data/vectors/semcor..4-8.counts.txt
08-Nov-19 12:25:37 - INFO - Writing rolling cosine similarities ...
08-Nov-19 12:25:37 - INFO - Written data/vectors/semcor..4-8.rolling_cosims.txt
08-Nov-19 12:25:37 - INFO - Writing lmms_train_config.json
08-Nov-19 12:25:37 - INFO - Written data/vectors/lmms_config.json
CPU times: user 1.58 s, sys: 235 ms, total: 1.81 s
Wall time: 3min 24s
```

6.7.3   Extend the Coverage of the Knowledge Graph

Next, we propagate the embeddings learnt during the previous training phase throughout the WordNet graph in order to also calculate embeddings for the senses that do not appear explicitly in the training corpus. There are three main levels at which such extension is performed:

1. **Synset Level:** For any sense without an embedding, we assign the embeddings of sibling senses, i.e. those that share the same synset.
2. **Hypernym Level:** After the synset-based expansion, those senses that do not have an associate embedding yet are assigned the average embedding of their hypernyms.
3. **Lexname Level:** After the hypernym-based expansion, top-level categories in WordNet called lexnames are assigned the average embedding of all its available underlying senses. Any senses that do not have an associated embedding after the previous two steps yet are assigned the embedding of their lexname.

The new embeddings resulting from the different extensions above described are saved in an additional file: **semcor_ext.3-512.vecs.npz**.

```
In [ ]: %%time
!python extend.py -sup_sv_path data/vectors/semcor..3-512.vecs.txt -ext_mode lexname
                  -out_path data/vectors/semcor_ext.3-512.vecs.npz

08-Nov-19 12:28:28 - INFO - Loading SensesVSM ...
08-Nov-19 12:28:37 - INFO - Processing ...
08-Nov-19 12:28:37 - INFO - Extension at synset 0 - 0
08-Nov-19 12:28:37 - INFO - Extension at synset 1000 - 144
08-Nov-19 12:28:37 - INFO - Extension at synset 2000 - 332
[...]
08-Nov-19 12:28:38 - INFO - Extension at synset 206000 - 22286
08-Nov-19 12:28:38 - INFO - Extension at hypernym 0 - 22442
[...]
08-Nov-19 12:28:45 - INFO - Extension at hypernym 206000 - 120933
08-Nov-19 12:28:45 - INFO - Preparing lexname vecs ...
08-Nov-19 12:28:50 - INFO - Extension at lexname 0 - 121236
08-Nov-19 12:28:50 - INFO - Extension at lexname 1000 - 121892
[...]
08-Nov-19 12:28:50 - INFO - Extension at lexname 206000 - 173546
08-Nov-19 12:28:50 - INFO - Writing vecs ...
08-Nov-19 12:28:50 - INFO - n_vecs: 206949 - 206949
08-Nov-19 12:28:50 - INFO - Coverage: 1.000000
CPU times: user 594 ms, sys: 81.3 ms, total: 676 ms
Wall time: 1min 22s
```

6.7.4 Evaluating a Transigrafo

The evaluation of the resulting embeddings is performed through the Java Scorer
script provided by the authors of the LMMS paper.

```
In [ ]: %cd external/wsd_eval/WSD_Evaluation_Framework/Evaluation_Datasets/
        !javac Scorer.java
        %cd /content/LMMS/

        /content/LMMS/external/wsd_eval/WSD_Evaluation_Framework/Evaluation_Datasets
        /content/LMMS
```

The SemCor corpus counts with five different test sets: **senseval2,senseval3,
semeval2007, semeval2013**, and **semeval2015**. Also, there is an additional test
set available that contains all the previous datasets ("**all**"). Next, we evaluate the
previously calculated embeddings against semeval2015.

```
In [ ]: %%time
!python eval_nn.py -backend transformers -sv_path data/vectors/semcor_ext.3-512.vecs.npz
                   -test_set semeval2015

08-Nov-19 12:29:44 - INFO - Loading SensesVSM ...
08-Nov-19 12:29:50 - INFO - Loaded SensesVSM
08-Nov-19 12:29:50 - INFO - Creating TransformerSentenceEncoder
[...]
08-Nov-19 12:29:51 - INFO - Model config {
  "attention_probs_dropout_prob": 0.1,
  "directionality": "bidi",
  "finetuning_task": null,
  "hidden_act": "gelu",
  "hidden_dropout_prob": 0.1,
  "hidden_size": 1024,
  "initializer_range": 0.02,
  "intermediate_size": 4096,
  "layer_norm_eps": 1e-12,
  "max_position_embeddings": 512,
  "num_attention_heads": 16,
  "num_hidden_layers": 24,
  "num_labels": 2,
  "output_attentions": false,
  "output_hidden_states": true,
  "output_past": true,
  "pooler_fc_size": 768,
  "pooler_num_attention_heads": 12,
  "pooler_num_fc_layers": 3,
  "pooler_size_per_head": 128,
  "pooler_type": "first_token_transform",
  "pruned_heads": {},
  "torchscript": false,
  "type_vocab_size": 2,
  "use_bfloat16": false,
  "vocab_size": 28996
}

08-Nov-19 12:30:02 - INFO - Created TransformerSentenceEncoder
config {'model_name_or_path': 'bert-large-cased', 'model_arch': 'BERT', 'min_seq_len': 3,
        'max_seq_len': 512, 'pooling_strategy': 'NONE', 'pooling_layer': [-4, -3, -2, -1],
        'tok_merge_strategy': 'mean', 'sent_special_tokens': [{'index': 0, 'tok_id': 101,
        'tok': '[CLS]'}, {'index': -1, 'tok_id': 102, 'tok': '[SEP]'}], 'tok_dim': 1024}
08-Nov-19 12:30:25 - DEBUG - ACC: 0.817 (278 32/138)
08-Nov-19 12:30:40 - DEBUG - ACC: 0.759 (457 64/138)
08-Nov-19 12:30:55 - DEBUG - ACC: 0.745 (635 96/138)
08-Nov-19 12:31:16 - DEBUG - ACC: 0.746 (929 128/138)
08-Nov-19 12:31:22 - DEBUG - ACC: 0.752 (1022 138/138)
```

```
08-Nov-19 12:31:22 - INFO - Supplementary Metrics:
08-Nov-19 12:31:22 - INFO - Avg. correct idx: 0.555773
08-Nov-19 12:31:22 - INFO - Avg. correct idx (failed): 2.245059
08-Nov-19 12:31:22 - INFO - Avg. num options: 5.484344
08-Nov-19 12:31:22 - INFO - Num. unknown lemmas: 0
08-Nov-19 12:31:22 - INFO - POS Failures:
08-Nov-19 12:31:22 - INFO - POS Confusion:
08-Nov-19 12:31:22 - INFO - NOUN - {'NOUN': 531, 'VERB': 0, 'ADJ': 0, 'ADV': 0}
08-Nov-19 12:31:22 - INFO - VERB - {'NOUN': 0, 'VERB': 251, 'ADJ': 0, 'ADV': 0}
08-Nov-19 12:31:22 - INFO - ADJ - {'NOUN': 0, 'VERB': 0, 'ADJ': 160, 'ADV': 0}
08-Nov-19 12:31:22 - INFO - ADV - {'NOUN': 0, 'VERB': 0, 'ADJ': 0, 'ADV': 80}
08-Nov-19 12:31:22 - INFO - Running official scorer ...
P=      75.2%
R=      75.2%
F1=      75.2%
CPU times: user 602 ms, sys: 83.4 ms, total: 686 ms
Wall time: 1min 44s
```

Precision, recall, and f1 scores are showed (around 75% in our implementation). We can also compare these results with the ones from the original LMMS paper in Table 6.2. The "LMMS 1024" row shows the results we are reproducing here. The "LMMS 2048" row shows some additional improvement, obtained through concatenation with the embeddings resulting from glosses and lemmas.

Table 6.2 Sense embeddings evaluation results—variations of the LMMS algorithm

	Senseval2	Senseval3	Semeval2007	Semeval2013	Semeval2015	ALL
MFS	66.8	66.2	55.2	63.0	67.8	65.2
LMMS-1024	75.4	74.0	66.4	72.7	75.3	73.8
LMMS-2048	76.3	75.6	68.1	75.1	77.0	75.4

6.7.5   Inspect Sense Embeddings in Transigrafo

As we previously did with the embeddings resulting from Vecsigrafo, using an extended version of Swivel, next we inspect the embeddings obtained to generate our Transigrafo, based on neural language models and transformers.

```
In [ ]: import numpy as np

        loader = np.load("data/vectors/semcor_ext.3-512.vecs.npz")
        labels = loader['labels'].tolist()
        vectors = loader['vectors']
        indices = {l: i for i, l in enumerate(labels)}
```

To this purpose, we define two functions, based on the k-NN algorithm, which allow obtaining the neighbors of a sense embedding in the Transigrafo vector space.

```
In [ ]: from sklearn.neighbors import KNeighborsClassifier
        import pandas

        pandas.set_option('display.max_colwidth', -1)
```

```
def get_knn (n_neighbors,vectors,labels):
  neigh = KNeighborsClassifier(n_neighbors=n_neighbors+1)
  neigh.fit(vectors,labels)
  return neigh

def get_neighbors_report(neigh,sense,i):
  sensekey2synset_map = {}
  for synset in nltk.corpus.wordnet.all_synsets():
        for lemma in synset.lemmas():
            sensekey2synset_map[lemma.key()] = synset

  print("SENSE: ", sense)
  print("SYNSET: ", str(sensekey2synset_map[sense])[8:-2])
  print("GLOSSA: ", sensekey2synset_map[sense].definition())


  print("\nK-NEIGHBORS")
  distance_list, neigh_list = neigh.kneighbors(vectors[i].reshape(1, -1))
  distance_list = distance_list[0].tolist()
  neigh_list = neigh_list[0].tolist()

  if i in neigh_list:
    distance_list.remove(distance_list[neigh_list.index(i)])
    neigh_list.remove(i)
  else:
    distance_list = distance_list[:-1]
    neigh_list = neigh_list[:-1]

  res=[labels[n] for n in neigh_list]

  glossas = []
  synsets = []
  for r in res:
    synsets.append(str(sensekey2synset_map[r])[8:-2])
    glossas.append(sensekey2synset_map[r].definition())
  table = [list(i) for i in zip(*[distance_list, res, synsets, glossas])]
  return table
```

Next, we generate a k-NN model with the embeddings:

```
In [ ]: neigh = get_knn(3,vectors,labels)
```

Executing the following cells in our notebook will display the 3-neighbors of some selected sample senses: **"long%3:00:02::"**, **"be%2:42:03::"**, and **"review%2:31:00::"**.

```
In [ ]: sense = "long%3:00:02::"
        table = get_neighbors_report(neigh, sense, indices[sense])
        pandas.DataFrame(table, columns=['distance','sense','synset', 'glossa'])

SENSE:   long%3:00:02::
SYNSET:  long.a.01
GLOSSA:  primarily temporal sense; being or indicating a relatively great or greater
         than average duration or passage of time or a duration as specified

Out[ ]:    distance ...                                              glossa
        0  19.909746 ...  for an extended time or at a distant time
        1  27.274618 ...  primarily spatial sense; of relatively great or greater than
                          average spatial extension or extension as specified
        2  28.726203 ...  a prolonged period of time

In [ ]: sense = "be%2:42:03::"
        table = get_neighbors_report(neigh, sense, indices[sense])
        pandas.DataFrame(table, columns=['distance', 'sense', 'synset', 'glossa'])
```

```
SENSE:  be%2:42:03::
SYNSET:  be.v.01
GLOSSA:  have the quality of being; (copula, used with an adjective or a predicate noun)

Out[ ]:    distance  ...                                              glossa
        0  0.0       ...  have the property of being packable or of compacting easily
        1  0.0       ...  be in equilibrium
        2  0.0       ...  have the property of being packable or of compacting easily

In [ ]: sense = "review%2:31:00::"
        table = get_neighbors_report(neigh, sense, indices[sense])
        pandas.DataFrame(table, columns=['distance','sense', 'synset', 'glossa'])

SENSE:  review%2:31:00::
SYNSET:  review.v.01
GLOSSA:  look at again; examine again

Out[ ]:    distance   ...                                    glossa
        0  25.646945  ...  evaluate professionally a colleague's work
        1  25.646945  ...  appraise critically
        2  25.646945  ...  evaluate professionally a colleague's work
```

6.7.6   Exploring the Stability of the Transigrafo Embeddings

One of the enhancements we added over the standard LMMS algorithm and its
implementation is a rolling cosine similarity measure calculated during the process
of learning the embeddings. For each sense, such measure collects cosine similarity
scores between the average vector until then and the current occurrence of the sense
in the training corpus. This value should converge to the average distance of the
sense with respect to its average in each iteration. Peaks and valleys in the expected
convergence may indicate issues, e.g. derived from a corpus that may be too small,
with underrepresented senses. Next, we include the implementation of our rolling
cosine similarity measure.

```
In [ ]: def read_rolling_cosims(base_path, ext='txt', sep=' '):
            def _float(s):
                try:
                    return float(s)
                except:
                    raise ValueError()
                    #print("Can't convert ", s.strip(), "to float")
                    #return 0.0

            result = {}
            with open(base_path +'.rolling_cosims.%s' % ext) as tsv_f:
                for line_idx, line in enumerate(tsv_f):
                    line = line.strip()
                    elems = line.split(sep)
                    #print("line ", line_idx, len(elems))
                    try:
                        result[elems[0]] = list(map(_float, elems[1:]))
                    except:
                        print('Error reading line %d\n%s\n%s' % (line_idx, line, elems))
            return result

In [ ]: blc = read_rolling_cosims('data/vectors/semcor..3-512')

In [ ]: len(blc)
```

```
Out[ ]: 33362

In [ ]: import statistics
def rcosim_stdevs(rcosims, start_occ=10, min_occs=20):
    return {
        sense: statistics.stdev(cosims[start_occ:]) for sense, cosims in rcosims.items()
        if len(cosims) > start_occ + min_occs
    }

In [ ]: def plot_senses(rcosims, sense_list=[], lemma=None):
        style = ['b-', 'g-', 'r-', 'c-', 'm-', 'y-', 'k-',
                 'b:', 'g:', 'r:', 'c:', 'm:', 'y:', 'k:',
                 'b--', 'g--', 'r--', 'c--', 'm--', 'y--', 'k--',
                 'bx', 'gx', 'rx']
        if lemma is not None:
            assert sense_list == []
            sense_list = [sense for sense in rcosims.keys()
                          if sense.startswith(lemma+"%")]
        if len(sense_list) > 6:
            for i in range(0, len(sense_list), 6):
                #print('plotting sense ', i, 'to', i+6)
                plot = plot_senses(rcosims, sense_list[i:i+6])
                plot.show()
            return
        for i, sense in enumerate(sense_list):
            x = len(rcosims[sense])
            #print(sense, x)
            #plt.scatter(range(len(rcosims[sense])), rcosims[sense])
            plt.plot(range(x), rcosims[sense], style[i],
                     label="%s n=%d $\mu$=%.3f $\sigma$=%.3f" % (
                sense, x,
                0.0 if x == 0 else statistics.mean(rcosims[sense]),
                0.0 if x < 2 else statistics.stdev(rcosims[sense])))
        plt.legend()
        plt.ylabel('Rolling cosim')
        plt.xlabel('sense occurrence in corpus')
        axes = plt.gca() # get current
        axes.set_xlim([0,100])
        axes.set_ylim([0,1.0])
        return plt
```

Next, we continue our analysis to understand the influence of the disambiguated corpus in the resulting embeddings and the information obtained from the rolling cosine similarity measure.

6.7.6.1 How Often Do Senses Occur in SemCor?

As we can see in Fig. 6.4, most of the senses in the SemCor corpus (20K out of 33K) only occur once or twice in the corpus. Only about 500 senses occur 100 times or more. This indicates that the corpus is probably too small, providing little signal to learn the task at hand. Therefore, future work in this area will require investing more effort in the generation of larger disambiguated corpus, following different approaches like, e.g. crowdsourcing.

```
In [ ]: import matplotlib.pyplot as plt
        plt.yscale('log')
        _ = plt.hist([len(rcosims) for sense, rcosims in blc.items()], bins=50)

In [ ]: _ = plt.hist([len(rcosims) for sense, rcosims in blc.items()], bins=50)
```

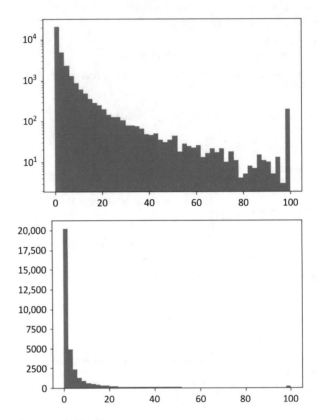

Fig. 6.4 Sense frequency in SemCor

6.7.6.2 What Do Frequent Sense rcosim Plots Look Like

As shown in Figs. 6.5, 6.6, 6.7, and 6.8, even the embeddings of the most frequent senses are quite unstable according to the rolling cosine similarity measure. This pattern becomes even more obvious with lower frequency senses and their lemmas.[18]

```
In [ ]: senses_byfreq = [kv[0] for kv in sorted(blc.items(), key=lambda kv: len(kv[1]))]

In [ ]: _ = plot_senses(blc, senses_byfreq[-6:]) # most frequent senses


In [ ]: # some less frequent senses, but still visible
        _ = plot_senses(blc, senses_byfreq[32000:32006])


In [ ]: # senses for lemma 'be'
        plot_senses(blc, lemma="be")
```

---

[18]Note the point of these figures is not to be able to see the pattern of each lemma, but rather that all the lemmas are quite unstable. We invite the reader to adapt the code in the notebook to plot a single lemma.

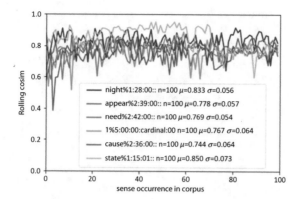

Fig. 6.5 Rolling cosine similarity for the most frequent senses in SemCor

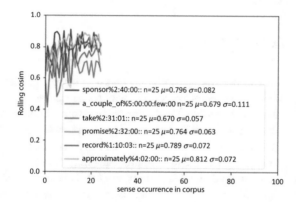

Fig. 6.6 Rolling cosine similarity for some less frequent senses, but still frequent enough to be visible in the plot

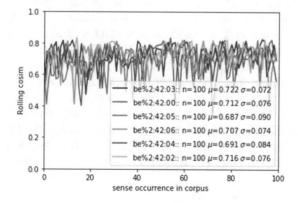

Fig. 6.7 Rolling cosine similarity for the senses corresponding to lemma *be*

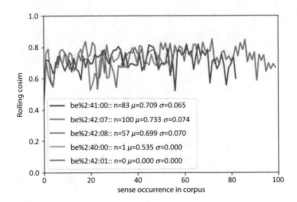

Fig. 6.8 Rolling cosine similarity for other senses of lemma *be* with lower frequency. The pattern of instability identified in Fig. 6.7 is even more acute due to the lower frequency of appearance of these senses in the corpus

6.7.7   *Additional Reflections*

The values obtained in the rolling similarity measure clearly indicate issues with the size and variety of the SemCor corpus, which can be addressed by creating new larger disambiguated corpora. In addition to an informed comparison between Vecsigrafo and Transigrafo, how to create such corpora, required to learn a more robust Transigrafo model, is also a research topic that will need to be addressed in the future. To this purpose, possible approaches may entail higher automation (SemCor is manually annotated, which surely limited its possible size) and crowd-sourcing, given the volume of disambiguated text that may be needed, as well as advanced tooling that enable knowledge engineers to curate the disambiguated corpora, following a semi-automatic approach where expert intervention is still needed.

Another key aspect that requires further research and improvement for a practical application of Transigrafo includes multi-lingualism. Currently, most neural language models are only available in a handful of languages in addition to English and, though useful, multi-lingual BERT (M-BERT) is also limited [143]. However, we expect that the solution to this issue will naturally unfold with the normal evolution of the deployment of neural language models among NLP researchers and practitioners. Indeed, this is happening as we write these lines, with BERT-based models already available in well-represented languages like French (CamemBERT [115]), German,[19] Italian (ALBERTo [144]), Spanish (BETO[20]), or Dutch (BERTje [184] and RobBERT [38]). Extending such coverage to underrepresented languages will require interesting and challenging research.

---

[19]https://deepset.ai/german-bert.

[20]https://github.com/dccuchile/beto.

6.8 Conclusion

This chapter presented two approaches for learning hybrid word and concept embeddings from large text corpora and knowledge graphs. The first approach requires disambiguating the training corpus prior to training. The second approach assumes that recent transformer-based language models somehow encode concept-level embeddings in some layers of the contextual embedding stack and derives the concept-level embeddings from examples in a pre-annotated corpus. By following the practical sections you will have been able to train embeddings based on both approaches and explore their results. We also discussed some of the properties of the representations resulting from both approaches. In the next chapter we look more thoroughly at different ways of evaluating word and concept embeddings, with special focus on corpus-based knowledge graph embeddings like Vecsigrafo.

Chapter 7
Quality Evaluation

Abstract In the previous chapters we have discussed various methods for generating embeddings for both words and concepts. Once you have applied some embedding learning mechanism you may wonder *how good are these embeddings?* In this chapter we look at methods for assessing the quality of the learned embeddings: from visualizations to intrinsic evaluations like predicting alignment with human-rated word similarity and extrinsic evaluations based on downstream tasks. As in the previous chapters, we provide hands-on practical sections for gaining experience in applying evaluation methods. We also discuss the methodology and results used for a real-world evaluation of Vecsigrafo compared to various other methods, which provides a sense for how thorough real-world evaluations can be performed.

7.1 Introduction

In the previous chapters, you have already seen several methods to generate embeddings for words and concepts. At the end of the day, having embeddings is not an end goal in and of itself; their purpose is to have a way to encode information in such a way that they are useful in achieving useful tasks. Indeed, in the subsequent chapters, you will see various applications of these embeddings for various text and knowledge graph tasks such as classification, KG interlinking, and analysis of fake news and disinformation. Since different methods for generating embeddings encode different information, some embeddings can be more suitable for some tasks than others. Therefore, once you have applied some embedding learning mechanism—or once you have found some pre-calculated embeddings online—you may wonder *how good are these embeddings?* In this chapter, we look at various generic ways to assess the quality of embeddings.

First, we will provide an overview of evaluation methods in Sect. 7.2 and then, in Sects. 7.3 and 7.4, we will practice evaluating some of the simple embeddings we have calculated in the previous chapters; this will give you practical experience in evaluating embeddings. Finally, in Sect. 7.5, we describe how we have applied some of these methods to evaluate a full version of Vecsigrafo embeddings. This last part

© Springer Nature Switzerland AG 2020
J. M. Gomez-Perez et al., *A Practical Guide to Hybrid Natural Language Processing*, https://doi.org/10.1007/978-3-030-44830-1_7

does not include practical exercises, but will give you an idea of how real-world embeddings can be evaluated and compared to other state-of-the-art embeddings.

7.2   Overview of Evaluation Methods

Common embedding evaluation methods can be divided into:

- **Visual Exploration**: whereby (a subsection of) the embeddings are displayed as a diagram. This is often used in combination with graphical user interfaces which enable querying, filtering, and selecting from a variety of projections. Good examples of this are TensorFlow's embedding Projector[1] and Parallax.[2] The main advantage of visualizations is that they provide an intuitive understanding of what the embedding algorithms are doing. However, since visualizations are often in 2D or 3D, they cannot correctly encode all of the information contained in the full embedding space. Furthermore, these methods are often limited to a few hundreds or thousands of embedding points. A final limitation of these methods is that they do not provide a unique numeric global score, making it difficult to assess whether one embedding space is better than another one.
- **Intrinsic Evaluation**: whereby the embeddings are used to perform a token-based task and the results are compared with a gold standard. The most common tasks used are word similarity, but datasets also exist for other tasks like word analogies and categorization. The main advantage of this method is that quite a few datasets are available and there is a tradition of using such datasets; therefore, it is easy to compare new embeddings against previously published results. On the other hand, the tasks in and of themselves are not that useful and some of the most common datasets have been criticized (for example, for failing to distinguish between word similarity and relatedness, or failing to decide whether antonyms should be considered to be similar or not). Below, we also provide practical experience with a **Word Prediction** method, whereby we look into using a test corpus to evaluate the embeddings by defining a word prediction task; this is an intrinsic evaluation method with a visual component.
- **Extrinsic Evaluation**: whereby a new model is learned (using the embeddings as inputs) to perform a downstream task like text classification. This is task dependent and, if you have a specific task in mind, should be your primary concern. However, these types of evaluations make it difficult to compare embedding spaces in a more general set of tests. Also, note that if you have a large number of downstream tasks, you may want to avoid maintaining separate embedding spaces for each of these tasks; instead, it is more likely that you will choose a single embedding space which performs reasonably well in a large number of tasks.

---

[1]https://projector.tensorflow.org/.

[2]https://github.com/uber-research/parallax.

KG embeddings tend to be evaluated using **graph completion** tasks, which we will also discuss briefly. With the recent popularity of language models, evaluation of individual word embeddings becomes more difficult, since words are assigned different embeddings depending on their context. As of the time of writing, there are no clear ways to evaluate embeddings for these systems; instead, these systems are evaluated using a battery of NLP tasks, the most widely used of which is the GLUE benchmark.[3]

7.2.1   Recommended Papers in This Area

Schnabel et al. [158] provide a good overview of methods and introduce terminology to refer to different types of evaluations. Baroni at al. [15] focused mostly on *intrinsic* evaluations and showed that predictive models like word2vec produce better results than count models (based on co-occurrence counting). Finally, Levy et al. [103] studied how various implementation or optimization "details" used in predictive models, which were not needed or used in count models, affect the performance of the resulting embeddings. Examples of such details are negative sampling, dynamic context windows, subsampling, and vector normalization. The paper shows that once such details are taken into account, the difference between count and predictive models is actually not that large.

7.3   Practice: Evaluating Word and Concept Embeddings

```
In [15]: %cd /content/tutorial
         !git pull
         %cd /content/

/content/tutorial
remote: Enumerating objects: 9, done.
remote: Counting objects: 100% (9/9), done.
remote: Compressing objects: 100% (1/1), done.
remote: Total 5 (delta 4), reused 5 (delta 4), pack-reused 0
Unpacking objects: 100% (5/5), done.
From https://github.com/hybridnlp/tutorial
   c433662..e57213f  master     -> origin/master
Updating c433662..e57213f
Fast-forward
 scripts/swivel/wordsim.py | 2 +-
 1 file changed, 1 insertion(+), 1 deletion(-)
/content
```

---

[3] https://gluebenchmark.com.

7.3.1 Visual Exploration

Tools like Embedding Projector[4] use dimensionality reduction algorithms such as t-SNE and PCA to visualize a subset of the embedding space and project points to a 2-D or 3-D space.

Pros
- Can give you a sense of whether the model has correctly learned meaningful relations. Especially if you have a small number of pre-categorized words.
- Easy to explore the space.

Cons
- Subjective: Neighborhoods may look good, but are they? There is no gold standard.
- It works best for a small subset of the embedding space. But how to identify such subset?
- The resulting projection can be deceiving: what looks close in 3-D space can be far in 300-D space (and vice versa).

7.3.2 Intrinsic Evaluation

Intrinsic evaluations are those where you can use embeddings to perform relatively simple, word-related tasks.

Schnabel et al. distinguish between:

- **Absolute Intrinsic**: You have a (human annotated) gold standard for a particular task and use the embeddings to make predictions.
- **Comparative Intrinsic**: You use the embedding space to present predictions to humans, who then rate them. Mostly used when there is no gold standard available.

The tasks used in intrinsic evaluation are the following:

- **Relatedness**: How well do embeddings capture human-perceived word similarity? Datasets typically consist of triples: two words and a similarity score (e.g., between 0.0 and 1.0). Several available datasets although interpretation of "word similarity" can vary.
- **Synonym Detection**: Can embeddings select a synonym for a given word and a set of options? Datasets are n-tuples where the first word is the input word and the other $n-1$ words are the options. Only one of the options is a synonym.
- **Analogy**: Do embeddings encode relations between words? Datasets are 4-tuples: the first two words define the relation, the third word is the source of

---
[4]http://projector.tensorflow.org.

the query, and the fourth word is the solution. Good embeddings should predict an embedding close to the solution word.

- **Categorization**: Can embeddings be clustered into hand-annotated categories? Datasets are word–category pairs. Standard clustering algorithms can then be used to generate k-clusters and the purity of the clusters can be computed.
- **Selectional Preference**: Can embeddings predict whether a noun–verb pair is more likely to represent a verb–subject or a verb–object relation? For example, `people-eat` is more likely to be found as a verb–subject.

7.3.2.1 Compute a Relatedness Score

Swivel comes with a `eval.mk` script that downloads and unzips various relatedness and analogy datasets. The script also compiles an `analogy` executable. It assumes you have a Unix environment and tools such as `wget`, `tar`, `unzip`, and `egrep`, as well as `make` and a `c++` compiler.

For convenience, we have included various relatedness datasets as part of this repo in `datasamples/relatedness`. We assume you have generated vectors as part of previous notebooks, which we will test here.

```
In [ ]: import os

In [5]: %ls /content/tutorial/datasamples/relatedness/

rarewords.ws.tab   simverb3500.ws.tab   ws353sim.ws.tab
simlex999.ws.tab   ws353rel.ws.tab

In [ ]: %cp /content/umbc/coocs/tlgs_wnscd_5K_ls_f/row_vocab.txt \
    /content/umbc/vec/tlgs_wnscd_5K_ls_f/vocab.txt
    umbc_5k_vec = '/content/umbc/vec/tlgs_wnscd_5k_ls_f/'
    umbc_full_vec = '/content/umbc/vec/vecsi_tlgs_wnscd_ls_f_6e_160d/'
```

You can use Swivel's `wordsim.py` to produce metrics for the k-cap embeddings we produced in previous notebooks:

```
In [16]: !python /content/tutorial/scripts/swivel/wordsim.py \
    --vocab={umbc_5k_vec}vocab.txt \
    --embeddings={umbc_5k_vec}vecs.bin \
    --word_prefix="lem_" \
    /content/tutorial/datasamples/relatedness/*.ws.tab

Opening vector from file /content/umbc/vec/tlgs_wnscd_5k_ls_f/vocab.txt
vocab size 5632 (unique 5632)
read rows
65 of 2034 pairs found
0.576 /content/tutorial/datasamples/relatedness/rarewords.ws.tab
288 of 999 pairs found
0.066 /content/tutorial/datasamples/relatedness/simlex999.ws.tab
1126 of 3500 pairs found
0.073 /content/tutorial/datasamples/relatedness/simverb3500.ws.tab
92 of 252 pairs found
0.371 /content/tutorial/datasamples/relatedness/ws353rel.ws.tab
57 of 203 pairs found
0.459 /content/tutorial/datasamples/relatedness/ws353sim.ws.tab

In [25]: %ls {umbc_full_vec}vocab.txt
    !python /content/tutorial/scripts/swivel/wordsim.py \
```

```
  --vocab=/content/umbc/vec/vecsi_tlgs_wnscd_ls_f_6e_160d/vocab.txt \
  --embeddings={umbc_full_vec}vecs.bin \
  --word_prefix="lem_" /content/tutorial/datasamples/relatedness/*.ws.tab

/content/umbc/vec/vecsi_tlgs_wnscd_ls_f_6e_160d/vocab.txt
Opening vector from file /content/umbc/vec/vecsi_tlgs_wnscd_ls_f_6e_160d/vocab.txt
vocab size 1499136 (unique 1499125)
read rows
1433 of 2034 pairs found
0.401 /content/tutorial/datasamples/relatedness/rarewords.ws.tab
999 of 999 pairs found
0.276 /content/tutorial/datasamples/relatedness/simlex999.ws.tab
3494 of 3500 pairs found
0.191 /content/tutorial/datasamples/relatedness/simverb3500.ws.tab
250 of 252 pairs found
0.529 /content/tutorial/datasamples/relatedness/ws353rel.ws.tab
202 of 203 pairs found
0.649 /content/tutorial/datasamples/relatedness/ws353sim.ws.tab
```

The numbers show that both embedding spaces only have a small coverage of the evaluation datasets. Furthermore, the correlation score achieved is in the range of 0.07–0.22, which is very poor, but expected given the size of the corpus.

For comparison state-of-the-art results are in the range of 0.65–0.8.

7.3.2.2   Conclusions for Intrinsic Evaluation

Intrinsic evaluations are the most direct way of evaluating (word) embeddings.

Pros
- They provide a single objective metric that enables easy comparison between different embeddings.
- There are several readily available evaluation datasets (for English).
- If you have an existing, manually crafted knowledge graph, you can generate your own evaluation datasets.

Cons
- Evaluation datasets are small and can be biased in terms of word selection and annotation.
- You need to take coverage into account (besides final metric).
- Existing datasets only support English words (few datasets in other languages, few compound words, few concepts).
- Tasks are low level and thus somewhat artificial: people care about document classification, but not about word categories or word similarities.

7.3.3   Word Prediction Plots

This can be seen as a task for intrinsic evaluation; however, the task is very close to the original training task used to derive the embeddings in the first place.

Recall that *predictive models* (such as `word2vec`) try to minimize the distance between a word embedding and the embeddings of the context words (and that over a whole corpus) (Fig. 7.1).

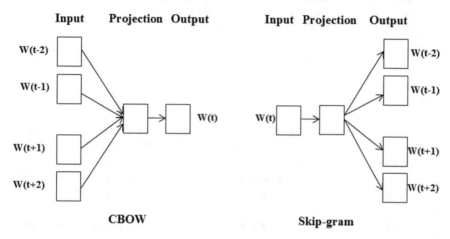

Fig. 7.1 word2vec diagrams

This means that, if we have a test corpus, we can use the embeddings to try to predict words based on their contexts. Assuming the test corpus and the training corpus contain similar language we should expect better embeddings to produce better predictions on average.

A major advantage of this approach is that we do not need human annotation. Also, we can reuse the tokenization pipeline used for training to produce similar tokens as those in our embedding space. For example, we can use word-sense disambiguation to generate a test corpus including lemmas and concepts.

The algorithm in pseudo-code is:

```
similarities = {}
for window in corpus:
  focus_word, context_words = window
  focus_vector = embedding(focus_word)
  context_vector = predict_embedding(context_words, focus_word)
  similarities[focus_word].append(cosine_similarity(focus_vector, context_vector))
return similarities.values().average()
```

The result is a single number that tells you how far the prediction embedding was from the actual word embedding over the whole test corpus. When using cosine similarity this should be a number between −1 and 1.

We can also use the intermediate `similarities` dictionary to plot diagrams which can provide further insight. For example, random embeddings result in a plot depicted in Fig. 7.2.

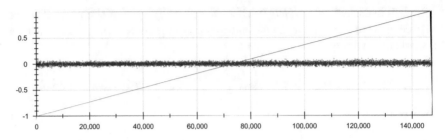

Fig. 7.2 Word prediction plot for random embeddings

The horizontal axis is the rank of the focus_word sorted by their frequency in the training corpus. (For example, frequent words such as be and the would be close to the origin, while infrequent words would be towards the end of the axis.)

The plot shows that, when words have random embeddings, on average the distance between the prediction for each word and the word embedding is close to 0.

These plots can be useful for detecting implementation bugs. For example, when we were implementing the CogitoPrep utility for counting co-occurrences for lemmas and concepts, we generated the following plot depicted in Fig. 7.3.

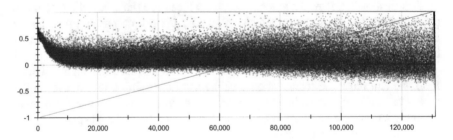

Fig. 7.3 Buggy embeddings

This showed that we were learning to predict frequent words and some non-frequent words, but that we were not learning most non-frequent words correctly.

After fixing the bug, we got the plot shown in Fig. 7.4.

This shows that now we were able to learn embeddings that improved word prediction across the whole vocabulary. But it also showed that prediction for the most frequent words lagged behind more uncommon words.

After applying some vector normalization techniques to Swivel and re-centering the vectors (we noticed that the centroid of all the vocabulary embeddings was not the origin), we got the plot shown in Fig. 7.5, which shows better overall prediction.

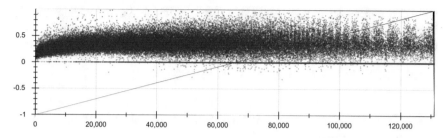

Fig. 7.4 Uncentered

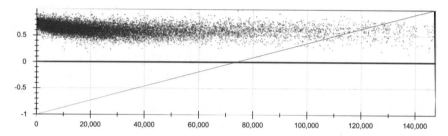

Fig. 7.5 Recentered

7.3.3.1   Conclusion for Word Prediction

Word prediction provides a single objective metric.

Pros
- It does not require human annotation (although it may require pre-processing of the test corpus).
- It allows reusing the tokenization steps used during embedding creation.
- It can be used to generate plots, which can provide insights about implementation or representation issues.

Cons
- There are no standard test corpora.
- It can be slow to generate the metric for large test corpus. We recommend balancing the size of the test corpus to maximize the vocabulary coverage while minimizing the time required to process the corpus.

7.3.4   Extrinsic Evaluation

In extrinsic evaluations, we have a more complex task we are interested in (e.g., text classification, text translation, image captioning), whereby we can use embeddings as a way to represent words (or tokens). Assuming we have (1) a model architecture and (2) a corpus for training and evaluation (for which the embeddings provide adequate coverage), we can then train the model using different embeddings and evaluate its overall performance. The idea is that better embeddings will make it easier for the model to learn the overall task.

7.4 Practice 2: Assessing Relational Knowledge Captured by Embeddings

In this practical section, we use the embrela library to study whether various embedding spaces capture certain lexico-semantic relations on WordNet. The approach behind embrela is described by Denaux and Gomez-Perez in [41].

The main idea here is that word/concept embeddings seem to capture many lexico-semantic relations. However evaluation methods like word similarity and word analogy have several drawbacks. Also, if you have an existing KG with relations that matter to you, you want to know how well word/concept embeddings capture those relations. The embrela pipeline is designed to help you do this by: (1) generating *word/concept pair datasets* from a KG, (2) creating and evaluating classifiers based on the embedding space(s), and (3) providing guidelines on how to analyze the evaluation results.

There are **pitfalls to all three of these steps**, which the embrela pipeline takes into account in order to *avoid concluding incorrectly that embeddings capture relational information* when in fact, the generated dataset may be biased or evaluation results may not be statistically significantly better than random guesses. The overall pipeline is depicted in Fig. 7.6.

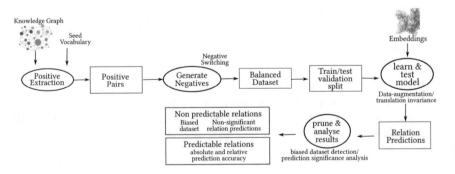

Fig. 7.6 embrela pipeline for assessing the lexico-semantic relational knowledge captured in an embedding space

7.4.1   *Download the embrela Project*

We put the main Python module on the main working folder to make importing of submodules a bit easier to read.

```
In [1]: !git clone https://github.com/rdenaux/embrelassess.git embrela_prj
        !ln -s embrela_prj/embrelassess embrelassess

Cloning into 'embrela_prj'...
remote: Enumerating objects: 304, done.
remote: Counting objects: 100% (304/304), done.
remote: Compressing objects: 100% (149/149), done.
remote: Total 304 (delta 138), reused 295 (delta 132), pack-reused 0
Receiving objects: 100% (304/304), 14.64 MiB | 6.98 MiB/s, done.
Resolving deltas: 100% (138/138), done.
```

7.4.2   *Download Generated Datasets*

Instead of generating datasets from scratch, which can be done by using the `embrela_prj/wnet-rel-pair-extractor`, in this section we will use a set of pre-generated datasets extracted from WordNet.

```
In [2]: !wget https://github.com/rdenaux/embrelassess/releases/download/
v0.1/vocabrels_wnet-switched-negs.zip
    !unzip vocabrels_wnet-switched-negs.zip
```

This should download and unzip the file containing the datasets. We can load the metadata of the generated relations as follows:

```
In [ ]: import embrelassess.learn as learn
        import os.path as osp
```

```
In [ ]: rel_path = osp.join('vocabrels_wn-switched-negs/')
        rels_df = learn.load_rels_meta(rel_path)
```

which gives us a pandas DataFrame with metadata about the datasets. You can print it by issuing command:

```
In [5]: rels_df
```

This will print a table with various fields. Here we only print a small part of that table:

```
Out[5]:
type   ...                                            file
lem2lem  ...  lem2lem_member_of_category_domain__9116.txt
lem2lem  ...                     lem2lem_synonym__74822.txt
lem2lem  ...                   lem2lem_entailment__1519.txt
lem2lem  ...                lem2lem_part_meronym__6403.txt
lem2lem  ...                  lem2lem_hypernym__110650.txt
lem2lem  ...              lem2lem_substance_holonym__369.txt
lem2lem  ...                   lem2lem_hyponym__110650.txt
lem2lem  ...                        lem2lem_cause__719.txt
lem2lem  ...               lem2lem_part_holonym__6403.txt
lem2lem  ...                 lem2lem_participle_of__81.txt

[27 rows x 4 columns]
```

The previous step should have printed a table with 27 rows. One for each generated dataset. All of the datasets are lem2lem, i.e. the *source* and *target*s are both lemmas. In the paper we also consider pairs of types lem2syn, syn2syn, and lem2pos, where syn is a synset (or syncon) and pos is part-of-speech.

The remaining columns in the table tell us:

- The name of the relation.
- cnt: the number of **positive** examples extracted from the KG, WordNet 3 in this case.
- The file name where we can find both the positive and negative examples.

Note that each dataset will have about twice the number of lines as the positive cnt, since we aim to build balanced datasets. For example for the entailment relation, we have 1519 positive pairs, but

```
In [6]: !wc -l vocabrels_wn-switched-negs/lem2lem_entailment__1519.txt

3039 vocabrels_wn-switched-negs/lem2lem_entailment__1519.txt
```

3039 lines in total. Further inspection of the file shows that it is a tab-separated-value with columns: source, target, label, and comment.

```
In [7]: !head -n 5 vocabrels_wn-switched-negs/lem2lem_antonym__9310.txt
```

This should print lines which correspond to the following table:

src word	tgt word	Label	Comment
specialize	diversify	1	Positive
give off	affirm	0	[NegSwitched]
beginning	ending	1	Positive
take off	dc	0	[NegSwitched]
hot	cold	1	Positive

7.4.3 Load the Embeddings to Be Evaluated

We will use the following embeddings:

- WordNet embeddings trained using **HolE**, which learns embeddings directly from the WordNet graph. This is a strong baseline.
- **fastText**.
- **GloVe**.

First, we download the pre-trained HolE embeddings. These have been trained for 500 epochs and have 150 dimensions.

```
In [9]: !wget https://github.com/rdenaux/embrela/releases/download/
        v0.1.1/wn-en-3.1.-HolE-500e-150d.vec.tar.gz
        !tar xzf wn-en-3.1.-HolE-500e-150d.vec.tar.gz

https://github.com/.../v0.1.1/wn-en-3.1.-HolE-500e-150d.vec.tar.gz
...
Saving to: 'wn-en-3.1.-HolE-500e-150d.vec.tar.gz'
wn-en-3.1.-HolE-500 100%[===================>]
... - 'wn-en-3.1.-HolE-500e-150d.vec.tar.gz' saved [369436200/369436200]
```

Next, we can load the embeddings. The `embrela` library, as well as `torchtext` has various convenience methods to do this. `torchtext` automatically downloads pre-trained embeddings published at the official fastText and GloVe sites.

```
In [ ]: import embrelassess.embloader as embloader
        #import torchtext
        from torchtext.vocab import Vectors, FastText, GloVe
```

`torchtext` defines a number of `aliases`[5] for pre-trained embeddings. We use: * the `glove.6B.100d` pre-trained embeddings. In the paper we have used the `glove.840B.300d`, but these take longer to download * the `fasttext.simple.300d` embeddings.

```
In [ ]: # uncomment next line if you want to use GloVe embeddings.
        # These can take a while to load
        # glove_en = GloVe(name='6B', dim=100)

In [ ]: holE_wnet_en = embloader.TSVVectors('wn-en-3.1-HolE-500e.vec')

In [46]: len(list(holE_wnet_en.stoi.keys()))

Out[46]: 264965
```

We will also use random vectors as another baseline and to filter out biased relations. We use the vocabulary of words and syncons used in the K-CAP'19 paper, which was derived from disambiguating the UN corpus using Cogito.

```
In [ ]: vocab_path = osp.join('embrela_prj/vocab_sensi_lemsyn_UN.txt')
        rnd_vecs = embloader.RandomVectors(vocab_path, dim=300)
```

The training phase expects to get a map of vector space ids to `VecPairLoader` instances, which will take care of mapping `source` and `target` words in the generated datasets into the appropriate embeddings. Here we define the data loaders to use. Uncomment others if you want to use other embedding spaces.

```
In [ ]: data_loaders = {
        #'glove_cc_en':    embloader.VecPairLoader(glove_en),
        #'ft_wikip_en':    embloader.VecPairLoader(ft_en),
        #'vecsi_wiki_en': embloader.VecPairLoader(vecsi_wiki_en),
        #'vecsi_un_en':   embloader.VecPairLoader(vecsi_un_en),
        'rand_en':        embloader.VecPairLoader(rnd_vecs),
        'holE_wnet_en':   embloader.VecPairLoader(holE_wnet_en)
}
```

---

[5]https://torchtext.readthedocs.io/en/latest/vocab.html#pretrained-aliases.

7.4.4 Learn the Models

Now that we have the datasets and the embeddings, we are ready to train some models. This step is highly configurable, but in this notebook we will:

- Only train models with the nn3 architecture (i.e., with three fully connected layers).
- Only train models for a couple of (the 27) relations to keep execution short.
- Only train three models per embedding/relation/architecture combination.
- Apply *input perturbation* as explained in the paper which shifts both source and target embeddings by the same amount.

The trained models and evaluation results will be written to an output folder. Even with this restricted setup, this step can take 5–10 min on current Google Colaboratory environments.

```
In [24]: model_archs = ['nn3']
         n_runs = 3
         my_rels = ['entailment', 'antonym']
         def only_with_names(relname_whitelist):
           return lambda df_row: df_row['name'] in relname_whitelist

         odir = 'experiment/trained_models/'

         learn_results = learn.learn_rels(
             rel_path, rels_df, data_loaders,
             models=model_archs, n_runs=n_runs,
             rel_filter=only_with_names(my_rels),
             train_input_disturber_for_vec=learn.pair_disturber_for_vectors,
             odir_path=odir, cuda=True)
```

Executing the previous commands will result in a long list of outputs as the program iterates through the relations, trains and evaluates models to try to predict relations. The results are stored in the learn_results, which is a list of trained models along with model metadata and evaluation results gathered during training and validation. It is a good idea to write these results to disk:

```
In [ ]: for lr in learn_results:
            learn.store_learn_result(odir, lr)
```

The previous step will have generated a directory structure in the specified output dir. The folder structure is as follows:

(odir)/(rel_type)/(rel_name)/(emb_id)/(arch_id)/run_(number)/

See the embrela README for more details about the generated files.

7.4.5 Analyzing Model Results

Now that we have trained (and evaluated) models for the selected datasets, we can load the results and analyze them.

7.4.5.1   Load and Aggregate Evaluation Results for the Trained Models

First we show how to load and aggregate evaluation data from disk once you have gone through the step of learning the models and you have a train result folder structure as described above. If you skipped that part, below we will load pre-aggregated results.

```
In [ ]: import embrelassess.analyse as analyse
```

```
In [ ]: lr_read = learn.load_learn_results(odir)
```

We will read the results from disk, aggregate the results, and put them into a pandas DataFrame for easier analysis:

```
In [43]: import pandas as pd
         aggs = []
         for learn_result in lr_read:
           rel_aggs = analyse.aggregate_runs(learn_result)
           aggs = aggs + rel_aggs

         aggs_df = pd.DataFrame(aggs)
```

We can inspect the resulting DataFrame:

```
In [45]: aggs_df
```

This should output a table similar to:

rel_type	rel_name	emb	Model	result_type
lem2lem	antonym	holE_wnet_en	nn3	test
lem2lem	antonym	holE_wnet_en	nn3	random
lem2lem	antonym	rand_en	nn3	test
lem2lem	antonym	rand_en	nn3	random
lem2lem	entailment	holE_wnet_en	nn3	test
lem2lem	entailment	holE_wnet_en	nn3	random
lem2lem	entailment	rand_en	nn3	test
lem2lem	entailment	rand_en	nn3	random

As we can see the DataFrame contains 22 columns, including `rel_type`, `rel_name`, `emb`, and `model`, which identify the model that was trained and on which relation dataset.

You will notice that for each combination we have two sets of results, but they have a different value for column `result_type`: * value `test` indicates results after training and * value `random` indicates baseline results when testing using a heuristic choosing a label at random.

As you can see, the training in this case does not produce very interesting results since there is no overlap between the words in the datasets and the HolE embeddings. To illustrate the analysis of results, we include results obtained by training on the same datasets using various embeddings. Below, we load the results into a DataFrame and continue analysis.

7.4.5.2   Loading Pre-aggregated Results

Since training models on a variety of embedding spaces and relations take a long while, here we will load pre-aggregated results which we will use to demonstrate how to analyze the data. We load two sets of aggregated results: * `aggregated_wn_results` contains results on training with the wnet datasets shown at the beginning of this notebook and * `aggregated_random_dataset_results.tsv` contains results of training a variety of models/embeddings on datasets generated at random. We use this to detect **baseline ranges for prediction metrics** as discussed below.

```
In [ ]: import pandas as pd
        wnet_results_df = pd.read_csv(
            'embrela_prj/eval_data/aggregated_wn_results.tsv')
        rand_ds_results_df = pd.read_csv(
            'embrela_prj/eval_data/aggregated_random_dataset_results.tsv')

In [ ]: aggs_df = pd.concat([wnet_results_df, rand_ds_results_df])

In [13]: aggs_df.sample(n=5)
```

This will print a sample of the table. As you can see, the data read from the tsv has the same columns as we would get by aggregating the results read from disk.

7.4.6   Data Pre-processing: Combine and Add Fields

Most of the columns in the DataFrame are aggregated values, but for further analysis it is useful to combine fields and relation metadata.

First we add column `rel_name_type`, which combines the `rel_name` and `rel_type`:

```
In [ ]: aggs_df['rel_name_type'] = aggs_df.apply(
        lambda row: '%s_%s' % (row['rel_name'], row['rel_type']), axis=1)
```

Next, we need to fix some terminology issues. We rename column `rel_type` to `pair_type` because values like `lem2lem` describe the types of pairs we tried to predict. We use `rel_type` to create high-level relation types like `similarity` and `lexical`, as described in the paper.

We will add a column `KG` to document that all the relations came from WordNet

```
In [ ]: aggs_df['KG'] = 'wnet'

In [ ]: aggs_df.rename(columns={'rel_type': 'pair_type'}, inplace=True)
```

The `embrela` project defines a utility script `relutil` which calculates the relation type based on the rows in the DataFrame:

```
In [ ]: !cp embrela_prj/relutil.py .

In [ ]: import relutil

In [ ]: aggs_df['rel_type'] = aggs_df.apply(
            relutil.calc_rel_type_for_dfrow_fn(rel_name_field='rel_name'), axis=1)
```

We also add column `emb_corpus_type` to distinguish between types of embeddings used:

```
In [ ]: def calc_emb_corpus_type(row):
            emb=row['emb']
            if emb.startswith('holE_'):
                return 'kg'
            elif emb.startswith('rand_'):
                return 'no-corpus'
            elif emb.startswith('swivelsyn_'):
                return 'concept-corpus'
            elif emb.startswith('ftsyn_'):
                return 'concept-corpus'
            elif emb.startswith('vecsi_'):
                return 'word-concept-corpus'
            elif emb.startswith('sw2v_umbc'):
                return 'word-corpus'
            else:
                return 'word-corpus'

In [ ]: aggs_df['emb_corpus_type'] = aggs_df.apply(calc_emb_corpus_type, axis=1)
```

Now we start merging the relation dataset metadata into the aggregated DataFrame. We first add a field `positive_examples`:

```
In [ ]: def calc_positive_examples(row):
            name = row['rel_name']
            ptype = row['pair_type']

            name_filter = rels_df['name'] == name
            ptype_filter = rels_df['type'] == ptype
            cnts = rels_df[name_filter & ptype_filter]['cnt'].values
            if len(cnts) > 0:
              return cnts[0]
            else:
              return 0

In [ ]:
aggs_df['positive_examples'] = aggs_df.apply(calc_positive_examples, axis=1)
```

7.4.7   Calculate the Range Thresholds and Biased Dataset Detection

Next, we can calculate range thresholds as described in the paper. $\tau_{\text{biased}}^{\upsilon_{\min}} = \mu_{\delta_{\text{rand},x}}^{\upsilon} - 2\sigma_{\delta_{\text{rand},x}}^{\upsilon}$ and $\tau_{\text{biased}}^{\upsilon_{\max}} = \mu_{\delta_{\text{rand},x}}^{\upsilon} + 2\sigma_{\delta_{\text{rand},x}}^{\upsilon}$. Any metrics within these ranges could be due to chance with 95% probability because several models trained on datasets with random pairs achieve values within these ranges.

```
In [ ]:
randomrel_filter = aggs_df['rel_name'].str.startswith('random_')

def calc_rand_avg_and_std(metric='f1', debug=False):
    test_result_filter = aggs_df['result_type']=='test'

    avg_field = '%s_avg' % metric
    std_field = '%s_std' % metric

    sub_df = aggs_df[randomrel_filter & test_result_filter]
    rand_metric_avg2 = sub_df[avg_field].mean()
    rand_metric_avg_std = sub_df[avg_field].std()
```

```
    rand_metric_std_avg = sub_df[std_field].mean()
    max_std = max(rand_metric_avg_std, rand_metric_std_avg)

    return {'avg': rand_metric_avg2, 'std': max_std}

In [26]: calc_rand_avg_and_std(debug=True)

Out[26]: {'avg': 0.4070040067097273, 'std': 0.12301846272363581}
```

The output shows that models trained on datasets of random pairs obtain values for $f1$ metrics with $\mu^{v}_{\delta_{\text{rand}}} = 0.407$ and $\sigma^{v}_{\delta_{\text{rand}}} = 0.123$. This gives us: $\tau^{v_{\min}}_{\text{biased}} = 0.161$ and $\tau^{v_{\max}}_{\text{biased}} = 0.653$. Any results within this range have a 95% probability of being the result of chance and are not necessarily due to the used embeddings encoding relational knowledge about the relation being predicted.

We define two filters to detect biased relations and test results:

```
In [ ]:
def partition_rel_name_types_at_mu_plus_sigma(
        sigma_factor=2.0, metric='f1'):
    randemb_filter = aggs_df['emb'] == 'rand_en'
    result = {'over': [], 'under': []}
    avg_std = calc_rand_avg_and_std(metric=metric)
    avg_threshold = avg_std['avg'] + sigma_factor * avg_std['std']
    avg_field = '%s_avg' % metric
    rnts = list(aggs_df['rel_name_type'].unique())
    for rnt in rnts:
        rnt_filter = aggs_df['rel_name_type'] == rnt
        randemb_df = aggs_df[
            rnt_filter & test_result_filter() & randemb_filter]
        randemb_avg = randemb_df[avg_field].mean()
        if randemb_avg > avg_threshold:
            result['over'].append(rnt)
        else:
            result['under'].append(rnt)
    return result

In [ ]:
def filter_biased_rel_types(sigma_factor=2.0, metric='f1'):
    rnt_partition_over = partition_rel_name_types_at_mu_plus_sigma(
        sigma_factor=sigma_factor, metric=metric)
    rnt_partition_under = partition_rel_name_types_at_mu_plus_sigma(
        sigma_factor=-sigma_factor, metric=metric)
    valid_rnts = set.intersection(set(rnt_partition_over['under']),
        set(rnt_partition_under['over']))
    return aggs_df['rel_name_type'].isin(valid_rnts)

In [ ]:
def test_result_filter():
    return aggs_df['result_type']=='test'

In [34]: aggs_df[filter_biased_rel_types() & test_result_filter()].sample(n=5)
```

This should print a sample of biased relations.

7.4.8   Finding Statistically Significant Models

We consider a dataset to be **biased** if models can perform well on them regardless of whether the embeddings used to train the model encode any information. Intuitively, these are datasets which are imbalanced in some way allowing the model to exploit this imbalance during prediction, but that do not reflect the knowledge encoded in the embeddings. To detect these, we look at model results for models trained on random embeddings (i.e., on models $m^{\delta_r, s_{\text{rand}}, t}$). We say that δ_r is biased if $\mu^{f1}_{\delta_r, s_{\text{rand}}}$ is outside of the $[\tau^{f1_{\min}}_{\text{biased}}, \tau^{f1_{\max}}_{\text{biased}}]$ range. The rationale is that even with random embeddings, such models were able to perform outside of the 95% baseline ranges.

```
In [ ]:
def calc_delta_to_rand_fn(whole_df, metric_field='f1_avg'):
    def calc_delta_to_rand(row):
        rel_name_type = row['rel_name_type']
        emb = row['emb']
        result_type = row['result_type']
        row_metric = row[metric_field]

        rel_filter = whole_df['rel_name_type'] == rel_name_type
        rand_filter = whole_df['emb'] == 'rand_en'
        result_type_filter = whole_df['result_type'] == result_type

        multi_filter = rel_filter & result_type_filter & rand_filter
        rand_metrics = whole_df[multi_filter][metric_field].values
        rand_metric = rand_metrics[0]

        delta = row_metric - rand_metric
        return delta
    return calc_delta_to_rand
```

We can store the delta between the model and the random predictions as a field in our DataFrame:

```
In [ ]: aggs_df['delta_f1_to_rand_emb'] = aggs_df.apply(
            calc_delta_to_rand_fn(aggs_df), axis=1)
```

And we specify this delta in terms of the σ, which we will store in another column:

```
In [ ]: def calc_sigmadelta_to_rand_fn(whole_df, metric='f1'):
            avg_metric_field = '%s_avg' % metric
            std_metric_field = '%s_std' % metric
            def calc_sigmadelta_to_rand(row):
                rel_name_type = row['rel_name_type']
                emb = row['emb']
                result_type = row['result_type']
                row_avg_metric = row[avg_metric_field]
                row_std_metric = row[std_metric_field]

                rel_filter = whole_df['rel_name_type'] == rel_name_type
                rand_filter = whole_df['emb'] == 'rand_en'
                result_type_filter = whole_df['result_type'] == result_type

                rand_df = whole_df[rel_filter & result_type_filter & rand_filter]
                rand_avg_metric = rand_df[avg_metric_field].values[0]
                rand_std_metric = rand_df[std_metric_field].values[0]

                max_std = max(row_std_metric, rand_std_metric)

                #print('rand_metric type', type(rand_metric))
                delta = row_avg_metric - rand_avg_metric
                sigma_delta = delta / max_std
                return sigma_delta
            return calc_sigmadelta_to_rand

In [38]:
aggs_df['sigdelta_f1_to_rand_emb'] = aggs_df.apply(
            calc_sigmadelta_to_rand_fn(aggs_df), axis=1)
```

This field allows us to define filters:

```
In [ ]: def sigdelta_over(value):
            return aggs_df['sigdelta_f1_to_rand_emb'] > value
        def sigdelta_under(value):
            return aggs_df['sigdelta_f1_to_rand_emb'] < value
```

Which we can use to find which embeddings resulted in models with statistically better results than their random counterparts.

```
In [41]: aggs_df[test_result_filter() & sigdelta_over(2.0)]['emb'].unique()

Out[41]: array(['glove_cc_en', 'ft_wiki_en', 'vecsi_UN_en', 'swiv_UN_en',
                'ft_wikip_en', 'vecsi_wiki_en', 'vecsi_un_en', 'holE_sensi_en',
                'ft_cc_en', 'ft_un_en', 'swivel_un_en', 'vecsi_un_en_ts',
                'swivel_wiki_en', 'ftsyn_wiki'], dtype=object)
```

7.4.8.1   Combining Filters

Now we have seen filters for:

- Detecting biased datasets
- Detecting statistically significant results

We have further filters for only selecting rows describing test results and results that were trained on non-random datasets. For example, to select only those results which significantly outperformed random predictions, we can use the following command:

```
In [46]: display_columns = ['datapoints', 'emb', 'f1_avg', 'model',
             'rel_name_type', 'KG', 'positive_examples',
             'sigdelta_f1_to_rand_emb']
         aggs_df[test_result_filter() & filter_biased_rel_types() &
         sigdelta_over(2.0) & ~randomrel_filter][display_columns]
```

This will show a table with 65 rows and 8 columns showing the embeddings which had the highest improvement compared to the random embeddings.

```
Out[46]:
emb               ...    positive_examples    sigdelta_f1_to_rand_emb
glove_cc_en       ...         110650                12.220272
glove_cc_en       ...         110650                12.317966
ft_wiki_en        ...         110650                12.244312
ft_wiki_en        ...         110650                12.517522
vecsi_UN_en       ...         110650                12.165311
...               ...            ...                    ...
vecsi_un_en       ...           1519                 3.217797
vecsi_un_en       ...           4944                 3.772919
glove_cc_en       ...           4944                 3.117599
holE_sensi_en ...               1519                 2.125610
vecsi_un_en       ...           1519                 3.097962

        [65 rows x 8 columns]
```

7.4.9   Conclusion of Assessing Relational Knowledge

In this practical part we used the `embrela` library for assessing how well various word/concept embeddings capture relational knowledge in WordNet.

The pipeline is straightforward, but takes into account a variety of pitfalls that can occur during dataset creation, training and interpreting the classification results.

7.5   Case Study: Evaluating and Comparing Vecsigrafo Embeddings

In the previous two sections, you had the opportunity to gain hands-on experience in evaluating embeddings. To keep the practical sessions short we typically used small embedding spaces or only used a few evaluation datasets. Based on what you have learned, you should be able to edit the accompanying notebooks to use your own embeddings or use alternative evaluation datasets. To further illustrate how real-world embeddings can be evaluated, in this section we present an example of an evaluation we performed to assess the quality of Vecsigrafo embeddings. As you will see, we applied a variety of methodologies to gather metrics that helped us to study how Vecsigrafo embeddings compared to other embedding learning mechanisms. Most of this evaluation was done at an academic level with the aim of publishing an academic paper. Note that for practitioners (e.g., in business settings) it may be sufficient to only perform a subset of the evaluations we present below.

7.5.1   Comparative Study

In this part of the evaluation, we study how Vecsigrafo-based embeddings compare to lexical and semantic embeddings produced by other algorithms.

7.5.1.1   Embeddings

Table 7.3 shows an overview of the embeddings used during the evaluations. We used five main methods to generate these. In general, we tried to use embeddings with 300 dimensions, although in some cases we had to deviate. In general, as can be seen in the table, when the vocabulary size is small (due to corpus size and tokenization), we required a larger number of epochs to let the learning algorithm converge.

- Vecsigrafo-based embeddings were first tokenized and word-disambiguated using Cogito. We explored two basic tokenization variants. The first is lemma-concept with filtered tokens ("ls filtered"), whereby we only keep lemmas and concept ids for the corpus. Lemmatization uses the known lemmas in Sensigrafo to combine compound words as a single token. The filtering step removes various types of words: dates, numbers, punctuation marks, articles, proper names (entities), auxiliary verbs, proper nouns, and pronouns which are not bound to a concept. The main idea of this filtering step is to remove tokens from the corpus which are not semantically relevant. We also trained a few embeddings without lemmatization and filtering. In such cases, we have kept the original surface form bound to the concept (including morphological variants) and we did not remove the tokens described above. For all the embeddings, we have used a minimum frequency of 5 and a window size of 5 words around the center word. We also used a harmonic weighting scheme (we experimented with linear and uniform weighting schemes but results did not differ substantially).

- Swivel[6] based embeddings use either a basic white-space tokenization of the input corpus or a lemma-based tokenization performed by Cogito. We have used the default parameters defined by the open-source project. For the Wikipedia corpus, we had to reduce the number of dimensions to 256, since otherwise, the main Swivel algorithm would run out of GPU memory during training. We also imposed a limit of 1M for the vocabulary for the same reason.
- GloVe embeddings trained by us were derived using the master branch on its GitHub repository[7] and we used the default hyperparameters defined therein.
- fastText embeddings trained by us were derived using the master branch on its GitHub repository[8] and we used the default hyperparameters defined therein.
- HolE embeddings were trained by us using the code on GitHub[9] after we exported the Sensigrafo to create a training set of 2.5M triples including covering over 800K lemmas and syncons and 93 relations, including hypernymy relations, but also hasLemma relations between concepts and lemmas. (We also tried to apply ProjE,[10] but various errors and slow performance made it impossible to apply it to our Sensigrafo corpus.) We trained HolE for 500 epochs using 150 dimensions and the default hyperparameters. The final evaluation after training reported an MRR of 0.13, a mean rank of 85,279, and Hits@10 of 19.48%.

Besides the embeddings trained by us, we also include, as part of our study, several pre-trained embeddings, notably the GloVe embeddings for CommonCrawl—code glove_840B provided by Stanford[11] —fastText embeddings based on a Wikipedia dump from 2017—code ft_en,[12] as well as the embeddings for BabelNet concepts (NASARI[13] and SW2V) since these require direct access to BabelNet indices. In Table 7.3, we share the details that are reported by the embedding providers.

---

[6]https://github.com/tensorflow/models/tree/master/research/swivel.

[7]https://github.com/stanfordnlp/GloVe.

[8]https://github.com/facebookresearch/fastText.

[9]https://github.com/mnick/holographic-embeddings.

[10]https://github.com/bxshi/ProjE.

[11]http://nlp.stanford.edu/data/glove.840B.300d.zip.

[12]https://s3-us-west-1.amazonaws.com/fasttext-vectors/wiki.en.vec.

[13]http://lcl.uniroma1.it/nasari/files/NASARIembed+UMBC_w2v.zip.

Table 7.3 Evaluated embeddings

Code	Corpus	Method	Tokenization	Epochs	Vocab	Concepts
	UN	vecsi	ls filtered	80	147K	76K
	UN	swivel	ws	8	467K	0
	UN	glove	?	15	541K	0
	UN	vecsi	ts	8	401K	83K
	UN	fastText	?	15	541K	0
	wiki	glove	?	25	2.4M	0
	wiki	swivel	ws	8	1.0M	0
	wiki	vecsi	ls filtered	10	824K	209K
ft_en	wiki	fastText	?	8	2.4M	0
	UMBC	w2v	?	?	1.3M	0
	wiki/UMBC	nasari	?	?	5.7M	4.4M
	Sensigrafo	HolE	n/a	500	825K	423K
	wiki'	fastText	?	?	2.5M	0
glove_cc	CommonCrawl	GloVe	?	?	2.2M	0

7.5.1.2 Word Similarity Results

Table 7.4 shows the Spearman correlation scores for the 14 word similarity datasets and the various embeddings generated based on the UN corpus. The last column in the table shows the average coverage of the pairs for each dataset. Since the UN corpus is medium sized and focused on specific domains, many words are not included in the learned embeddings, hence the scores are only calculated based on a subset of the pairs.

Table 7.6 shows the results for the embeddings trained on larger corpora and directly on the Sensigrafo. We have not included results for vectors trained with NASARI (concept-based) and SW2V on UMBC, since these perform considerably worse than the remaining embeddings (e.g., NASARI scored 0.487 on MEN-TR-3k and SW2V scored 0.209 for the same dataset, and see Table 7.5 for the overall average score). We have also not included word2vec on UMBC since it does not achieve the best score for any of the reported datasets; however, overall it performs a bit better than Swivel but worse than Vecsigrafo. For example, it achieves a score of 0.737 for MEN-TR-3k).

Table 7.5 shows the aggregate results. Since some of the word similarity datasets overlap—SIMLEX-999 and WS-353-ALL were split into its subsets, MC-30 is a subset of RG-65—and other datasets—RW-STANFORD, SEMEVAL17, VERB-143, and MTurk-287—have non-lemmatized words (plurals and conjugated verb forms) which penalize embeddings that use some form of lemmatization during tokenization, we take the average Spearman score over the remaining datasets. We discuss the lessons we can extract from these results in Sect. 7.5.2 (Table 7.6).

Table 7.4 Spearman correlations for word similarity datasets and **UN**-based embeddings

Dataset	ft	glove	swivel	swivel l f	vecsi ls f	vecsi ls f c	vecsi ts	vecsi ts c	avg$_{perc}$
MC-30	0.602	0.431	0.531	0.572	0.527	0.405	0.481	**0.684**	82.5
MEN-TR-3k	0.535	0.383	0.509	0.603	**0.642**	0.525	0.558	0.562	82.0
MTurk-287	0.607	0.438	0.519	0.559	**0.608**	0.578	0.500	0.540	69.3
MTurk-771	0.473	0.398	0.416	0.539	**0.599**	0.497	0.520	0.520	94.6
RG-65	0.502	0.378	0.443	0.585	0.614	0.441	0.515	**0.664**	74.6
RW-STANFORD	0.492	0.263	0.356	0.444	**0.503**	0.439	0.419	0.353	49.2
SEMEVAL17	0.541	0.395	0.490	0.595	**0.635**	0.508	0.573	0.610	63.0
SIMLEX-999	0.308	0.253	0.226	0.303	**0.382**	0.349	0.288	0.369	96.1
SIMLEX-999-Adj	0.532	0.267	0.307	0.490	**0.601**	0.559	0.490	0.532	96.6
SIMLEX-999-Nou	0.286	0.272	0.258	0.337	**0.394**	0.325	0.292	0.384	94.7
SIMLEX-999-Ver	0.253	0.193	0.109	0.186	0.287	**0.288**	0.196	0.219	100.0
SIMVERB3500	0.233	0.164	0.155	0.231	0.306	**0.328**	0.197	0.318	94.4
VERB-143	**0.382**	0.226	0.116	0.162	0.085	-0.089	0.234	0.019	76.2
WS-353-ALL	0.545	0.468	0.516	0.537	**0.588**	0.404	0.502	0.532	91.9
WS-353-REL	0.469	0.434	0.465	0.478	**0.516**	0.359	0.447	0.469	93.4
WS-353-SIM	0.656	0.553	0.629	0.642	**0.699**	0.454	0.619	0.617	91.5
YP-130	0.432	0.350	0.383	0.456	**0.546**	0.514	0.402	0.521	96.7

The column names refer to the method used to train the embeddings, the tokenization of the corpus (lemma, syncon, and/or text and whether the tokens were filtered), and whether concept-based word similarity was used instead of the usual word-based similarity. Bold values are either the best results, or results worth highlighting, in which case they are further discussed in the text

Table 7.5 Aggregated word similarity results

Method	Corpus	avg ρ	avg coverage %
glove	cc	0.629	100.0
vecsi ls f c 25e	wiki	0.622	99.6
vecsi ls f 25e	wiki	0.619	98.6
sw2v c	umbc	0.615	99.9
ft 8e	wiki	0.613	100.0
vecsi ls f c 10e	wiki	0.609	99.6
ft	wiki17	0.606	98.9
HolE c 500e	sensi	0.566	99.6
w2v	umbc	0.566	98.9
swivel 8e	wiki	0.542	99.9
vecsi ls f 80e	UN	0.538	93.1
vecsi ts c 8e	UN	0.505	97.9
swivel l f	UN	0.480	92.9
ft 15e	UN	0.451	88.6
vecsi ts 8e	UN	0.443	91.0
glove 25e	wiki	0.438	100.0
vecsi ls f c 80e	UN	0.433	83.4
swivel 8e	UN	0.403	87.9
HolE 500e	sensi	0.381	99.6
glove 15e	UN	0.364	88.6
nasari c	umbc	0.360	94.0
sw2v	umbc	0.125	100.0

Table 7.6 Spearman correlations for word similarity datasets on large corpora (UMBC, Wikipedia, and CommonCrawl)

Corpus	sensi		umbc	wiki17			wiki18			cc	
Dataset	HolE	HolE c	sw2v c	ft en	ft	glove	swivel	vecsi ls f	vecsi ls f c	glove	avg_perc
MC-30	0.655	**0.825**	0.822	0.812	0.798	0.565	0.768	0.776	0.814	0.786	100.0
MEN-TR-3k	0.410	0.641	0.731	0.764	0.760	0.607	0.717	**0.785**	0.773	**0.802**	99.9
MTurk-287	0.272	0.534	0.633	0.679	0.651	0.473	**0.687**	0.675	0.634	**0.693**	85.6
MTurk-771	0.434	0.577	0.583	0.669	0.649	0.504	0.587	**0.685**	0.578	**0.715**	99.9
RG-65	0.589	0.798	0.771	0.797	0.770	0.639	0.733	0.803	**0.836**	0.762	100.0
RW-STANFORD	0.216	0.256	0.395	0.487	**0.492**	0.124	0.393	0.463	0.399	0.462	81.9
SEMEVAL17	0.475	0.655	**0.753**	0.719	0.728	0.546	0.683	0.723	0.692	0.711	81.8
SIMLEX-999	0.310	0.380	**0.488**	0.380	0.368	0.268	0.278	0.374	0.420	0.408	99.4
SIMLEX-999-Adj	0.246	0.201	0.556	0.508	0.523	0.380	0.323	0.488	**0.564**	**0.622**	99.5
SIMLEX-999-Nou	0.403	0.484	**0.493**	0.410	0.383	0.321	0.331	0.422	0.464	0.428	100.0
SIMLEX-999-Ver	0.063	0.133	**0.416**	0.231	0.233	0.105	0.103	0.219	0.163	0.196	97.7
SIMVERB3500	0.227	0.318	**0.417**	0.258	0.288	0.131	0.182	0.271	0.331	0.283	98.8
VERB-143	0.131	-0.074	-0.084	0.397	**0.452**	0.228	0.335	0.207	0.133	0.341	75.0
WS-353-ALL	0.380	0.643	0.597	0.732	**0.743**	0.493	0.692	0.708	0.685	0.738	98.5
WS-353-REL	0.258	0.539	0.445	0.668	**0.702**	0.407	0.652	0.649	0.609	0.688	98.2
WS-353-SIM	0.504	0.726	0.748	0.782	**0.805**	0.615	0.765	0.775	0.767	0.803	99.1
YP-130	0.315	0.550	**0.736**	0.533	0.562	0.334	0.422	0.610	0.661	0.571	98.3

Bold values are either the best results, or results worth highlighting, in which case they are further discussed in the text

7.5.1.3 Inter-Embedding Agreement

The word similarity datasets are typically used to assess the correlation between the similarity of word pairs assigned by embeddings and a gold standard defined by human annotators. However, we can also use the word similarity datasets to assess how similar two embedding spaces are. We do this by collecting all the similarity scores predicted for all the pairs in the various datasets and calculating the Spearman's ρ metric between the various embedding spaces. We present the results in Fig. 7.7; darker colors represent higher inter-agreement between embeddings. For example, we see that `wiki17 ft` has high inter-agreement with `ft` and very low with `HolE c`. We discuss these results in Sects. 7.5.2.1 and 7.5.2.2.

7.5.1.4 Word–Concept Prediction

One of the disadvantages of word similarity (and relatedness) datasets is that they only provide a single metric per dataset. In [40] we introduced word prediction plots, a way to visualize the quality of embeddings by performing a task that is very similar to the loss objective of word2vec. Given a test corpus (ideally different from the corpus used to train the embeddings), iterate through the sequence of tokens using a context window. For each center word, take the (weighted) average of the embeddings for the context tokens and compare it to the embedding for the center word using cosine similarity. If the cosine similarity is close to 1, this essentially correctly predicts the center word based on its context. By aggregating all such cosine similarities for all tokens in the corpus we can (1) plot the average cosine similarity for each term in the vocabulary that appears in the test corpus and (2) get an overall score for the test corpus by calculating the (weighted by token frequency) average over all the words in the vocabulary.

Table 7.7 provides an overview of the test corpora we have chosen to generate word and concept prediction scores and plots. The corpora are:

- webtext [108] is a topic-diverse corpus of contemporary text fragments (support fora, movie scripts, ads) from publicly accessible websites, popular as training data for NLP applications.
- NLTK Gutenberg selections[14] contain a sample of public-domain literary texts by well-known authors (Shakespeare, Jane Austen, Walt Whitman, etc.) from Project Gutenberg.
- Europarl-10k: We have created a test dataset based on the Europarl [98] v7 dataset. We used the English file that has been parallelized with Spanish, removed the empty lines, and kept only the first 10K lines. We expect Europarl to be relatively similar to the UN corpus since they both provide transcriptions of proceedings in similar domains.

---

[14]https://raw.githubusercontent.com/nltk/nltk_data/gh-pages/packages/corpora/gutenberg.zip.

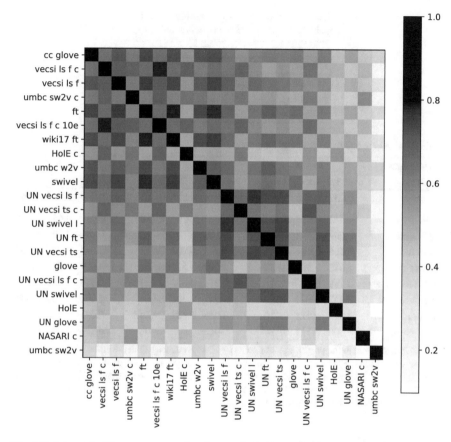

Fig. 7.7 Inter-embedding agreement for the word similarity datasets in the same order as Table 7.5. Embeddings that do not mention a corpus were trained on Wikipedia 2018

Figure 7.8 shows the word prediction plots for various embeddings and the three test corpora. Table 7.8 shows (1) the token coverage relative to the embedding vocabulary (i.e., the percentage of the embedding vocabulary found in the tokenized test corpus); (2) the weighted average score, this is the average cosine similarity per prediction made (however, since frequent words are predicted more often, this may skew the overall result if infrequent words have worse predictions); (3) the "token average" score, this is the average of the average score per token. This gives an indication of how likely it is to predict a token (word or concept) given its context if a token is selected from the embedding vocabulary at random, i.e. without taking into account its frequency in general texts. As with previous results, we will draw conclusions about these results in Sect. 7.5.2.

Table 7.7 Overview—test corpora used to gather word and concept prediction data

	Tokens		
Corpus	Text	Lemmas	Concepts
webtext	300K	209K	198K
gutenberg	1.2M	868K	832K
Europarl-10k	255K	148K	143K

Table 7.8 Aggregate word prediction values

Test corpus	webtext			gutenberg			Europarl-10k		
emb	Coverage	w avg	t avg	Coverage	w avg	t avg	Coverage	w avg	t avg
cc glove	0.007	**0.855**	**0.742**	0.016	**0.859**	0.684	0.005	**0.868**	**0.764**
wiki swivel	0.013	0.657	**0.703**	0.027	0.664	**0.718**	0.010	0.654	0.666
UN vecsi ts	0.069	**0.688**	**0.703**	0.103	0.701	0.715	0.062	0.700	**0.717**
wiki ft	0.006	0.684	0.702	0.013	**0.702**	0.712	0.004	**0.702**	0.700
umbc w2v	0.012	0.592	0.638	0.030	0.574	0.662	0.008	0.566	0.649
UN vecsi ls f	0.138	0.630	0.617	0.214	0.652	0.628	0.128	0.681	0.636
wiki vecsi ls	0.037	0.603	0.593	0.057	0.606	0.604	0.026	0.601	0.588
HolE ls	0.035	0.414	0.416	0.056	0.424	0.424	0.026	0.400	0.398
wiki glove	0.006	0.515	0.474	0.013	0.483	0.408	0.004	0.468	0.566

The coverage refers to the percentage of tokens (words and concepts) in the embedding vocabulary that were found in the test corpus. The "w avg" is the average cosim weighted by token frequency and "t avg" is the average cosine similarity for all the token predictions regardless of their frequency in the corpus. Bold values are either the best results, or results worth highlighting, in which case they are further discussed in the text

7.5.1.5 Relation Prediction

Word (and concept) similarity and prediction tasks are good for getting a sense of the embedding quality. However, ultimately the relevant quality metric for embeddings is whether they can be used to improve the performance of systems that perform more complex tasks such as document categorization or knowledge graph completion. For this reason we include an evaluation for predicting specific types of relations in a knowledge graph between pairs of words, following recent work in the area [102, 180, 191]. At Expert System, such a system would help our team of knowledge engineers and linguists to curate the Sensigrafo.

To minimize introducing bias, rather than using Sensigrafo as our knowledge graph, we have chosen to use WordNet since we have not used it to train HolE embeddings and it is different from Sensigrafo (hence any knowledge used during disambiguation should not affect the results). For this experiment, we chose the following relations:

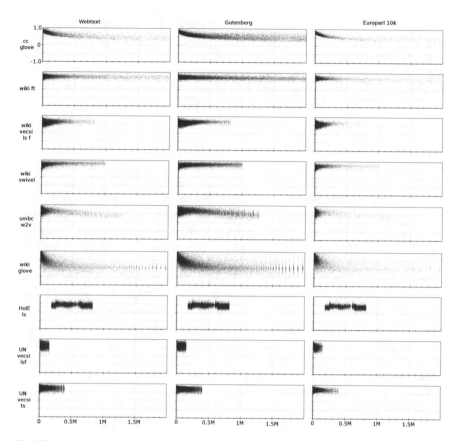

Fig. 7.8 Word and concept prediction plots. The horizontal axis contains the word ids sorted by frequency on the training corpus; although different embeddings have different vocabulary sizes, we have fixed the plotted vocabulary size to 2M tokens to facilitate comparison. Since HolE is not trained on a corpus, hence the frequencies are unknown, the vocabulary is sorted alphabetically. The vertical axis contains the average cosine similarity between the weighted context vector and the center word or concept

- verb group, relating similar verbs to each other, e.g. "shift"-"change" and "keep"-"prevent."
- entailment, which describes entailment relations between verbs, e.g. "peak"-"go up" and "tally"-"count."

Datasets

We built a dataset for each relation by (1) starting with the vocabulary of UN vecsi ls f (the smallest vocabulary for the embeddings we are studying) and look up all the synsets in WordNet for the lemmas. Then we (2) searched for all the connections to other synsets using the selected relations, which gives us a list of positive examples. Finally, (3) we generate negative pairs based on the list of positive examples for the same relation (this *negative switching* strategy has been recommended in order to avoid models simply memorizing words associated with positive pairs [103]). This resulted in a dataset of 3039 entailment pairs (1519 positives) and 9889 verb group pairs (4944 positives).

Training

Next, we trained a neural net with two fully connected hidden layers on each dataset, using a 90% training, 5 validation, 5 test split. The neural nets received as their input the concatenated embeddings for the input pairs (if the input verb was a multi-word like "go up," we took the average embedding of the constituent words when using word embeddings rather than lemma embeddings). Therefore, for embeddings with 300 dimensions, the input layer had 600 nodes, while the two hidden layers had 750 and 400 nodes. The output node has two one-hot-encoded nodes. For the HolE embeddings, the input layer had 300 nodes and the hidden layers had 400 and 150 nodes. We used dropout (0.5) between the hidden nodes and an Adam optimizer to train the models for 12 epochs on the verb group dataset and 24 epochs on the entailment dataset. Also, to further avoid the neural net to memorize particular words, we include a random embedding perturbation factor, which we add to each input embedding; the idea is that the model should learn to categorize the input based on the difference between the pair of word embeddings. Since different embedding spaces have different values, the perturbation takes into account the minimum and maximum values of the original embeddings.

Results

Table 7.9 shows the results of training various embeddings: cc glove, wiki ft,[15] HolE, UN vecsi ls f, and wiki vecsi ls f. Since constructing such datasets is not straightforward [103], we also include a set of random embeddings. The idea is that, if the dataset is well constructed, models trained with the random embeddings should have an accuracy of 0.5, since no relational information should be encoded in the random embeddings (as opposed to the trained embeddings).

The main finding was that the Vecsigrafo-based embeddings learnt from the medium-sized UN corpus outperform the rest at the prediction of both target relations. Surprisingly the Vecsigrafo UN embeddings also outperformed the Wikipedia-based embeddings; a possible explanation for this is the greater

---

[15]For GloVe and fastText only the optimal results, based on the larger corpus (cc, wiki) , are shown.

specificity of the UN corpus compared to Wikipedia, which spans across a large variety of topics. This could provide a stronger signal for the relation prediction task since there are less potentially ambiguous entries and the model can better leverage the relational knowledge explicitly described in the KG.

Table 7.9 Entailment and verb group average prediction accuracy and standard deviation over five training runs

	Entailment	Verb group
ft_wikip	0.630 ± 0.022	0.661 ± 0.021
glove_cc	0.606 ± 0.008	0.628 ± 0.013
holE_sensi	0.603 ± 0.011	0.558 ± 0.009
vecsi_un	0.684 ± 0.003	0.708 ± 0.009
vecsi_wiki	0.608 ± 0.009	0.587 ± 0.032
rand_en	0.566 ± 0.011	0.572 ± 0.003

7.5.2 Discussion

7.5.2.1 Vecsigrafo (and SW2V) Compared to Conventional Word Embeddings

From Tables 7.4 and 7.5 we can draw the conclusion that, for the UN corpus (a medium-sized corpus):

- **Co-training lemmas and concepts produces better embeddings than training them using conventional word embedding methods**. In particular we see that: $\rho_{vecsi_{lsf}} > \rho_{swivel_l} \simeq \rho_{ft} \succ \rho_{vecsi_{ts}} \succ \rho_{swivel} \simeq \rho_{glove}$, where $>$ means that the difference is statistically significant (t-test $p < 0.01$), $\succ$ means slightly significance ($p < 0.05$), and $\simeq$ means difference is not statistically significant. As in the ablation study, we see that for the same tokenization strategy, adding concepts significantly improves the quality of the word embeddings. The comparative study furthermore shows that just lemmatizing and filtering achieves a similar quality as that of fastText (which also performs pre-processing and uses subword information as discussed in Sect. 2.3).

For larger corpora such as Wikipedia and UMBC:

- **There is no statistically significant difference between fastText, Vecsigrafo,**[16] **or SW2V.**[17] Similarly, GloVe performs at roughly the same level as these other

---

[16]Either concept-based or lemma-based similarity.

[17]Concept-based only.

embeddings but requires a very large corpus such as CommonCrawl to match them.

- **fastText, Vecsigrafo, and SW2V significantly outperform Standard Swivel and GloVe.**
- **Both lemma and concept embeddings are of high quality for Vecsigrafo-based embeddings.** For SW2V-based embeddings, concept embeddings are of high quality, but the co-trained word embeddings are of poor quality. Since both methods are similar, it is not clear why this is the case.

We were surprised to see how NASARI concept embeddings (based on lexical specificity) compare poorly to the other embeddings. This was unexpected, since results in [29] were very good for similar word similarity tests, although restricted to a few of the smaller (and thus less stable) datasets. We note that the pre-trained embeddings we used only provide embeddings for concepts which are nouns even though the method should support concepts for verbs and other grammar types. However, even for noun-based datasets we could not reproduce the results reported in [29]: for MC-30 we measured 0.68 ρ vs 0.78 reported, for SIMLEX-999-Nou we measured 0.38 instead of 0.46, and WS-353-SIM it was 0.61 instead of 0.68. An explanation for the different results may be that we do not apply any filtering by POS, as this is not specified in the concept-based word similarity evaluation method. Instead, we find all the concepts matching the words in the word pair and return the maximum cosine similarity, regardless of whether the concepts are nouns or verbs. Also, since we do not have access to the full BabelNet, we used the REST API to download a mapping from words to BabelNet concepts. It may be the case that [29] used an internal API which performs a more thorough mapping between words and concepts, which affects the results.

In terms of inter-embedding agreement, from Fig. 7.7 we see that, even if those concepts are derived from a different semantic net (BabelNet and Sensigrafo), **concept-based embeddings tend to have a higher agreement with other concept-based embeddings. Similarly, word and lemma-based embeddings tend to be aligned with other word-based embeddings.** Since both types of embeddings achieve high scores for word similarity (against the gold standard), **this suggests that a hybrid word similarity evaluation approach could yield better results**.

Furthermore, we clearly see that for the medium-sized corpus, all lexical embeddings tend to have a high inter-agreement with each other, but less so with lexical embeddings trained on larger corpora. For larger corpora, both lexical and concept embeddings show high inter-agreement with other similar embeddings even when trained with other corpora. For such large corpora, we see that the method used to train the embeddings (Vecsigrafo, fastText, SW2V, etc.) or the method used to predict word similarity (word-based vs concept-based) has a higher impact on the measured inter-agreement.

From the word prediction plots (Fig. 7.8) and results (Table 7.8), we see very different learning patterns for the various word embedding algorithms:

- GloVe tends to produce skewed predictions excelling at predicting very high-frequency words (with little variance), but as words become less frequent the average prediction accuracy drops and variance increases. This pattern is particularly clear for GloVe trained on CommonCrawl. The same pattern applies for `wiki glove`; however, the plot shows that for most words (except the most frequent ones) these embeddings barely perform better than random (average cosine similarity is close to 0). This suggests that there is an issue with the default hyperparameters, or that GloVe requires a much higher number of epochs compared to other algorithms (note we initially trained most of the embeddings with 8 epochs, but due to poor performance we increased the presented GloVe embeddings for Wikipedia to 25 epochs).

- fastText produces very consistent results: prediction quality does not change depending on word frequency.
- word2vec applied to UMBC has a pattern in between that of fastText and GloVe. It shows a high variance in prediction results, especially for very high-frequency words and shows a linearly declining performance as words become less frequent.
- Swivel with standard tokenization also shows mostly consistent predictions; however, very frequent words show a higher variance in prediction quality which is almost the opposite of GloVe: some high-frequency words tend to have a poor prediction score, but the average score for less frequent words tends to be higher. The same pattern applies to Vecsigrafo (based on Swivel), although it is less clear for `wiki vecsi ls`. Due to the relatively small vocabulary sizes for the studied Vecsigrafos trained on the UN corpus, it is hard to identify a learning pattern when normalizing the vocabulary to 2M words.

By comparing the word prediction results between `wiki swivel` and the three Vecsigrafo-based embeddings we can see a few counter-intuitive results.

- First, on average word prediction quality *decreases* by using Vecsigrafo, which is surprising (especially since word embedding quality improves significantly based on the word similarity results as discussed above). One possible reason for this is that the context vector for Vecsigrafo-based predictions will typically be the average of twice as many context tokens (since it will include both lemmas and concepts). However, the results for `UN vecsi ts` would suffer from the same issue, but this is not the case. In fact, `UN vecsi ts` performs as well as `wiki swivel` at this task.
- Second, both UN-based Vecsigrafo embeddings outperform the wiki-based Vecsigrafo embedding for this task. When comparing `UN vecsi ls f` and `wiki vecsi ls`, we see that due to the vocabulary size, the UN-based embeddings had to perform fewer predictions for fewer tokens; hence maybe less frequent words are introducing noise when performing word prediction. Further studies are needed in order to explain these results. For now, the results indicate that, for the word prediction task, Vecsigrafo embeddings based on smaller corpora outperform those trained on larger corpora. This is especially relevant for tasks such as Vecsigrafo-based disambiguation, for which standard word embeddings would not be useful.

Other results from the word prediction study are:

- Most embeddings perform better for the Gutenberg test corpus than for webtext. The only exceptions are `cc glove` and `wiki glove`. This may be a result of the size of the test corpus (Gutenberg is an order of magnitude larger than webtext) or the formality of the language. We assume that webtext contains more informal language, which is not represented in either Wikipedia or the UN corpus, but could be represented in CommonCrawl. Since the average differences are quite small, we would have to perform further studies to validate these new hypotheses.
- The training and test corpora matter: for most embeddings we see that the token average for Europarl is similar or worse than for webtext (and hence worse than for Gutenberg). However, this does not hold for the embeddings that were trained on the UN corpus, which we expect to have a similar language and vocabulary as Europarl. For these embeddings—UN `vecsi ts` and Un `vecsi ls f`— the Europarl predictions are better than for the Gutenberg dataset. Here again, the GloVe-based embeddings do not conform to this pattern. Since the `wiki glove` embeddings are of poor quality, this is not that surprising. For `cc glove`, it is unclear why results would be better than for both webtext and Gutenberg.
- Finally and unsurprisingly, lemmatization clearly has a *compacting effect on the vocabulary size*. This effect can provide practical advantages: for example, instead of having to search for the top-k neighbors in a vocabulary of 2.5M words, we can limit our search to 600K lemmas (and avoid finding many morphological variants for the same word).

From the verb relation prediction results in Table 7.9, we see that, once again, UN `vecsi ls f` outperforms other embeddings, including `wiki vecsi ls f`. The fact that the random embeddings result in an average accuracy of around 0.55 indicates that the dataset is well formed and the results are indicative of how well the trained models would perform for new pairs of words. We can see that both tasks are relatively challenging, with the models performing at most at around 70% accuracy.

7.5.2.2   Vecsigrafo Compared to KG Embeddings

Table 7.5 shows that for KG-based embeddings, the lemma embeddings (`HolE 500e`) perform poorly, while the concept-based similarity embeddings perform relatively well (`HolE c 500e`). However, the concept embeddings learned using HolE perform significantly worse than those based on the top-performing word embedding methods (fastText on wiki and GloVe on CommonCrawl) and concept-embedding methods (SW2V and Vecsigrafo). This result supports our hypothesis that **corpus-based concept-embeddings improve on graph-based embeddings since they can refine the concept representations by taking into account tacit knowledge from the training corpus**, which is not explicitly captured in a knowledge graph. In particular, and unsurprisingly, lemma embeddings derived from KGs are of much poorer quality than those derived from (disambiguated) text corpora.

The inter-embedding agreement results from Fig. 7.7 show that HolE embeddings have a relatively low agreement with other embeddings, especially conventional word embeddings. Concept-based HolE similarity results have a relatively high agreement with other concept-based similarities (Vecsigrafo, SW2V, and NASARI).

Results from the word prediction task are consistent with those of the word similarity task. HolE embeddings perform poorly when applied to predicting a center word or concept from context tokens.

In Fig. 7.8 we see that the first 175K words in the HolE vocabulary are not represented in the corpus. The reason for this is that these are quoted words or words referring to entities (hence capitalized names for places, people) which have been filtered out due to the `ls f` tokenization applied to the test corpus. Also, we see a jump in token prediction quality around word 245K which is maintained until word 670K. This corresponds to the band of concept tokens, which are encoded as `en#concept-id`. Hence words between 175K and 245K are lemmas starting from "a" to "en" and words after 670K are lemmas from "en" to "z." This again indicates that HolE is better at learning embeddings for concepts rather than lemmas (leaf nodes in the Sensigrafo KG).

7.6 Conclusion

This chapter was all about ways to evaluate the quality of your embeddings. We saw that there is a plethora of methods that can be used to evaluate embeddings with various trade-offs. Some methods are easier to apply since datasets already exist and results for various pre-trained embeddings are readily available for comparison. Other methods require more effort and interpreting the results may not be as easy. Finally, we saw that, depending on what you want to do with your embeddings, you may decide to focus on one type of evaluation over another.

The overview of existing evaluation methods combined with practical exercises for applying a variety of these methods and the case study should provide you with plenty of ideas on how to evaluate a range of embeddings for your particular use cases.

Chapter 8
Capturing Lexical, Grammatical, and Semantic Information with Vecsigrafo

Abstract Embedding algorithms work by optimizing the distance between a word and its context(s), generating an embedding space that encodes their distributional representation. In addition to single words or word pieces, other features, which result from a deeper analysis of the text, can be used to enrich such representations with additional information. Such features are influenced by the tokenization strategy used to chunk the text and can include not only lexical and part-of-speech information but also annotations about the disambiguated sense of a word according to a structured knowledge graph. In this chapter we analyze the impact that explicitly adding lexical, grammatical and semantic information during the training of Vecsigrafo has in the resulting representations and whether or not this can enhance their downstream performance. To illustrate this analysis we focus on corpora from the scientific domain, where rich, multi-word expressions are frequent, hence requiring advanced tokenization strategies.

8.1 Introduction

As we have already seen, distributed word representations in the form of dense vectors, known as word embeddings, have become extremely popular for NLP tasks such as part-of-speech tagging, chunking, named entity recognition, semantic role labeling, and synonym detection. Such interest was significantly sparkled by the word2vec algorithm proposed in [117], which provided an efficient way to learn word embeddings from large corpora based on word context and negative sampling, and continues to date. Much research has been put into the development of increasingly effective means to produce word embeddings, resulting in algorithms like GloVe [138], Swivel [164], or fastText [23]. Lately, much of this effort has focused on neural language models that produce contextual word representations at a scale never seen before, like ELMo [139], BERT [44], and XLNet [195].

In general, word embedding algorithms are trained to minimize the distance between a token and its usual context of neighboring tokens in a document corpus. The set of tokens that occur in text after some tokenization is applied may include, e.g. words ("making"), punctuation marks (";"), multi-word expressions ("day-care

© Springer Nature Switzerland AG 2020

J. M. Gomez-Perez et al., *A Practical Guide to Hybrid Natural Language Processing*, https://doi.org/10.1007/978-3-030-44830-1_8

Table 8.1 Tokenizations for the first window of size $W = 3$ for the sentence: *With regard to breathing in the locus coeruleus, ...*

Context	t^{i-3}	t^{i-2}	t^{i-1}	t^i	t^{i+1}	t^{i+2}	t^{i+3}
t	With	regard	to	breathing	in	the	locus coeruleus
sf	With regard to	breathing	in	the	locus coeruleus	$\varnothing$	
l	With regard to	breathe	$\varnothing$	$\varnothing$	locus coeruleus	$\varnothing$	
c	en#216081	en#76230	$\varnothing$	$\varnothing$	en#101470452	$\varnothing$	
g	PRE	VER	PRE	ART	NOU	PNT	

First we show basic space-based tokenization. Next, sequences for surface forms, lemmas, syncons, and grammar type

center") or combinations of words and punctuation marks ("However,"). Indeed, the information that is actually encoded in the resulting embeddings depends not only on the neighboring context of a word or its frequency in the corpus but also on the strategies used to chunk the text into sequences of individual tokens.

In Table 8.1 we show several examples of tokenizations that can be produced by processing a sentence following different strategies. In the example, the original text is annotated with information on space-separated tokens (t) and surface forms (sf). Additional lexical, grammatical, and semantic annotations can also be extracted from the text, like the lemma (l) associated with each token, the corresponding sense or concept[1] extracted through word-sense disambiguation (c), and part-of-speech information (g) about the role each token plays in the context of a particular sentence.

As can be seen, the resulting sequences of tokens used to train the embeddings differ significantly both in number of tokens and complexity. This can have a decisive impact on what information is actually encoded in the embeddings. As a matter of fact, the analysis and selection of optimal tokenization strategies and their application to train word embeddings working at either word (word2vec), character (ELMo), byte-pair encoding (BPEmb [76]), or word-piece (BERT) levels is already well covered in the literature. However, none of these approaches investigate the role that explicit linguistic and semantic annotations (henceforth, generically linguistic annotations) like the ones above-mentioned, as well as their combinations, can play in the training of the embeddings.

In this chapter we make use of this observation to investigate how linguistic annotations extracted from the text can be used to produce enriched, higher-quality embeddings. In doing so, we focus on the scientific domain as a field with a significantly complex terminology, rich in multi-word expressions and other linguistic artifacts. Scientific resources like Springer Nature's SciGraph [73], which contains over 3M scholarly publications, can be considerably rich in domain-specific multi-word expressions. As shown in Table 8.2, this is particularly noticeable in the

---

[1]Note that in the example, concept information is linked to a knowledge graph through a unique identifier.

Table 8.2 Multi-word expressions (mwe) vs. single-word expressions (swe) per grammar type (PoS) in SciGraph

Part-of-speech	Example	#Single-word expressions	#Multi-word expressions
ADJ	single+dose	104.7	0.514
ADV	in+situ	21	1.98
CON	even+though	34.6	3.46
ENT	august+2007	1.5	1.24
NOU	humid+climate	216.9	15.24
NPH	Ivor+Lewis	0.917	0.389
NPR	dorsal+ganglia	22.8	5.22
PRO	other+than	13.89	0.005
VER	take+place	69.39	0.755

Number of swe and mwe occurrences are in millions

case of grammar types like adverbs (ADV), nouns (NOU), noun phrases (NPH), proper names (NPR), or entities (ENT), while others like conjunctions (CON) or propositions (PRO) are domain-independent.

We quantify the impact of each individual type of linguistic annotation and their possible combinations on the resulting embeddings following different approaches. First, intrinsically, through word similarity and analogical reasoning tasks. In this regard, we observe that word similarity and analogy benchmarks are of little help in domains which, like science, have highly specialized vocabularies, highlighting the need for domain-specific benchmarks. Second, we also evaluate extrinsically in two downstream tasks: a word prediction task against scientific corpora extracted from SciGraph and Semantic Scholar [3], as well as general-purpose corpora like Wikipedia and UMBC [74], and a classification task based on the SciGraph taxonomy of scientific disciplines.

Next, we address different ways to capture various types of linguistic and semantic information in a single embedding space (Sect. 8.2) and report experimental results based on that (Sect. 8.3). Some interesting findings include the following. Embeddings learnt from corpora enriched with sense information consistently improve word similarity and analogical reasoning, while the latter additionally tends to benefit from surface form embeddings. Other results show the impact of using part-of-speech information to generate embeddings in the target domain, with significant improvements in precision for the classification task while penalizing word prediction.

8.2 Approach

The method used is based on Vecsigrafo [39], which allows jointly learning word, lemma, and concept embeddings using different tokenization strategies, as well as linguistic annotations.

8.2.1 Vecsigrafo: Corpus-Based Word-Concept Embeddings

As introduced in Chap. 6, Vecsigrafo [39] is a method that jointly learns word and concept embeddings using a text corpus and a knowledge graph. Like word2vec, it uses a sliding window over the corpus to predict pairs of center and context words. Unlike word2vec, which relies on a simple tokenization strategy based on space-separated tokens (t), in Vecsigrafo the aim is to learn embeddings also for linguistic annotations, including surface forms ($sf \in SF$), lemmas ($l \in L$), grammar information like part-of-speech ($g \in G$) and knowledge graph concepts ($c \in C$). To derive such additional information from a text corpus, appropriate tokenization strategies and a word-sense disambiguation pipeline are required.

In contrast to simple tokenization strategies based on space separation, surface forms are the result of a grammatical analysis where one or more tokens can be grouped using the part-of-speech information, e.g. in noun or verb phrases. Surface forms can include multi-word expressions that refer to concepts, e.g. "Cancer Research Center." A lemma is the base form of a word, e.g. surface forms "is," "are," "were" all have lemma "be."

Due to the linguistic annotations that are included in addition to the original text, the word2vec approach is no longer directly applicable. The annotated text is a sequence of words and annotations and hence sliding a context window from a central word needs to care about both words and annotations. For this reason, Vecsigrafo extends the Swivel [164] algorithm to first use the sliding window to count co-occurrences between pairs of linguistic annotations in the corpus, which are then used to estimate the pointwise mutual information (PMI) between each pair. The algorithm then tries to predict all the pairs as accurately as possible. In the end, Vecsigrafo produces an embedding space: $\Phi = \{(x, e) : x \in SF \cup L \cup G \cup C, e \in \mathbf{R}^n\}$. That is, for each entry x, it learns an embedding of dimension n, such that the dot product of two vectors predicts the PMI of the two entries.

8.2.2 Joint Embedding Space

To use Vecsigrafo embeddings we need to annotate a corpus D with the linguistic annotations used to learn the embeddings. An annotated document in D is a sequence of annotation tuples $D_j = ((sf, l, g, c)_i)_{i=0}^{|D_j|-1}$. Then we need to generate out of D a vocabulary for each linguistic annotation $V(D) = \{v : v \in SF_D \cup L_D \cup G_D \cup C_D\}$ and represent any annotated document as a finite sequence of items in this vocabulary $S(D_j) = (sf_i, l_i, g_i, c_i)_{i=0}^{|D_j|-1}$. Following this approach there is a direct mapping between any sequence element in $S(D_j))$ and Vecsigrafo embeddings in Φ.

In addition, it is possible to merge Vecsigrafo embeddings, for example, surface form and concept embeddings, in a similar way as embeddings are merged for contextualized embeddings [44, 139] or to create multi-modal embedding spaces [179].

Different operations can be applied on the embeddings, including concatenation, average, addition, and dimension reduction techniques such as principal component analysis PCA, singular vector decomposition SVD, or neural auto-encoders.

8.2.3 Embeddings Evaluation

The different approaches to evaluating embeddings can be classified either as intrinsic methods [158], which assess whether the embedding space actually encodes the distributional context of words, or extrinsic methods, where evaluation is done according to the performance of a downstream task. Here, we focus on the following.

Word similarity [150] is an intrinsic evaluation method that assesses whether the embedding space captures the semantic relatedness between words. The relatedness score, defined by human judgment, is compared with an embedding similarity measure. To work with the concept embeddings produced by Vecsigrafo we use a concept-based word similarity measure, where each pair of words is mapped to concepts, using the most frequent word meaning as reference, and similarity is calculated on the corresponding concept embeddings.

Word analogy [121] is another intrinsic evaluation method where the goal is to find y such that given x the relation x:y resembles a sample relation a:b by operating on the corresponding word vectors.

Word prediction, introduced in [39], proposes to use a test corpus to model how accurately the resulting embeddings can predict a linguistic annotation (t, sf, l, c, or g). This essentially emulates the word2vec skipgram loss function on a test corpus unseen during training. It iterates through the sequence of tokens in a corpus using a context window. For each center word or linguistic annotation, take the (weighted) average of the embeddings for the context tokens and compare it to the embedding for the center word using cosine similarity. If the cosine similarity is close to 1, the center word is being correctly predicted based on its context. We use this to plot the similarities for the whole embedding vocabulary, providing insights about possible disparities in the quality of common and uncommon words, as well as the applicability of the resulting embeddings to a different corpus.

Text classification: Since word embeddings are usually at the input of neural architectures to solve NLP tasks, the performance of the latter can be used as an indicator of the fitness of the former. Here, we select classification as one of the most widely used tasks in NLP. In contrast to models frequently used for text classification [113] like Naive Bayes and support vector machines (SVM) [189] that work in a highly dimensional space, deep neural networks work on a compressed space thanks to the use of fixed length embeddings. Neural networks with convolutional layers CNN [100] using a single layer [36, 96] or multiple-layers [155, 200] have shown state-of-the-art performance for NLP tasks without the need of hand-crafted features [36], one of the main limitations of traditional approaches.

8.3   Evaluation

Next, we describe the corpus, embeddings learnt from the linguistic annotations, and the experiments carried out to get insights on their usefulness in the different evaluation tasks. We present a comprehensive experimental study on the quality of embeddings generated from a scientific corpus using additional, explicit annotations with linguistic and semantic information extracted from the text. To this purpose, we follow the approach proposed by Vecsigrafo. However, in contrast to the experiments described in [39], which used general domain corpora, here we rely on domain-specific text from scientific publications and include the use of grammatical information (part-of-speech) in the experimentation. We cover all the possible combinations of the resulting embeddings, including those related to space-separated tokens, surface forms, lemmas, concepts, and grammatical information. Finally, we add an extrinsic evaluation task on scientific text classification to further assess the quality of the embeddings.

8.3.1   Dataset

The scientific corpus used in the following experiments is extracted from Sci-Graph [73], a knowledge graph for scientific publications. From it, we extract titles and abstracts of articles and book chapters published between 2001 and 2017. The resulting corpus consists roughly of 3.2 million publications, 1.4 million distinct words, and 700 million tokens.

Next, we use Cogito, Expert System's NLP suite, to parse and disambiguate the text and add the linguistic annotations associated with each token or group of tokens. To this purpose, Cogito relies on its own knowledge graph, Sensigrafo. Note that we could have used any other NLP toolkit as long as the generation of the linguistic annotations used in this work were supported.

Table 8.3 Account of token types and embeddings learnt from the text in the title and abstracts from research articles and book chapters in English published between 2001 and 2017 and available in SciGraph

Algorithm	Types	Total	Distinct	Embeddings
Swivel	t	707M	1,486,848	1,486,848
Vecsigrafo	sf	805M	5,090,304	692,224
	l	508M	4,798,313	770,048
	g	804M	25	8
	c	425M	212,365	147,456

The corpus parsing and annotations generated by Cogito are reported in Table 8.3. For space-separated tokens we learnt an initial set of embeddings using Swivel, which is the reference algorithm for Vecsigrafo. For the remaining linguistic annotations (*sf*, *l*, *g*, *c*), as well as their combinations including two and three elements, we learnt their embeddings using Vecsigrafo. The difference in the number of distinct number of annotations and actual embeddings is due to filtering. Following previous findings [39], we filtered out elements with grammar type article, punctuation mark, or auxiliary verbs and generalize tokens with grammar type entity or person proper noun, replacing the original token with special tokens *grammar#ENT* and *grammar#NPH*, respectively.

8.3.2 Word Similarity

In Table 8.4 we report the 16 datasets used in the word similarity evaluation task. During training of the Vecsigrafo embeddings we tested them at each step of the learning process against these datasets. We present in Table 8.5 the similarity results calculated for the Vecsigrafo embeddings in a subset of 11 datasets, although the average reported in the last column is for the 16 datasets. Note that we only applied concept-similarity in those combinations where *sf* or *l* were not present.

From the data we observe that there is a clear evidence that embeddings learnt from linguistic annotations, individually or jointly learnt, perform better in the similarity task than using token embeddings. An individual analysis of each linguistic annotation shows that *c* embeddings outperform *l* embeddings, which in turn are superior to *sf* embeddings. Note that most of the similarity datasets in Table 8.4 contain mainly nouns and lemmatized verbs. Thus, semantic and lemma embeddings are better representations for these datasets since they condense different words and morphological variations in one representation while surface forms may generate several embeddings, for the different morphological variations of words, that might not be necessary for this task and can hamper the similarity estimation.

Regarding Vecsigrafo embeddings jointly learnt for two or more linguistic annotations, semantic embeddings *c* improve the results in all the combinations where they were used. That is, concept embeddings enhance the lexical representations based on surface forms and the grouped morphological variations represented by lemmas in the similarity task. On the other hand, grammatical information *g* seems to hamper the performance of Vecsigrafo embeddings, except when they are jointly learnt with the semantic embeddings *c*. If we focus the analysis on the top five results in Table 8.5, *l* and *c* embeddings, jointly or individually learnt, are the common elements in the embedding combinations that perform best in the similarity task. The performance of embeddings from surface forms *sf*, on the other hand, and related combinations is at the bottom of the table. In general, embeddings based on *l* and *c*, individually or jointly, seem to be better correlated to the human notion of similarity than embeddings based on *l* and *g*.

Table 8.4 Similarity and relatedness datasets used for embeddings evaluation

Dataset	Main content	Word pairs	Raters per pair
The RG-65 [154]	Nouns	65	51
MC-30 [122]	Nouns	30	51
WS-353-ALL [60]	Nouns	353	13–16
WS-353-REL [1]	Nouns	252	13–17
WS-353-SIM [1]	Nouns	203	13–18
YP-130 [194]	Verbs	130	6
VERB-143 [13]	Conjugated verbs	143	10
SIMVERB3500 [64]	Lemmatized verbs	3500	10
MTurk-287 [148]	Nouns	287	23
MTurk-771 [98]	Nouns	771	20
MEN-TR-3K [26]	Nouns	3000	10
SIMLEX-999-Adj [77]	Adjectives	111	50
SIMLEX-999-Nou [77]	Nouns	666	50
SIMLEX-999-Ver [77]	Verbs	222	50
RW-STANFORD [111]	Noun, Verbs, Adj	2034	10
SEMEVAL17 [28]	Named entities, MWE	500	3

To summarize, from the results obtained in the similarity task, embeddings seem to benefit from the additional semantic information contributed by the linguistic annotations. Lexical variations presented at the level of surface forms are better representations in this regard than space-separated tokens, while the conflation of these variations in a base form at the lemma level and their link to an explicit concept increase performance in the prediction of word relatedness. Jointly learnt embeddings for surface forms, lemmas, and concepts achieve the best overall similarity results.

The analysis in [39] evaluates in the same settings Vecsigrafo embeddings for lemmas and concepts learnt from a 2018 dump of Wikipedia, achieving a Spearman's rho of 0.566, which contrasts with the 0.380 achieved by the same embeddings learnt from the SciGraph corpus. These results may not be directly comparable due to the difference of corpora size (3B tokens in Wikipedia vs. 700M in SciGraph). Another factor is the general-purpose nature of Wikipedia, while SciGraph is specialized in the scientific domain.

Table 8.5 Average Spearman's rho for a subset of all the similarity datasets and the final learnt Vecsigrafo and Swivel embeddings

Embed.	MC_30	MEN_TR_3k	MTurk_771	RG_65	RW_STANFORD	SEMEVAL17	SIMLEX_999	SIMVERB3500	WS_353_ALL	YP_130	Average ↓
sf_l_c	**0.6701**	0.6119	0.4872	0.6145	**0.2456**	0.4241	0.2773	0.1514	**0.4915**	0.4472	**0.4064**
c	0.6214	0.6029	0.4512	0.5340	0.2161	**0.5343**	0.2791	0.2557	0.4762	0.4898	0.3883
l_g_c	0.5964	**0.6312**	**0.5103**	0.5206	0.1916	0.4535	0.2903	0.1745	0.4167	0.4576	0.3826
l_c	0.5709	0.5787	0.4355	0.5607	0.1888	0.4912	0.2627	0.2378	0.4462	0.5180	0.3807
l	0.6494	0.6093	0.4908	**0.6972**	0.2002	0.4554	0.2509	0.1297	0.4410	0.3324	0.3763
g_c	0.4458	0.5663	0.4046	0.4985	0.1803	0.5280	**0.3040**	**0.2637**	0.3957	**0.5322**	0.3671
sf_l	0.5390	0.5853	0.4229	0.5448	0.2139	0.3870	0.2493	0.1374	0.4670	0.3627	0.3652
sf_c	0.5960	0.5603	0.4430	0.4788	0.2013	0.4958	0.2722	0.2433	0.3957	0.4835	0.3607
sf_g_c	0.5319	0.6199	0.4565	0.4690	0.2315	0.3938	0.2789	0.1452	0.4201	0.2663	0.3559
sf	0.5150	0.5819	0.4387	0.4395	0.2325	0.3855	0.2673	0.1524	0.4370	0.3630	0.3538
sf_l_g	0.5096	0.5645	0.4008	0.3268	0.2077	0.3427	0.2376	0.1100	0.3909	0.3179	0.3220
l_g	0.5359	0.5551	0.4238	0.5230	0.1648	0.3791	0.2139	0.1204	0.3087	0.3853	0.3057
sf_g	0.5016	0.5239	0.3950	0.3448	0.1681	0.3469	0.1979	0.1028	0.3699	0.3322	0.2990
t	0.1204	0.3269	0.1984	0.1546	0.0650	0.2417	0.1179	0.0466	0.1923	0.2523	0.1656

The results are sorted in descending order on the average of all datasets in the last column. Bold values indicate the largest correlation

8.3.3 Analogical Reasoning

For the analogy task we use the Google analogy test set[2] that contains 19,544 question pairs (8869 semantic and 10,675 syntactic questions) and 14 types of relations (9 syntactic and 5 semantic). The accuracy of the embeddings in the analogy task is reported in Table 8.6.

Table 8.6 Results of the analogy tasks sorted in descending order on the overall results

Embeddings	Analogy task		
	Semantic	Syntactic	Overall
sf_c	11.72%	**14.17%**	**12.94%**
sf_g_c	14.13%	11.65%	12.89%
sf_l_c	9.27%	12.10%	10.69%
l_g_c	**14.83%**	3.09%	8.96%
sf_l	7.18%	8.63%	7.91%
l_c	10.47%	4.06%	7.26%
sf	6.69%	6.43%	6.56%
sf_l_g	6.60%	5.74%	6.17%
sf_g	6.07%	3.79%	4.93%
l	4.07%	1.27%	2.67%
l_g	2.33%	0.79%	1.56%
t	0.64%	0.09%	0.37%

Bold values indicate the largest accuracy

Similarly to the word similarity results, in this task the linguistic annotations also generate better embeddings than space-separated tokens. However, in this case surface forms are more relevant than lemmas. Surface form embeddings achieve large accuracy in both semantic and syntactic analogies. However, lemma embeddings accuracy is large for semantic analogies and really small for syntactic analogies. In this case, embeddings generated taking into account the morphological variations of words are better than using the base forms. For example, some syntactic analogies actually require to work at the surface form level, e.g., "bright-brighter cold-colder" since the lemmas of *brighter* and *colder* are *bright* and *cold*, respectively, and therefore in the lemma embedding space there is no representation for *brighter* and *colder*.

Jointly learning *sf* and *c* embeddings achieves the highest accuracy over the board and in fact these two linguistic annotations are in the top 3 results along with *g* or *l*. As in word similarity, semantic embeddings *c* improve every combination in which they are used. If we focus on the semantic analogies, we can see that *l*, *g*, and *c* reach the highest accuracy. Nevertheless the performance of this combination is

---

[2] Analogy dataset available at: https://aclweb.org/aclwiki/Google_analogy_test_set_(State_of_the_art).

very poor on syntactic analogies given that l do not include morphological variations of words that are heavily represented in the syntactic analogies. In general the worst results are obtained when the combinations do not include c.

In Shazeer et al. [164] Swivel embeddings learnt from Wikipedia and Gigaword achieved an analogy accuracy in the same dataset used in this experiments of 0.739, while the best result reported in our analysis is 0.129. As in the similarity evaluation, the rather smaller size of the SciGraph corpus and domain specificity seem to hamper the results in this generic evaluation tasks.

8.3.4 Word Prediction

We have selected 17,500 papers from Semantic Scholar, which are not in the SciGraph corpus, as the unseen text on which we try to predict the embeddings for certain words (or linguistic annotations) according to the context. We applied the same annotation pipeline to the test corpus so that we can use the embeddings learnt from SciGraph. As baselines we used pre-trained embeddings learnt for linguistic annotations that we derived from *generic*, i.e. non-scientific, corpora: a dump of Wikipedia from January 2018 containing 2.89B tokens and UMBC [74], a web-based corpus of 2.95B tokens.

The overall results are shown in Table 8.7. We also plot the full results for some of the prediction tasks in Fig. 8.1. The results show a clear pattern: embeddings learnt from linguistic annotations significantly outperform the plain space-separated token embeddings (t). That is, the cosine similarity between the predicted embedding for the linguistic annotation on Semantic Scholar and the actual embeddings learnt from SciGraph is higher. Recall that the predicted embedding is calculated by averaging the embeddings of the words or their annotations in the context window.

In general, embeddings learnt from linguistic annotations on SciGraph are better at predicting embeddings in the Semantic Scholar corpus. For these embeddings it was easier to predict surface forms embeddings, followed by lemma and concept embeddings. We assume this is because *sf* annotations contain more information, since they keep morphological information. Similarly, concept information may be more difficult to predict due to possible disambiguation errors or because the specific lemma used to refer to a concept may still provide useful information for the prediction task.

Jointly learning embeddings for *sf* and other annotations (c or l) produce *sf* embeddings which are slightly harder to predict than when trained on their own. However, jointly learning l and c embeddings produces better results; i.e. jointly learning lemmas and concepts has a synergistic effect.

When comparing to the baselines, we see that SciGraph-based embeddings outperform both the Wikipedia and UMBC-based embeddings. The out-of-vocabulary (oov) numbers provide an explanation: both baselines produce embeddings which miss many terms in the test corpus but which are included in the SciGraph embeddings. Wikipedia misses 116K lemmas, UMBC 93K, but SciGraph only misses 81K of the lemmas in the test corpus. Wikipedia misses most concepts

Table 8.7 Prediction results of embeddings for linguistic annotations

Corpus	Embed.	pred	Cosine Sim.	#tokens	Out-of-voc oov	oov %
SciGraph	sf	sf	0.765	3,841,378	617,094	16.064
SciGraph	sf_c	sf	0.751	3,841,378	617,144	16.066
SciGraph	sf_l	sf	0.741	3,841,378	617,121	16.065
SciGraph	l_c	l	0.733	2,418,362	81,087	3.353
SciGraph	l	l	0.730	2,418,362	81,041	3.351
SciGraph	l_c	c	0.690	2,012,471	1481	0.074
SciGraph	c	c	0.690	2,012,471	1572	0.078
Wiki	l_c	l	0.676	2,418,362	116,056	4.799
UMBC	l_c	l	0.674	2,418,362	93,169	3.853
UMBC	l_c	c	0.650	2,012,471	1102	0.055
Wiki	l_c	c	0.650	2,012,471	2216	0.110
SciGraph	t	t	0.576	3,396,730	205,154	6.040

(2.2K), followed by SciGraph (1.5K) and UMBC (1.1K); however, despite missing more concepts, the SciGraph-based embeddings outperform both baselines.

Manual inspection of the missing words shows that UMBC is missing nearly 14K lemmas (mostly for scientific terms) which the SciGraph-based embeddings contain, such as "negative bias temperature instability," "supragranular," "QHD." Inversely, the SciGraph vocabulary is missing nearly 7K lemmas for generic entities such as "Jim Collins," "Anderson School of Management," but also misspellings. However, most of the missing words (around 42K) are in neither UMBC nor SciGraph and include very specific metrics ("40 kilopascal"), acronyms ("DB620"), and named entities ("Victoria Institute of Forensic Medicine"). We observe a similar pattern when comparing missing concepts.

8.3.5   Classification of Scientific Documents

Leveraging SciGraph metadata, we formulate a multi-label classification task that aims at predicting one or more 22 first-level categories such as Mathematical Sciences, Engineering, or Medical and Health Sciences. To learn the classifier we use a vanilla CNN implementation available in Keras, with 3 convolutional layers with 128 filters and a 5-element window size, each followed by a max-pooling layer, a fully connected 128-unit ReLU layer, and a sigmoid output. Recall that our goal is not to design the best classifier, but to evaluate the different types of embeddings through its performance.

To evaluate the classifiers we select articles published in 2011 and use tenfold cross-validation. We define a vocabulary size of 20K elements and max sequence size of 1000. As baseline, we train a classifier that learns from embeddings generated randomly, following a normal distribution. As upper bound we learn a

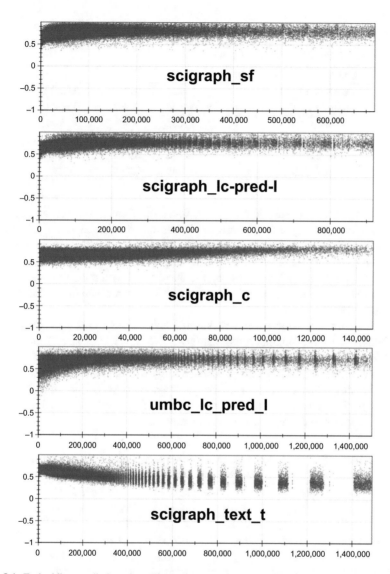

Fig. 8.1 Embedding prediction plots. The horizontal axis aligns with the terms in the vocabulary sorted by frequency. The vertical axis is the average cosine similarity (which can range from 0 to 1) between the predicted embedding on the Semantic Scholar corpus and the actual learnt embedding from SciGraph. According to this task the closer to 1 the better. Blank spaces indicates lack of coverage

classifier that is able to optimize the embeddings during task-specific training. In addition, we train classifiers using embeddings generated for t, sf, l, and c.

The performance of the classifiers measured in terms of precision, recall, and f-measure is shown in Table 8.8. l embeddings contribute to learn the best classifier,

Table 8.8 Learning results using token-based embeddings generated randomly (baseline) and learnt by the convolutional neural network (upper bound), and Swivel embeddings for t, sf, l, and c

Embed. Algorithm	Types	P	R	f-Measure
Random normal	t	0.7596	0.6775	0.7015△
Learnt by CNN	t	0.8062	0.767	0.7806▽
Swivel	t	0.8008	0.7491	0.7679
Vecsigrafo	sf	0.8030	0.7477	0.7684
Vecsigrafo	l	0.8035	0.7539	0.7728
Vecsigrafo	c	0.7945	0.7391	0.7583

followed by sf and t embeddings. If we focus on f-measure, we can see again that grammatical analysis (l, sf) performs better than the lexical level (t). However, the performance of c embeddings for this task is rather low. The low number of c embeddings (see Table 8.3) seems to affect negatively the learning process. On the other hand, all the classifiers including the one trained with c improve the baseline of random embeddings. However none of the classifiers reached the performance of the upper bound.

Next, we train classifiers using Vecsigrafo embeddings from all the ten possible combinations of the linguistic annotations (sf, l, g, c) with size 2 and 3. The classifiers were trained using the merging techniques described in Sect. 8.2.2: combinations of single embeddings per each linguistic annotation type and merging the embeddings using vector operators as average, concatenate, and PCA. The average performance of the classifiers is presented in Table 8.9. Each column is sorted according to the reported evaluation metric.

Table 8.9 Average performance of the classifiers trained using different strategies to mix and merge Vecsigrafo embeddings

Precision		Recall		f-Measure	
Types	Average ↓	Types	Average ↓	Types	Average ↓
sf_l_g	0.8126	sf_l	0.7605	sf_l	0.7776
sf_g	0.8091	l_c	0.7556	sf_l_g	0.7750
l_g	0.8090	sf_l_c	0.7538	l_g_c	0.7730
sf_g_c	0.8084	l_g_c	0.7524	l_c	0.7728
l_g_c	0.8073	sf_l_g	0.7524	sf_l_c	0.7720
g_c	0.8060	sf_c	0.7520	sf_g_c	0.7716
sf_l	0.8056	sf_g_c	0.7504	l_g	0.7702
sf_l_c	0.8031	l_g	0.7477	sf_c	0.7699
l_c	0.8021	sf_g	0.7374	sf_g	0.7638
sf_c	0.8006	g_c	0.7338	g_c	0.7599

Each column is sorted in descending order of the corresponding metric

Regarding precision, the top three classifiers are learnt from different combination of sf, l, and g, indicating that, precision-wise, grammatical information is more relevant than semantic information (c). However, note that the common linguistic element in the 6 first classifiers is g, even when combining it with c, and in general removing g embeddings produced the least precise classifiers. This means that grammar information makes the difference regardless of the other linguistic elements, although the influence of g is enhanced when used in combination with sf and l. Note that the precision of the top five classifiers is better than the upper bound classifier (Table 8.8), where the embeddings were learnt at classification training time, although the linguistic-based embeddings were not learnt for this specific purpose.

The recall analysis shows a different picture since grammar embeddings g do not seem to have a decisive role on the performance of the classifier recall-wise, while c gain more relevance. sf and l help in learning the best classifier. The combination of c and l seems to benefit recall since, as seen in 3 of the top 4 classifiers. In contrast when concepts are combined with sf the recall is lower. The fact that l embeddings are more directly related to c than sf seems to make a difference in the recall analysis when these three elements are involved. In general, g-based embedding combinations generate classifiers with lower recall.

Finally, the f-measure data shows more heterogeneous results since by definition it is the harmonic mean of precision and recall, and hence the combinations that generate the best f-measure need a high precision and a high recall. sf and l combination is at the top (best recall), followed by their combination with g (best precision). c appears in positions 3 to 6 in the ranking, however when combined solely with sf or g the f-measure results are the worst. g, on the other hand, when combined with at least two other elements ranks high in f-measure, while when it is combined with a single linguistic annotation type the resulting performance of the classifiers is the worst.

8.4 Discussion

Although the different evaluation tasks assess the embeddings from different perspectives, in all of them we have observed that the embeddings learnt from linguistic annotations outperform space-separated token embeddings. In the intrinsic evaluation tasks, the embeddings learnt from linguist annotations have different performance mainly due to the vocabulary used in the evaluation datasets. For example, in the analogical reasoning datasets, syntactic analogies are more represented compared to semantic analogies. Also, most of the syntactic analogies often include morphological variations of the words, which are better covered by surface form embeddings than lemma embeddings, where morphological variations are conflated in a single base form. For example, comparative and superlative analogies like *cheap-cheaper* and *cold-colder* may require to use morphological variations of the verb by adding the *-er* and *-(e)st* suffixes, and although some adjectives and adverbs may produce irregular forms, the only ones included in the dataset are *good-better*, *bad-worse*, *good-best*, and *bad-worst*.

In contrast, in the similarity datasets (see Table 8.4) most of the word pairs available for evaluation are either nouns, named entities, or lemmatized verbs—only the Verb-143 dataset contains conjugated verbs. Thus, most of the word pairs are non-inflected word forms and therefore concept and lemma embeddings are the representations more fitted for this task which is in line with the evaluation results reported in Table 8.5.

Remarkably, in the analogy task, surface form embeddings jointly learnt with concept embeddings achieve the highest performance, and in the similarity task jointly learning concepts and lemma embeddings also improves the lemma embeddings performance in the task. Therefore, including concept embeddings in the learning process of other embeddings generally helps to learn better distributional representations.

The word prediction task provides additional insight in the sense that embeddings learnt from linguistic features seem to better capture the distributional context, as evaluated against unseen text. Surface form and lemma embeddings were the easiest to predict.

Finally, in the text classification task, single embeddings from lemma and surface form annotations were more useful than space-separated token embeddings. Nevertheless, in this task concept embeddings perform worst mainly due to the low coverage offered by these embeddings with respect to the whole vocabulary, indicating that the knowledge graph used to annotate the text possibly provides a limited coverage of the domain. We also show that jointly learning lemma and surface form embeddings helps to train the best classifier in term of f-measure and recall. Furthermore, adding grammar embeddings produced the best overall precision.

Next, we illustrate with actual code some of the experiments performed in this chapter. The notebook is available online[3] as part of the tutorial accompanying this book.

8.5   Practice: Classifying Scientific Literature Using Surface Forms

Here we show a practical exercise of how to use Vecsigrafo and a surface form-based tokenization strategy to classify scientific literature from Springer Nature SciGraph. Articles are classified in one or more of the 22 first-level categories in SciGraph. Previously we have extracted from SciGraph the papers published in 2011. For each paper we consider only the text in the title and the abstract.

---

[3]https://colab.research.google.com/github/hybridnlp/tutorial/blob/master/
09_classification_of_scholarly_communications.ipynb.

8.5.1   Import the Required Libraries

```
In [0]: from keras.preprocessing.text import Tokenizer
        from keras.preprocessing.sequence import pad_sequences
        from keras.layers import Embedding, Input, Conv1D, MaxPooling1D, Flatten, Dense
        from keras.layers import Dropout, LSTM
        from keras.models import Model, Sequential
        from keras.metrics import categorical_accuracy
        from keras.utils import to_categorical
        from sklearn.preprocessing import MultiLabelBinarizer
        from sklearn.metrics import classification_report, f1_score, precision_score
        from sklearn.metrics import recall_score
        from sklearn.model_selection import KFold
        from tqdm import tqdm
        from random import sample
        import numpy as np
        import json
        import re
        import h5py
        import mmap
```

8.5.2   Download Surface form Embeddings and SciGraph Papers

8.5.2.1   Downloading Data from Google Drive

```
In [3]: pip install gdown

Out[3]: Requirement already satisfied: gdown in /usr/local/lib/python3.6/dis...
        Requirement already satisfied: six in /usr/local/lib/python3.6/dist-...
...

In [4]: import gdown
        url = 'https://drive.google.com/uc?id=1MRL2mYnJUb-qGitAZ53BFeNi4HLyqKlN'
        out = 'data-embeddings.zip'
        gdown.download(url,out,False)

Out[4]: Downloading...
        From: https://drive.google.com/uc?id=1MRL2mYnJUb-qGitAZ53BFeNi4HLyqKlN
        To: /content/data-embeddings.zip
        1.13GB [00:45, 24.8MB/s]
        'data-embeddings.zip'
```

Unzip the content and set the variables that point to the data and embeddings

```
In [5]: !unzip data-embeddings.zip

Out[5]: Archive:  data-embeddings.zip
          inflating: data/scigraph-2011-sf.json
          inflating: embeddings/row_embedding.tsv
```

8.5.3   Read and Prepare the Classification Dataset

To speed up the classifier learning process, we take a sampe of the whole dataset. If you want to use the whole dataset, please comment the second-to-last line below.

```
In [6]: sample_size = 10000
        texts = []
        labels_index = {}
        labels = []
        word_index = {}
        dataset_file="data/scigraph-2011-sf.json"
        embeddings_file="embeddings/row_embedding.tsv"

        # Read the articles dataset that will be used to train and validate the model.
        with open(dataset_file, "r", encoding="utf-8", errors="surrogatepass") as file:
            dataset = json.load(file)

        file.close()

        #Prepare data
        for doc in tqdm(dataset,total = len(dataset), desc="extracting labels") :
            # Extract the 2-number field code, that is, the most general one.
            fields = [x for x in doc["fieldcodes"] if len(x)==2]
            label_ids = set()
            for field in fields:
                # if the field is not already stored assign a new label to it.
                if field not in labels_index:
                    label_id = len(labels_index)
                    labels_index[field] = label_id
                else:
                    label_id = labels_index[field]
                # Add the corresponding field label
                label_ids.add(label_id)
            labels.append(label_ids)
            # Extract the title and abstract of each article
            texts.append(doc["sf"])

        #To speed up the training we obtain a sample of sample_size of the data.
        #To work with the full dataset comment the line below
        labels, texts = zip(*sample(list(zip(labels, texts)), sample_size))
        print('\n'+str(len(texts))+' papers')
Out[6]: extracting labels: 100% 187795/187795 [00:00<00:00, 350375.49it/s]
        10000 papers
```

Get data and label tensors (using Keras tokenizer)

```
In [7]: max_nb_words = 40000
        max_sequence_length = 1000
        #standar keras tokenizer filters except the + symbol which is used
        #in our sf to glue multiword expressions
        tokenizer_filters = '!"#$%&()*,-./:;<=>?@[\\]^_`{|}~\t\n'

        # Tokenize the sentences of all the articles
        tokenizer = Tokenizer(num_words=max_nb_words, filters=tokenizer_filters)
        tokenizer.fit_on_texts(texts)
        sequences = tokenizer.texts_to_sequences(texts)

        # Get the vocabulary index
        word_index = { w:c for (w,c) in tokenizer.word_index.items() if c < max_nb_words}

        print("Found %s unique tokens." % len(word_index))

        # Fit the sequences into the maximum length
        data = pad_sequences(sequences, maxlen=max_sequence_length, padding="post",
        truncating="post")
        print("Shape of data tensor:", data.shape)

        # Transform the labels into a binary vector, with one element for each category
        mlb = MultiLabelBinarizer()
```

```
labels_cat = mlb.fit_transform(labels)

print("Shape of label tensor:", labels_cat.shape)

print("Found %s unique tokens." % len(word_index))
```

```
Out[7]: Found 39999 unique tokens.
        Shape of data tensor: (10000, 1000)
        Shape of label tensor: (10000, 22)
        Found 39999 unique tokens.
```

Glance at the vocabulary gathered by the tokenizer. Note that surface forms of multi-word expression use the + symbol to concatenate the single words.

```
In [8]: list(word_index.keys())[-20:]
```

```
Out[8]: ['moseri',
         'gilbert',
         'acanthocephalan',
         'obscurus',
         'rbcs',
         'inelastic+collision',
         'percutaneous+coronary+intervention',
         'october+2006',
         'pisaura',
         'mirabilis',
         'slits',
         'polaritons',
         'spps',
         'cell+division+cycle',
         'side+effect',
         'photochemical+reaction',
         'sulfosalicylaldehyde',
         'displace',
         'israeli+ibd',
         'electrophiles']
```

8.5.4 Surface form Embeddings

In the following we use pre-trained Vecsigrafo (surface form) embeddings learnt from SciGraph. Let us load Vecsigrafo embeddings:

```
In [9]: dimensions = 300

        def get_num_lines(file_path):
            fp = open(file_path, "r+")
            buf = mmap.mmap(fp.fileno(), 0)
            lines = 0
            while buf.readline():
                lines += 1
            return lines

        file_size = get_num_lines (embeddings_file)
        print("loading file"+embeddings_file)

        # Load the word embeddings
        file = open(embeddings_file, "r", encoding="utf-8", errors="surrogatepass")
        embeddings_index = {}

        with open(embeddings_file) as infile:
            for line in tqdm(infile, total = file_size, desc="Embeddings file") :
```

```
        values = line.split()
        wordlimit=len(values)-dimensions
        vector = np.asarray(values[wordlimit:], dtype='float32')
        word = values[0]
        index=0
        for value in values[1:wordlimit]:
            word = word + "+"+value
        embeddings_index[word] = vector

    print('Found %s word vectors.' % len(embeddings_index))
```

```
Out[9]: loading fileembeddings/row_embedding.tsv
        Embeddings file: 100% 692224/692224 [00:48<00:00, 14275.49it/s]
        Found 692214 word vectors.
```

Glance at some of the surface forms contained in the embeddings files

```
In [10]: l=[w for w,e in embeddings_index.items()]
         print(*l[10000:10010],sep='\n' )
```

```
Out[10]:
        irrigated
        sequelae
        chronic+diseases
        landolt-börnstein+homepage+volume+iv
        tick
        vte
        until+now
        bootstrap
        2+%
        authentic
```

8.5.5   Create the Embeddings Layer

The embedding layer is a matrix with all the embeddings corresponding to all the
vocabulary words. In other words, the rows are the words in the vocabulary and the
columns the embeddings dimensions.

```
In [11]: embedding_dimensions = len(list(embeddings_index.values())[0])

         #dictionary_size = len(word_index)
         dictionary_size = list(word_index.values())[-1]

         print("dim ->"+str(embedding_dimensions))
         print("word_index len ->"+str(len(word_index) + 1))
         print("last position in the dictionary ->"+ str(dictionary_size))

         embedding_matrix = np.zeros((dictionary_size + 1, embedding_dimensions))
         for word, i in word_index.items():
             embedding_vector = embeddings_index.get(word)
             if embedding_vector is not None:
                 # Words not found in the embedding index will be all-zeros
                 embedding_matrix[i] = embedding_vector

         # Create an embedding layer based on the embedding matrix
         # This layer is not trainable: the embeddings will not be changed
         embedding_layer = Embedding(dictionary_size + 1,
                                     embedding_dimensions,
                                     weights = [embedding_matrix],
                                     input_length = max_sequence_length,
                                     trainable = False)
```

```
Out[11]:    dim ->300
            word_index len ->40000
            last position in the dictionary ->39999
```

8.5.6   Train a Convolutional Neural Network

```
In [12]:precisions = []
        recalls = []
        f1s = []
        kfold = KFold(n_splits=10, shuffle=True)

        for train, test in kfold.split(data, labels_cat):
            # Define, train and validate the neural network model
            sequence_input = Input(shape=(max_sequence_length,), dtype="int32")
            embedded_sequences = embedding_layer(sequence_input)
            x = Conv1D(128, 5, activation="relu")(embedded_sequences)
            x = MaxPooling1D(5)(x)
            x = Conv1D(128, 5, activation="relu")(x)
            x = MaxPooling1D(5)(x)
            x = Conv1D(128, 5, activation="relu")(x)
            x = MaxPooling1D(35)(x)
            x = Flatten()(x)
            x = Dense(128, activation="relu")(x)
            preds = Dense(len(labels_index), activation="sigmoid")(x)
            model = Model(sequence_input, preds)
            model.compile(loss="binary_crossentropy", optimizer="rmsprop",
                          metrics=[categorical_accuracy])
            model.fit(data[train], labels_cat[train],
                      validation_data=(data[test],labels_cat[test]),
                      epochs=5, batch_size=128)

            # Evaluate the model assigning zeros and ones according to a threshold
            pred = model.predict(data[test], batch_size=128)
            pred[pred >= 0.5] = 1
            pred[pred < 0.5] = 0
            print(classification_report(labels_cat[test], pred, digits=4))
            precisions.append(precision_score(labels_cat[test], pred, average="weighted"))
            recalls.append(recall_score(labels_cat[test], pred, average="weighted"))
            f1s.append(f1_score(labels_cat[test], pred, average="weighted"))
        print("Precision: %.4f (+/- %.4f)" % (np.mean(precisions), np.std(precisions)))
        print("Recall: %.4f (+/- %.4f)" % (np.mean(recalls), np.std(recalls)))
        print("F1 Score: %.4f (+/- %.4f)" % (np.mean(f1s), np.std(f1s)))
```

```
Out[12]: Train on 9000 samples, validate on 1000 samples
Epoch 1/5
9000/9000 [==============================] - 8s 902us/step - loss: 0.1578
- categorical_accuracy: 0.3662 - val_loss: 0.1181 - val_categorical_accuracy: 0.5390
Epoch 2/5
9000/9000 [==============================] - 3s 299us/step - loss: 0.0991
- categorical_accuracy: 0.5926 - val_loss: 0.0959 - val_categorical_accuracy: 0.5740
Epoch 3/5
9000/9000 [==============================] - 3s 300us/step - loss: 0.0829
- categorical_accuracy: 0.6673 - val_loss: 0.0824 - val_categorical_accuracy: 0.6540
Epoch 4/5
9000/9000 [==============================] - 3s 301us/step - loss: 0.0734
- categorical_accuracy: 0.7080 - val_loss: 0.0835 - val_categorical_accuracy: 0.6620
Epoch 5/5
9000/9000 [==============================] - 3s 302us/step - loss: 0.0653
- categorical_accuracy: 0.7396 - val_loss: 0.0808 - val_categorical_accuracy: 0.6750
```

	precision	recall	f1-score	support
0	0.8595	0.9007	0.8796	292
1	0.8871	0.3929	0.5446	140
2	0.7864	0.7788	0.7826	104

3	1.0000	0.0526	0.1000	38
4	0.8214	0.6133	0.7023	75
5	0.6667	0.7742	0.7164	31
6	0.7861	0.8395	0.8119	162
7	0.0000	0.0000	0.0000	18
8	0.2857	0.3333	0.3077	6
9	0.7778	0.1061	0.1867	66
10	0.7105	0.5294	0.6067	51
11	0.0000	0.0000	0.0000	19
12	0.0000	0.0000	0.0000	6
13	0.4103	0.8889	0.5614	36
14	0.2857	0.2222	0.2500	9
15	0.0000	0.0000	0.0000	3
16	0.0000	0.0000	0.0000	10
17	0.0000	0.0000	0.0000	11
18	0.0000	0.0000	0.0000	1
19	0.0000	0.0000	0.0000	12
20	0.0000	0.0000	0.0000	0
21	0.0000	0.0000	0.0000	0
micro avg	0.7719	0.6211	0.6884	1090
macro avg	0.3762	0.2924	0.2932	1090
weighted avg	0.7442	0.6211	0.6351	1090
samples avg	0.6258	0.6290	0.6184	1090

8.6   Conclusion

In this chapter we presented an experimental study on the use of linguistic annotations for learning embeddings in domains, like the scientific one, which are particularly challenging in terms of multi-word expressions and rich lexicon. The experiments showed that embeddings learnt from linguistic annotations perform better than conventional space-separated tokens in all the evaluation tasks. Moreover, the experiments also show that the vocabulary, and its grammatical characteristics, used in each evaluation task is directly related to the quality of the embeddings trained using linguistic annotations.

Based on the results of this study there is clearly not a single type of linguistic annotation that always produces the best results consistently. However, it is possible to identify some patterns that may help practitioners to select the most suitable combinations for each specific task and dataset.

In the similarity task, learning embeddings based on lemmas generally works better given the high rate of nouns, named entities, and multi-word expressions contained in those datasets. On the contrary, in the analogy dataset there was a majority of syntactic analogies containing morphological variations of words that were better represented by single surface form embeddings. Jointly learning embeddings for concepts and either lemmas or surface forms improve the quality of each individual type of embeddings in all the evaluation tasks. In the word prediction task the embeddings learnt from linguistic annotations showed to better capture the distributional context of words in an unseen text compared to space-separated embeddings. In classification, jointly learnt lemma and surface form embeddings help to train the best classifier and, if grammar embeddings are also used, then the highest precision is also achieved.

In the future we will use linguistic annotations to enhance neural language models like BERT and assess whether such linguistic annotations can also help to learn better language models, improving performance when fine-tuned for various downstream tasks. In this regard, a path to explore addresses the extension of the current transformer-based architectures used to learn language models so that not only word pieces but also other kinds of linguistic annotations like the ones discussed in this chapter can be ingested and their effect propagated across the model.

Chapter 9
Aligning Embedding Spaces
and Applications for Knowledge Graphs

Abstract In previous chapters we have seen a variety of ways to train models to derive embedding spaces for words and concepts and other nodes in knowledge graphs. As you often do not have control over the full training procedure, you may find yourself with several embedding spaces which have (conceptually) overlapping vocabularies. *How can you best combine such embedding spaces?*. In this chapter we look at various techniques for aligning disparate embedding spaces. This is particularly useful in hybrid settings like when using embedding spaces for knowledge graph curation and interlinking.

9.1 Introduction

In the real world, NLP often can be used to extract value by analyzing texts in highly specific domains and settings, e.g. scientific papers on economics, computer science, or literature in English and Spanish. In order to build effective NLP pipelines, you may find yourself trying to combine embedding spaces with different but overlapping vocabularies. For example, some embedding spaces may be derived from generic but large corpora and only include words in the individual languages (English and Spanish). Other embeddings may be derived from smaller corpora which have been annotated with concepts, hence these embeddings include lemmas as well as concepts. Finally, other embeddings may have been derived directly from custom knowledge graphs for the specific domains. In many cases, you may even have separate knowledge graphs for different languages as they may have been built by different teams to address different goals in different markets (e.g., United States vs Latin America).

Since maintaining separate embedding spaces and KGs is expensive, ideally you want to reduce the number of embedding spaces and KGs or at least align them with each other so that downstream systems, e.g. a classifier or a rule-engine, that depend on a particular embedding space or KG can be reused.

© Springer Nature Switzerland AG 2020

J. M. Gomez-Perez et al., *A Practical Guide to Hybrid Natural Language Processing*, https://doi.org/10.1007/978-3-030-44830-1_9

In the symbolic world, KG curation and interlinking has been an active area of research for decades [52]. In the machine learning world, recent techniques have also been proposed. In this chapter we will briefly look at some of these techniques. In Sect. 9.2 we start by providing a brief overview of existing approaches that have been proposed; this section also provides an overview of how these techniques can be applied to a variety of problems. Then, in Sect. 9.3 we look at some basic embedding space alignment techniques and apply these to find a mapping between word embeddings in two different languages. We wrap this chapter with a practical exercise for finding alignments between old and modern English in Sect. 9.4.

9.2   Overview and Possible Applications

In one of the original word2vec papers [120], Mikolov et al. already proposed ways for aligning embeddings learned from corpora in different languages.[1] This initial technique relied on the assumption that the learned embedding spaces can be aligned via a linear transformation. Unfortunately, the geometry of embedding spaces is non-linear. Among others, the resulting spaces have issues such as hubness [45], which means that there are clusters of many words in the vocabulary which are very close to each other, i.e. the vectors are not evenly distributed across the space. It is unclear how embedding learning algorithms can be manipulated to avoid such areas or whether this is desirable.

Even if we managed to avoid geometrical issues with the embedding spaces, differences in the vocabularies and the underlying training data would result in words being assigned different areas in the space. Consider words *cat* in English and *gato* in Spanish, although both primarily refer to felines, in Spanish, this word is also commonly used to refer to a mechanical *jack* for lifting heavy objects. Therefore at the word level, the embedding for these words must occupy different areas in the space since we want the Spanish word to be close to other words related to the felines, but also close to words related to mechanical instruments (which is not the case for the English word). This means that in recent years, there have been many works looking at non-linear alignment of pre-computed embedding spaces [37, 70]. Of course, deep learning systems are really good at finding non-linear functions; therefore, it is also possible to tackle this alignment problem using standard machine learning. In Sect. 9.3.2 we look at how this can be implemented.

Most of the work in this area has traditionally focused on aligning multi-lingual word embeddings. However, the same techniques can be applied to a multitude of alignment problems. In the area of hybrid neural/symbolic systems, it is interesting to consider how embeddings can be used to improve knowledge graphs. As we have seen in previous chapters, KGs are crucial in knowledge management and complex information systems [135], but they are expensive to build and maintain.

---

[1]We will apply the proposed approach in Sect. 9.3.1.

This involves work finding whether there are new concepts that should be added to the KG (including deciding what the correct place should be in the graph, or whether there are already concepts which are related or even the same). Such KG curation also includes finding errors in the KG due to human input error or automatically derived knowledge. In the next subsections we provide an overview of work being done in these areas.

9.2.1 Knowledge Graph Completion

Knowledge graph completion (KGC) is the task of predicting whether an existing, incomplete, graph should add a vertex between two specific nodes. For example, in DBpedia, you may want to generate new links between pages and categories. Since KGs are often incomplete, several algorithms have been proposed to improve these representations by filling in its missing connections [125]. The main approach to solve this task is based on statistical models that use concept embeddings to represent entities and relations (for a complete overview, see Sect. 2.5).

Indeed, as introduced in Chap. 2, machine learning algorithms are able to learn these vector representations and use them to solve several tasks such as *entity resolution* or *link prediction* [188]. The most representative *translational* algorithms used to predict links in KG are the TransE model [25] and all its improvements TransH [190], TransR [106], TransD [54], TransM [57], TorusE [48], TranSparse [30], and TranSparse-DT [85]. *Bi-linear models* are RESCAL [131] and DISTMULT [193]. Extensions of DISTMULT are ComplEx [181], ComplEx-N3 [99].

A wide variety of algorithms are implemented using neural network architectures. Recurrent neural networks are used in IRN [165] and PTransE-RNN [105]. Instead, HolE [130] (*holographic embeddings*) is inspired by holographic models of associative memory [61]. Other neural network models are SME [24] (*semantic matching energy*), NTN model [171] (*neural tensor network*), and ProjE [167]. Models based on convolutional neural networks are ConvE [43], ConvKB [126], Conv-TransE [163], and CapsE [128].

Algorithms that implement language models to solve the KG completion task are presented in RDF2Vec [152] and KG-BERT [196]. Lastly, among the most recent research experiments can be mentioned CrossE [199], GRank [49], RotatE [174], SimplE [90], and TuckER [14].

Although embeddings for knowledge graphs are more suitable for this kind of task, word (and cross-modal) embeddings can also provide valuable input, since they involve information from complementary modalities in addition to the content of KG, like text or images.

9.2.2   Beyond Multi-Linguality: Cross-Modal Embeddings

In this section we show an example of an alignment technique used to align cross-modal embeddings at the conceptual level. Thoma et al. [179] describe in *Towards Holistic Concept Representations: Embedding Relational Knowledge, Visual Attributes, and Distributional Word Semantics* a way to combine KG, word, and visual embeddings. The authors use three pre-trained models for creating embeddings for the same concept:

- For the visual part they use Inception-v3 [176],
- For words they use word2vec, and
- For the KG they use DBpedia embeddings derived using TransE.

Then they average and concatenate these embeddings into a single embeddings for the concept using pre-existing mappings between ImageNet, WordNet, and DBpedia.

As part of their evaluations, the authors studied the problem of entity-type prediction (a subtask of knowledge graph completion), using a subgraph of DBpedia that provided coverage for the 1.538 concepts. Their results showed a clear improvement when using multi-modal embeddings, compared to just using the knowledge graph embeddings (see the original paper [179] for further details). In Chap. 10 of this book you will see another way of exploiting cross-modality.

9.3   Embedding Space Alignment Techniques

In this practical section we will implement a few alignment techniques. We start by implementing a simple linear alignment technique and later on expand to using non-linear alignments.

9.3.1   Linear Alignment

The most straightforward alignment between two embedding spaces can be achieved by using a *translation matrix*, as shown in [120]. Basically, a translation matrix W is such that $z=Wx$, where z is a vector belonging to the target vector space and x is the equivalent in the source.

To calculate the translation matrix, you need a **dictionary** that provides mappings for a subset of your vocabularies. You can then use existing linear algorithms to calculate the pseudo inverse. For optimal results, it is recommended to use very large corpora. If this is not possible, when using smaller corpora, it is a good idea to use parallel corpora so that the same words are encoded in similar ways.

In the following example, we use pre-trained embeddings for the most frequent 5K lemmas in the *United Nations parallel corpus* [202].

We first get the tutorial code and import the libraries we will be using.

```
In [ ]: %cd /content
        !git clone https://github.com/hybridnlp/tutorial.git
        from tutorial.scripts.swivel import vecs
        import os
        import pandas as pd
        import numpy as np
        from IPython.display import display
```

This should output something along the lines of:

```
/content
Cloning into 'tutorial'...
remote: Enumerating objects: 592, done.
remote: Total 592 (delta 0), reused 0 (delta 0), pack-reused 592
Receiving objects: 100% (592/592), 47.53 MiB | 39.32 MiB/s, done.
Resolving deltas: 100% (337/337), done.
```

Next, we load the pre-trained embeddings:

```
In [ ]: en_path = '/content/tutorial/datasamples/UNv1.0/en_lemma_5k/'
        es_path = '/content/tutorial/datasamples/UNv1.0/es_lemma_5k/'
        en_vecs = vecs.Vecs(en_path + 'vocab.txt',
                            en_path + 'vecs.bin')
        es_vecs = vecs.Vecs(es_path + 'vocab.txt',
                            es_path + 'vecs.bin')
```

This should produce something like:

```
Opening vector with expected size 5000 from file
  /content/tutorial/datasamples/UNv1.0/en_lemma_5k/vocab.txt
vocab size 5000 (unique 5000)
read rows
Opening vector with expected size 5000 from file
  /content/tutorial/datasamples/UNv1.0/es_lemma_5k/vocab.txt
vocab size 5000 (unique 5000)
read rows
```

Let us check a couple of words in each embedding space as we have done in previous chapters:

```
In [ ]: import pandas as pd
        pd.DataFrame(en_vecs.k_neighbors('knowledge'))
```

```
Out[ ]:      cosim          word
        0  1.000000     knowledge
        1  0.631812         skill
        2  0.603642      know-how
        3  0.574704       sharing
        4  0.537305   information
        5  0.536732      learning
        6  0.534542    innovation
        7  0.533146    technology
        8  0.531260 understanding
        9  0.513664       science
```

```
In [ ]: pd.DataFrame(es_vecs.k_neighbors('conocimiento'))
```

```
Out[ ]:      cosim           word
        0  1.000000   conocimiento
        1  0.780866  conocimientos
        2  0.603392        aptitud
        3  0.586549     comprensión
        4  0.557678     intercambio
        5  0.537809       capacidad
        6  0.526911        difusión
        7  0.525315      científico
        8  0.521962     información
        9  0.516031        fomentar
```

Besides the embeddings for English and Spanish, we also provide a **dictionary** that was generated automatically to map 1K English lemmas into Spanish.

```
In [ ]:
en2es_dict_path = '/content/tutorial/datasamples/UNv1.0/en2es-lemma-dict-1k.txt'
!head -n 5 {en2es_dict_path}
```

This will print the first five lines in the dictionary file:

```
be:ser
by:por conducto de
report:informe
state:estado
country:estado
```

Let us load the dictionary into a python object.

```
In [ ]: def load_dict(path, invert=False):
            result = {}
            with open(path, 'r') as lines:
                for line in lines:
                    (key, val) = line.split(':')
                    if invert:
                        result[val.strip('\n')] = key
                    else:
                        result[key] = val.strip('\n')
            return result

In [ ]: en2es = load_dict(en2es_dict_path)
        es2en = load_dict(en2es_dict_path, invert=True)
        len(en2es), len(es2en)

Out[ ]: (1000, 882)
```

We can see from the reported numbers that some English lemmas were mapped to the same Spanish lemma. Let us inspect some of the entries in the dictionary:

```
In [ ]: min = 5
        max = min + 5
        for en in list(en2es)[min:max]:
            print(en, '->', en2es[en])
        print('')
        for es in list(es2en)[min:max]:
            print(es, '->', es2en[es])
```

This should produce an output like:

```
also -> también
provide -> proporcionar
all -> todo
development -> intensificación
other -> otro

proporcionar -> supply
todo -> all
intensificación -> development
otro -> another
programar -> programme
```

In order to create the translation matrix, we need to create two **aligned** matrices:

- M_{en} will contain n English embeddings from the dictionary
- M_{es} will contain n Spanish embeddings from the dictionary

However, since the dictionary was generated automatically, it may be the case that some of the entries in the dictionary are not in the English or Spanish vocabularies. We only need the ids in the respective vecs:

```
In [ ]: en_dict_ids = []
        es_dict_ids = []
        es_dict_voc = []
        for es in es2en:
            es_id = es_vecs.word_to_idx.get(es)
            en_id = en_vecs.word_to_idx.get(es2en[es])
            if en_id and es_id :
                es_dict_voc.append(es)
                en_dict_ids.append(en_id)
                es_dict_ids.append(es_id)
        print(len(en_dict_ids), len(es_dict_ids))
```
477 477

From the 1K dictionary entries, only 477 pairs were both in the English and the Spanish vecs. In order to verify that the translation works, we can split this into 450 pairs that we will use to calculate the translation matrix and we keep the remaining 27 for testing:

```
In [ ]: train_en_dict_ids = en_dict_ids[:450]
        train_es_dict_ids = es_dict_ids[:450]
        test_en_ids = en_dict_ids[450:]
        test_es_ids = es_dict_ids[450:]
        print(len(train_en_dict_ids), len(test_en_ids))
```
450 27

Before calculating the translation matrix, let us verify that we need one. We chose three example words:

- *conocimiento* and *proporcionar* are in the training set,
- *tema* is in the test set.

For each word, we get:

- the five Spanish neighbors for the English vector,
- the five Spanish neighbors for the Spanish translation according to the dictionary.

```
In [ ]:
es_examples = ['conocimientos', 'proporcionar', 'tema']
from IPython.display import display
for i, es in enumerate(es_examples):
    print(es, '->', es2en[es])
    print('top k for Spanish vector in English vector space:')
    k = 5
    df1 = pd.DataFrame(en_vecs.k_neighbors(es_vecs.lookup(es), k=k,
        result_key_suffix='_es_vec'))
    print('top k for English translation in English vector space:')
    df2 = pd.DataFrame(en_vecs.k_neighbors(es2en[es], k=k,
        result_key_suffix='_en'))
    df3 = pd.concat([df1, df2], axis=1)
    display(df3)
```

This should output tables for the three search words which translate based on the dictionary to *knowledge*, *supply*, and *theme*. The tables should be similar to:

cosim_es_vec	word_es_vec	cosim_en	word_en
0.195447	jewish	1.000000	knowledge
0.194971	concept	0.631812	skill
0.185432	once	0.603642	know-how
0.183663	theme	0.574704	sharing
0.183211	cross	0.537305	information
0.175961	sister	0.536732	learning
0.175771	saudi	0.534542	innovation
0.172918	business	0.533146	technology
0.169612	united kingdom	0.531260	understanding
0.165519	pronounce	0.513664	science

cosim_es_vec	word_es_vec	cosim_en	word_en
0.222659	candidate	1.000000	supply
0.195560	arrest warrant	0.748887	supplies
0.187525	king	0.542984	spare part
0.185336	trading	0.537591	purchase
0.183837	selection	0.500451	fuel
0.183204	select	0.499277	medical
0.179192	commit	0.483074	transportation
0.179038	pool	0.482907	ration
0.174210	rule	0.480970	service
0.172928	business plan	0.470521	shortage

cosim_es_vec	word_es_vec	cosim_en	word_en
0.204613	accumulate	1.000000	theme
0.202783	per cent	0.695908	topic
0.190149	wood	0.636073	panel discussion
0.179899	go on	0.634660	thematic
0.174604	than	0.612211	cross-cutting
0.174476	ten	0.565744	sustainable development
0.171583	accumulation	0.562757	round table
0.167805	correctly	0.547525	discussion
0.167107	vision	0.541553	high-level
0.166883	scene	0.536971	focus

Clearly, simply using the Spanish vector in the English space does not work. Let us get the matrices:

```
In [ ]: m_en = en_vecs.vecs[train_en_dict_ids]
        m_es = es_vecs.vecs[train_es_dict_ids]
        print(m_en.shape, m_es.shape)
```

```
(450, 300) (450, 300)
```

As expected, we get two matrices of 450×300, since embeddings are of dimension 300 and we have 450 training examples. Now, we can calculate the translation matrix and define a method for linearly translating a point in the Spanish embedding space into a point in the English embedding space.

```
In [ ]: tm_es2en = np.linalg.pinv(m_es).dot(m_en)
        def es_vec_to_en_vec(es_vec):
            return np.dot(es_vec, tm_es2en)
        print(tm_es2en.shape)
```

```
(300, 300)
```

As we can see, the translation matrix is just a 300×300 matrix. Now that we have the translation matrix, Let us inspect the example words to see how it performs:

```
In [ ]:
for i, es in enumerate(es_examples):
    print(es, '->', es2en[es])
    k = 5
    print('\t%s: Spanish vector for "%s" in English vector space' % ('es_vec', es))
    df1 = pd.DataFrame(en_vecs.k_neighbors(es_vecs.lookup(es), k=k,
        result_key_suffix='_es_vec'))
    print('\t%s: English vector for "%s" in English vector space' % ('en', es2en[es]))
    df2 = pd.DataFrame(en_vecs.k_neighbors(es2en[es], k=k, result_key_suffix='_en'))
    print('\t%s: Spanish vector for "%s" *mapped* to English space using tm_es2en' % (
        'tm_es_vec', es))
    df3 = pd.DataFrame(en_vecs.k_neighbors(es_vec_to_en_vec(es_vecs.lookup(es)), k=k,
        result_key_suffix='_tm_es_vec'))
    df4 = pd.concat([df1,df2,df3], axis=1)
    display(df4)
```

The output with the three updated tables for the query words is shown below. For spacing we have omitted the first column as they are shown above. The first three columns are the same as above: results when looking up the Spanish vector directly in the English embedding space, the results when looking up the translation according to the dictionary. The final two columns are the results obtained using the translation matrix:

word_es_vec	cosim_en	word_en	cosim_tm_es_vec	word_tm_es_vec
jewish	1.000000	knowledge	0.894568	knowledge
concept	0.631812	skill	0.652778	skill
once	0.603642	know-how	0.597379	know-how
theme	0.574704	sharing	0.581842	technology
cross	0.537305	information	0.568328	capacity
sister	0.536732	learning	0.566806	information
saudi	0.534542	innovation	0.564072	technical
business	0.533146	technology	0.563809	sharing
united kingdom	0.531260	understanding	0.551107	scientific
pronounce	0.513664	science	0.545087	training

word_es_vec	cosim_en	word_en	cosim_tm_es_vec	word_tm_es_vec
candidate	1.000000	supply	0.742566	supply
arrest warrant	0.748887	supplies	0.577888	supplies
king	0.542984	spare part	0.442933	food
trading	0.537591	purchase	0.427956	provision
selection	0.500451	fuel	0.423716	provide
select	0.499277	medical	0.419686	service
commit	0.483074	transportation	0.419077	purchase
pool	0.482907	ration	0.411310	medical
rule	0.480970	service	0.411244	spare part
business plan	0.470521	shortage	0.401046	transportation

word_es_vec	cosim_en	word_en	cosim_tm_es_vec	word_tm_es_vec
accumulate	1.000000	theme	0.772404	theme
per cent	0.695908	topic	0.610194	topic
wood	0.636073	panel discussion	0.602442	session
go on	0.634660	thematic	0.585061	discussion
than	0.612211	cross-cutting	0.576319	thematic
ten	0.565744	sustainable development	0.550427	agenda
accumulation	0.562757	round table	0.549161	high-level
correctly	0.547525	discussion	0.539559	panel discussion
vision	0.541553	high-level	0.538621	meeting
scene	0.536971	focus	0.533962	discuss

As we can see, the results provided by the translation matrix are similar to what we would get if we had a perfect dictionary between the two languages. Note that these results also apply to words which are not in the seed vocabulary, like *tema*. Feel free to explore with other words.

9.3.2 Non-linear Alignment

The linear alignment seems to work OK for this set of embeddings. In our experience, when dealing with larger vocabularies (and vocabularies mixing lemmas and concepts), this approach does not scale, since the number of parameters is limited to the $d \times d$ translation matrix.

For such cases it is possible to follow the same approach, but instead of deriving a pseudo-inverse matrix, we train a neural network to learn a non-linear translation function. The non-linearities can be introduced by using activation functions such as ReLUs. See *Towards a Vecsigrafo: Portable Semantics in Knowledge-based Text Analytics* [40] for more details.

Instead of using simple neural networks, there are also libraries which attempt to learn mappings using mathematical and statistical analysis. In particular the MUSE library by Facebook AI[2] is worth trying out, especially since it provides both supervised and unsupervised methods with and without a seed dictionary.

9.4 Exercise: Find Correspondences Between Old and Modern English

The purpose of this exercise is to use two Vecsigrafos, one built on UMBC and WordNet and another one produced by directly running Swivel against a corpus of Shakespeare's complete works, to try to find correlations between old and modern English, e.g. "thou" -> "you", "dost" -> "do", "raiment" -> "clothing". For example, you can try to pick a set of 100 words in "ye olde" English corpus and see how they correlate to UMBC over WordNet.

Next, we prepare the embeddings from the Shakespeare corpus and load a UMBC Vecsigrafo, which will provide the two vector spaces to correlate.

9.4.1 Download a Small Text Corpus

First, we download the corpus into our environment. We will use the Shakespeare's complete works corpus, published as part of Project Gutenberg and publicly available.[3] If you have not cloned the tutorial yet, you can do so now:

```
In [ ]: !git clone https://github.com/hybridnlp/tutorial
```

---

[2]https://github.com/facebookresearch/MUSE.

[3]http://www.gutenberg.org.

Let us see if the corpus is where we think it is:

```
In [ ]: %cd tutorial/lit
        %ls

/content/tutorial/lit
coocs/  shakespeare_complete_works.txt  swivel/  wget-log
```

9.4.2   Learn the Swivel Embeddings over the Old Shakespeare Corpus

To do this, we assume you already downloaded and extracted a version of Swivel. See Sect. 4.4 for instructions on downloading and using Swivel.

9.4.2.1   Calculating the Co-occurrence Matrix

```
In [ ]: corpus_path = './lit/shakespeare_complete_works.txt'
        coocs_path = './lit/coocs'
        shard_size = 512
        freq=3
        !python ./scripts/swivel/prep.py --input={corpus_path} \
          --output_dir={coocs_path} \
          --shard_size={shard_size} \
          --min_count={freq}
```

This should output something like:

```
running with flags
...

vocabulary contains 23552 tokens
Computing co-occurrences: 140000..., last lid 1820, sum(1820)=188.256746
writing shard 2116/2116
Wrote vocab and sum files to /content/tutorial/lit/coocs
Wrote vocab and sum files to /content/tutorial/lit/coocs
done!
```

```
In [ ]: %ls {coocs_path} | head -n 10
```

The output should be similar to:

```
col_sums.txt
col_vocab.txt
row_sums.txt
row_vocab.txt
shard-000-000.pb
shard-000-001.pb
shard-000-002.pb
shard-000-003.pb
shard-000-004.pb
shard-000-005.pb
```

9.4.2.2   Learning the Embeddings from the Matrix

```
In [ ]: vec_path = './lit/vec/'
        !python ./scripts/swivel/swivel.py --input_base_path={coocs_path} \
            --output_base_path={vec_path} \
            --num_epochs=20 --dim=300 \
            --submatrix_rows={shard_size} --submatrix_cols={shard_size}
```

The output will show messages from TensorFlow and progress learning the embeddings. Next, we check the context of the "vec" directory. Should contain checkpoints of the model plus .tsv files for column and row embeddings.

```
In [ ]: os.listdir(vec_path)

Out[ ]: ['model.ckpt-0.index',
         'model.ckpt-42320.index',
         'model.ckpt-42320.data-00000-of-00001',
         'model.ckpt-0.data-00000-of-00001',
         'row_embedding.tsv',
         'checkpoint',
         'col_embedding.tsv',
         'model.ckpt-42320.meta',
         'model.ckpt-0.meta',
         'graph.pbtxt',
         'events.out.tfevents.1539004459.46972dad0a54']
```

Converting tsv to bin:

```
In [ ]: !python ./scripts/swivel/text2bin.py --vocab={vec_path}vocab.txt \
            --output={vec_path}vecs.bin \
            {vec_path}row_embedding.tsv \
            {vec_path}col_embedding.tsv
```

Which will result in:

```
executing text2bin
merging files ['./lit/vec/row_embedding.tsv', './lit/vec/col_embedding.tsv'] into
output bin
```

Finally, you can inspect the generated files with the following command:

```
In [ ]: %ls {vec_path}
```

9.4.2.3   Read Stored Binary Embeddings and Inspect Them

```
In [ ]:
import importlib.util
spec = importlib.util.spec_from_file_location("vecs", "./scripts/swivel/vecs.py")
m = importlib.util.module_from_spec(spec)
spec.loader.exec_module(m)
shakespeare_vecs = m.Vecs(vec_path + 'vocab.txt', vec_path + 'vecs.bin')
```

This will load the vectors you previously created:

```
Opening vector with expected size 23552 from file /content/tutorial/lit/vec/vocab.txt
vocab size 23552 (unique 23552)
read rows
```

Define a basic method to print the k nearest neighbors for a given word

```
In [ ]:
def k_neighbors(vec, word, k=10):
    res = vec.neighbors(word)
    if not res:
        print('%s is not in the vocabulary, try e.g. %s' % (
            word, vecs.random_word_in_vocab()))
    else:
        for word, sim in res[:10]:
            print('%0.4f: %s' % (sim, word))
```

And use it to explore the neighbors of some words. For example:

```
In [ ]: k_neighbors(shakespeare_vecs, 'strife')
```

```
1.0000: strife
0.4599: tutors
0.3981: tumultuous
0.3530: future
0.3368: daughters'
0.3229: cease
0.3018: Nought
0.2866: strike.
0.2852: War
0.2775: nature.
```

```
In [ ]: k_neighbors(shakespeare_vecs,'youth')
1.0000: youth
0.3436: tall,
0.3350: vanity,
0.2945: idleness.
0.2929: womb;
0.2847: tall
0.2823: suffering
0.2742: stillness
0.2671: flow'ring
0.2671: observation
```

9.4.3 Load Vecsigrafo from UMBC over WordNet

Next, you can adapt the steps presented in Sect. 10.4.3 to load Vecsigrafo embeddings trained on the UMBC corpus and see how they compare to the embeddings trained on the Shakespeare corpus in the previous section (Sect. 9.4.2).

Either follow the instructions given in Sect. 9.3.1 to find a linear alignment between the two embedding spaces or, attempt to use the MUSE library. The goal is to find correlation between terms in old English extracted from the Shakespeare corpus and terms in modern English extracted from UMBC. If you choose to try a linear alignment, you will need to generate a dictionary relating pairs of lemmas between the two vocabularies and use it to produce a pair of translation matrices to transform vectors from one vector space to the other. Then apply the k_neighbors method to identify the correlations.

9.4.4 Exercise Conclusion

This exercise proposes the use of Shakespeare's complete works and UMBC to provide the student with embeddings that can be exploited for different operations between the two vector spaces. Particularly, we propose to identify terms and their correlations over such spaces. If you want to contribute your solution, we encourage you to submit your solution as a pull request for the corresponding tutorial notebook on GitHub.[4]

9.5 Conclusion

This chapter presented the issue of dealing with multiple, overlapping embedding spaces. In practice, you will often need to build applications that need to combine models and results from different embedding spaces; which means sooner or later you may have to deal with this issue. In this chapter, we have presented a few methods to deal with this problem and provided practical exercises. We also highlighted specific applications of such embedding alignment approaches for more general problems such as knowledge graph completion, multi-linguality, and multi-modality.

---

[4]https://github.com/hybridnlp/tutorial/blob/master/06_shakespeare_exercise.ipynb.

Part III
Applications

Chapter 10
A Hybrid Approach to Disinformation Analysis

Abstract Disinformation and fake news are complex and important problems where natural language processing can play an important role in helping people navigate online content. In this chapter, we provide various practical tutorials where we apply several of the hybrid NLP techniques involving neural models and knowledge graphs introduced in earlier chapters to build prototypes that solve some of the pressing issues posed by disinformation.

10.1 Introduction

In this chapter we will build a prototype for a real-world application in the context of disinformation analysis. The prototype we will build shows how deep learning approaches for NLP and knowledge graphs can be combined to benefit from the best of both machine learning and symbolic approaches.

Among other things, we will see that injecting concept embeddings into simple deep learning models for text classification can improve such models. Similarly, we will show that the output of deep learning classifiers for identifying misinforming texts can be used as input for propagating such signals in social knowledge graphs.

This chapter has four main sections:

- Section 10.2 provides an overview of the area of disinformation detection and a high-level idea of what we want to build in the rest of the chapter,
- in Sect. 10.3 we build a database of claims that have been manually fact-checked as well as a neural index in order to, given a query sentence, find similar claims that have been previously fact-checked,
- in Sect. 10.4 we use hybrid word/concept embeddings to build a model for detecting documents which show signs of using deceptive language, and
- Section 10.5 shows how we can combine information provided by human and machine-learning based annotations and the structure of a knowledge graph to propagate credibility scores. This allows us to estimate the credibility of nodes for which we do not yet have direct evidence.

© Springer Nature Switzerland AG 2020

J. M. Gomez-Perez et al., *A Practical Guide to Hybrid Natural Language Processing*, https://doi.org/10.1007/978-3-030-44830-1_10

10.2   Disinformation Detection

In this first section, we provide some background information about what we understand by *disinformation* and provide context as to what we are trying to build. This section does not contain any practical steps.

10.2.1   Definition and Background

Disinformation and misinformation is, at the time of writing, a hot research topic. Although disinformation has always been a prevalent phenomenon in societies, it has gained further impact in the era of decentralized and social media. While disinformation used to require control of mass communication media, nowadays anyone with a social media account is able to spread (mis)information. Furthermore, it is much harder to control the spread of misinformation, since the threshold to spread messages has been greatly reduced. In this section we provide a summary of what has been published in academic research related to disinformation and discuss how it has impacted our design for what we will build in the remaining sections of this chapter.

To start, it is useful to have a precise definition of disinformation to inform our design. Fallis et al. [56] consider various philosophical aspects such as the relation (and differences) between disinforming and lying. The analysis identifies that when speaking about disinformation it is crucial to take into account the intention of the source as well as the communication process (besides the information being disseminated as such). The author arrives at the following formal definition for disinformation. You disinform X if and only if:

- You disseminate information
- You believe that p is false
- You foresee that X is likely to infer from the content of information I that p
- p is false
- It is reasonable for X to infer from the content of information I that p

While this seems to be a very good formal definition of disinformation, in practice, it poses several technical difficulties. The main difficulty is that current NLP systems only have limited support of propositional level analysis of the content: i.e. NLP systems can identify actors, entities, emotions, topics, and themes from the content of the information, but have very limited extraction of propositions. Even in these cases, current systems have trouble understanding negations within propositions, which makes it very hard to determine whether the proposition is true or not. For these reasons, when developing our disinformation detection module, we use a weakened form of detection: we assign a disinformation score to a document which represents the likelihood that the document contains disinformation. This opens the possibility to use statistical methods while not having to deal with propositional level knowledge.

On the other hand, recent transformer-based language models perform reasonably well in sentence semantic similarity tasks. Therefore, if we know the accuracy level of a particular claim p, such models should help us to find paraphrases or similar formulations for the same claim. In Sect. 10.3 we will look at how this can be done using sentence-level embeddings.

From the area of psychology, Porter et al. [145] state that deception is a "fundamental aspect of human behavior," since people admit to lying in 14% of emails, 27% of face-to-face interactions, and 37% of phone calls. From this point of view, it is also worth noting how difficult detection is, even using the best case scenario: having access to all modalities (visual, audio, linguistic style) and direct interaction (without time to conceal a lie) and spreading a high-stake lie, people are bad at detecting lies. There is little reason to believe that machines, which have a much narrower view of the information spectrum, can perform any better than humans. This view of disinformation further reinforces the design for our module: by choosing to report a discredibility score, we can expect many documents to include some form of discredibility, at the same time, the discredibility score is purely meant as a flag. Useful to draw the attention of human agents (e.g., journalists, law enforcement) to certain documents, but not enough to say for sure that a document contains disinformation.

One of the richest sources of information available to automated system is text-based documents. In the area of linguistics, Hancock et al. [75] have tried to detect lies by analyzing transcripts of dialogues, they take into account various linguistic cues that are associated with deception such as word quantity, pronoun use, emotion words, and cognitive complexity.

Disinformation detection is highly related to the area of fact-checking, which is in between purely scientific and industrial research, with several news organizations and internet companies doing intensive research in this area. A good review of the state of the art in this area by Babakar et al. [9] looks at fact-checking as a 4-stage problem. Spotting claims is the task of extracting claims given a large document. In terms of checking claims, [9] suggest three main ways to do this. Checking claims by reference could be achieved by using third-party KBs such as generic knowledge graphs like DBpedia, Wikidata, or EventKB. Recently, specialized knowledge graphs are also being constructed such as ClaimsKG [177]. In Sect. 10.3 we will implement a similar knowledge graph of claims that have previously been fact-checked by humans. Finally, checking claims contextually can be done by using metadata related to the documents and looking at the information we have about the document author or publisher; in Sect. 10.5 we look at a way to exploit this type of information.

When looking at contextual ways to check claims, or more generally, to assess how trustworthy is a source, given a social network another research area that is relevant is that of *network analysis*, which includes work by Ziegler et al. [201] and by Jiang et al. [86]. These approaches have been mostly applied (and require) knowledge about social networks (e.g., Facebook and Twitter relations between users). There are many types of such network analysis algorithms, but the idea is that: if you can give some of the users in the network a trust score, you can estimate how trustworthy other users are likely to be.

Finally, *computational text analysis* is being used to build complex models of disinformation, such as [8] and [2], which look at determining the attitude of a short text towards a claim. The idea is that this can be applied to social networks: if a first tweet makes a claim (or shares a document making a claim) and many of the replies are either pro or against something (presumably the claim), that is a good indicator that the initial tweet is controversial and may include disinformation.

10.2.2   Technical Approach

The scientific research presented suggests various directions in terms of implementing a disinformation detection system or component. In this section, we describe the design for such a component in technical terms. In the next sections we will go through the process of producing a prototype implementation for various subcomponents.

First of all, we should try to reuse information that is already published online by reputable fact-checkers as much as possible. This requires that we build a database of claims that have already been fact-checked. The main problem with current material available online is that fact-checking is a recent phenomenon and publishing the fact-checked claims in a format that is easy to collect is only now being adopted by the fact-checking community. Also, the number of fact-checkers worldwide is still relatively small and the number of claims that have been fact-checked is very small compared to the number of claims or sentences that can be found online. Therefore, we not only need a database of claims, but also a way to find relevant claims given a query sentence we may find online. In Sect. 10.3 we will build a prototype for such a database and index.

Besides the database of claims and annotations provided by fact-checkers, it would be useful to use automated classifiers to further provide input about the credibility of texts we find online. While the claim database works at the level of individual sentences, there are datasets available which can help us estimate the credibility of documents. In Sect. 10.4 we will look at how we can implement a model for detecting deceptive language. In reality, there are multiple such models we could implement that could look at different aspects of a document.

Finally, we assume that we can eventually build a database of documents and claims as well as sufficient metadata, e.g.:

- which sentences in a document are similar to claims in our database
- who is the author of a particular document
- where and when was a document published

Having such a database means we have a knowledge graph of documents, claims, persons (authors, reviewers, journalists, etc.), and publishers. Only for a fraction of all of these, we have reputable assessments of their accuracy (via fact-checkers). For a larger part of the nodes, we can also get estimates about the credibility of textual documents based on machine learning models. However, for the vast majority of the nodes in this graph, we will not have a reliable estimate about their credibility. Therefore, we need a method for propagating the knowledge that we have to other nodes in the graph. In Sect. 10.5 we will implement a prototype for such a subcomponent.

10.3 Application: Build a Database of Claims

In this section we will build a semantic search engine for fact-checked claims using BERT. The overall approach will be to:

1. create a fine-tuned version of BERT that is able to produce claim embeddings in such a way that semantically similar claims are close to each other in the embedding space and
2. use the resulting BERT claim encoder to create an index for a dataset of fact-checked claims that can be used to find claims.

10.3.1 Train a Semantic Claim Encoder

As explained above, we want to train a deep learning model that is capable of:

- Given a claim c, produce an embedding for that claim v_c in such a way that:
- if c_1 and c_2 are semantically similar (e.g., they are paraphrases of each other), then $f_{dist}(v_{c_1}, v_{c_2}) \approx 0$ for some distance function f_{dist}.

10.3.1.1 Training Dataset: STS-B

Fortunately, the SemEval[1] series of workshops/challenges have produced many tasks that aim to test exactly such *semantic similarity*.

Various of these SemEval task datasets have been bundled together[2] into what is known as the **STS-B: Semantic Textual Similarity Benchmark**, which is part of the GLUE collection of NLP benchmark datasets.[3]

STS-B consists of pairs of sentences which have been manually rated on a scale between 0 (no semantic similarity) and 5 semantically equivalent.

We can download and load the dataset into a pandas `DataFrame`:

```
In [ ]:
!wget http://ixa2.si.ehu.es/stswiki/images/4/48/Stsbenchmark.tar.gz
!tar -xzf Stsbenchmark.tar.gz
```

---

[1] https://aclweb.org/aclwiki/SemEval_Portal.

[2] http://ixa2.si.ehu.es/stswiki/index.php/STSbenchmark.

[3] https://gluebenchmark.com/tasks.

The output should be something like:

```
...
Stsbenchmark.tar.gz 100%[==================>]

... - 'Stsbenchmark.tar.gz' saved [409630/409630]
```

Unfortunately, we cannot use the standard pandas `read_csv` method, because some lines in the csv have additional fields which are not well documented and cause the pandas parser to fail. We implement our own:

```
In [ ]: import pandas as pd
def read_sts_csv(path, columns=['source', 'type', 'year', 'id',
        'score', 'sent_a', 'sent_b']):
  rows = []
  with open(path, mode='r', encoding='utf-8') as f:
    lines = f.readlines()
    print('Reading', len(lines), 'lines from', path)
    for lnr, line in enumerate(lines):
      cols = line.split('\t')
      assert len(cols) >= 7, 'line %s has %s columns instead of %s:\n\t%s' % (
          lnr, len(cols), 7, "\n\t".join(cols)
      )
      cols = cols[:7]
      assert len(cols) == 7
      rows.append(cols)
  result = pd.DataFrame(rows, columns=columns)
  # score is read as a string, so add a copy with correct type
  result['score_f'] = result['score'].astype('float64')
  return result

In [ ]: sts_dev_df = read_sts_csv('stsbenchmark/sts-dev.csv')
        sts_train_df = read_sts_csv('stsbenchmark/sts-train.csv')

Reading 1500 lines from stsbenchmark/sts-dev.csv
Reading 5749 lines from stsbenchmark/sts-train.csv
```

You can explore the dataset by looking at a small sample:

```
In [ ]: sts_train_df.sample(n=5)

Out[ ]:             source   ...   score_f
        3946     main-news   ...     2.400
        4836     main-news   ...     5.000
        4794     main-news   ...     2.600
        3281     main-news   ...     4.333
        5534     main-news   ...     1.800

        [5 rows x 8 columns]
```

10.3.1.2   Load the BERT Model

We will use BERT as a starting point, since it is the current state of the art in deep learning architectures for NLP tasks and is a representative of a Transformer-based deep learning model. The advantage of using BERT is that it has already been pre-trained on a large corpus, so we only need to *fine-tune it* on the STS-B dataset.

We will use the Huggingface PyTorch-Transformers[4] library as an interface to the BERT model. We can install it on our environment, as follows:

```
In [ ]: !pip install PyTorch-transformers
```

---

[4]https://github.com/huggingface/PyTorch-transformers.

This will install the required library and its dependencies. Next, we can import various libraries:

```
In [ ]: import torch
        from PyTorch_transformers import *
        import torch.nn.functional as F
```

And we can load BERT, which consists of two main parts:

1. The **model** itself, it:

   - receives as input a sequence of *token ids* according to a vocabulary defined during pre-training,
   - has an initial embedding layer that combines non-contextual and positional embeddings, and
   - *n* Transformer layers (seq 2 seq), which produce contextual embeddings for the input tokens of increasing complexity.

2. A **tokenizer** that converts the input sentence into a sequence of *token ids*

   - BERT (and other Transformer-based architectures) usually tokenizes the input sentence based on word pieces or subword units. See the **sentencepiece** repo[5] for more information about variants.
   - as part of the tokenization, BERT (and other models) adds special tokens that help the model understand where sentences begin and end; useful during training.

BERT has two main variants: `base` (has 12 layers) and `large` (24 layers). In this notebook we will use the `bert-base-cased` variant, but feel free to explore alternative pre-trained models.[6] We load the tokenizer and the model as follows:

```
In [ ]: bert_model_name = 'bert-base-cased'
tokenizer = BertTokenizer.from_pretrained(bert_model_name,
    do_lower_case=False)
bert = BertModel.from_pretrained(bert_model_name,
    output_hidden_states=True)
if torch.cuda.is_available():
  bert = bert.cuda()
```

Now that we have the Bert tokenizer and model, we can pass it a sentence, but we need to define which output of BERT we want to use as the sentence embedding. We have several options:

- Input sequences are pre-prended with a special token `[cls]` which is meant to be used for classification of the sequence.
- We can combine the final layer of contextual embeddings, e.g. by concatenating or pooling them (take the sum or average).
- We can combine any combination of layers (e.g., the final four layers).

Also, since the model and tokenizer need to be used together, we define a `tok_model` dict that we can pass to the function. We will split the implementation into the following methods:

---

[5]https://github.com/google/sentencepiece.

[6]https://huggingface.co/transformers/pretrained_models.html.

1. `pad_encode` creates token ids of a uniform sequence length for a given sentence.
2. `tokenize` tokenizes a batch of sentences and produces a tensor that can be fed to the model.
3. `embedding_from_bert_output` produces a sentence embedding from the outputs of a BERT model, based on some encoding strategy.
4. `calc_sent_emb` receives a list of sentences and produces a tensor of sentence embeddings. Orchestrates by calling the other methods.

```
In [ ]:
def pad_encode(text, tokenizer, max_length=50):
    """creates token ids of a uniform sequence length for a given sentence"""
    tok_ids = tokenizer.convert_tokens_to_ids(tokenizer.tokenize(text))
    tok_ids2 = tokenizer.add_special_tokens_single_sentence(tok_ids)
    att_mask = [1 for _ in tok_ids2]
    n_spectoks = len(tok_ids2) - len(tok_ids)
    if len(tok_ids2) > max_length: # need to truncate
        #print('Truncating from', len(tok_ids2))
        n_to_trunc = len(tok_ids2) - max_length
        tok_ids2 = tokenizer.add_special_tokens_single_sentence(tok_ids[:-n_to_trunc])
        att_mask = [1 for _ in tok_ids2]
    elif len(tok_ids2) < max_length: # need to pad
        padding = []
        for i in range(len(tok_ids2), max_length):
            padding.append(tokenizer.pad_token_id)
        att_mask += [0 for _ in padding]
        tok_ids2 = tok_ids2 + padding
    assert len(tok_ids2) == max_length
    assert len(att_mask) == max_length
    return tok_ids2, att_mask

def tokenize_batch(sentences, tok_model, max_len=50, debug=False):
    assert type(sentences) == list
    encoded = [pad_encode(s, tokenizer=tok_model['tokenizer'],
                          max_length=max_len)[0] for s in sentences]
    att_masks = [pad_encode(s, tokenizer=tok_model['tokenizer'],
                          max_length=max_len)[1] for s in sentences]
    input_ids = torch.tensor(encoded)
    att_masks = torch.tensor(att_masks)
    if debug: print(input_ids.shape)

    if torch.cuda.is_available():
        input_ids = input_ids.cuda()
        att_masks = att_masks.cuda()
    return input_ids, att_masks

def embedding_from_bert_output(bert_output, strategy="pooled"):
    """Given the output tensor from a BERT model, return embeddings for the batch.
    :param strategy can be:
        1. a tuple ("reduce_mean_layer", n) where n is the index of the layer in model
        2. a tuple ("layer", n)
        2. "pooled" returns the default pooled embedding for the model. E.g. for BERT,
           this is the last output for token [CLS]
    """
    assert len(bert_output) == 3, "Expecting 3 outputs, make sure to output hidden states"
    last_layer, pooled, hidden_layers = bert_output
    if strategy == "pooled":
        return pooled
    if not type(strategy) == tuple:
        raise ValueError("Expecting a tuple, but found %s " % (type(strategy)))
    strat_name, strat_val = strategy
    if strat_name == "reduce_mean_layer":
        layer_index = strat_val
        layer_to_pool = hidden_layers[layer_index]
        pooled_layer = torch.sum(layer_to_pool, dim=1) / (layer_to_pool.shape[1] + 1e-10)
```

```
      if debug: print('pooled layer %s of %s' % (layer_index, len(hidden_layers)),
                         pooled_layer.shape,
                         'pooled from', layer_to_pool.shape)
      return pooled_layer
  if strat_name == "layer":
    layer_index = strat_val
    return hidden_layers[layer_index]
  raise ValueError("Unsupported strategy %s " % strategy)

def calc_sent_emb(sentences, tok_model, strategy="pooled", seq_len=50, debug=False):
  """Returns the embeddings for the input sentences, based on the `tok_model`
  :param tok_model dict with keys `tokenizer` and `model`
  :param strategy see `embedding_from_bert_output`
  """
  input_ids, att_masks = tokenize_batch(sentences, tok_model, debug=debug,
    max_len=seq_len)

  model = tok_model['model']
  model.eval() # needed to deactivate any Dropout layers

  with torch.no_grad():
    model_out = model(input_ids, attention_mask=att_masks)

  return embedding_from_bert_output(model_out, strategy)
```

The pre-trained BERT model is optimized to predict masked tokens or the next sentence in a pair of sentences. This means that we cannot expect the pre-trained BERT to perform well in our task of semantic similarity. Therefore, we need to fine-tune the model. In PyTorch, we can do this by defining a PyTorch Module as follows:

```
In [ ]:
class BERT_Finetuned_Encoder(torch.nn.Module):
  def __init__(self,
                bert_model_name='bert-base-cased',
                pooling_strategy="pooled",
                train_from_layer=6,
                seq_len=50):
    super(BERT_Finetuned_Encoder, self).__init__()
    tokenizer = BertTokenizer.from_pretrained(bert_model_name, do_lower_case=False)
    bert_model=BertModel.from_pretrained(bert_model_name, output_hidden_states=True)
    if train_from_layer is not None:
      assert type(train_from_layer) == int
      assert train_from_layer >= 0 and train_from_layer <= len(bert_model.encoder.layer)
      print("Freezing wordpiece embeddings")
      for param in bert_model.embeddings.parameters():
        param.requires_grad = False
      for i, layer in enumerate(bert_model.encoder.layer):
        if i < train_from_layer:
          print("Freezing layer", i)
          for param in layer.parameters():
            param.requires_grad = False
        else:
          print("Trainable layer", i)
      print("Trainable pooling layer") # pooler layer is always trained
    self.tokenizer = tokenizer
    self.bert_model = bert_model
    self.pooling_strategy = pooling_strategy
    self.seq_len = seq_len

    # power func parameters
    self.min_val = 0.8
    self.k = 1.0
```

```python
def forward(self, sentences, sents_to_compare=None):
  assert type(sentences) == list
  if sents_to_compare is not None:
    return self.predict_similarity(sentences, sents_to_compare)
  else:
    return self.encode(sentences)

def predict_encoded_similarity(self, semembs_as, semembs_bs):
  cosim = F.cosine_similarity(semembs_as, semembs_bs) # (batch_size, 1)
  # make prediction a value between 0.0 and 1.0
  return self.power_fun_cosim2predfn(cosim)

def predict_similarity(self, sentsA, sentsB):
  """Predict pairwise similarity between two lists of sentences
  Predicted values range from 0 (no similarity) and 1(semantically equal)
  """
  assert type(sentsB) == list
  assert len(sentsB) == len(sentsA)
  #print('semembs_as', type(semembs_as))
  return self.predict_encoded_similarity(
      self.encode(sentsA), self.encode(sentsB))

def power_fun_cosim2predfn(self, cosim, min_val=0.8, k=25, steps=100):
  """Converts a cosine similarity result onto a value in range [0.0, 1.0] using
  a non-linear mapping. This is useful because cosine similarities between
  vectors in embedding spaces are usually skewed towards a specific value."""
  assert min_val < 1.0
  cosim_step = (1.0-min_val)/steps
  val = torch.clamp(cosim, min=min_val, max=1.0)
  step_i = (val - min_val)/cosim_step
  pred = (step_i/steps)**k
  assert len(pred.shape) == 1, pred.shape # (batch_size)
  return torch.clamp(pred, min=0.0, max=1.0)

def linear_cosim2predfn(self, cosim):
  """Alternative mapping from a cosim tensor to a prediction range
  Use `power_fun_cosim2predf` instead since it better aligns with the
  distribution of cosine similarities.
  """
  return (cosim + 1.0) / 2.0 # make prediction a value between 0.0 and 1.0

def encode(self, sentences):
  # essentially the same as calc_sent_emb, but without explicitly setting model
  # for evaluation (since we can be in training mode)
  input_ids, att_masks = tokenize_batch(sentences, {"tokenizer": self.tokenizer,
      "model": self.bert_model}, max_len=self.seq_len)
  model_out = self.bert_model(input_ids, attention_mask=att_masks)
  return embedding_from_bert_output(model_out, self.pooling_strategy)
```

10.3.1.3 Define Training Method

We are now ready to define the main training loop. This is a pretty standard loop for PyTorch. The main thing here is that we:

- iterate over batches of the STS-B dataset and produce encodings for both sentences,
- then we calculate the cosine similarity between the two encodings and map that onto a predicted similarity score in a range between 0 and 1, and
- we use the STS-B value (normalized to the same range) to define a loss and train the model.

```
In [ ]:
import time
import copy
from scipy import stats

def train_semantic_encoder(semantic_encoder,
                           dataloaders,
                           optimizer, criterion, scheduler, num_epochs=25,
                           device="cuda"):
  """ Trains a semantic encoder model
  :param semantic_encoder maps a list of sentences onto a semantic embedding
    space
  :param dataloaders a dict with keys `train` and `val`, the values must be PyTorch
    DataLoader instances providing STS-B item batches
  :param cosim2predfn a function that maps a cosine similarity metric onto a
    value in the range [0.0, 1.0]
  """
  since = time.time()

  assert getattr(semantic_encoder, 'state_dict', None) is not None, "No model to train!!"

  def run_epoch(phase):
    """Execute a single epoch through the datasets.
    :param phase can be `train` or `val`
    returns a result dict with `loss` and `pearson`
    """

    def run_step(sts_itembatch):
      """Execute a step in this epoch, i.e. process a batch.
      Returns a triple with the batch (loss int, labels floats, predictions floats)
      """
      #print('sts_itembatch', type(sts_itembatch))
      sent_as = [item['sent_a'][0] for item in sts_itembatch]
      sent_bs = [item['sent_b'][0] for item in sts_itembatch]
      assert type(sent_as[0]) == str
      label_scores = torch.tensor([float(item['score'][0]) for item in sts_itembatch])

      label_scores = label_scores.to(device)
      optimizer.zero_grad()

      with torch.set_grad_enabled(phase == 'train'):
        pred_score = semantic_encoder(sent_as, sent_bs)
        loss = criterion(pred_score, label_scores/5.0) # make label between 0.0 and 1.0

        if phase == 'train':
          loss.backward()
          optimizer.step()
      return loss.item(), label_scores.tolist(), pred_score.tolist()

    # run epoch:
    if phase == 'train':
      semantic_encoder.train()   # Set model to training mode
    else:
      semantic_encoder.eval()    # Set to evaluate mode (important for Dropout layers)

    running_loss, _label_scores, _pred_scores = 0.0, [], []
    for sts_itembatch in dataloaders[phase]: # Iterate over data in epoch
      batch_loss, batch_labels, batch_preds = run_step(sts_itembatch)
      running_loss += batch_loss # * len(sts_itembatch) # update state
      _label_scores += batch_labels
      _pred_scores += batch_preds

    if phase == 'val' and scheduler is not None:
      scheduler.step(running_loss) #

    epoch_loss = running_loss / len(dataloaders[phase])
    epoch_correl, p_val = stats.pearsonr(_label_scores, _pred_scores)
```

```
print('{} Loss: {:.4f}, Pearson: r={:.4f} p={:.4f} n={}'.format(
    phase, epoch_loss, epoch_correl, p_val, len(_label_scores)))
return {"loss": epoch_loss,
        "pearson": {"r": epoch_correl,
                    "p": p_val,
                    "n": len(_label_scores)}}  # run_epoch

def is_better_result(current_best, new_val):
  return new_val['pearson']['r'] > current_best['pearson']['r']

best_weights = copy.deepcopy(semantic_encoder.state_dict())
print('Validating initial model')
best_val = run_epoch('val')  # run a validation epoch before the actual training

for epoch in range(num_epochs):
  print('Epoch {}/{}'.format(epoch, num_epochs - 1))
  print('-' * 10)

  # Each epoch has a training and validation phase
  for phase in ['train', 'val']:
    epoch_result = run_epoch(phase)
    if phase == 'val' and is_better_result(best_val, epoch_result):
      best_val = epoch_result   # store state of best model
      best_weights = copy.deepcopy(semantic_encoder.state_dict())
  print()

time_elapsed = time.time() - since
print('Training complete in {:.0f}m {:.0f}s'.format(
    time_elapsed // 60, time_elapsed % 60))
print('Best loss: {:4f} correl: {:.4f}'.format(best_val['loss'],
                                               best_val['pearson']['r']))

# load best model weights
semantic_encoder.load_state_dict(best_weights)
return semantic_encoder
```

The `train_semantic_encoder` method expects the data to be provided via PyTorch's Dataset[7] and DataLoader[8] mechanisms. So, we need to wrap our STS train and dev sets (at the moment a pandas `DataFrame`) into classes:

```
In [ ]:
import torch.utils.data
import math

class STSDataset(torch.utils.data.Dataset):
  def __init__(self, sts_df, batch_size=20):
    super(STSDataset).__init__()
    self.sts_df = sts_df
    self.batch_size = batch_size

  def __len__(self):
    n_sents = self.sts_df.shape[0]
    n_batch = n_sents/self.batch_size
    result = math.ceil(n_batch)
    return result

  def __getitem__(self, index):
    begin, end = index*self.batch_size, (index+1)*self.batch_size
    values = self.sts_df[begin:end].values
    result = []
    for row in values:
```

---

[7]https://PyTorch.org/docs/stable/data.html?highlight=dataset#torch.utils.data.Dataset.

[8]https://PyTorch.org/docs/stable/data.html#torch.utils.data.DataLoader.

```
    result.append({col: row[i] for i, col in enumerate(self.sts_df.columns.values)})
    return result

def __iter__(self):
  raise NotImplementedError()
  #return self.sts_df.iterrows()
```

We are now ready to train the model, by defining the data loaders:

```
In [ ]: dataloaders = {
    'train': torch.utils.data.DataLoader(STSDataset(sts_train_df, batch_size=64)),
    'val':   torch.utils.data.DataLoader(STSDataset(sts_dev_df,   batch_size=64))}
```

We also create the model to fine-tune:

```
In [ ]: bert_finetuned_semencoder = BERT_Finetuned_Encoder(train_from_layer=8)
        if torch.cuda.is_available():
            bert_finetuned_semencoder = bert_finetuned_semencoder.cuda()
```

To train the model we need to create the optimizer. In the next lines we also start the training (this can take about 10 min in a regular GPU):

```
In [ ]: # using learning rate for fine-tuning as suggested in BERT paper
adam_optim = AdamW(
    [p for p in bert_finetuned_semencoder.parameters() if p.requires_grad],
    lr=5e-5)

bert_finetuned_semencoder = train_semantic_encoder(
    bert_finetuned_semencoder,
    dataloaders=dataloaders,
    optimizer=adam_optim,
    criterion=torch.nn.SmoothL1Loss(reduction='sum'),
    scheduler=torch.optim.lr_scheduler.ReduceLROnPlateau(adam_optim),
    num_epochs=5)
```

The output should be something like:

```
Validating initial model
val Loss: 5.2647, Pearson: r=0.1906 p=0.0000 n=1500
Epoch 0/5
...
Epoch 5/5
...
Training complete in 9m 20s
Best loss: 1.688949 correl: 0.7717
```

Note that before training, we validate using the dev part of the dataset and achieve $r_{pearson} = 0.1906$, which is what the pre-trained BERT produces. This shows that the default BERT embeddings are not very *semantic*, or at least not well-aligned with what humans regard as semantic similarity. The fine-tuned model should achieve a $r_{pearson}$ score close to 0.8, which is much better aligned with human ratings.

10.3.2   Create a Semantic Index of Embeddings and Explore It

Now that we have a model for producing semantic embeddings of sentences, we can create a simple semantic index and define methods to populate and query it.

Our semantic index is simply a Python `dict` with fields `sent_encoder`, our semantic encoder, and `sent2emb` a `dict` from the sentence to its embedding.

```
In [ ]:    index = {
                'sent_encoder': bert_finetuned_semencoder,
                'sent2emb': {}
           }
```

10.3.2.1   Define a Method to Populate the Index

```
In [ ]:
def populate_index(sentence_generator, index, debug=False):
  """Populates a semantic sentence index with sentences from a generator
  Returns the `index` with the new embeddings."""

  def add_batch(index, batch):
    with torch.no_grad():
      batch_embs = index['sent_encoder'](batch)
      assert batch_embs.shape[0] == len(batch)
      for i, s in enumerate(batch):
        index['sent2emb'][s] = batch_embs[i]

  index['sent_encoder'].eval() # put into evaluation mode

  batch = []
  for snr, sentence in enumerate(sentence_generator):
    batch.append(sentence)
    if len(batch) > 32:
      if debug: print('At', snr, "processing batch..", )
      add_batch(index, batch)
      batch = []
  if len(batch) > 0:
    add_batch(index, batch)

  print('Index now has', len(index['sent2emb']), 'sentences')
  return index
```

And a method to iterate over all the STS-B items in one of the `DataFrames` we loaded at the beginning of the section:

```
In [ ]: def sts_df_as_sent_generator(df):
            """Create a sentence generator given a DataFrame with STS-B rows"""
            for rnr, row in df.iterrows():
              for s in [row['sent_a'], row['sent_b']]:
                yield s
```

10.3.3   Populate Index with STS-B dev

```
In [ ]: index = populate_index(sts_df_as_sent_generator(sts_dev_df), index)
```

```
Index now has 2941 sentences
```

To explore the newly populated dataset, we can define a method to find the top k elements in the index for a given sentence:

```
In [ ]:
def find_most_similar(text, semb_index, k=5):
  text_emb = semb_index['sent_encoder']([text])
```

```
if len(text_emb.shape) == 2:
  text_emb = text_emb[0]
assert len(text_emb.shape) == 1, "" + str(text_emb.shape)
s2cosim = {}
for s, s_emb in semb_index['sent2emb'].items():
  assert len(s_emb.shape) == 1, "%s" % (s_emb.shape)
  s2cosim[s] = F.cosine_similarity(text_emb, s_emb, dim=0).item()
sorted_s2cosim = sorted(s2cosim.items(), key=lambda kv: kv[1], reverse=True)
results = [{'sentence': kv[0], 'cosim': kv[1]} for kv in sorted_s2cosim[:k]]
return pd.DataFrame(results).sort_values(by=['cosim'], ascending=False)
```

In the remainder of this section, we will explore the dataset using some examples. We start by querying for a sentence related to news about traffic accidents in China:

```
In [ ]: find_most_similar("3 traffic accidents leave 56 dead in China", index)
```

cosim	Sentence
0.993376	'Around 100 dead or injured' after China earthquake
0.992287	Hundreds dead or injured in China quake\n
0.990573	Floods leave six dead in Philippines
0.989853	At least 28 people die in Chinese coal mine explosion\n
0.989653	Heavy rains leave 18 dead in Philippines\n

Let us explore another example on the topic of the economic output of the USA:

```
In [ ]:
find_most_similar("US' industrial output growth slows to 9.2 pct in July", index)
```

This should print a table along the lines of:

cosim	Sentence
0.9973	North American markets grabbed early gains Monday morning,...
0.9969	North American markets finished mixed in directionless trading Monday ...
0.9966	S. Korean economic growth falls to near 3-year low\n
0.9963	The blue-chip Dow Jones industrial average .DJI climbed 164 points, ...
0.9962	That took the benchmark 10-year note US10YT=RR down 9/32, its yield ...

10.3.4   Create Another Index for a Claims Dataset

So the results on STS-B dev seem OK. Now, let us create an index for a dataset of checked facts from Data Commons' Fact Check.[9] First, let us download the dataset:

```
In [ ]:
!wget https://storage.googleapis.com/datacommons-feeds/claimreview/latest/data.json
!mv data.json datacommons-factcheck.json

... - 'data.json' saved [9801768/9801768]
```

---

[9]https://www.datacommons.org/factcheck/download#research-data.

10.3.5   Load Dataset into a Pandas DataFrame

This dataset is formatted using JSON-LD, so we can simply parse it as JSON

```
In [ ]:
import json
with open('datacommons-factcheck.json', mode='r', encoding='utf-8') as f:
  js_datafeed = json.load(f)
```

We can also define a method to convert the nested Python `dict` into a pandas `DataFrame`. We are not interested in all the data in the json feed, so we only populate a few columns.

```
In [ ]:
def load_datacommons_feed_df(js_datafeed):
  claims = []
  for feed_item in js_datafeed['dataFeedElement']:
    claim_items = feed_item.get('item', [])
    if claim_items is None:
      claim_items = []
    for claim_in_feed in claim_items:
      claim = claim_in_feed.get('claimReviewed', None)
      if claim is not None:
        claims.append({
          'claimReviewed': claim,
          'reviewed_by': claim_in_feed.get('author', {}).get('name', 'unknown'),
          'review_altName': claim_in_feed.get('reviewRating', {}).get('alternateName', ""),
          'claim_date': claim_in_feed.get('itemReviewed', {}).get('datePublished', None),
          'claimed_by': claim_in_feed.get('itemReviewed', {}).get('author', {}).get('name',
            None)
        })
  return pd.DataFrame(claims)
```

```
In [ ]: claims_df = load_datacommons_feed_df(js_datafeed)
        claims_df.shape
```

```
Out[ ]: (5647, 5)
```

```
In [ ]: claims_df.sample(n=4)
```

This should display a table along the lines of:

claimReviewed	reviewed_by
"Sumber daya yang sebelumnya dikuasai asing, berhasil …"	Tempo.co
The push by Assembly Democrats seeking Americans with …	PolitiFact
The EU sends Northern Ireland €500 million a year	Fact Check NI
A claim that herdsmen walked into the terminal …	DUBAWA

10.3.5.1   Create Claim Iterator

The datafeed contains claims in many different languages, and since our model only works for English, we should only take into account English claims. Unfortunately, the feed does not include a language tag, so we need to filter the feed.

```
In [ ]: !pip install langdetect
```

Your output should be similar to:

```
Collecting langdetect
...
Installing collected packages: langdetect
Successfully installed langdetect-1.0.7

In [ ]:
from langdetect import detect

def is_english(sentence):
  try:
    return detect(sentence) == 'en'
  except:
    # e.g. because sentence is empty
    return False

In [ ]:
is_english("Tin bài hàng đầu"), is_english(
    "Claim: H Raja and S Ve Sekher supporters fighting in BJP TN office"), is_english(" ")

Out[ ]: (False, True, False)

In [ ]:
def claims_df_english_row_generator(df):
  for rnr, row in df.iterrows():
    s = row['claimReviewed']
    if is_english(s):
      yield row.to_dict()
```

10.3.5.2 Populate a claim_index

We could just reuse the `populate_index` method we defined above, but we already have some interesting metadata about reviewed claims, so it is interesting to keep those in our index. Therefore, we define a slightly modified version:

```
In [ ]:
def populate_claim_index(claim_rows, index, debug=False):
    """Populates a semantic sentence index with sentences from a generator
    Returns the `index` with the new embeddings."""

    def add_batch(index, batch):
      sent_batch = [row['claimReviewed'] for row in batch]
      with torch.no_grad():
        batch_embs = index['sent_encoder'](sent_batch)
      assert batch_embs.shape[0] == len(batch)
      for i, s in enumerate(sent_batch):
        index['sent2emb'][s] = batch_embs[i]
        index['claim_meta'][s] = {
            'review_altName': batch[i]['review_altName'],
            'reviewed_by': batch[i]['reviewed_by']
            }

    index['sent_encoder'].eval() # put into evaluation mode

    batch = []
    for snr, claim_row in enumerate(claim_rows):
      batch.append(claim_row)
      if len(batch) > 32:
        if debug: print('At', snr, "processing batch..", )
        add_batch(index, batch)
        batch = []
    if len(batch) > 0:
```

```
    add_batch(index, batch)

  print('Index now has', len(index['sent2emb']), 'sentences')
  return index
In [ ]:
claim_index = {
      'sent_encoder': bert_finetuned_semencoder,
      'sent2emb': {},
      'claim_meta': {}
  }
In [ ]: claim_index = populate_claim_index(
             claims_df_english_row_generator(claims_df), claim_index)
```

You should see something like:

```
Index now has 3519 sentences
```

10.3.5.3   Explore Dataset

We define a custom version of `find_most_similar` to display more relevant info about the most similar claims:

```
In [ ]:
def find_most_similar_claim(text, claim_index, k=5):
  text_emb = claim_index['sent_encoder']([text]) # shape (1, emb_dim)
  s2cosim = {}
  s2pred = {}
  for s, s_emb in claim_index['sent2emb'].items():
    ts_emb = s_emb.unsqueeze(0) # shape (1, emb_dim)
    pred_score = claim_index['sent_encoder'].predict_encoded_similarity(
        text_emb, ts_emb)

    s2pred[s] = pred_score.item()


  sorted_s2pred = sorted(s2pred.items(), key=lambda kv: kv[1], reverse=True)
  claim_meta = claim_index['claim_meta']
  results = [{'claim': claim,
              'true?': claim_meta[claim].get('review_altName', '??'),
              'reviewed by': claim_meta[claim].get('reviewed_by', "??"),
              'pred': pred

             } for claim, pred in sorted_s2pred[:k]]

  return pd.DataFrame(results).sort_values(by=['pred'], ascending=False)
```

Now we can use this method to explore the neighboring claims in the index for query sentences. First, we try to find claims related to a claim about Brexit

```
In [ ]: find_most_similar_claim("Most people in UK now want Brexit", claim_index)
```

The results in our run are depicted in Table 10.4. The numerical value for the predictions is what the model outputs, i.e. the range is between 0 (not similar at all) and 1 (semantically very similar). In this case, we see that a related, but narrower, claim was found with semantic similarity score of 0.76. Other results are below 0.7 and are not about Brexit at all.

Next, we use a query claim related to Northern Ireland and EU contributions:

Table 10.4 Claim search results for "Most people in UK now want Brexit"

Claim	Pred	True?
77% of young people in the UK don't want Brexit	0.766	Inaccurate. Polls for Great Britain show support from those aged 18–24 for remaining in the EU at between 57% and 71%; for Northern Ireland, betwe...
A claim that says Nigeria's Independent National Electoral Commission [INEC] ban phones at polling stations	0.681	The claim that INEC has banned the use of phones and cameras at polling stations is NOT ENTIRELY FALSE. While you are not banned from going to the...
The DUP at no point has ever agreed to establish an Irish Language Act with the UK government, with the Irish government, with Sinn Féin or anybod...	0.636	Accurate. The St Andrew's Agreement committed the UK Government to an Irish Language Act, but subsequent legislation compelled the Northern Ire-lan...
Says there could be a potential mass shooting at a Walmart nearby	0.636	It's a widespread hoax message
Claim video claiming Muslims protesting in Kashmir after Eid prayers against article 370 dissolution	0.630	FALSE

```
In [ ]: find_most_similar_claim(
    "Northern Ireland receives yearly half a billion pounds from the European Union",
    claim_index)
```

Table 10.5 Claim search results for "Northern Ireland receives yearly half a billion pounds from the European Union"

Claim	Pred	True?
The EU sends Northern Ireland €500 million a year	0.752	ACCURATE WITH CONSIDERATION. The €500 million figure quoted by the SDLP is substantiated by European Commission figures for EU regional funding of...
Northern Ireland is a net contributor to the EU	0.747	This claim is false, as we estimate that Northern Ireland was a net recipient of £74 million in the 2014/15 financial year. Others have claimed th...
Arlene Foster, the leader of the Democratic Unionist Party, said that the party delivered "an extra billion pounds" for Northern Ireland	0.736	ACCURATE. The £1bn is specific to the jurisdiction of Northern Ireland and is in addition to funding pledged as a result of the Stormont House Agr...
Northern Ireland were once net contributors of revenue to HM Treasury	0.732	True, up until the 1930s. But data show that Northern Ireland has run a fiscal deficit since 1966. The most recent figure, from 2013–2014, is a subv...

The results are shown in Table 10.5. In this case we see that the first two matches are on topics with scores above 0.74. Notice that the only words that appear both in the query and the result for the top result are "Northern Ireland." The rest of the top 5 is still about money and Northern Ireland, but no longer relate to the EU, even though the similarity score is still in the range of [0.73, 0.74].

Let us explore a final example: **State hacking of digital devices.**

```
In [ ]: find_most_similar_claim("The state can hack into any digital device",
    claim_index)
```

Table 10.6 Claim search results for "The state can hack into any digital device"

Claim	Pred	True?
Claim: All computers can now be monitored by government agencies	0.704	Fact Crescendo Rating: True
Claim unrelated image from a random FB profile used to recirculate an old incident	0.641	FALSE
EVMs hacked by JIO network	0.641	Fact Crescendo Rating: False
A video of Mark Zuckerberg shows him talking about controlling "billions of people's stolen data" to control the future	0.633	Pants on Fire

The results are shown in Table 10.6. In this final example, we see that one claim has score above 0.7 and is again a related claim. The other results are somewhat related, but not directly relevant to assess the query claim.

10.3.6   Conclusion of Building a Database of Claims

In this practical section we saw how transformer-based models like BERT can be used to create a neural index for finding semantically similar claims. The examples shown above provide an indication of how well these models work. Although in many cases the model is able to find semantically similar sentences, simply having a cosine similarity does not provide enough information about whether the most similar claims found are truly a paraphrasing of the query sentence or not. Fortunately, the `ClaimReview` format provides a rich context which can help us to collect more information about the credibility of the claims and documents. In the next sections we will see how to analyze longer documents to get a prediction about whether they contain deceptive language (Sect. 10.4) and how we can combine different signals about the credibility of a document (typically obtained from human-annotated claims or machine learning models) and the knowledge graph structure provided by `ClaimReviews` to estimate the credibility of other nodes in the graph (Sect. 10.5).

10.4   Application: Fake News and Deceptive Language Detection

In this section, we will look at how we can use hybrid embeddings in the context of NLP tasks. In particular, we will see how to use and adapt deep learning architectures to take into account hybrid knowledge sources to classify documents.

10.4.1   Basic Document Classification Using Deep Learning

First, we will introduce a basic pipeline for training a deep learning model to perform text classification.

10.4.1.1   Dataset: Deceptive Language (Fake Hotel Reviews)

As a first dataset, we will use the deceptive opinion spam dataset.[10]   See the exercises below for a couple of more challenging datasets on fake news detection.

This corpus contains:

- 400 truthful positive reviews from TripAdvisor
- 400 deceptive positive reviews from Mechanical Turk
- 400 truthful negative reviews from Expedia, Hotels.com, Orbitz, Priceline, TripAdvisor, and Yelp
- 400 deceptive negative reviews from Mechanical Turk

The dataset is described in more detail in the papers by Ott et al. [133, 134]. For convenience, we have included the dataset as part of our GitHub tutorial repository.

```
In [ ]: %ls
```

```
In [ ]: %cd /content
        !git clone https://github.com/hybridnlp/tutorial
        !head -n2 /content/tutorial/datasamples/deceptive-opinion.csv
```

The last two lines show that the dataset is distributed as a comma-separated-value file with various fields. For our purposes, we are only interested in fields:

- `deceptive`: this can be either *truthful* or *deceptive*
- `text`: the plain text of the review

The other fields: `hotel` (name), `polarity` (positive or negative), and `source` (where the review comes from) are not relevant for us in this practical section.

Let us first load the dataset in a format that is easier to feed into a text classification model. What we need is an object with fields:

- `texts`: an array of texts
- `categories`: an array of textual tags (e.g., *truthful* or *deceptive*)

---

[10]http://myleott.com/op-spam.html.

- `tags`: an array of integer tags (the categories)
- `id2tag`: a map from the integer identifier to the textual identifier for the tag

The following cell produces such an object:

```
In [ ]: import pandas as pd # for handling tables a DataFrames
        import tutorial.scripts.classification as clsion # for text classification

In [ ]:
hotel_df = pd.read_csv('/content/tutorial/datasamples/deceptive-opinion.csv',
        names=["deceptive", "hotel", "polarity", "source", "text"])
hotel_df = hotel_df[1:].reset_index() # first row is the header, so remove
hotel_wnscd_df = pd.read_csv(
    '/content/tutorial/datasamples/deceptive-opinion.tlgs_wnscd',
    names=['text_tlgs_wnscd'])
hotel_df = pd.concat([hotel_df, hotel_wnscd_df], axis=1)
raw_hotel_ds = clsion.read_classification_corpus(
    hotel_df, text_fields=['text'], tag_field='deceptive')
raw_hotel_wnscd_ds = clsion.read_classification_corpus(
    hotel_df, text_fields=['text_tlgs_wnscd'], tag_field='deceptive')
```

The previous cell has in fact loaded two versions of the dataset:

- `raw_hotel_ds` contains the actual texts as originally published and
- `raw_hotel_wnscd_ds` provides the WordNet disambiguated `tlgs` tokenization (see Sect. 6.5 on Vecsigrafo for more details about this format).

This is needed because we do not have a Python method to automatically disambiguate a text using WordNet, so we provide this disambiguated version as part of the GitHub repo for this tutorial.

```
In [ ]: hotel_df[:5]
```

We can print a couple of examples from both datasets.

```
In [ ]: clsion.sanity_check(raw_hotel_ds)
```

```
In [ ]: clsion.sanity_check(raw_hotel_wnscd_ds)
```

Cleaning the raw text often produces better results; we can do this as follows:

```
In [ ]: cl_hotel_ds = clsion.clean_ds_texts(raw_hotel_ds)
        clsion.sanity_check(cl_hotel_ds)
```

10.4.1.2   Tokenize and Index the Dataset

As we said above, the raw datasets consist of `texts`, `categories`, and `tags`. There are different ways to process the texts before passing it to a deep learning architecture, but typically they involve:

- **Tokenization**: How to split each document into basic forms which can be represented as vectors. In this section we will use tokenizations which result in words and synsets, but there are also architectures that accept character-level or n-grams of characters.

- **Indexing** of the text: In this step, the tokenized text is compared to a **vocabulary** (or, if no vocabulary is provided, it can be used to create a vocabulary), a list of words, so that you can assign a unique integer identifier to each token. You need this so that tokens will then be represented as embedding or vectors in a matrix. So having an identifier will enable you to know which row in the matrix corresponds to which token in the vocabulary.

The `clsion` library, included in the tutorial GitHub repo, already provides various indexing methods for text classification datasets. In the next cell we apply *simple indexing*, which uses white-space tokenization and creates a vocabulary based on the input dataset.

```
In [ ]: csim_hotel_ds = clsion.simple_index_ds(cl_hotel_ds)
```

Since the vocabulary was created based on the dataset, all tokens in the dataset are also in the vocabulary. In the next sections, we will see examples where embeddings are provided during indexing.

The following cell prints a couple of characteristics of the indexed dataset:

```
In [ ]: print(
            'vocab size:', len(csim_hotel_ds['vocab_embedding']['w2i']),
            'dim:', csim_hotel_ds['vocab_embedding']['dim'],
            'vectors:', csim_hotel_ds['vocab_embedding']['vecs'])
```

The output allows us to see that the vocabulary is quite small (about 11K words). By default, it specifies that the vocabulary embeddings should be of dimension 150, but no vectors are specified. This means the model can assign random embeddings to the 11K words.

10.4.1.3 Define the Experiment to Run

The `clsion` allows us to specify experiments to run: given an indexed dataset, we can execute a text classification experiment by specifying various hyperparameters as follows:

```
In [ ]: experiment1 = {
            'hotel_csim': {
                'indexed_dataset': csim_hotel_ds,
                'executor': clsion.execute_experiment,
                'hparams': clsion.merge_hparams([
                    clsion.common_hparams, clsion.biLSTM_hparams,
                    clsion.calc_hparams(csim_hotel_ds),
                    {
                        'epochs': 20
                    }
                ])
            }
        }
```

Under the hood, the library creates a bidirectional LSTM model as requested (the library also can create other model architectures such as convolutional NNs).

Since our dataset is fairly small, we do not need a very deep model. A fairly simple bidirectional LSTM should be sufficient. The generated model will consist of the following layers:

- The **input layer**: is a tensor of shape $(l,)$, where l is the number of tokens for each document. The empty second parameter will let us pass the model different number of input documents, as long as they all have the same number of tokens.
- The **embedding layer** converts the each input document (a sequence of word ids) into a sequence of embeddings. Since we are not yet using pre-computed embeddings, these will be generated at random and trained with the rest of parameters in the model.
- The **lstm layer**s: one or more bidirectional LSTMs. Explaining these in detail is out of the scope of this tutorial. Suffice it to say, each layer goes through each embedding in the sequence and produces a new embedding taking into account previous and posterior embeddings. The final layer only produces a single embedding, which represents the full document.
- The **dense layer**: is a fully connected neural network that maps the output embedding of the final layer to a vector of 2 dimensions which can be compared to the manual labeled tag.

Finally, we can run our experiment using the `n_cross_val` method. Depending on whether you have an environment with a GPU this can be a bit slow, so we only train a model once. (In practice, model results may vary due to random initializations, so it is usually a good idea to run the same model several times to get an average evaluation metric and an idea of how stable the model is.)

```
In [ ]: ex1_df, ex1_best_run = clsion.n_cross_val(experiment1, n=1)
```

The first element of the result is a DataFrame containing test results and a record of the used parameters. You can inspect it by executing:

```
In [ ]: ex1_df
```

10.4.1.4   Discussion

Bidirectional LSTMs are really good at learning patterns in text and were one of the most used architectures before transformer-based architectures were introduced. However, this way of training a model will tend to overfit the training dataset. Since our dataset is fairly small and narrow: it only contains texts about hotel reviews, we should not expect this model to be able to detect fake reviews about other products or services. Similarly, we should not expect this model to be applicable to detecting other types of deceptive texts such as fake news.

The reason why such a model is very tied to the training dataset is that even the vocabulary is derived from the dataset: it will be biased towards words (and senses of those words) related to hotel reviews. Vocabulary about other products, services, and topics cannot be learned from the input dataset.

Furthermore, since no pre-trained embeddings were used, the model had to learn the embedding weights from scratch based on the signal provided by the "deceptive" tags. It did not have an opportunity to learn more generic relations between words from a wider corpus.

For these reasons it is a good idea to use pre-trained embeddings as we show in the following sections.

10.4.2   Using HolE Embeddings

In this section we use embeddings learned using `HolE` and trained on WordNet 3.0. As we have seen in the previous chapters, in particular Chap. 5, such embeddings capture the relations specified in the WordNet knowledge graph. As such, synset embeddings tend to encode useful knowledge. However, lemma embeddings tend to be of poorer quality when learned from the KG (compared to learning them from large corpora of text).

10.4.2.1   Download the Embeddings

Execute the following cell to download and unpack the embeddings. If you recently executed previous notebooks as part of this tutorial, you may still have these in your environment.

```
In [ ]:
!mkdir /content/vec/
%cd /content/vec/
!wget https://zenodo.org/record/1446214/files/wn-en-3.0-HolE-500e-150d.tar.gz
!tar -xzf wn-en-3.0-HolE-500e-150d.tar.gz

In [ ]: %ls /content/vec/
```

10.4.2.2   Load the Embeddings and Convert to the Format Expected by `clsion`

The provided embeddings are in `swivel`'s binary + vocab format. However, the `clsion` library expects a different Python data structure. Furthermore, it will be easier to match the lemmas in the dataset to plain text rather than the `lem_<lemma_word>` format used to encode the HolE vocabulary; hence, we need to do some cleaning of the vocabulary. This occurs in the following cells:

```
In [ ]:
import tutorial.scripts.swivel.vecs as vecs
vocab_file = '/content/vec/wn-en-3.1-HolE-500e.vocab.txt'
holE_voc_file = '/content/vec/wn-en-3.1-HolE-500e.clean.vocab.txt'
with open(holE_voc_file, 'w', encoding='utf_8') as wf:
  with open(vocab_file, 'r', encoding='utf_8') as f:
    for word in f.readlines():
      word = word.strip()
      if not word:
        continue
      if word.startswith('lem_'):
        word = word.replace('lem_', '').replace('_', ' ')
      print(word, file=wf)
vecbin = '/content/vec/wn-en-3.1-HolE-500e.tsv.bin'
wnHolE = vecs.Vecs(holE_voc_file, vecbin)
```

```
In [ ]:
import array
import tutorial.scripts.swivel.vecs as vecs

def load_swivel_bin_vocab_embeddings(bin_file, vocab_file):
    vectors = vecs.Vecs(vocab_file, bin_file)
    vecarr = array.array(str('d'))
    for idx in range(len(vectors.vocab)):
        vec = vectors.vecs[idx].tolist()[0]
        vecarr.extend(float(x) for x in vec)
    return {'itos': vectors.vocab,
            'stoi': vectors.word_to_idx,
            'vecs': vecarr,
            'source': 'swivel' + bin_file,
            'dim': vectors.vecs.shape[1]}
wnHolE_emb=load_swivel_bin_vocab_embeddings(vecbin, holE_voc_file)
```

Now that we have the WordNet HolE embedding in the right format, we can explore some of the "words" in the vocabulary:

```
In [ ]: wnHolE_emb['itos'][150000] # integer to string
```

10.4.2.3   Tokenize and Index the Dataset

As in the previous case (see Sect. 10.4.1.2), we need to tokenize the raw dataset. However, since we now have access to the WordNet HolE embeddings, it makes sense to use the WordNet disambiguated version of the text (i.e., raw_hotel_wnscd_ds). The clsion library already provides a method index_ds_wnet to perform tokenization and indexing using the expected WordNet encoding for synsets.

```
In [ ]: wn_hotel_ds = clsion.index_ds_wnet(raw_hotel_wnscd_ds, wnHolE_emb)
```

```
In [ ]: print(
            'vocab size:', len(wn_hotel_ds['vocab_embedding']['w2i']),
            'dim:', wn_hotel_ds['vocab_embedding']['dim'])
```

The above produces an ls tokenization of the input text, which means that each original token is mapped to both a lemma and a synset. The model will then use both of these to map each token to the concatenation of the lemma and synset embedding. Since the WordNet HolE has 150 dimensions, each token will be represented by a 300 dimensional embedding (the concatenation of the lemma and synset embedding).

10.4.2.4   Define the Experiment and Run

We define the experiment using this new dataset as follows, the main change is that we do not want the embedding layer to be trainable, since we want to maintain the knowledge learned via HolE from WordNet. The model should only train the LSTM and dense layers to predict whether the input text is deceptive or not.

```
In [ ]: experiment2 = {
            'hotel_wn_holE': {
                'indexed_dataset': wn_hotel_ds,
                'executor': clsion.execute_experiment,
                'hparams': clsion.merge_hparams([
```

```
                    clsion.common_hparams, clsion.biLSTM_hparams,
                    clsion.calc_hparams(wn_hotel_ds),
                    {
                        'epochs': 20,
                        'emb_trainable': False
                    }
                ])
            }
        }
```

```
In [ ]: ex2_df, ex2_best_run = clsion.n_cross_val(experiment2, n=1)
```

Like before, you can inspect the results of training as follows:

```
In [ ]: ex2_df
```

10.4.2.5   Discussion

Although the model performs worse than the `csim` version, we can expect the model to be applicable to closely related domains. The hope is that, even if words did not appear in the training dataset, the model will be able to exploit embedding similarities learned from WordNet to generalize the "deceptive" classification.

10.4.3   Using Vecsigrafo UMBC WNet Embeddings

10.4.3.1   Download the Embeddings

If you executed previous notebooks, you may already have the embedding in your environment.

```
In [ ]:
%mkdir /content/umbc
%mkdir /content/umbc/vec
full_precomp_file = 'vecsigrafo_umbc_tlgs_ls_f_6e_160d_row_embedding.tar.gz'
full_precomp_url = 'https://zenodo.org/record/1446214/files/' + full_precomp_file
full_precomp_targz = '/content/umbc/vec/tlgs_wnscd_ls_f_6e_160d_row_embedding.tar.gz'
!wget {full_precomp_url} -O {full_precomp_targz}
```

```
In [ ]: !tar -xzf {full_precomp_targz} -C /content/umbc/vec/
        full_precomp_vec_path = '/content/umbc/vec/vecsi_tlgs_wnscd_ls_f_6e_160d'
```

Since the embeddings were distributed as `tsv` files, we can use the `load_tsv_embeddings` method. Training models with all 1.4M vocab elements requires a lot of RAM, so we limit ourselves to only the first 250K vocab elements (these are the most frequent lemmas and synsets in UMBC).

```
In [ ]:
def simple_lemmas(word):
  if word.startswith('lem_'):
    return word.replace('lem_', '').replace('_', ' ')
  else:
    return word

wn_vecsi_umbc_emb = clsion.load_tsv_embeddings(
```

```
full_precomp_vec_path + '/row_embedding.tsv',
max_words=250000,
word_map_fn=simple_lemmas
)
```

10.4.3.2   Tokenize and Index Dataset

```
In [ ]:
wn_v_umbc_hotel_ds = clsion.index_ds_wnet(raw_hotel_wnscd_ds, wn_vecsi_umbc_emb)

In [ ]: print(
            'vocab size:', len(wn_v_umbc_hotel_ds['vocab_embedding']['w2i']),
            'dim:', wn_v_umbc_hotel_ds['vocab_embedding']['dim'])
```

10.4.3.3   Define the Experiment and Run

```
In [ ]: experiment3 = {
            'hotel_wn_vecsi_umbc': {
                'indexed_dataset': wn_v_umbc_hotel_ds,
                'executor': clsion.execute_experiment,
                'hparams': clsion.merge_hparams([
                    clsion.common_hparams, clsion.biLSTM_hparams,
                    clsion.calc_hparams(wn_v_umbc_hotel_ds),
                    {
                        'epochs': 20,
                        'emb_trainable': False
                    }
                ])
            }
        }

In [ ]: ex3_df, ex3_best_run = clsion.n_cross_val(experiment3, n=1)

In [ ]: ex3_df
```

10.4.4   Combine HolE and UMBC Embeddings

One of the advantages of embeddings as a knowledge representation device is that they are trivial to combine. In the previous experiments we have tried to use lemma and synset embeddings derived from:

- WordNet via HolE: these embeddings *encode* the knowledge derived from the structure of the WordNet knowledge graph
- the shallow connectivity disambiguation of the UMBC corpus: these embeddings *encode* the knowledge derived from trying to predict the lemmas and synsets from their contexts.

Since the embeddings encode different types of knowledge, it can be useful to use both embeddings at the same time when passing them to the deep learning model, as shown in this section.

10.4.4.1   Combine the Embeddings

We use the `concat_embs` method, which will go through the vocabularies of both input embeddings and concatenate them. Missing embeddings from one vocabulary will be mapped to the zero vector. Note that since `wnHolE_emb` has dimension 150 and `wn_vecsi_umbc_emb` has dimension 160, the resulting embedding will have dimension 310. (Besides concatenation, you could also experiment with other merging operations such as summation, subtraction, or averaging of the embeddings.)

```
In [ ]: wn_vh_emb = clsion.concat_embs(wn_vecsi_umbc_emb, wnHolE_emb)

In [ ]:
synsets = [w for w in wn_vh_emb['itos'] if w.startswith('wn31_')]
print('vocab has ', len(wn_vh_emb['itos']), '"words"', len(synsets),
    'of which are synsets')

In [ ]: wn_vh_hotel_ds = clsion.index_ds_wnet(raw_hotel_wnscd_ds, wn_vh_emb)

In [ ]: experiment4 = {
            'hotel_wn_vecsi_umbc': {
                'indexed_dataset': wn_vh_hotel_ds,
                'executor': clsion.execute_experiment,
                'hparams': clsion.merge_hparams([
                    clsion.common_hparams, clsion.biLSTM_hparams,
                    clsion.calc_hparams(wn_vh_hotel_ds),
                    {
                        'epochs': 20,
                        'emb_trainable': False
                    }
                ])
            }
        }

In [ ]: ex4_df, _ = clsion.n_cross_val(experiment4, n=1)
```

10.4.5   Discussion and Results

In this section we have shown how to use different types of embeddings as part of a deep learning text classification pipeline. We have not performed detailed experiments on the WordNet-based embeddings used in this notebook and, because the dataset is fairly small, the results can have quite a bit of variance depending on the initialization parameters. However, we have performed studies based on Cogito-based embeddings. The tables below show some of our results:

The first set of results corresponds to experiment 1 above. We trained the embeddings but explored various tokenizations strategies.

Code	μ acc	σ acc	tok	vocab	emb	Trainable
sim	0.8200	0.023	ws	ds	random	y
tok	0.8325	0.029	keras	ds	random	y
csim	0.8513	0.014	clean ws	ds	random	y
ctok	0.8475	0.026	clean keras	ds	random	y

As discussed above, this approach produces the best test results, but the trained models are very specific to the training dataset. The current practice when using BiLSTMs or similar architectures is therefore to use pre-trained word-embeddings (although this is now being replaced by simply fine-tuning transformer-based architectures, which we leave as an exercise). fastText embeddings tend to yield the best performance. We got the following results:

Code	μ acc	σ acc	tok	vocab	emb	Trainable
ft-wiki	0.7356	0.042	ws	250K	`wiki-en.vec`	n
ft-wiki	0.7775	0.044	clean ws	250K	`wiki-en.vec`	n

Next, we tried using HolE embedding trained on sensigrafo 14.2, which had very poor results:

Code	μ acc	σ acc	tok	vocab	emb	Trainable
HolE_sensi	0.6512	0.044	cogito s	250K	`HolE-en.14.2_500e`	n

Next we tried Vecsigrafo trained on both Wikipedia and UMBC, either using only lemmas, only syncons, or both lemmas and syncons. Using both lemmas and syncons always proved better.

Code	μ acc	σ acc	tok	vocab	emb	Trainable
v_wiki_l	0.7450	0.050	cogito l	250K	`tlgs_ls_f_6e_160d`	n
v_wiki_s	0.7363	0.039	cogito s	250K	`tlgs_ls_f_6e_160d`	n
v_wiki_ls	0.7450	0.032	cogito ls	250K	`tlgs_ls_f_6e_160d`	n
v_umbc_ls	0.7413	0.038	cogito ls	250K	`tlgs_ls_6e_160d`	n
v_umbc_l	0.7350	0.041	cogito l	250K	`tlgs_ls_6e_160d`	n
v_umbc_s	0.7606	0.032	cogito s	250K	`tlgs_ls_6e_160d`	n

Finally, like in the experiment 4 above, we concatenated Vecsigrafos (both lemmas and syncons) with HolE embeddings (only syncons, since lemmas tend to be poor quality). This produced the best results with a mean test accuracy of 79.31%. This is still lower than `csim`, but we expect this model to be more generic and applicable to other domains besides hotel reviews.

Code	μ acc	σ acc	tok	vocab	emb	Trainable
vw_H_s	0.7413	0.033	cogito s	304K	`tlgs_lsf,HolE`	n
vw_H_ls	0.7213	0.067	cogito ls	250K	`tlgs_lsf,HolE`	n
vw_ls_H_s	0.7275	0.041	cogito ls	250K	`tlgs_lsf,HolE`	n
vu_H_s	0.7669	0.043	cogito s	309K	`tlgs_ls,HolE`	n
vu_ls_H_s	0.7188	0.043	cogito ls	250K	`tlgs_ls,HolE`	n
vu_ls_H_s	0.7225	0.033	cogito l	250K	`tlgs_ls,HolE`	n

Code	μ acc	σ acc	tok	vocab	emb	Trainable
vu_ls_H_s	0.7788	0.033	cogito s	250K	tlgs_ls, HolE	n
vu_ls_H_s	0.7800	0.035	cl cog s	250K	tlgs_ls, HolE	n
vu_ls_H_s	0.7644	0.044	cl cog l	250K	tlgs_ls, HolE	n
vu_ls_H_s	**0.7931**	0.045	cl cog ls	250K	tlgs_ls, HolE	n
vu_ls_H_s	0.7838	0.028	cl cog s	500K	tlgs_ls, HolE	n
vu_ls_H_s	?	?	cl cog l	500K	tlgs_ls, HolE	n
vu_ls_H_s	0.7819	0.035	cl cog ls	500K	tlgs_ls, HolE	n

Finally, we started experimenting with contextual embeddings, in particular ELMo, described in [107]. However, we did not manage to reproduce good results with this approach.

Code	μ acc	σ acc	tok	vocab	emb	Trainable
elmo	0.7250	0.039	nltk sent	∞	elmo-5.5B	n (0.1 dropout)
elmo	0.7269	0.038	nltk sent	∞	elmo-5.5B	n (0.5 dropout, 20ep)

We have not yet tried applying more recent contextual embeddings, but based on results reported elsewhere we assume these should produce very good results. We encourage you to use the Huggingface transformer library introduced back in Sect. 3.4.2.1 to fine-tune BERT for this task.

In this practical section, we looked at what is involved in creating a model to detect deceptive language. We saw that combining embeddings from different sources can improve the performance of the model. We also saw that when training such models, there is always a consideration about how well the model will perform with data that is different from the training set.

In Sect. 10.3 we created a database of claims which have already been reviewed by human fact-checkers. The main drawback of that database is that it is quite limited; therefore, we said that it would be useful to have more automated ways of figuring out whether a document should be trusted or not; in this section, we have now created a model which does this. The presented model is just one of the many automated models that can be implemented to estimate the credibility of a textual document (see Sect. 10.2 for other methods). Assuming we are able to implement or use such models that others have implemented, the next problem is: *how can we combine automatic estimates and our database of human-annotated claims?* In the next section we look at a way to do this.

10.5   Propagating Disinformation Scores Through a Knowledge Graph

In the previous sections we have seen how to build a classifier to detect deceptive language in text, and we saw that it is not easy to build such a model in a way that generalizes well. We also saw that we can build deep learning models to determine whether two sentences are semantically similar. In this notebook, we look at how we can use a knowledge graph of entities and claims to assign credibility values for all entities based on a limited number of human-rated credibility scores.

In this section we will use the kg-disinfo library[11] to obtain an estimation of (dis)credibility, based on knowledge graphs (KGs). Given a KG and a few seed nodes which contain (lack of) credibility scores (represented as a numerical value), the system uses a metric propagation algorithm to estimate the (lack of) credibility of neighboring nodes (for which no previous score is available). The used knowledge graph is created from the Data Commons claimReview datafeed.[12] `kg-disinfo` implements a credibility score propagation algorithm called `appleseed`, first published in [201].

10.5.1   Data Commons ClaimReview Knowledge Graph

To construct the knowledge graph, we process the Data Commons claimReview datafeed.[13] This is a json-ld[14] graph, consisting of a list of `claimReviews`. An example of such a claimReview looks as follows:

```
{'@type':'DataFeedItem',
 'dateCreated':'2019-09-26T04:54:30.135723+00:00',
 'item': [{
  '@context':'http://schema.org',
  '@type':'ClaimReview',
  'author': {
    '@type':'Organization',
    'name':'Fact Crescendo',
    'url':'https://www.factcrescendo.com/'},
 'claimReviewed':'police found weapons hidden in a motorcycle in Jammu and Kashmir',
 'datePublished':'2019-09-25',
 'itemReviewed': {
   '@type':'Claim',
   'author': {
     '@type':'Person',
     'name':'Dinesh Gajera'},
   'datePublished':'2019-09-24',
   'firstAppearance':{
     '@type':'CreativeWork',
     'url':'https://www.facebook.com/dinesh.gajera.5015/videos/224778855168984/'}},
```

---

[11] https://github.com/rdenaux/kg-disinfo.

[12] https://github.com/rdenaux/kg-disinfo.

[13] https://storage.googleapis.com/datacommons-feeds/claimreview/latest/data.json.

[14] https://json-ld.org.

```
'reviewRating': {
  '@type':'Rating',
  'alternateName':'FALSE'},
'sdPublisher': {
  '@type':'Organization',
  'name':'Google Fact Check Tools',
  'url':'https://g.co/factchecktools'}}],
'url':'https://www.factcrescendo.com/fact-check-...-police-...-in-jammu-and-kashmir/'}
```

In this section we will only use a few of the entities in the graph, namely those accessible through paths:

- `claimReviewed`,
- `itemReviewed->author->name`,
- `itemReviewed->firstAppearance->url`, and
- `reviewRating->alternateName` or `reviewRating->rantingValue`, when available.

10.5.1.1   KG Schema and Credibility Injections

To create the required knowledge graph, we need to know how to specify the graph and injections[15] in the format that `kg-disinfo` expects. The main points are:

- The graph is just a list of weighted and directed edges between nodes.
- The `injections` assign initial values to some nodes for the metric that should be propagated. In our case these are discredibility scores.
- The `weights` of edges control how the injected values propagate between nodes in the graph. You can define different weights depending on the nodes.

At the schema level, the graph and propagation weights could look as follows:

```
{
  "edges" : [ {
    "src-node" : "claim",
    "tgt-node" : "author",
    "meta" : {
      "weight" : 0.7,
      "explanation" : "Credibility of an author is based on the credibility of his claims",
      "name" : "hasAuthor"
    }
  }, {
    "src-node" : "author",
    "tgt-node" : "claim",
    "meta" : {
      "weight" : 0.5,
      "explanation" : "Credibility of a claim depends on who claims it",
      "name" : "AuthorOf"
    }
  }, {
    "src-node" : "claim",
    "tgt-node" : "publisherDomain",
    "meta" : {
      "weight" : 0.7,
      "explanation" : "Credibility of a publisher depends on the credibility of its claims",
      "name" : "published_in"
```

---

[15]https://github.com/rdenaux/kg-disinfo#specifying-graphs-and-injections.

```
      }
    }, {
      "src-node" : "publisherDomain",
      "tgt-node" : "claim",
      "meta" : {
        "weight" : 0.5,
        "explanation" : "Credibility of a claim depends on who publishes it",
        "name" : "published"
      }
    }, {
      "src-node" : "claim",
      "tgt-node" : "article",
      "meta" : {
        "weight" : 0.7,
        "explanation" : "Credibility of an article depends on its claims",
        "name" : "appears_in"
      }
    }, {
      "src-node" : "article",
      "tgt-node" : "claim",
      "meta" : {
        "weight" : 0.5,
        "explanation" : "If an article is not credible, its claims are also less credible",
        "name" : "includes_claim"
      }
    }, {
      "src-node" : "claimReview_altName",
      "tgt-node" : "claim",
      "meta" : {
        "weight" : 1.0,
        "explanation" : "ClaimReview is the source of credibility",
        "name" : "is_reviewAltNameOf"
      }
    }
  ]
}
```

Note that weights were arbitrarily defined by us, taking into account how much we think a certain relation between two nodes should propagate a discredibility value. In reality, the schema of the graph may be implicit; when you convert the Data Commons ClaimReview dataset into this format, you will only see *instance level* relations between nodes in the graph, as we show in the next section.

10.5.1.2   Data Commons ClaimReview Knowledge Graph Instances

Once we processed the Data Commons claimReview datafeed, the knowledge graph in JSON notation is something like this:

```
{
    "edges": [
        {
            "src-node": "Kamel Daoud Sentenced in Algeria for Injuries on His Wife",
            "tgt-node": "Oumma",
            "meta": {
                "weight": 0.7,
                "name": "hasAuthor",
                "explanation": "Credibility of an author is based on their claims"
            }
        },
        {
            "src-node": "Oumma",
```

```
                "tgt-node": "Kamel Daoud Sentenced in Algeria for Injuries on His Wife",
                "meta": {
                    "weight": 0.5,
                    "name": "AuthorOf",
                    "explanation": "Credibility of a claim depends on who claims it"
                }
            },
            {
                "src-node": "Kamel Daoud Sentenced in Algeria for Injuries on His Wife",
                "tgt-node": "oumma.com",
                "meta": {
                    "weight": 0.7,
                    "name": "published_in",
                    "explanation": "Credibility of a publisher depends on published claims"
                }
            },
            {
                "src-node": "oumma.com",
                "tgt-node": "Kamel Daoud Sentenced in Algeria for Injuries on His Wife",
                "meta": {
                    "weight": 0.5,
                    "name": "published",
                    "explanation": "Credibility of a claim depends on who publishes it"
                }
            },
            {
                "src-node": "Kamel Daoud Sentenced in Algeria for Injuries on His Wife",
                "tgt-node": "https//oumma.com/kamel-daoud-condamne-en-...-contre-sa-femme/",
                "meta": {
                    "weight": 0.7,
                    "name": "appears_in",
                    "explanation": "Credibility of an article depends on its claims"
                }
            },
            {
                "src-node": "https//oumma.com/kamel-daoud-condamne-en-...-contre-sa-femme/",
                "tgt-node": "Kamel Daoud Sentenced in Algeria for Injuries on His Wife",
                "meta": {
                    "weight": 0.5,
                    "name": "includes_claim",
                    "explanation": "If an article is not credible, neither are its claims"
                }
            },
            {
                "src-node": "Wrong. Kamel Daoud reacted to the news and denied it",
                "tgt-node": "Kamel Daoud Sentenced in Algeria for Injuries on His Wife",
                "meta": {
                    "weight": 0.85,
                    "name": "is_reviewAltnameOf",
                    "explanation": "ClaimReview is the source of credibility"
                }
            }, ...
        ]
}
```

10.5.1.3   Data Commons ClaimReview Discredibility Scores

ClaimReviews contain `reviewRatings`, this is a numerical value between a range. However, often `reviewRating` values are missing. In such cases we use the claimReview's `alternateName` value. To obtain the discredibility scores, we normalize the numerical values of rantingValues when is possible, and if not, we apply heuristic rules on the alternateNames to obtain a discredibility score.

Here is an example of the credibility scores for various claimReviews:

```
{
    "injection": {
        "Wrong. Kamel Daoud reacted to the news and denied it": 1.0,
        "Three Pinocchios": 0.8,
        "MISLEADING": 0.75,
        "FALSE": 1.0,
        "Sesat": 0.75,
        "Falso": 1.0,
        "Error": 0.0,
        "Partial error": 0.25,
        "Wrong. The doctor was sentenced to 18 months in prison, including 6 farms.": 0.75,
        "False": 0.4,
        "We Explain the Research": 0.5,
        "To know is to see the face of God": 0.33333333333333337,
        "THis is custom text": 0.5,
        "Pants on Fire": 0.4444444444444444,
        "Mostly False": 0.6666666666666667,
        "Who, really... can ever know?": 1.0,
        "Half True": 0.7777777777777778,
        "Half true": 0.5,
        "Stunt ad makes false claim": 0.5,
        "Ryan Allowed Them": 0.5,
        "This is misleading": 0.75,
        "False.": 1.0,
        "True": 0.0,
        "This is misleading.": 0.75,
        "This is exaggerated.": 0.75,
        "This is misleading. ": 0.75,
        "True.": 0.0,
        "Maybe.": 0.5,
        "False. ": 1.0
    }
}
```

We can see that there are some cases when the discredibility is 0.0 ("Error": 0.0), but it should be 1.0, this is because the given rating might be incorrectly encoded in the source dataset. In some other cases ("We Explain the Research": 0.5), we cannot know the discredibility score, and in that case we assign a 0.5 by default. Therefore these ratings should not be treated as a ground truth (someone could have created a false claimReview), but as an estimation of credibility.

10.5.2   Discredibility Scores Propagation

10.5.2.1   Discredibility Propagation at Schema Level

To better understand how the propagation works, we will first demonstrate it at the schema level. To run it, we need to get:

- The code for the tutorial, as it contains KG data we will be using and
- the kg-disinfo distribution. This is a java jar file.

```
In [ ]: %cd /content
        !git clone https://github.com/hybridnlp/tutorial
```

```
In [ ]: !wget https://github.com/rdenaux/kg-disinfo/releases/download/0.2.0/\
  kg-disinfo-0.2.0-standalone.jar
```

```
... - 'kg-disinfo-0.2.0-standalone.jar' saved [23612836/23612836]
```

Now we can execute the `kg-disinfo` on an example graph. The main arguments for the application are:

- `-g` a path to the json graph (a list of edges as shown above)
- `-i` a path to the json injections (a map from nodes in the graph to initial discredibility values)
- `--generate-viz` is an optional parameter which tells `kg-disinfo` to generate visualizations of the graph.

```
In [ ]: !java -jar kg-disinfo-0.2.0-standalone.jar \
  -g tutorial/datasamples/datacommons-claimreview-kg/datacommons_schema_graph.json \
  -i tutorial/datasamples/datacommons-claimreview-kg\
  /datacommons_schema_graph_injections.json \
  --generate-viz svg
```

To see the injected scores (before propagation):

```
In [ ]: from IPython.display import SVG, display
```

```
In [ ]:dir = 'tutorial/datasamples/datacommons-claimreview-kg/'
    SVG(filename= dir + 'datacommons_schema_graph_base_with_seed.svg')
```

This should print a figure like that shown in Fig. 10.2. The idea is that the "claimReview_altName" node has an injection of a discredibility score of 1.0. This score is then propagated through the neighbors when running the kg-disinfo application. The scores after propagation are shown in Fig. 10.3.

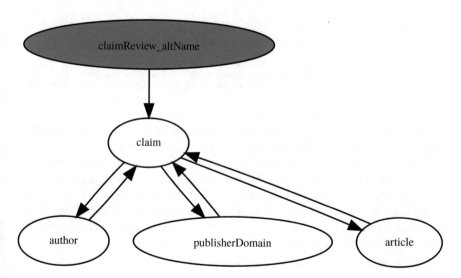

Fig. 10.2 KG schema with initial injection for node `claimReview_altName`

```
In [ ]:SVG(filename= dir + 'datacommons_schema_graph_base_scored.svg')
```

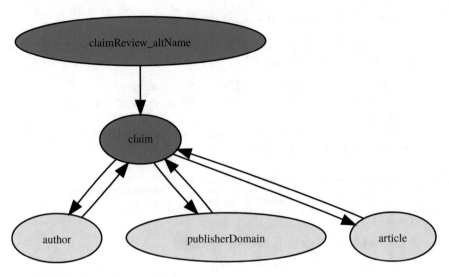

Fig. 10.3 KG schema after propagation

Here we can see that the discredibility of `claimReview_altName` is propagated first to `claim`, and from there it is propagated through the neighboring nodes.

10.5.2.2 Discredibility Propagation at Instance Level

Now is time to run `kg-disfo` with the Data Commons claimReview knowledge graph to see how the discredibility scores propagate through the graph.

```
In [ ]: !java -jar kg-disinfo-0.2.0-standalone.jar \
    -g tutorial/datasamples/datacommons-claimreview-kg/datacommons-graph.json \
    -i ntutorial/datasamples/datacommons-claimreview-kg/datacommons-graph_injections.json \
    --generate-viz svg
```

The output printed by the program should allow you to see that it does not take too much time since we created the knowledge graph with a small part (100 claimReviews) of the datafeed (more than 2000 claimReviews).

The command outputs SVG files to visualize the graph. However, even for a relatively small graph of 100 claimReviews, the graph is difficult to inspect visually without tooling to allow filtering and zooming. We encourage you to load the generated files on your browser or another SVG viewer. If you are executing this section along on a Jupyter environment or Google Colaboratory, you can inspect the SVG using the following commands:

```
In [ ]: SVG(filename= dir + 'datacommons-graph_base_with_seed.svg')
```

If you do that, you should be able to see that our knowledge graph has subgraphs that are not connected with other subgraphs, and that the only nodes with some color are those with an initial discredibility score. These correspond to nodes of type claimReview_altNames.

You can similarly display the graph after propagation:

```
In [ ]: SVG(filename= dir + 'datacommons-graph_base_scored.svg')
```

You should be able to see that there are some nodes that previously did not have a score of discredibility with an estimation. This does not only happen with the claims, but also with authors, articles, and publisher domains.

Naturally, we can also get the estimated numerical numbers for each node.

```
In [ ]:
import json
with open( dir + 'datacommons-graph_propagated.json') as json_file:
    data = json.load(json_file)

In [ ]: from collections import OrderedDict
        sorted_data = OrderedDict(sorted(data['scores'].items(),
                                  key=lambda kv: kv[1], reverse=True))
```

This should output a long list of values, among which:

```
Out[ ]: OrderedDict([
    ('Donald J. Trump', 0.6922187686181025),
    ('Falso', 0.4331510797439524),
    ('Who, really... can ever know?', 0.39875357252315535),
    ('Kamel Daoud Sentenced in Algeria for Injuries on His Wife',
     0.38533736548491027),
    ('False. ', 0.38211341999853476),
    ('FALSE', 0.38099321691560617),
    ...,
    ('Rubber bullets are supposed to be banned in Catalonia', 0.0),
    ('Error', 0.0),
    ('According to the Internet, "Papaya is the king of many medicines, and the US Dep',
     0.0),
    ('Pablo Iglesias', 0.0),
    ('True', 0.0)])
```

Based on the knowledge graph discredibility propagation, one of the least credible nodes, besides the `claimReview_altName` nodes, is "Donald J. Trump."

10.5.2.3 Discussion and Further Improvements

The algorithm distributes the initial injections throughout the graph, but the sum of all scores at the end of the propagation is the same as the initial injections. This means the initial weights are *diluted*, which makes interpreting the final scores difficult. A final normalization step could help with this.

At the moment the algorithm only propagates discredibility scores. However, we often have also a score about the confidence of the score. It would be good to have a way to also propagate this confidence information.

At the moment, we can only propagate discredibility scores between a range of 0.0 and 1.0. Arguably, a more natural way of thinking about credibility is as a range between −1 (not credible) and 1 (fully credible).

Finally, it is worth noting that credibility injections can come from a variety of sources. ClaimReviews come from reputable fact-checker organizations, but alternative sources can also be considered. For example, there are various sites/services which provide reputation scores for internet domains.

10.6   Conclusion

In this chapter, we have implemented several prototypes, applying hybrid NLP techniques introduced in the previous chapters, for addressing the issue of disinformation and fake news. Since this is a complex problem, there are no easy solutions and the implemented prototypes show that, although many of the current technologies can be useful in this area, they require a lot of work to get right: data gathering, data cleaning, model training or fine-tuning, model evaluation, model result aggregation (via rules), etc. Most of the techniques presented can be applied to other problem domains besides disinformation, so after following the practical parts in this chapter you should be able to improve on the presented components or apply them to your own complex NLP problems.

Chapter 11
Jointly Learning Text and Visual Information in the Scientific Domain

Abstract In this chapter we address multi-modality in domains where not only text but also images or, as we will see next, scientific figures and diagrams are important sources of information for the task at hand. Compared to natural images, understanding scientific figures is particularly hard for machines. However, there is a valuable source of information in scientific literature that until now remained untapped: the correspondence between a figure and its caption. In this chapter we show what can be learnt by looking at a large number of figures and reading their captions, and describe a figure-caption correspondence learning task that makes use of such observation. Training visual and language networks without supervision other than pairs of unconstrained figures and captions is shown to successfully solve this task. We also follow up on previous chapters and illustrate how transferring lexical and semantic knowledge from a knowledge graph significantly enriches the resulting features. Finally, the positive impact of such hybrid and semantically enriched features is demonstrated in two transfer learning experiments involving scientific text and figures: multi-modal classification and machine comprehension for question answering.

11.1 Introduction

This is almost the last stop of our journey towards hybrid natural language processing. The readers that made it this far are now familiar with the concept of Vecsigrafo and its evolution based on neural language models, how to apply such representations in actual applications like disinformation analysis, and how to inspect their quality. In this chapter we make things a step more complex and propose to deal not only with text but also with other modalities of information, including images, figures, and diagrams. Here, too, we show the advantages of hybrid approaches involving not only neural representations but also knowledge graphs and show the reader how to master them for different tasks in this context.

To this purpose, as in Chap. 8 we focus on the scientific domain, lexically complex and full of information that can be presented in many forms, not only text. Previous analysis [72] produced an inventory of the different types of knowledge

© Springer Nature Switzerland AG 2020
J. M. Gomez-Perez et al., *A Practical Guide to Hybrid Natural Language Processing*, https://doi.org/10.1007/978-3-030-44830-1_11

involved in scientific disciplines like Chemistry, Biology, or Physics, with several fine-grained knowledge types like, e.g. factual, procedural, taxonomic, mathematical, diagrammatic, or tabular knowledge. Therefore, successfully reading and understanding scientific literature either by humans or machines requires addressing such different modalities, a task that remains challenging nowadays.

Like many other manifestations of human thought, the scientific discourse usually adopts the form of a narrative, a scientific publication where related knowledge is presented in mutually supportive ways over different modalities. In the case of scientific figures, like charts, images, and diagrams, these are usually accompanied by a text paragraph, a caption, that elaborates on the analysis otherwise visually represented. The approach described herein taps on the potential of learning from such enormous source of free supervision available in the scientific literature, with millions of figures and their captions, by simply looking at the figures, reading their captions, and learning if they correspond or not.

Understanding natural images has been a major area of research in computer vision, with well-established datasets like ImageNet [42], Flickr8K [80], Flickr30K [198], and COCO [104]. However, reasoning with other visual representations like scientific figures and diagrams has not received the same attention yet and entails additional challenges: Scientific figures are more abstract and symbolic, their captions tend to be significantly longer and use specialized lexicon, and the relation between a scientific figure and its caption is unique, i.e. in a scientific publication there is only one caption that corresponds with one figure and vice versa.

The figure-caption correspondence (FCC) task subject of study in this chapter is a form of co-training [22], where there are two views of the data and each view provides complementary information. Similar two-branch neural architectures focus on image-sentence [50, 187] and audio-video [5] matching. Others like [172] learn common embeddings from images and text. However, in such cases one or both networks are typically pre-trained.

Some authors [161] focus on geometry and maximize the agreement between text and visual data. In [27], the authors apply machine vision and natural language processing to extract data from figures and their associated text in bio-curation tasks. In [92], they parse diagram components and connectors as a Diagram Parse Graph (DPG), semantically interpret the DPG and use the resulting features in a diagram question answering model.

Knowledge fusion approaches like [179] investigate the potential of complementing knowledge graph embeddings with text and natural images by integrating information across the three modalities in a single latent representation. However, in doing so they assume pre-trained entity representations exist in each individual modality, e.g. the visual features encoding the image of a ball, the word embeddings associated with the token "ball," and the knowledge graph embeddings related to the ball entity, which are then stitched together. In contrast, FCC co-trains text and visual features from figures and their captions and supports the enrichment of such features with lexical and semantic knowledge transferred from a knowledge graph during training.

More details on the work described in this chapter can be found in [69], including a complete qualitative study on the activation of the model that shows evidence of improved textual and visual semantic discrimination over the equivalent uni-modal cases. All the code and data, including the corpora extracted from the different datasets, are also available in GitHub.[1]   Practical examples, including code to train the FCC model, a qualitative inspection, a comparison with image-sentence matching approaches, and application in classification and question answering, are shown in Sect. 11.8.

11.2   Figure-Caption Correspondence Model and Architecture

The main idea of this task is to learn the correspondence between scientific figures and their captions as they appear in a scientific publication. The information captured in the caption explains the corresponding figure in natural language, providing guidance to identify the key features of the figure and vice versa. By seeing a figure and reading the textual description in its caption the aim is to learn representations that capture, e.g. what it means that two plots are similar or what gravity looks like.

In essence, FCC is a binary classification task that receives a figure and a caption and determines whether they correspond or not. For training, positive pairs are actual figures and their captions from a collection of scientific publications. Negative pairs are extracted from combinations of figures and any other randomly selected captions. The network is then made to learn text and visual features from scratch, without additional labeled data.

The two-branch neural architecture (Fig. 11.1) proposed for the FCC task is very simple. It has three main parts: the vision and language subnetworks, respectively, extracting visual and text features, and a fusion subnetwork that takes the resulting features from the visual and text blocks and uses them to evaluate figure-caption correspondence.

The **vision subnetwork** follows a VGG-style [170] design, with four blocks of conv+conv+pool layers. Based on [96], the **language subnetwork** has three convolutional blocks and a 300-D embedding layer at the input, with a maximum sequence length of 1000 tokens.[2]   Vision and language subnetworks produce each a 512-D vector in the last convolutional block. The **fusion subnetwork** calculates the element-wise product of the 512-D visual and text feature vectors into a single vector r to produce a 2-way classification output (correspond or not). The probability of each choice is the softmax of r, i.e. $\hat{y} = softmax(r) \in \mathbb{R}^2$. During training, the negative log probability of the correct choice is minimized.

---

[1] https://github.com/hybridNLP/look_read_and_enrich.

[2] Note that the architecture of both vision and language subnetworks can be replaced by others, including (bi)LSTMs or based on neural language models. In this case CNNs were chosen for simplicity and ease of inspection.

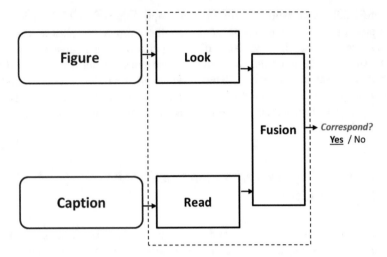

Fig. 11.1 Two-branch architecture of the FCC task

Now, let V the vocabulary of words from a collection of documents D. Also, let L the lemmas of such words, i.e. base forms without morphological or conjugational variations, and C the concepts (or senses) in a knowledge graph. Each word w_k in V, e.g. *made*, has one lemma l_k (*make*) and may be linked to one or more concepts c_k in C (*create or produce something*).

For each word w_k, the FCC task learns a d-D embedding $\mathbf{w}_k$, which can be combined with pre-trained word ($\mathbf{w}'_k$), lemma ($\mathbf{l}_k$), and concept ($\mathbf{c}_k$) embeddings to produce a single vector $\mathbf{t}_k$. If no pre-trained knowledge is transferred from an external source, then $\mathbf{t}_k = \mathbf{w}_k$. Note that D was previously lemmatized and disambiguated against the knowledge graph in order to select the right pre-trained lemma and concept embeddings for each particular occurrence of w_k. Equation (11.1) shows the different combinations of learnt and pre-trained embeddings considered: (a) learnt word embeddings only, (b) learnt and pre-trained word embeddings, and (c) learnt word embeddings and pre-trained semantic embeddings, including both lemmas and concepts, in line with recent findings [39].

$$\mathbf{t}_k = \begin{cases} \mathbf{w}_k & (a) \\ [\mathbf{w}_k; \mathbf{w}'_k] & (b) \\ [\mathbf{w}_k; \mathbf{l}_k; \mathbf{c}_k] & (c) \end{cases} \qquad (11.1)$$

During experimentation concatenation proved optimal to combine the embeddings learnt by the network and the pre-trained embeddings, compared to other methods like summation, multiplication, average, or learning a task-specific weighting of the different representations as in [139]. Since some words may not have associated pre-trained word, lemma, or concept embeddings, padding is used when needed. The dimensionality of t_k is fixed to 300, i.e. the size of each sub-vector in configurations (a), (b), and (c) is 300, 150, and 100, respectively. Training used tenfold cross-validation, Adam optimization [97] with learning rate 10^{-4} and weight decay 10^{-5}. The network was implemented in Keras and TensorFlow, with batch size 32. The number of positive and negative cases is balanced within the batches.

Knowledge graph embedding approaches like HolE [130] and Vecsigrafo [39] can be used to learn semantic embeddings that enrich the pre-trained FCC features. In contrast to Vecsigrafo, which requires both a text corpus and a knowledge graph, HolE follows a graph-based approach where embeddings are learnt exclusively from the knowledge graph. As Sect. 11.4 will show, this gives Vecsigrafo a certain advantage in the FCC task. Following up with previous work [39], the knowledge graph used here is also Sensigrafo, which underlies Expert System's Cogito NLP platform. As introduced earlier in the book, Sensigrafo is conceptually similar to WordNet. Cogito was used to disambiguate the text corpora prior to training Vecsigrafo. All the semantic (lemma and concept) embeddings produced with HolE or Vecsigrafo are 100-D.

Next, we compare the actual FCC task against two supervised baselines and inspect the resulting features from a qualitative point of view. Then, we situate the task of learning the correspondence between scientific figures and captions in the more general context of image-sentence matching in order to illustrate the additional complexity compared to natural images.

11.3 Datasets

The following datasets were used for training and evaluation:

The Semantic Scholar corpus [3] (SemScholar) is a large dataset of scientific publications made available by AI2. From its 39M articles, 3.3M PDFs were downloaded (the rest were behind paywalls, did not have a link or it was broken) and extracted 12.5M figures and captions through PDFFigures2 [34]. A randomly selected sample of 500K papers was used to train the FCC task on their figures and captions and another 500K to train Vecsigrafo on the text of their titles and abstracts.

Springer Nature's SciGraph[3] contains 7M scientific publications organized in 22 scientific fields or categories. Since SciGraph does not provide a link to the PDF of the publication, the intersection with SemScholar was selected, producing a smaller corpus of 80K papers (in addition to the 1M papers from SemScholar mentioned above) and 82K figures that used for training certain FCC configurations and supervised baselines (Sect. 11.4).

The Textbook Question Answering corpus [93] includes 1076 lessons and 26,260 multi-modal test questions from middle school science curricula. Its complexity and scope make it a challenging textual and visual question answering dataset.

---

[3]https://www.springernature.com/gp/researchers/scigraph.

Wikipedia. The January 2018 English Wikipedia dataset as one of the corpora on which to train Vecsigrafo. As opposed to SciGraph or SemScholar, specific of the scientific domain, Wikipedia is a source of general-purpose information.

Flickr30K and COCO, as image-sentence matching benchmarks.

11.4 Evaluating the Figure-Caption Correspondence Task

The method is evaluated in the task it was trained to solve: determining whether a figure and a caption correspond. We also compare the performance of the FCC task against two supervised baselines, training them on a classification task against the SciGraph taxonomy. For such baselines we first train the vision and language networks independently and then combine them. The feature extraction parts of both networks are the same as described in Sect. 11.2. On top of them, a fully connected layer with 128 neurons and ReLU activation and a softmax layer is attached, with as many neurons as target classes.

The **direct combination** baseline computes the figure-caption correspondence through the scalar product between the softmax outputs of both networks. If it exceeds a threshold, which was heuristically fixed on 0.325, the result is positive. The **supervised pre-training** baseline freezes the weights of the feature extraction trunks from the two trained networks, assembles them in the FCC architecture as shown in Sect. 11.2, and trains the FCC task on the fully connected layers. While direct combination provides a notion of the agreement between the two branches, supervised pre-training is the most similar supervised approach to our method.

Table 11.1 FCC and supervised baselines results (% accuracy)

	Corpus	Word rep.	Acc_{vgg}.	Acc.
Direct	SciGraph	$\mathbf{w}_k$	60.30	
Pre-train		$\mathbf{w}_k$	68.40	
FCC$_1$		$\mathbf{w}_k$	78.09	78.48
FCC$_2$	SciGraph	$[\mathbf{w}_k; \mathbf{w}'_{k\_sem}]$	79.75	80.35
FCC$_3$		$[\mathbf{w}_k; \mathbf{l}_{k\_holE}; \mathbf{c}_{k\_holE}]$	78.64	78.08
FCC$_4$		$[\mathbf{w}_k; \mathbf{l}_{k\_wiki}; \mathbf{c}_{k\_wiki}]$	79.71	80.50
FCC$_5$		$[\mathbf{w}_k; \mathbf{l}_{k\_sem}; \mathbf{c}_{k\_sem}]$	**80.50**	**81.97**
FCC$_6$	SemScholar	$\mathbf{w}_k$	80.42	81.44
FCC$_7$		$[\mathbf{w}_k; \mathbf{l}_{k\_sem}; \mathbf{c}_{k\_sem}]$	**82.21**	**<u>84.34</u>**

Bold is the best result in each column per each corpus type while bold underscored is the absolute best

Table 11.1 shows the results of the FCC task and the supervised baselines. FCC$_k$ denotes the corpus and word representation used to train the FCC task. Acc_{vgg} shows the accuracy after replacing our visual branch with pre-trained VGG16 features learnt on ImageNet. This provides an estimate of how specific of the scientific domain scientific figures and therefore the resulting visual features can be compared to natural images. As the table shows, the results obtained using pre-trained visual features are clearly worse in general (only slightly better in FCC_3), suggesting that the visual information contained in scientific figures indeed differs from natural images.

The FCC network was trained on two different scientific corpora: SciGraph (FCC_{1-5}) and SemScholar (FCC_{6-7}). Both FCC_1 and FCC_6 learnt their own word representations without transfer of any pre-trained knowledge. Even in its most basic form our approach substantially improves over the supervised baselines, confirming that the visual and language branches learn from each other and also that figure-caption correspondence is an effective source of free supervision.

Adding pre-trained knowledge at the input layer of the language subnetwork provides an additional boost, particularly with lemma and concept embeddings from Vecsigrafo (FCC_5). Vecsigrafo clearly outperformed HolE (FCC_3), which was also beaten by pre-trained fastText [23] word embeddings (FCC_2) trained on SemScholar.

Although the size of Wikipedia is almost triple of our SemScholar corpus, training Vecsigrafo on the latter resulted in better FCC accuracy (FCC_4 vs. FCC_5), suggesting that domain relevance is more significant than sheer volume, in line with previous findings [62]. Training FCC on SemScholar, much larger than SciGraph, further improves accuracy, as shown in FCC_6 and FCC_7.

11.5 Figure-Caption Correspondence vs. Image-Sentence Matching

We put the FCC task in the context of the more general problem of image-sentence matching through a bidirectional retrieval task where images are sought given a text query and vice versa. While Table 11.2 focuses on natural images datasets (Flickr30K and COCO), Table 11.3 shows results on scientific datasets (SciGraph and SemScholar) rich in scientific figures and diagrams. The selected baselines (Embedding network, 2WayNet, VSE++, and DSVE-loc) report results obtained on the Flickr30K and COCO datasets, also included in Table 11.2. Performance is measured in recall at k (Rk), with $k = \{1, 5, 10\}$. From the baselines, DSVE-loc was successfully reproduced using the code made available by the authors,[4] and trained it on SciGraph and SemScholar.

The FCC task was trained on all the datasets, both in a totally unsupervised way and with pre-trained semantic embeddings, with focus on the best FCC configuration. As shown in Table 11.1, such configuration leverages semantic enrichment using Vecsigrafo (indicated with subscript vec). The bidirectional retrieval task is then run using the resulting text and visual features. Further experimentation included pre-trained VGG16 visual features extracted from ImageNet (subscript vgg), with more than 14 million hand-annotated images. Following common

---

[4]https://github.com/technicolor-research/dsve-loc.

practice in image-sentence matching, the splits are 1000 samples for test and the rest for training.

We can see a marked division between the results obtained on natural images datasets (Table 11.2) and those focused on scientific figures (Table 11.3). In the former case, VSE++ and DSVE-loc clearly beat all the other approaches. In contrast, FCC performs poorly on such datasets although results are ameliorated with pre-trained visual features ("FCC$_{vgg}$" and "FCC$_{vgg-vec}$"). Interestingly, the situation changes radically with the scientific datasets. While the recall of DSVE-loc drops dramatically in SciGraph, and even more in SemScholar, FCC shows the opposite behavior in both figure and caption retrieval. Using visual features enriched with pre-trained semantic embeddings from Vecsigrafo during training of the FCC task further improves recall in the bidirectional retrieval task.

Unlike in Flickr30K and COCO, replacing the FCC visual features with pre-trained ones from ImageNet brings us little benefit in SciGraph and even less in SemScholar, where the combination of FCC and Vecsigrafo ("FCC$_{vec}$") obtains the best results across the board. This and the extremely poor performance of the best image-sentence matching baseline (DSVE-loc) in the scientific datasets shows evidence that dealing with scientific figures is considerably more complex than natural images. Indeed, the best results in figure-caption correspondence ("FCC$_{vec}$" in SemScholar) are still far from the SoA in image-sentence matching (DSVE-loc in COCO).

Table 11.2 Bidirectional retrieval

| Model | Flickr30K | | | | | | COCO | | | | | |
| | Caption-to-image | | | Image-to-caption | | | Caption-to-image | | | Image-to-caption | | |
	R1	R5	R10	R1	R5	R10	R1	R5	R10	R1	R5	R10
Emb. net [187]	29.2	59.6	71.7	40.7	69.7	79.2	39.8	75.3	86.6	50.4	79.3	89.4
2WayNet [50]	36.0	55.6	n/a	49.8	67.5	n/a	39.7	63.3	n/a	55.8	75.2	n/a
VSE++ [55]	**39.6**	n/a	**79.5**	**52.9**	n/a	**87.2**	52.0	n/a	92.0	64.6	n/a	95.7
DSVE-loc [53]	34.9	**62.4**	73.5	46.5	**72.0**	82.2	**55.9**	**86.9**	**94**	**69.8**	**91.9**	**96.6**
FCC$_{vgg}$	3.4	14.0	23.2	4.7	16.4	24.8	11.7	39.7	58.8	15.2	40.0	56.1
FCC	0.4	1.3	2.8	0.2	1.5	3.2	2.6	10.3	18.0	2.5	9.3	17.3
FCC$_{vgg-vec}$	5.4	17.8	27.8	6.8	20.3	32.0	12.8	40.9	59.7	17.3	41.2	57.4
FCC$_{vec}$	0.6	2.9	5.3	1.2	3.7	6.5	4.0	14.6	25.3	4.4	15.6	25.9

FCC vs. image-sentence matching baselines (%recall@k). Natural images datasets (Flick30K, COCO). Bold values indicate column best

Next, the visual and text features learnt in the FCC task are put to the test in two different transfer learning settings: (1) classification of scientific figures and captions according to a given taxonomy and (2) multi-modal machine comprehension for question answering given a context of text, figures, and images.

Table 11.3 Bidirectional retrieval

Model	SciGraph						SemScholar					
	Caption-to-figure			Figure-to-caption			Caption-to-figure			Figure-to-caption		
	R1	R5	R10	R1	R5	R10	R1	R5	R10	R1	R5	R10
Emb. net [187]	n/a	n/a	n/a	n/a	n/a	n/a	n/a	n/a	n/a	n/a	n/a	n/a
2WayNet [50]	n/a	n/a	n/a	n/a	n/a	n/a	n/a	n/a	n/a	n/a	n/a	n/a
VSE++ [55]	n/a	n/a	n/a	n/a	n/a	n/a	n/a	n/a	n/a	n/a	n/a	n/a
DSVE-loc [53]	0.7	3.1	5.3	1.4	1.4	2.4	0.9	3	4.5	0.8	0.8	1.3
FCC_{vgg}	1.4	6.6	11.3	1.3	6.4	10.6	2.9	9.5	17.4	3.1	12.1	18.0
FCC	0.7	5.7	11.4	1.2	4.9	10.0	2.8	11.4	18.8	2.1	10.6	18.2
$FCC_{vgg-vec}$	**1.7**	7.8	14.2	2.1	7.7	15.8	2.9	13.9	24.0	**4.7**	14.9	23.2
FCC_{vec}	1.5	**9.0**	**14.9**	**2.6**	**9.7**	**16.1**	**3.9**	**15.5**	**25.1**	4.4	**16.6**	**25.6**

FCC vs. image-sentence matching baselines (%recall@k). Scientific datasets (SciGraph, SemScholar). Bold values indicate column best

11.6 Caption and Figure Classification

We evaluate the language and visual representations emerging from FCC in the context of two classification tasks that aim to identify the scientific field an arbitrary text fragment (a caption) or a figure belong to, according to the SciGraph taxonomy. The latter is a particularly hard task due to the whimsical nature of the figures that appear in our corpus: figure and diagram layout is arbitrary; charts, e.g. bar and pie charts, are used to showcase data in any field from health to engineering; figures and natural images appear indistinctly, etc. Also, note that only the actual figure is used, not the text fragment where it is mentioned in the paper.

The study picks the text and visual features that produced the best FCC results with and without pre-trained semantic embeddings (see Table 11.1) and use the language and vision subnetworks presented in Sect. 11.2 to train our classifiers on SciGraph in two different scenarios. First, only the fully connected and softmax layers are fine-tuned, freezing the text and visual weights (non-trainable in the table). Second, all the parameters are fine-tuned in both networks (trainable). In both cases, a baseline using the same networks initialized with random weights without FCC training is used for comparison. In doing so, the first, non-trainable scenario seeks to quantify the information contributed by the FCC features, while training from scratch on the target corpus should provide an upper bound for figure and caption classification. Additionally, for figure classification, the baseline freezes the pre-trained VGG16 model. Training uses tenfold cross-validation and Adam. For the caption classification task, the learning rate is 10^{-3} and batch size 128. In figure classification, learning rate 10^{-4}, weight decay 10^{-5}, and batch size 32 are selected.

The results in Table 11.4 show that using FCC features amply beats the baselines, including the upper bound (training from scratch on SciGraph). The delta is particularly noticeable in the non-trainable case for both caption and figure classification and is considerably increased in FCC_7, which uses pre-trained semantic embeddings. This includes both the random and VGG baselines and

Table 11.4 Caption and figure classification (%accuracy)

| Model | Non-trainable | Trainable | Non-trainable | Trainable |
| | Caption | | Figure | |
	Non-trainable	Trainable	Non-trainable	Trainable
Random	39.92	78.20	44.19	61.21
VGG16	n/a	n/a	58.43	n/a
FCC6	61.31	**_79.24_**	58.57	**_63.60_**
FCC7	**_67.40_**	79.11	**60.19**	63.49

The significance of underscore bold is the absolute best for figure and caption

Table 11.5 TQA results (% accuracy)

Model	Text	Visual	Word representation	Figure rep.	Inspired by	MC_{text}	MC_{diag}
Random	x	x	n/a	n/a	Random	22.7	25.0
BiDAF	✓	x	w_k	n/a	BiDAF [162]	32.2	30.1
TQA_1	✓	x	w_k	n/a	MemoryNet [192]	32.9	29.9
TQA_2	✓	✓		VGG19	VQA [4]	n/a	29.9
TQA_3	✓	✓		DPG	DSDP-NET [93]	n/a	31.3
TQA_4	✓	✓		FCC_6	FCC	33.89	34.27
TQA_5	✓	✓		FCC_7		33.73	_33.52_
TQA_6	✓	x	$[w_k + l_{k\_sem} + c_{k\_sem}]$	n/a	MemoryNet [192]	35.41	34.57
TQA_7	✓	✓		VGG19	VQA [4]	36.26	32.58
TQA_8	✓	✓		DPG	DSDP-NET [93]	n/a	n/a
TQA_9	✓	✓		FCC_6	FCC	**36.56**	**35.30**
TQA_{10}	✓	✓		FCC_7		35.84	33.94

FCC vs. random, BiDAF, MemoryNet, VQA and DSDP-NET baselines. Bold values indicate column best

illustrates again the additional complexity of analyzing scientific figures compared to natural images, even if the latter is trained on a considerably larger corpus like ImageNet. Fine-tuning the whole networks on SciGraph further improves accuracies. In this case, FCC_6, which uses FCC features without additional pre-trained embeddings, slightly outperforms FCC_7, suggesting a larger margin to learn from the task-specific corpus.

11.7 Multi-Modal Machine Comprehension for Textbook Question Answering

We leverage the TQA dataset and the baselines in [93] to evaluate the features learnt by the FCC task in a multi-modal machine comprehension scenario. We study how the FCC model, which was not originally trained for this task, performs against state-of-the-art models specifically trained for diagram question answering and textual reading comprehension in a very challenging dataset. We also study how pre-trained semantic embeddings impact in the TQA task: first, by enriching the visual features learnt in the FCC task as shown in Sect. 11.2 and then by using pre-trained semantic embeddings to enrich word representations in the TQA corpus.

We focus on multiple-choice questions, which represent 73% of all the questions in the dataset. Table 11.5 shows the performance of the FCC model against the results reported in [93] for five TQA baselines: random, BiDAF (focused on text machine comprehension), text only (TQA_1, based on MemoryNet), text+image (TQA_2, VQA), and text+diagrams (TQA_3, DSDP-NET). The TQA_1 and TQA_2 architectures were successfully reproduced. The latter was also adapted.[5] Then, the visual features in TQA_2 were replaced with those learnt by the FCC visual subnet-work both in a completely unsupervised way (FCC_6 in Table 11.1) and with pre-trained semantic embeddings (FCC_7), resulting in TQA_4 and TQA_5, respectively.

While TQA_{1-5} used no pre-trained embeddings at all, TQA_{6-10} were trained including pre-trained Vecsigrafo semantic embeddings. Unlike FCC, where concatenation was used to combine pre-trained lemma and concept embeddings with the word embeddings learnt by the task, in the case of TQA element-wise addition showed to work best.

Following the recommendations in [93], the TQA corpus was pre-processed to: (1) consider knowledge from previous lessons in the textbook in addition to the lesson of the question at hand and (2) address challenges like long question contexts with a large lexicon. In both text and diagram MC, applying the Pareto principle to reduce the maximum token sequence length in the text of each question, their answers and context improved accuracy considerably. This optimized the amount of text to consider for each question, improving the signal to noise ratio. Finally, the most relevant paragraphs for each question were obtained through tf–idf.[6] The models were trained using tenfold cross-validation, Adam, learning rate 10^{-2} and batch size 128. Text MC also used 0.5 dropout and recurrent dropout in the LSTM layers.

Fitting multi-modal sources into a single memory, the use of visual FCC features clearly outperforms all the TQA baselines in diagram MC. Enhancing word representation with pre-trained semantic embeddings during training of the TQA task provides an additional boost that results in the highest accuracies for both text MC and diagram MC. These are significantly good results since, according to the authors of the TQA dataset [93], most diagram questions in it would normally require a specific rich diagram parse.

11.8   Practice with Figure-Caption Correspondence

As in previous chapters, next we illustrate in a Jupyter notebook,[7] the methods described in this chapter. The notebook is structured around the following experiments:

---

[5]While VGG19 produces a 7-by-7 grid of 512-D image patch vectors, our visual subnetwork produces a 512-D vector. To align dimensions, we add a 7-max pooling layer.

[6]Future work includes paragraph selection through semantic similarity and language models.

[7]https://colab.research.google.com/github/hybridnlp/tutorial/blob/master/ 08_scientific_information_management.ipynb.

1. **Training and evaluation of the FCC task**, used to jointly learn text and visual features from scientific bibliography. **This includes the use of pre-trained embeddings from a knowledge graph learnt through the Vecsigrafo approach**.
2. **A qualitative analysis of the resulting features** so that you can see by yourself the information captured by them.
3. **A comparison between state-of-the-art algorithms used in image-sentence matching and the FCC task**. This will allow you to better understand the limitations of applying state-of-the-art image-sentence matching techniques to the scientific domain.
4. **Textual and visual classification over the SciGraph taxonomy** using figures and their captions as input.
5. **Multi-modal question answering** involving text but also diagrams over the TQA dataset.

In addition to this notebook, all the related code and data used for the experimentation in the paper can be found in GitHub.

11.8.1   Preliminary Steps

First, we import the Python libraries necessary to run our experiments.

```
In [ ]: !pip install scipy==1.1.0

Requirement already satisfied: scipy==1.1.0
in /usr/local/lib/python3.6/dist-packages (1.1.0)
Requirement already satisfied: numpy>=1.8.2
in /usr/local/lib/python3.6/dist-packages (from scipy==1.1.0) (1.16.5)
```

```
In [ ]: import json
        import cv2
        from pandas import DataFrame
        import matplotlib.pyplot as plt
        from tqdm import tqdm
        from PIL import Image
        import numpy as np
        from keras.preprocessing.text import Tokenizer
        from keras.preprocessing.sequence import pad_sequences
        from keras.models import Sequential, Model
        from keras.layers import InputLayer, Conv2D, BatchNormalization,
            MaxPooling2D, Flatten, Embedding, Concatenate,
            Conv1D, MaxPooling1D, Multiply, Dense
        from keras.optimizers import Adam
        from keras.utils import plot_model
```

```
import random
from sklearn.model_selection import train_test_split
from sklearn.preprocessing import LabelBinarizer
from collections import Counter
from vis.visualization import visualize_cam
```
Using TensorFlow backend.

The datasets we use for training and evaluation are SciGraph, Semantic Scholar, and TQA, as described in Sect. 11.3. For practical reasons, in the notebook the size of the dataset is limited to 400 figures and captions to train the FCC task. As can be expected, this is not sufficient to train a performant model. So, when necessary we use the weights resulting from training over the whole corpus.

Next, we clone the repository with the datasets and other materials.

```
In [ ]: !git clone https://github.com/hybridnlp/tutorial.git
```

```
Cloning into 'tutorial'...
remote: Enumerating objects: 53, done.
remote: Counting objects: 100% (53/53), done.
remote: Compressing objects: 100% (52/52), done.
remote: Total 382 (delta 30), reused 0 (delta 0), pack-reused 329
Receiving objects: 100% (382/382), 450.66 MiB | 11.94 MiB/s, done.
Resolving deltas: 100% (192/192), done.
Checking out files: 100% (92/92), done.
```

We uncompress the zip files:

```
In [ ]: !unzip -q tutorial/datasamples/scigraph.zip
        !unzip -q tutorial/datasamples/tqa.zip
```

The figures and captions are structured as json files. Let us take a look at them:

```
In [ ]: index = 0 #first figure and caption

        with open("./tutorial/datasamples/scigraph_wordnet.json", "r",
            encoding="utf-8", errors="surrogatepass") as file:
              dataset = json.load(file)

        print("FIGURE PATH: ./scigraph/" + dataset[index]["img_file"])
        print("CAPTION: " + dataset[index]["captions"][0])

        im = cv2.imread("./scigraph/"+dataset[index]["img_file"])
        plt.imshow(im)
        plt.show()
```
```
FIGURE PATH: ./scigraph/1752-1947-8-200-Figure2-1.png
CAPTION: Abdominal X-ray revealing several air-fluid levels of the small
        bowel and a large air-fluid level of the sigmoid colon.
```

11.8.2 Figure-Caption Correspondence

As introduced in Sect. 11.2, FCC is a binary classification task that receives a figure and a caption and determines whether they correspond or not. The positive pairs are actual figures and their captions from a collection of scientific publications. Negative pairs are extracted from combinations of figures and other captions ad random.

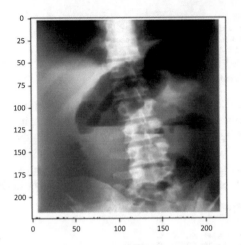

Fig. 11.2 Sample image obtained from the FCC datasets, in this case SciGraph

11.8.2.1 Loading the Dataset

To illustrate the training of the FCC task, we focus on the SciGraph corpus. First, we save in a list all the figures and their captions. For the text part, we keep not only the tokens but also their associated WordNet synsets resulting from word-sense disambiguation. This is a necessary step to enrich the text features with the semantic (lemma and synset) embeddings of each token (Fig. 11.2).

As in previous notebooks, we use Cogito to tokenize the text and WordNet as the knowledge graph used for word-sense disambiguation. In the original paper [69] Sensigrafo, Expert System's proprietary knowledge graph, was used instead.

```
In [ ]: list_figures_paths = []
        list_captions_tokens = []
        list_captions_synsets = []


        with open("./tutorial/datasamples/scigraph_wordnet.json", "r",
            encoding="utf-8", errors="surrogatepass") as file:
          dataset = json.load(file)

        for doc in dataset:
          list_figures_paths.append("./scigraph/" + doc["img_file"])
          list_captions_tokens.append(doc["captions_tokens"][0])
          list_captions_synsets.append(doc["captions_synsets"][0])

        print("Number of figures = " + str(len(list_figures_paths)))
        print("Number of captions (tokens) = " + str(len(list_figures_paths)))
        print("Number of captions (synsets) = " + str(len(list_figures_paths)))

Number of figures = 400
Number of captions (tokens) = 400
Number of captions (synsets) = 400
```

Once we have our three lists with figure paths, caption tokens, and caption synsets, we transform them into tensors.

First, we create numpy arrays from the figures using the PIL library:

```
In [ ]: figures = []
        for figure_path in tqdm(list_figures_paths,total=len(list_figures_paths)):
            f_img = open(figure_path, 'rb')
            im = Image.open(f_img)
            arr = np.array(im.convert(mode='RGB'))
            im.close()
            f_img.close()
            figures.append(arr)
        figures = np.array(figures)
        print("SHAPE OF FIGURES TENSOR: " + str(np.shape(figures)))
```

```
100% 400/400 [00:00<00:00, 1040.83it/s]
```

```
SHAPE OF FIGURES TENSOR: (400, 224, 224, 3)
```

Then, we:

1. create two Keras tokenizers, one for caption tokens and another for their synsets,
2. create word indexes for both modalities, and
3. transform the captions in sequence arrays with a length of 1000 tokens each.

```
In [ ]: MAX_SEQ_LEN = 1000
```

```
In [ ]: caption_types = [list_captions_tokens, list_captions_synsets]
        tokenizers = []
        captions = []

        for lst_cpt in caption_types:
          tokenizer = Tokenizer(filters='')
          tokenizer.fit_on_texts(lst_cpt)
          tokenizers.append(tokenizer)
          sequences = tokenizer.texts_to_sequences(lst_cpt)
          data_text = pad_sequences(sequences, maxlen=MAX_SEQ_LEN, padding="post",
            truncating="post")
          captions.append(data_text)
        tokenizer_tokens, tokenizer_synsets = tokenizers
        captions_tokens, captions_synsets = captions

        print("SIZE OF TOKENS VOCABULARY: " + str(len(tokenizer_tokens.word_index)))
        print("SIZE OF SYNSETS VOCABULARY: " + str(len(tokenizer_synsets.word_index)))
        print("SHAPE OF TOKENS SEQUENCES: " + str(np.shape(captions_tokens)))
        print("SHAPE OF SYNSETS SEQUENCES: " + str(np.shape(captions_synsets)))
```

```
SIZE OF TOKENS VOCABULARY: 2934
SIZE OF SYNSETS VOCABULARY: 1559
SHAPE OF TOKENS SEQUENCES: (400, 1000)
SHAPE OF SYNSETS SEQUENCES: (400, 1000)
```

11.8.2.2 Semantic Embeddings

As described in Eq. (11.1), for each word w_k in the vocabulary, the FCC network learns an embedding $\mathbf{w}_k$ that can be combined with pre-trained word $\mathbf{w}'_k$, lemma $\mathbf{l}_k$, and concept $\mathbf{c}_k$ embeddings to produce a single vector $\mathbf{t}_k$. If no pre-trained knowledge is transferred from an external source, then $\mathbf{t}_k = \mathbf{w}_k$. The options shown in Eq. (11.1) include:

(a) Only word embeddings learnt by the network upon training over the corpus.
(b) Learnt and pre-trained word embeddings.

(c) Learnt word embeddings and pre-trained semantic (lemma and concept) embeddings.

```
In [ ]: index = 0   #first figure

        caption_token = dataset[index]["captions_tokens"][0]
        caption_synset = dataset[index]["captions_synsets"][0]

        tab1 = [list(i) for i in zip(*[caption_token.split(" "), caption_synset.split(" ")])]

        DataFrame(tab1,columns=["tokens","synsets"])
```

```
Out[ ]:             tokens              synsets
        0         abdominal    wn31_abdominal.a.01
        1             x-ray         wn31_x-ray.v.01
        2          revealing    wn31_bring+out.v.01
        3            several   wn31_respective.a.01
        4               air       wn31_air+out.v.01
        5                 -                   None
        6             fluid      wn31_fluent.a.01
        7            levels       wn31_level.n.05
        8                of                   None
        9               the                   None
        10            small       wn31_small.a.01
        11            bowel    wn31_intestine.n.01
        12              and                   None
        13                a                   None
        14            large       wn31_large.a.01
        15              air       wn31_air+out.v.01
        16                -                   None
        17            fluid      wn31_fluent.a.01
        18            level       wn31_level.n.05
        19               of                   None
        20              the                   None
        21    sigmoid+colon  wn31_sigmoid+colon.n.01
        22                .                   None
```

For conciseness, here we focus on option (*c*), where word, lemma, and concept embeddings are concatenated in a 300 dimension vector (100 dimensions for words, lemmas, and embeddings each). All the .tsv files of the embeddings are also available in GitHub.

```
In [ ]: EMB_FILE = "./tutorial/datasamples/scigraph_wordnet.tsv"
        DIM = 100
```

First we extract the embeddings from the .tsv and put them in two dictionaries (embeddings_index_tokens and embeddings_index_synsets):

```
In [ ]: file = open(EMB_FILE, "r", encoding="utf-8", errors="surrogatepass")
        embeddings_index_tokens = {}
        embeddings_index_synsets = {}

        for line in file:
          values = line.split()
          comp_len = len(values)-DIM
          word = "+".join(values[0:comp_len])
          if (line.startswith("wn31")):
            vector = np.asarray(values[comp_len:], dtype='float32')
            embeddings_index_synsets[word] = vector
          else:
            if (line.startswith("grammar#")):
              continue
            else:
              vector = np.asarray(values[comp_len:], dtype='float32')
```

```
            embeddings_index_tokens[word] = vector
    file.close()

    embedding_indexes =
        [embeddings_index_tokens, embeddings_index_synsets]

    print("NUMBER OF TOKENS IN THE EMBEDDINGS: " +
        str(len(embeddings_index_tokens)))
    print("NUMBER OF SYNSETS IN THE EMBEDDINGS: " +
        str(len(embeddings_index_synsets)))
```

```
NUMBER OF TOKENS IN THE EMBEDDINGS: 19438
NUMBER OF SYNSETS IN THE EMBEDDINGS: 9232
```

Now we take every word and its disambiguated synset and fetch their pre-trained embeddings from the dictionaries to build the embeddings matrices for the model. In case of out-of-vocabulary words we use an array of zeros for that token during the training of the FCC task.

```
In [ ]: embedding_matrices = []
        for tok_i in range(len(tokenizers)):
            embedding_matrix = np.zeros((len(tokenizers[tok_i].word_index) + 1, DIM))
            for word, i in tokenizers[tok_i].word_index.items():
                embedding_vector = embedding_indexes[tok_i].get(word)
                if embedding_vector is not None:
                    embedding_matrix[i] = embedding_vector
            embedding_matrices.append(embedding_matrix)
        embedding_matrix_tokens, embedding_matrix_synsets = embedding_matrices

        print("SHAPE OF TOKENS MATRIX: " + str(np.shape(embedding_matrix_tokens)))
        print("SHAPE OF SYNSETS MATRIX: " + str(np.shape(embedding_matrix_synsets)))
```

```
SHAPE OF TOKENS MATRIX: (2935, 100)
SHAPE OF SYNSETS MATRIX: (1560, 100)
```

11.8.2.3 FCC Network Architecture

As shown in Sect. 11.1, we use a two-branch neural architecture with three main parts: the vision and language subnetworks, respectively, extracting visual and text features, and a fusion subnetwork to evaluate figure-caption correspondence (Fig. 11.3).

The **vision subnetwork** follows a VGG-style [170] design, with 3×3 convolutional filters, 2×2 max-pooling layers with stride 2 and no padding. It contains four blocks of conv+conv+pool layers, where inside each block the two convolutional layers have the same number of filters, while consecutive blocks have doubling number of filters (64, 128, 256, 512). The input layer receives $224 \times 224 \times 3$ images. The final layer produces a 512-D vector after 28×28 max-pooling. Each convolutional layer is followed by batch normalization [83] and ReLU layers.

```
In [ ]: modelFigures = Sequential()
        modelFigures.add(InputLayer(input_shape=(224,224,3)))
        modelFigures.add(Conv2D(64, (3,3), padding = "same", activation="relu"))
        modelFigures.add(BatchNormalization())
        modelFigures.add(Conv2D(64, (3,3), padding = "same", activation="relu"))
        modelFigures.add(BatchNormalization())
        modelFigures.add(MaxPooling2D(2))
        modelFigures.add(Conv2D(128, (3,3), padding = "same", activation="relu"))
        modelFigures.add(BatchNormalization())
        modelFigures.add(Conv2D(128, (3,3), padding = "same", activation="relu"))
```

```
modelFigures.add(BatchNormalization())
modelFigures.add(MaxPooling2D(2))
modelFigures.add(Conv2D(256, (3,3), padding = "same", activation="relu"))
modelFigures.add(BatchNormalization())
modelFigures.add(Conv2D(256, (3,3), padding = "same", activation="relu"))
modelFigures.add(BatchNormalization())
modelFigures.add(MaxPooling2D(2))
modelFigures.add(Conv2D(512, (3,3), padding = "same", activation="relu"))
modelFigures.add(BatchNormalization())
modelFigures.add(Conv2D(512, (3,3), padding = "same", activation="relu"))
modelFigures.add(BatchNormalization())
modelFigures.add(MaxPooling2D((28,28),2))
modelFigures.add(Flatten())

print(modelFigures.summary())
```

```
Model: "sequential_1"
_____
Layer (type)                 Output Shape              Param #
=================================================================
conv2d_1 (Conv2D)            (None, 224, 224, 64)      1792

batch_normalization_1 (Batch (None, 224, 224, 64)      256

conv2d_2 (Conv2D)            (None, 224, 224, 64)      36928

batch_normalization_2 (Batch (None, 224, 224, 64)      256

max_pooling2d_1 (MaxPooling2 (None, 112, 112, 64)      0

conv2d_3 (Conv2D)            (None, 112, 112, 128)     73856

batch_normalization_3 (Batch (None, 112, 112, 128)     512

conv2d_4 (Conv2D)            (None, 112, 112, 128)     147584

batch_normalization_4 (Batch (None, 112, 112, 128)     512

max_pooling2d_2 (MaxPooling2 (None, 56, 56, 128)       0

conv2d_5 (Conv2D)            (None, 56, 56, 256)       295168

batch_normalization_5 (Batch (None, 56, 56, 256)       1024

conv2d_6 (Conv2D)            (None, 56, 56, 256)       590080

batch_normalization_6 (Batch (None, 56, 56, 256)       1024

max_pooling2d_3 (MaxPooling2 (None, 28, 28, 256)       0

conv2d_7 (Conv2D)            (None, 28, 28, 512)       1180160

batch_normalization_7 (Batch (None, 28, 28, 512)       2048

conv2d_8 (Conv2D)            (None, 28, 28, 512)       2359808

batch_normalization_8 (Batch (None, 28, 28, 512)       2048

max_pooling2d_4 (MaxPooling2 (None, 1, 1, 512)         0

flatten_1 (Flatten)          (None, 512)               0
=================================================================
Total params: 4,693,056
Trainable params: 4,689,216
Non-trainable params: 3,840
_____

None
```

Based on [96], the **language subnetwork** has three convolutional blocks, each with 512 filters and a 5-element window size with ReLU activation. Each convolutional layer is followed by a 5-max pooling layer, except for the final layer, which produces a 512-D vector after 35-max pooling. The language subnetwork has a 300-D embeddings layer at the input, with a maximum sequence length of 1000 tokens.

```
In [ ]: modelCaptionsScratch = Sequential()
        modelCaptionsScratch.add(Embedding(len(tokenizer_tokens.word_index)+1,
            DIM,embeddings_initializer="uniform", input_length=MAX_SEQ_LEN, trainable=True))
        modelCaptionsVecsiTokens = Sequential()
        modelCaptionsVecsiTokens.add(Embedding(len(tokenizer_tokens.word_index) + 1,
            DIM,weights = [embedding_matrix_tokens], input_length = MAX_SEQ_LEN,
            trainable = False))
        modelCaptionsVecsiSynsets = Sequential()
        modelCaptionsVecsiSynsets.add(Embedding(len(tokenizer_synsets.word_index) + 1,
            DIM,weights = [embedding_matrix_synsets], input_length = MAX_SEQ_LEN,
            trainable = False))
        modelMergeEmbeddings = Concatenate()([modelCaptionsScratch.output,
            modelCaptionsVecsiTokens.output,modelCaptionsVecsiSynsets.output])
        modelMergeEmbeddings = Conv1D(512, 5, activation="relu")(modelMergeEmbeddings)
        modelMergeEmbeddings = MaxPooling1D(5)(modelMergeEmbeddings)
        modelMergeEmbeddings = Conv1D(512, 5, activation="relu")(modelMergeEmbeddings)
        modelMergeEmbeddings = MaxPooling1D(5)(modelMergeEmbeddings)
        modelMergeEmbeddings = Conv1D(512, 5, activation="relu")(modelMergeEmbeddings)
        modelMergeEmbeddings = MaxPooling1D(35)(modelMergeEmbeddings)
        modelMergeEmbeddings = Flatten()(modelMergeEmbeddings)
        modelCaptions = Model([modelCaptionsScratch.input,modelCaptionsVecsiTokens.input,
            modelCaptionsVecsiSynsets.input], modelMergeEmbeddings)

        print(modelCaptions.summary())
```

Model: "model_1"

Layer (type)	Output Shape	Param #	Connected to
embedding_1_input (InputLayer)	(None, 1000)	0	
embedding_2_input (InputLayer)	(None, 1000)	0	
embedding_3_input (InputLayer)	(None, 1000)	0	
embedding_1 (Embedding)	(None, 1000, 100)	293500	embedding_1_input[0][0]
embedding_2 (Embedding)	(None, 1000, 100)	293500	embedding_2_input[0][0]
embedding_3 (Embedding)	(None, 1000, 100)	156000	embedding_3_input[0][0]
concatenate_1 (Concatenate)	(None, 1000, 300)	0	embedding_1[0][0] embedding_2[0][0] embedding_3[0][0]
conv1d_1 (Conv1D)	(None, 996, 512)	768512	concatenate_1[0][0]
max_pooling1d_1 (MaxPooling1D)	(None, 199, 512)	0	conv1d_1[0][0]
conv1d_2 (Conv1D)	(None, 195, 512)	1311232	max_pooling1d_1[0][0]
max_pooling1d_2 (MaxPooling1D)	(None, 39, 512)	0	conv1d_2[0][0]
conv1d_3 (Conv1D)	(None, 35, 512)	1311232	max_pooling1d_2[0][0]
max_pooling1d_3 (MaxPooling1D)	(None, 1, 512)	0	conv1d_3[0][0]
flatten_2 (Flatten)	(None, 512)	0	max_pooling1d_3[0][0]

Total params: 4,133,976

```
Trainable params: 3,684,476
Non-trainable params: 449,500
```

None

The **fusion subnetwork** calculates the element-wise product of the 512-D visual and text feature vectors produced by last blocks of each subnetwork into a single vector r to produce a 2-way classification output (correspond or not). The probability of each choice is the softmax of r, i.e. $\hat{y} = softmax(r) \in \mathbb{R}^2$.

```
In [ ]: adam = Adam(lr=1e-4,decay=1e-5)

        mergedOut = Multiply()([modelCaptions.output,modelFigures.output])
        mergedOut = Dense(128, activation='relu')(mergedOut)
        mergedOut = Dense(2, activation='softmax')(mergedOut)
        model = Model([modelCaptionsScratch.input,modelCaptionsVecsiTokens.input,
            modelCaptionsVecsiSynsets.input, modelFigures.input], mergedOut)

        model.compile(loss="categorical_crossentropy", optimizer=adam,
            metrics=["categorical_accuracy"])

        plot_model(model, show_shapes=True, to_file='model.png', dpi=60)
```

11.8.2.4   Quantitative Analysis

FCC is evaluated in the task it was trained to solve: determining whether a figure and a caption correspond. Next, we define some hyperparameters:

```
In [ ]: EPOCHS = 4
        BATCH_SIZE = 16
```

The next generator introduces 32 inputs for every batch, balanced in terms of positive and negative cases within the batches:

- 16 positive cases with a figure and its correct caption.
- 16 negative cases with a randomly selected caption for the same figure.

For each word in the caption, three text sub-vectors are considered: token, lemma, and synset.

```
In [ ]: def generator(indexes):
            while True:
                np.random.shuffle(indexes)
                for i in range(0, len(indexes), BATCH_SIZE):
                    batch_indexes = indexes[i:i+BATCH_SIZE]
                    batch_indexes.sort()

                    bx,by = get_batches(batch_indexes)

                    yield (bx, by)

        def get_batches(batch_indexes):
            tuples_to_shuffle = []
            for batch_ind in batch_indexes:
                tuple1 = []
                tuple1.append(captions_tokens[batch_ind])
                tuple1.append(captions_tokens[batch_ind])
                tuple1.append(captions_synsets[batch_ind])
```

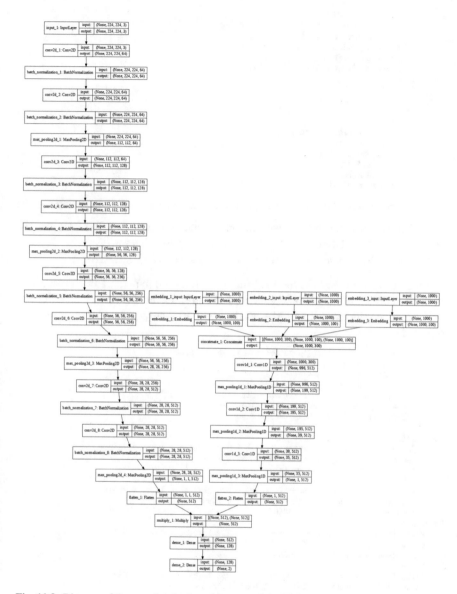

Fig. 11.3 Diagram of the complete basic architecture of the FCC model

```
tuple1.append(figures[batch_ind])
tuple1.append(np.array([0,1]))
tuples_to_shuffle.append(tuple1)
rand_ind = random.choice([x for x in range(len(captions_tokens))
    if x != batch_ind])
tuple2 = []
tuple2.append(captions_tokens[rand_ind])
tuple2.append(captions_tokens[rand_ind])
```

```
        tuple2.append(captions_synsets[rand_ind])
        tuple2.append(figures[batch_ind])
        tuple2.append(np.array([1,0]))
        tuples_to_shuffle.append(tuple2)
        random.shuffle(tuples_to_shuffle)
    bx0 = []
    bx1 = []
    bx2 = []
    bx3 = []
    y = []
    for tup in tuples_to_shuffle:
      bx0.append(tup[0])
      bx1.append(tup[1])
      bx2.append(tup[2])
      bx3.append(tup[3])
      y.append(tup[4])

    return [np.array(bx0),np.array(bx1),np.array(bx2),np.array(bx3)], np.array(y)
```

Before we train the model, we randomly select the train and test indexes. We choose a 90% train size and a 10% test size of the whole dataset.

```
In [ ]: train, test = train_test_split(range(len(captions_tokens)), test_size=0.1)
```

Finally, we train the FCC model. With the corpus and hyperparameters proposed in the notebook, training should take around **2 min**. Given the very small subset of data we have selected as input, the results will very likely be rather far from those reported in paper.

```
In [ ]: model.fit_generator(generator(train), epochs=EPOCHS,
            validation_data=generator(test),
            steps_per_epoch=len(train)//BATCH_SIZE,
            validation_steps=len(test)//BATCH_SIZE)
        modelFigures.save_weights("modelFigures_weights.h5")
        modelCaptions.save_weights("modelCaptions_weights.h5")
        model.save_weights("model_weights.h5")

Epoch 1/4
    22/22 [==============================] - 37s 2s/step - loss: 0.7349 -
    categorical_accuracy: 0.4659 - val_loss: 0.7147 -
    val_categorical_accuracy: 0.4844
Epoch 2/4
    22/22 [==============================] - 27s 1s/step - loss: 0.7063 -
    categorical_accuracy: 0.4646 - val_loss: 0.7369 -
    val_categorical_accuracy: 0.3750
Epoch 3/4
    22/22 [==============================] - 22s 1s/step - loss: 0.6925 -
    categorical_accuracy: 0.5057 - val_loss: 0.7157 -
    val_categorical_accuracy: 0.4583
Epoch 4/4
    22/22 [==============================] - 23s 1s/step - loss: 0.6833 -
    categorical_accuracy: 0.5201 - val_loss: 0.7366 -
    val_categorical_accuracy: 0.2812
```

Due to limited size of the training set used in this notebook, the results (around 50% accuracy) are merely testimonial.

Once you have trained the FCC task, you will have three files with the resulting text and visual features, along with the weights of the model. Such features can be used for the transfer learning tasks proposed in the notebook.

However, since their performance is very limited by the small amount of data used here, their actual use in transfer learning tasks is very limited. To overcome this, **in the remainder of the notebook we use FCC features that were previously**

learnt from a larger SciGraph selection (82K figures and captions). You are invited to experiment with different alternatives and check the results.

```
In [ ]: from tutorial.scripts import lre_aux

        !tar -zxvf tutorial/datasamples/model_weights.tar.gz

        captions_tokens, captions_synsets = lre_aux.get_captions(list_captions_tokens,
            list_captions_synsets)
        model = lre_aux.get_model()[2]

model_weights_BIG.h5
```

11.8.2.5 Qualitative Analysis

Now, we inspect the features learnt by the FCC task to gain a deeper understanding of the syntactic and semantic patterns captured for figure and caption representation (Figs. 11.4, 11.5, 11.6, 11.7, 11.8, and 11.9).

Vision features

The analysis was carried out on an unconstrained variety of charts, diagrams, and natural images from SciGraph, without filtering by figure type or scientific field. To obtain a representative sample of what the FCC network learns, we focus on the 512-D vector resulting from the last convolutional block before the fusion subnetwork.

```
In [ ]: modelF = lre_aux.get_figure_vis_model()
```

Let us pick the feature with the most significant activation over the whole dataset and select the figure that activate them most and show its heatmap. We prioritize such features with a higher maximum activation against the average activation:

```
In [ ]: feat_n = 2
        img_n = 2
```

With the next code we can generate the heatmap:

```
In [ ]: features = modelF.predict(figures[test])

        diff_list = []
        for i in range(512):
            media = np.mean(features[:,i])
            maximo = np.amax(features[:,i])
            diff_list.append(maximo-media)
        arr = np.array(diff_list)
        feats = arr.argsort()[-feat_n:][::-1]
        for feat in feats:
            args = list(features[:,feat].argsort()[-img_n:][::-1])
            count = 0
            for arg in args:
                count = count +1
                print("feat"+str(feat)+"-top"+str(count)+".png: \n" +
                        list_captions_tokens[test[arg]] +"\n\n")
                data = figures[test[arg],:,:,:]
                img = Image.fromarray(data, 'RGB')
                grads= visualize_cam(modelF, -1, feat, data)
                cam = cv2.applyColorMap(np.uint8(255*grads), cv2.COLORMAP_JET)
                cam = np.float32(cam) + np.float32(img)
                cam = 255 * cam / np.max(cam)
```

```
cv2.imwrite("./scigraph/"+str(feat)+"-top"+str(count)+".png", cam)
im = cv2.imread(list_figures_paths[test[arg]])
plt.imshow(im)
plt.show()
im = cv2.imread("./scigraph/"+str(feat)+"-top"+str(count)+".png")
plt.imshow(im)
plt.show()
```

feat255-top1.png:

fracture line of the first premolar confirmed surgically in a 61-year-old
man. (a) dental radiograph of the left upper+jaw reveals vertical
root fracture of the first premolar as a radiolucent line (arrowheads
) that approximates the root filling . the apex of the root had been
resected (large arrow) . the periodontal ligament is enlarged (small
arrows) . (b) magnified axial ct+scan of the left upper+jaw (original
magnification , 34) reveals a buccolingually oriented root fracture of
the first premolar (large arrow) that extends from the outer surface of
the tooth to the surface facing the oral+cavity . the adjacent segments
are separated widely . the periodontal ligament is enlarged (small arrows
) .

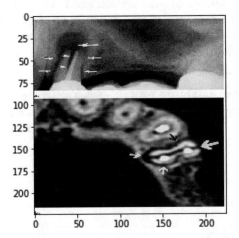

Fig. 11.4 Sample image

feat204-top2.png:

proportion of infected individuals during a boarding+school influenza
outbreak with _ = 1.66 / day and _ = 0.4545 / day (keeling and rohani
2008) . in each plot , the solid black line is the numerical solution
of the model (1) with an appropriate number of stages , and the dashed
line is the exponential growth curve with the rate determined by eq. (4
) shown on a logarithmic scale. a one - stage model with _ _ 1.2055 ,
b two - stage model with _ _ 1.4035 , c three - stage model with _ _
1.4762 , d five - stage model with _ _ 1.534 . in each case note that in
the earliest stages the exponential approximation is virtually identical
to the infection curve

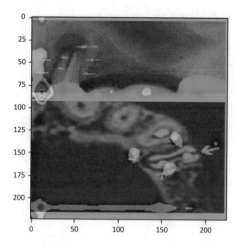

Fig. 11.5 Sample image with activation. Lighter means higher activation, focusing on the arrows in the lower half of the image

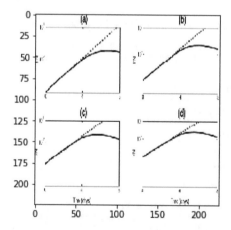

Fig. 11.6 Sample figure

Text features

Similar to the visual case, we select the feature from the last block of the language subnetwork with the highest activation and show it heatmap.

```
In [ ]: modelEmbeddings, modelVisualize, modelC = lre_aux.get_caption_vis_model()
```

The next parameters can change the number of features or captions for each feature you want to analyze.

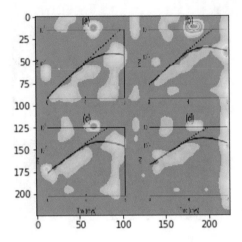

Fig. 11.7 Sample figure with activation. Activation is stronger on the curves and the characters identifying each plot. Also, strong activation appears on the right edge of the image

```
In [ ]: feat_n = 2
        capt_n = 1
```

With the next code we can generate the heatmap

```
In [ ]: features = modelC.predict([captions_tokens[test],
        captions_tokens[test],captions_synsets[test]])

        diff_list = []
        for i in range(512):
            media = np.mean(features[:,i])
            maximo = np.amax(features[:,i])
            diff_list.append(maximo-media)
        arr = np.array(diff_list)
        feats = arr.argsort()[-feat_n:][::-1]
        for feat in feats:
            args = list(features[:,feat].argsort()[-capt_n:][::-1])
            count = 0
            for arg in args:
                count = count +1
                data = modelEmbeddings.predict([
                        np.expand_dims(captions_tokens[test[arg]],axis=0),
                        np.expand_dims(captions_tokens[test[arg]],axis=0),
                        np.expand_dims(captions_synsets[test[arg]],axis=0)])
                grads = lre_aux.grad_cam(modelVisualize,data,feat,-2)
                res = np.sum(np.array(grads),axis=1)

                question_len = len(list_captions_tokens[test[arg]].split(' '))
                alphaX = [list_captions_tokens[test[arg]].split(' ')[j]
                        for j in range(question_len)]

                fig = plt.figure(figsize=(21, 12), dpi= 80,
                    facecolor='w', edgecolor='k')
                ax = fig.add_subplot(211)
                ax.matshow(np.expand_dims(res[0:question_len],axis=0),
                    cmap='jet', vmin=0., vmax=55.)
                ax.set_xticks(list(range(-1,question_len+1)))
                ax.set_xticklabels([''] +alphaX, rotation = 90, ha="right")
```

```
ax.set_yticks(list(range(1)))
ax.set_yticklabels([''])
plt.savefig("feat"+str(feat)+"-top"+str(count)+".png")
```

Fig. 11.8 Attention on each word of a sample caption (darker means higher activation): "The Aliev–Panfilov model with $\alpha = 0.01$, $\gamma = 0.002$, $b = 0.15$, $c = 8$, $\mu 1 = 0.2$, $\mu 2 = 0.3$. The phase portrait depicts trajectories for distinct initial values φ 0 and r 0 (*filled circles*) converging to a stable equilibrium point (*top*). Non-oscillatory normalized time plot of the non-dimensional action potential φ and the recovery variable r (*bottom*)"

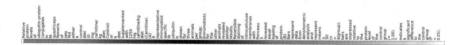

Fig. 11.9 Attention on each word of a sample caption (darker means higher activation): "Relative protein levels of ubiquitin-protein conjugates in M. quadriceps femoris of rats fed either a control diet (0 mg carnitine/kg diet; Control) or a diet supplemented with 1250 mg carnitine/kg diet (Carnitine). (**a**) A representative immunoblot specific to ubiquitin is shown for three animals per group; immunoblots for the other animals revealed similar results. Reversible staining of nitrocellulose membranes with Ponceau S revealed equal loading of protein. (**b**) Bars represent data from densitometric analysis and represent means $\pm$ SD ($n = 6$/group); bars are expressed relative to the protein level of the control group (=1.00). * indicates a significant difference to the control group ($P < 0.05$)"

11.8.3 Image-Sentence Matching

Next, we illustrate how to run the bidirectional retrieval (caption -> figure and figure -> caption) tasks against a small Scigraph sample (40 figures and captions). Of course, the results will differ from those in the previous tables in Sect. 11.5. Actually, as you will see they are much better because the search space is much smaller.

11.8.3.1 Best Baseline (DSVE-loc)

From the baselines, we successfully reproduced DSVE-loc, using the code made available by the authors, and trained it on SciGraph. Since downloading and installing the materials to run the DSVE-loc testing takes approximately **15 min**, we will skip this step but you can run it on your own.

```
In [ ]: !pip install --upgrade torch
        !pip install --upgrade visual_genome
        !pip install --upgrade sru[cuda]
        !pip install --upgrade scipy
        !pip install --upgrade torchvision
        !pip install --upgrade pycocotools
        !pip install --upgrade nltk
        !pip install --upgrade gdown
        !pip install --upgrade opencv-python
        !pip install numpy==1.16.1

        import nltk
        nltk.download('punkt')
```

First, we clone the original DSVE-loc repository and the necessary materials indicated there:

```
In [ ]: !git clone https://github.com/technicolor-research/dsve-loc.git
        !wget http://www.cs.toronto.edu/~rkiros/models/utable.npy
        !wget http://www.cs.toronto.edu/~rkiros/models/dictionary.txt
```

Next, we download a DSVE-loc model pre-trained offline over the overall 82K SciGraph samples and a random selection of 40 new SciGraph samples in DSVE-loc-compatible format for evaluation:

```
In [ ]: !gdown https://drive.google.com/uc?id=1xQkYpeeAxK_bx0t1tIvKL5lp4hfKQGSV
        !unzip -o tutorial/datasamples/dsve-loc.zip
```

Now, we run the bidirectional retrieval task. The results are two arrays with values of recall @ 1, 5, and 10. The first array contains figure retrieval (given a caption, obtain the corresponding figure) results, while the second contains caption retrieval results.

```
In [ ]: !python ./dsve-loc/eval_retrieval.py -p "best_scigraph.pth.tar" -te

Loading model from: best_scigraph.pth.tar
Error when loading pretrained resnet weldon
Dataset size:  200
### Beginning of evaluation ###

best_scigraph.pth.tar test [array([12.5, 12.5, 22.5]),
                            array([12.5, 45. , 65. ]), 27.5, 5.0]
```

11.8.3.2　Bidirectional Retrieval Based on FCC

To evaluate this task we implement the following algorithm:

1. Take each figure and its caption,
2. Take the score returned by the FCC model based on the probability that they correspond, expressed as a one-hot vector [0,1],

3. Compare it with the scores obtained by the rest of the captions (or figures, if the task is figure retrieval): If there are less than 10 captions/figures with a better score than the correct one, it means that we have one more recall@10 point. Similar with recall@5 (less than 5) and recall@1 (only 1).

The final count is divided by the number of samples in the test split, producing the final recall values.

```
In [ ]: r_at_1 = 0
        r_at_5 = 0
        r_at_10 = 0
        for i in tqdm(test,total=len(test)):
            bx = []
            bx.append(np.expand_dims(captions_tokens[i],axis=0))
            bx.append(np.expand_dims(captions_tokens[i],axis=0))
            bx.append(np.expand_dims(captions_synsets[i],axis=0))
            bx.append(np.expand_dims(figures[i],axis=0))
            count_cand = 0
            good_pred = model.predict(bx)
            for j in test:
              if i == j:
                continue
              bx[-1] = np.expand_dims(figures[j],axis=0)
              cand_pred = model.predict(bx)
              if cand_pred[:,1] > good_pred[:,1]:
                count_cand = count_cand + 1
              if count_cand >= 10:
                break
            if count_cand < 10:
              r_at_10 = r_at_10 + 1
            if count_cand < 5:
              r_at_5 = r_at_5 + + 1
            if count_cand < 1:
              r_at_1 = r_at_1 + 1

        print("\n")
        print ("FIGURE RETRIEVAL (r@1: {}% r@5: {}% r@10: {}%"
              .format((r_at_1*100)/(len(test)),
              (r_at_5*100)/(len(test)),
              (r_at_10*100)/(len(test))))

100%| 40/40 [00:38<00:00,  1.00it/s]


FIGURE RETRIEVAL (r@1: 17.5% r@5: 45.0% r@10: 77.5%

In [ ]: r_at_1 = 0
        r_at_5 = 0
        r_at_10 = 0
        for i in tqdm(test,total=len(test)):
            bx = []
            bx.append(np.expand_dims(captions_tokens[i],axis=0))
            bx.append(np.expand_dims(captions_tokens[i],axis=0))
            bx.append(np.expand_dims(captions_synsets[i],axis=0))
            bx.append(np.expand_dims(figures[i],axis=0))
            count_cand = 0
            good_pred = model.predict(bx)
            for j in test:
              if i == j:
                continue
              bx[0] = np.expand_dims(captions_tokens[j],axis=0)
              bx[1] = np.expand_dims(captions_tokens[j],axis=0)
```

```
            bx[2] = np.expand_dims(captions_synsets[j],axis=0)
            cand_pred = model.predict(bx)
            if cand_pred[:,1] > good_pred[:,1]:
               count_cand = count_cand + 1
            if count_cand >= 10:
               break
        if count_cand < 10:
           r_at_10 = r_at_10 + 1
        if count_cand < 5:
           r_at_5 = r_at_5 + + 1
        if count_cand < 1:
           r_at_1 = r_at_1 + 1

   print("\n")
   print ("CAPTION RETRIEVAL (r@1: {}% r@5: {}% r@10: {}%"
          .format((r_at_1*100)/(len(test)),
          (r_at_5*100)/(len(test)),
          (r_at_10*100)/(len(test))))
```
100%| 40/40 [00:35<00:00, 1.03it/s]

CAPTION RETRIEVAL (r@1: 12.5% r@5: 50.0% r@10: 67.5%

11.8.4   Caption/Figure Classification

We take the pre-trained text and visual features resulting from training the FCC task and use the architecture of the language and vision subnetworks to train our classifiers against the SciGraph taxonomy. Note that here we train using fine-tuning over the whole model over a subset of 400 samples from SciGraph, hence the results will differ from those reported in Sect. 11.6.

The first step is to obtain the categories of each figure and caption from the dataset file:

```
In [ ]: categories = []

        for doc in dataset:
           categories.append(doc["category"])

        lb = LabelBinarizer()
        labels = lb.fit_transform(categories)


        print("SHAPE OF LABELS = " + str(np.shape(labels)))
```
SHAPE OF LABELS = (400, 5)

11.8.4.1   Caption Classification

For this task, we train the model during five epochs with a batch size of 128:

```
In [ ]: EPOCHS = 5
        BATCH_SIZE = 128
```
Then we take the model with the weights already loaded (modelCaptions) and add two fully connected layers to classify the inputs into the five different categories that we previously selected (health, engineering, math, biology, and computer science).

```
In [ ]: modelCaptions = lre_aux.get_model()[1]

        modelCaptionsClassOut = Dense(128, activation='relu')(modelCaptions.output)
        modelCaptionsClassOut = Dense(5, activation='softmax')(modelCaptionsClassOut)
        modelCaptionsClass = Model(modelCaptions.inputs, modelCaptionsClassOut)

        print(modelCaptionsClass.summary())
```

Model: "model_10"

Layer (type)	Output Shape	Param #	Connected to
embedding_13_input (InputLayer)	(None, 1000)	0	
embedding_14_input (InputLayer)	(None, 1000)	0	
embedding_15_input (InputLayer)	(None, 1000)	0	
embedding_13 (Embedding)	(None, 1000, 100)	10236300	embedding_13_input[0][0]
embedding_14 (Embedding)	(None, 1000, 100)	10236300	embedding_14_input[0][0]
embedding_15 (Embedding)	(None, 1000, 100)	2281700	embedding_15_input[0][0]
concatenate_5 (Concatenate)	(None, 1000, 300)	0	embedding_13[0][0] embedding_14[0][0] embedding_15[0][0]
conv1d_13 (Conv1D)	(None, 996, 512)	768512	concatenate_5[0][0]
max_pooling1d_13 (MaxPooling1D)	(None, 199, 512)	0	conv1d_13[0][0]
conv1d_14 (Conv1D)	(None, 195, 512)	1311232	max_pooling1d_13[0][0]
max_pooling1d_14 (MaxPooling1D)	(None, 39, 512)	0	conv1d_14[0][0]
conv1d_15 (Conv1D)	(None, 35, 512)	1311232	max_pooling1d_14[0][0]
max_pooling1d_15 (MaxPooling1D)	(None, 1, 512)	0	conv1d_15[0][0]
flatten_9 (Flatten)	(None, 512)	0	max_pooling1d_15[0][0]
dense_9 (Dense)	(None, 128)	65664	flatten_9[0][0]
dense_10 (Dense)	(None, 5)	645	dense_9[0][0]

```
Total params: 26,211,585
Trainable params: 13,693,585
Non-trainable params: 12,518,000
```

None

Finally, we train the model with the same train and test split of the dataset of the FCC task. This will take **10 s** approx.

```
In [ ]: adam = Adam()

        modelCaptionsClass.compile(loss="categorical_crossentropy",
            optimizer=adam, metrics=["categorical_accuracy"])
        modelCaptionsClass.fit([captions_tokens[train], captions_tokens[train],
            captions_synsets[train]],labels[train], epochs=EPOCHS,
            batch_size=BATCH_SIZE, validation_data=[[captions_tokens[test],
            captions_tokens[test], captions_synsets[test]],labels[test]])
```

```
Train on 360 samples, validate on 40 samples
Epoch 1/5
```

```
360/360 [==============================] - 7s 18ms/step - loss: 1.3672 -
categorical_accuracy: 0.4111 - val_loss: 1.0357 -
val_categorical_accuracy: 0.5500
Epoch 2/5
360/360 [==============================] - 1s 3ms/step - loss: 0.9989 -
categorical_accuracy: 0.5667 - val_loss: 0.9662 -
val_categorical_accuracy: 0.6000
Epoch 3/5
360/360 [==============================] - 1s 3ms/step - loss: 0.7514 -
categorical_accuracy: 0.7694 - val_loss: 0.7769 -
val_categorical_accuracy: 0.7500
Epoch 4/5
360/360 [==============================] - 1s 3ms/step - loss: 0.5679 -
categorical_accuracy: 0.8306 - val_loss: 0.6897 -
val_categorical_accuracy: 0.7000
Epoch 5/5
360/360 [==============================] - 1s 3ms/step - loss: 0.4117 -
categorical_accuracy: 0.8667 - val_loss: 0.6567 -
val_categorical_accuracy: 0.7250
```

11.8.4.2   Figure Classification

In this case, we train the model during six epochs with a batch size of 32:

```
In [ ]: EPOCHS = 6
        BATCH_SIZE = 32
```

Then we load the weights from the FCC task and we add two fully connected layers to classify the inputs into the five different categories.

```
In [ ]: modelFiguresClass = lre_aux.get_model()[0]
        modelFiguresClass.add(Dense(128, activation='relu'))
        modelFiguresClass.add(Dense(5, activation='softmax'))

        modelFiguresClass.summary()
```

Model: "sequential_22"

Layer (type)	Output Shape	Param #
conv2d_41 (Conv2D)	(None, 224, 224, 64)	1792
batch_normalization_41 (Batc	(None, 224, 224, 64)	256
conv2d_42 (Conv2D)	(None, 224, 224, 64)	36928
batch_normalization_42 (Batc	(None, 224, 224, 64)	256
max_pooling2d_21 (MaxPooling	(None, 112, 112, 64)	0
conv2d_43 (Conv2D)	(None, 112, 112, 128)	73856
batch_normalization_43 (Batc	(None, 112, 112, 128)	512
conv2d_44 (Conv2D)	(None, 112, 112, 128)	147584
batch_normalization_44 (Batc	(None, 112, 112, 128)	512
max_pooling2d_22 (MaxPooling	(None, 56, 56, 128)	0
conv2d_45 (Conv2D)	(None, 56, 56, 256)	295168
batch_normalization_45 (Batc	(None, 56, 56, 256)	1024

conv2d_46 (Conv2D)	(None, 56, 56, 256)	590080
batch_normalization_46 (Batc	(None, 56, 56, 256)	1024
max_pooling2d_23 (MaxPooling	(None, 28, 28, 256)	0
conv2d_47 (Conv2D)	(None, 28, 28, 512)	1180160
batch_normalization_47 (Batc	(None, 28, 28, 512)	2048
conv2d_48 (Conv2D)	(None, 28, 28, 512)	2359808
batch_normalization_48 (Batc	(None, 28, 28, 512)	2048
max_pooling2d_24 (MaxPooling	(None, 1, 1, 512)	0
flatten_10 (Flatten)	(None, 512)	0
dense_13 (Dense)	(None, 128)	65664
dense_14 (Dense)	(None, 5)	645

```
=================================================================
Total params: 4,759,365
Trainable params: 4,755,525
Non-trainable params: 3,840
```

Finally, we train the model with the same train and test split of the dataset of the FCC task. It may take round **45 s**.

```
In [ ]: adam = Adam(lr=1e-4,decay=1e-5)

        modelFiguresClass.compile(loss="categorical_crossentropy",
            optimizer=adam, metrics=["categorical_accuracy"])
        modelFiguresClass.fit(figures[train],labels[train], epochs=EPOCHS,
            batch_size=BATCH_SIZE, validation_data=[figures[test],labels[test]])

Train on 360 samples, validate on 40 samples
Epoch 1/6
360/360 [==============================] - 15s 42ms/step - loss: 3.8686 -
categorical_accuracy: 0.3278 - val_loss: 1.1655 -
val_categorical_accuracy: 0.6250
Epoch 2/6
360/360 [==============================] - 10s 29ms/step - loss: 1.3191 -
categorical_accuracy: 0.7028 - val_loss: 1.0230 -
val_categorical_accuracy: 0.7000
Epoch 3/6
360/360 [==============================] - 10s 29ms/step - loss: 0.7367 -
categorical_accuracy: 0.7611 - val_loss: 0.8064 -
val_categorical_accuracy: 0.7000
Epoch 4/6
360/360 [==============================] - 10s 29ms/step - loss: 0.4728 -
categorical_accuracy: 0.8278 - val_loss: 0.7028 -
val_categorical_accuracy: 0.7250
Epoch 5/6
360/360 [==============================] - 10s 29ms/step - loss: 0.3348 -
categorical_accuracy: 0.9139 - val_loss: 0.6324 -
val_categorical_accuracy: 0.8000
Epoch 6/6
360/360 [==============================] - 10s 29ms/step - loss: 0.2425 -
categorical_accuracy: 0.9417 - val_loss: 0.7058 -
val_categorical_accuracy: 0.6750
```

11.8.5   Textbook Question Answering

We leverage the TQA dataset[8] developed by Kembhavi et al. to evaluate the textual
and visual features learnt by the FCC task in a multi-modal machine comprehension
scenario involving multiple-choice question answering over text and diagrams.
Next, we go through the different steps to train and evaluate a TQA model using
FCC features and semantic embeddings (TQA10).

11.8.5.1   Loading the Dataset

In this notebook, we focus on a subset of 401 diagram questions from the TQA
corpus. First we save in a list all the images and text (tokens and synsets) of this
subset. The TQA dataset comprises six types of textual information (paragraph,
question, answer A, answer B, answer C, and answer D) and two types of visual
information (paragraph image and question image). Also, we save in a list the
correct answer of each question as a one-hot vector (Fig. 11.10).

```
text_tokens = [[] for _ in range(6)]
text_synsets = [[] for _ in range(6)]
image_paths = [[] for _ in range(2)]
correct_answers = []

with open("./tutorial/datasamples/tqa_wordnet.json", "r") as file:
    dataset = json.load(file)
for doc in dataset:
    text_tokens[0].append(doc["paragraph_tokens"])
    text_synsets[0].append(doc["paragraph_synsets"])
    if doc["paragraph_img"] == "":
        image_paths[0].append(doc["paragraph_img"])
    else:
        image_paths[0].append("./tqa/"+doc["paragraph_img"])
    text_tokens[1].append(doc["question_tokens"])
    text_synsets[1].append(doc["question_synsets"])
    if doc["question_img"] == "":
        image_paths[1].append(doc["question_img"])
    else:
        image_paths[1].append("./tqa/"+doc["question_img"])
    text_tokens[2].append(doc["answer_a_tokens"])
    text_synsets[2].append(doc["answer_a_synsets"])
    text_tokens[3].append(doc["answer_b_tokens"])
    text_synsets[3].append(doc["answer_b_synsets"])
    text_tokens[4].append(doc["answer_c_tokens"])
    text_synsets[4].append(doc["answer_c_synsets"])
    text_tokens[5].append(doc["answer_d_tokens"])
    text_synsets[5].append(doc["answer_d_synsets"])
    correct_answer = doc["correct_answer"]
    correct_array = np.zeros(4)
    letter_list=["a","b","c","d"]
    for i in range(4):
        if letter_list[i]==correct_answer:
            correct_array[i]=1
    correct_answers.append(correct_array)
correct_answers = np.array(correct_answers)

print("Number of paragraphs (tokens): " + str(len(text_tokens[0])))
```

---

[8]http://vuchallenge.org/tqa.html.

```
print("Number of paragraphs (synsets): " + str(len(text_synsets[0])))
print("Number of paragraph images: " + str(len(image_paths[0])))
print("Number of questions (tokens): " + str(len(text_tokens[1])))
print("Number of questions (synsets): " + str(len(text_synsets[1])))
print("Number of question images: " + str(len(image_paths[1])))
print("Number of answers A (tokens): " + str(len(text_tokens[2])))
print("Number of answers A (synsets): " + str(len(text_synsets[2])))
print("Number of answers B (tokens): " + str(len(text_tokens[3])))
print("Number of answers B (synsets): " + str(len(text_synsets[3])))
print("Number of answers C (tokens): " + str(len(text_tokens[4])))
print("Number of answers C (synsets): " + str(len(text_synsets[4])))
print("Number of answers D (tokens): " + str(len(text_tokens[5])))
print("Number of answers D (synsets): " + str(len(text_synsets[5])))
print("Number of correct_answers: " + str(len(correct_answers)))
```

```
Number of paragraphs (tokens): 401
Number of paragraphs (synsets): 401
Number of paragraph images: 401
Number of questions (tokens): 401
Number of questions (synsets): 401
Number of question images: 401
Number of answers A (tokens): 401
Number of answers A (synsets): 401
Number of answers B (tokens): 401
Number of answers B (synsets): 401
Number of answers C (tokens): 401
Number of answers C (synsets): 401
Number of answers D (tokens): 401
Number of answers D (synsets): 401
Number of correct_answers: 401
```

Let us take a look at the corpus. You can change the index variable to retrieve different samples as you like.

```
index = 4
```

```
print("PARAGRAPH: " + text_tokens[0][index])
try:
  im = cv2.imread(image_paths[0][index])
  plt.imshow(im)
  plt.show()
except:
  print("No paragraph image\n")

print("QUESTION: " + text_tokens[1][index])
im = cv2.imread(image_paths[1][index])
plt.imshow(im)
plt.show()


print("ANSWERS:\n")
print("a. " + text_tokens[2][index])
print("b. " + text_tokens[3][index])
print("c. " + text_tokens[4][index])
print("d. " + text_tokens[5][index]+"\n")

print("CORRECT ANSWER: "+ str(correct_answers[index]))
```

PARAGRAPH:
eventually , the sediment in ocean water is deposited . deposition occurs
where waves and other ocean motions slow . the smallest particles ,
such+as silt and clay , are deposited away from shore . this is where
water is calmer . larger particles are deposited on the beach . this is
where waves and other motions are strongest .

QUESTION: where is eroded intertidal beach sediment deposited in a storm
weather beach system ?

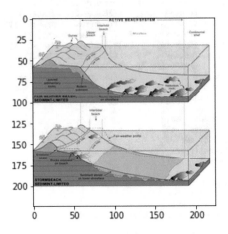

Fig. 11.10 Example of diagram question from the TQA dataset

ANSWERS:
a. dunes
b. continental+shelf
c. shoreface
d. intertidal beach

CORRECT ANSWER: [0. 0. 0. 1.]

Next, we transform these lists into tensors. For images, we transform the images
into numpy arrays and then extract the features after being processed with our pre-
trained model:

```
modelImages = lre_aux.get_model()[0]

images = [[] for _ in range(2)]
for i, img_path_type in enumerate(image_paths):
  for img_path in tqdm(img_path_type,total=len(img_path_type)):
    f_img = open(figure_path, 'rb')
    im = Image.open(f_img)
    arr = np.array(im.convert(mode='RGB'))
    im.close()
    f_img.close()
    feat = modelImages.predict(np.expand_dims(arr,axis=0))
    images[i].extend(feat)
images[0] = np.array(images[0])
images[1] = np.array(images[1])
print("\nSHAPE OF PARAGRAPH IMAGES TENSOR: " + str(np.shape(images[0])))
print("SHAPE OF QUESTION IMAGES TENSOR: " + str(np.shape(images[1])))

100%| 401/401 [00:10<00:00, 38.95it/s]
100%| 401/401 [00:09<00:00, 43.80it/s]


SHAPE OF PARAGRAPH IMAGES TENSOR: (401, 512)
SHAPE OF QUESTION IMAGES TENSOR: (401, 512)
```

We generate the tokenizers for caption tokens and synsets:

```
text_types = [text_tokens, text_synsets]
tokenizers = []

for lst_txt in text_types:
  text_full = []
  for elem in lst_txt:
    text_full.extend(elem)
  tokenizer = Tokenizer(filters='')
  tokenizer.fit_on_texts(text_full)
  tokenizers.append(tokenizer)

tokenizer_tokens, tokenizer_synsets = tokenizers

print("SIZE OF TOKENS VOCABULARY: " + str(len(tokenizer_tokens.word_index)))
print("SIZE OF SYNSETS VOCABULARY: " + str(len(tokenizer_synsets.word_index)))

SIZE OF TOKENS VOCABULARY: 3509
SIZE OF SYNSETS VOCABULARY: 1375
```

Next, we transform the captions into sequence arrays with a different length for each one. We apply the Pareto principle to select the best maximum length possible, covering the 80% of the tokens in the dataset for each type of text information.

```
txt_tokens = [[] for _ in range(6)]
txt_synsets = [[] for _ in range(6)]
max_lens = []
txt = [txt_tokens,txt_synsets]

for i, lst_txt in enumerate(text_types):
  for j, elem in enumerate(lst_txt):
    dict_count = Counter([len(x.split(" ")) for x in elem])
    threshold = 0.8*sum([len(x.split(" ")) for x in elem])
    sorted_by_key = sorted(dict_count.items(), key=lambda kv: kv[0])
    count = 0
    for e in sorted_by_key:
      if count >= threshold:
        break
      else:
        max_len = e[0]
        count = count + e[0]*e[1]
    sequences = tokenizers[i].texts_to_sequences(elem)
    txt[i][j] = pad_sequences(sequences, maxlen=max_len,
        padding="post", truncating="post")
    max_lens.append(max_len)

print("SHAPE OF PARAGRAPH TOKENS SEQUENCES: " + str(np.shape(txt_tokens[0])))
print("SHAPE OF QUESTION TOKENS SEQUENCES: " + str(np.shape(txt_tokens[1])))
print("SHAPE OF ANSWER A TOKENS SEQUENCES: " + str(np.shape(txt_tokens[2])))
print("SHAPE OF ANSWER B TOKENS SEQUENCES: " + str(np.shape(txt_tokens[3])))
print("SHAPE OF ANSWER C TOKENS SEQUENCES: " + str(np.shape(txt_tokens[4])))
print("SHAPE OF ANSWER D TOKENS SEQUENCES: " + str(np.shape(txt_tokens[5])))
print("SHAPE OF PARAGRAPH SYNSETS SEQUENCES: " + str(np.shape(txt_synsets[0])))
print("SHAPE OF QUESTION SYNSETS SEQUENCES: " + str(np.shape(txt_synsets[1])))
print("SHAPE OF ANSWER A SYNSETS SEQUENCES: " + str(np.shape(txt_synsets[2])))
print("SHAPE OF ANSWER B SYNSETS SEQUENCES: " + str(np.shape(txt_synsets[3])))
print("SHAPE OF ANSWER C SYNSETS SEQUENCES: " + str(np.shape(txt_synsets[4])))
print("SHAPE OF ANSWER D SYNSETS SEQUENCES: " + str(np.shape(txt_synsets[5])))

SHAPE OF PARAGRAPH TOKENS SEQUENCES: (401, 230)
SHAPE OF QUESTION TOKENS SEQUENCES: (401, 15)
SHAPE OF ANSWER A TOKENS SEQUENCES: (401, 6)
SHAPE OF ANSWER B TOKENS SEQUENCES: (401, 7)
SHAPE OF ANSWER C TOKENS SEQUENCES: (401, 6)
SHAPE OF ANSWER D TOKENS SEQUENCES: (401, 6)
```

```
SHAPE OF PARAGRAPH SYNSETS SEQUENCES: (401, 230)
SHAPE OF QUESTION SYNSETS SEQUENCES: (401, 15)
SHAPE OF ANSWER A SYNSETS SEQUENCES: (401, 6)
SHAPE OF ANSWER B SYNSETS SEQUENCES: (401, 7)
SHAPE OF ANSWER C SYNSETS SEQUENCES: (401, 6)
SHAPE OF ANSWER D SYNSETS SEQUENCES: (401, 6)
```

11.8.5.2   Building the Model

We adapt the text+image baseline, replacing the visual features with those learnt by the FCC visual subnetwork and including pre-trained Vecsigrafo semantic embeddings, as we did in the previous experiments. In this case, we use element-wise addition to combine pre-trained lemma and concept embeddings with the word embeddings learnt by the network.

First, we load the embedding matrices as we did for the FCC task:

```
embedding_matrices = []
for tok_i in range(len(tokenizers)):
  embedding_matrix = np.zeros((len(tokenizers[tok_i].word_index) + 1, DIM))
  for word, i in tokenizers[tok_i].word_index.items():
    embedding_vector = embedding_indexes[tok_i].get(word)
    if embedding_vector is not None:
      embedding_matrix[i] = embedding_vector
  embedding_matrices.append(embedding_matrix)
embedding_matrix_tokens, embedding_matrix_synsets = embedding_matrices

print("SHAPE OF TOKENS MATRIX: " + str(np.shape(embedding_matrix_tokens)))
print("SHAPE OF SYNSETS MATRIX: " + str(np.shape(embedding_matrix_synsets)))

SHAPE OF TOKENS MATRIX: (3510, 100)
SHAPE OF SYNSETS MATRIX: (1376, 100)
```

Since our TQA model is rather large,[9] we use our lre_aux library (also available in our GitHub) to load it. To compile the model we use Adam optimization with learning rate 0.01. No dropout is used in this experiment.

```
dout = 0.0            #dropout
rdout = 0.0           #recurrent dropout
adam = Adam(lr=1e-2)

tqa_model = lre_aux.get_TQAmodel(DIM,embedding_matrix_tokens,
    embedding_matrix_synsets,dout, rdout, tokenizers, max_lens)
tqa_model.compile(loss="categorical_crossentropy", optimizer=adam,
    metrics=['categorical_accuracy'])
```

11.8.5.3   Training and Evaluation

In this case, we train our model during five epochs, with a batch size of 128 multiple-choice questions:

```
BATCH_SIZE = 128
EPOCHS = 5
```

---

[9]The exact number of parameters in our TQA model is as follows. Total parameters: 1,287,668, trainable parameters: 799,068, non-trainable parameters: 488,600.

We build the input data following our model's structure:

```
train, test = train_test_split(range(np.shape(txt_tokens[0])[0]), test_size=0.1)
X_train = []
X_test = []
for x in range(6):
  X_train.append(txt_tokens[x][train])
  X_train.append(txt_tokens[x][train])
  X_train.append(txt_synsets[x][train])
  if (x <= 1):
    X_train.append(images[x][train])
  X_test.append(txt_tokens[x][test])
  X_test.append(txt_tokens[x][test])
  X_test.append(txt_synsets[x][test])
  if (x <= 1):
    X_test.append(images[x][test])
y_train = correct_answers[train]
y_test = correct_answers[test]
```

Finally, we train the model and we are ready to answer the TQA questions!

```
tqa_model.fit(X_train, y_train, batch_size=BATCH_SIZE, epochs=EPOCHS,
    validation_data=(X_test, y_test), verbose=1)

Train on 360 samples, validate on 41 samples
Epoch 1/5
360/360 [==============================] - 9s 26ms/step - loss: 1.4496 -
categorical_accuracy: 0.2417 - val_loss: 1.3862 -
val_categorical_accuracy: 0.2927
Epoch 2/5
360/360 [==============================] - 2s 5ms/step - loss: 1.3237 -
categorical_accuracy: 0.3722 - val_loss: 1.5633 -
val_categorical_accuracy: 0.1951
Epoch 3/5
360/360 [==============================] - 2s 5ms/step - loss: 1.1962 -
categorical_accuracy: 0.4889 - val_loss: 1.4156 -
val_categorical_accuracy: 0.2439
Epoch 4/5
360/360 [==============================] - 2s 5ms/step - loss: 1.0357 -
categorical_accuracy: 0.6250 - val_loss: 2.2010 -
val_categorical_accuracy: 0.2683
Epoch 5/5
360/360 [==============================] - 2s 5ms/step - loss: 0.8948 -
categorical_accuracy: 0.6111 - val_loss: 1.9704 -
val_categorical_accuracy: 0.1951
```

11.9   Conclusion

There is a wealth of knowledge in scientific literature and only a fraction of it is text. However, understanding scientific figures is a challenging task for machines, which is beyond their ability to process natural images.

In this chapter, we showed empirical evidence of this. The unsupervised co-training of text and visual features from a large corpus of scientific figures and their captions in a correspondence task (FCC) is certainly an effective, flexible, and elegant means towards overcoming such complexity. Furthermore, as shown above such features can be significantly enriched with additional information sources following the methods and techniques described throughout this book. Indeed, FCC enrichment using knowledge graphs provided the largest performance boost, with results generally beyond the state of the art.

Down the road of hybrid methods to natural language processing (and computer vision, as shown herein), it will be interesting to further the study of the interplay between the semantic concepts explicitly represented in different knowledge graphs, contextualized embeddings, e.g. from SciBERT [19], and the text and visual features learnt in the FCC task. Additionally, chartering the knowledge captured in such features is still a due task at the moment of writing these lines.

Chapter 12
Looking into the Future of Natural Language Processing

Abstract It has been a long journey, from theory to methods to code. We hope the book took you painlessly through experiments and real NLP exercises, as much as this is possible, and that you enjoyed it as much as we did. Now, it is time to wrap up. Here, we provide guidelines for future directions in hybrid natural language processing and share our final remarks, additional thoughts, and vision. As a bonus, we also include the personal view of a selection of experts on topics related to hybrid natural language processing. We asked them to comment on their vision, foreseeable barriers to achieve such vision, and ways to navigate towards it, including opportunities and challenges in promising research fields and areas of industrial application. Now it is up to you. Hopefully this book gave you the necessary tools to build powerful NLP systems. Use them!

12.1 Final Remarks, Thoughts and Vision

Recent breakthroughs in artificial intelligence have revolutionized the field of natural language processing. A good example of this is neural language models (Chap. 3). Trained on massive datasets with no prior knowledge about human language or the pragmatics of language and the world, BERT, ELMo, GPT, and others have rapidly advanced the state of the art on many NLP tasks [178] like reading comprehension, machine translation, question answering, and summarization.

The advances brought about by language models are undeniable. However, further levels of abstraction are still needed in order to achieve overall human-level comprehension: Language models like GPT-2 can be used to generate perfectly valid text that continues a cue sentence. However, while lexically and syntactically correct, the output may still be semantically incorrect or against commonsense.[1]

The adoption of language models in Aristo, a system that captures and reasons with scientific knowledge, significantly contributed to achieve amazing success on

---

[1]For a collection of examples using the GPT-2 language model, see: https://thegradient.pub/gpt2-and-the-nature-of-intelligence/.

© Springer Nature Switzerland AG 2020
J. M. Gomez-Perez et al., *A Practical Guide to Hybrid Natural Language Processing*, https://doi.org/10.1007/978-3-030-44830-1_12

the Grade 8 New York Regents Science Exams scoring over 90% on non-diagram, multiple-choice questions, where 3 years before the best systems scored less than 60%.[2] However, this still falls short with certain types of questions involving discrete reasoning, mathematical knowledge, or machine reading comprehension.

We believe that the combination of neural and knowledge-based approaches will be key for the next leap forward in NLP, addressing such challenges through reliably represented meaning that supports reasoning. Knowledge graphs have a key role to play in this regard. They already are a valuable asset to structure information in expressive, machine-actionable ways in many organizations public and corporate. Plus, the increasing adoption of knowledge graph embeddings is having a noticeable impact in the development of new and more effective ways to create, curate, query, and align knowledge graphs (Chap. 9), accelerating take up. Similar to the impact word embeddings (Chaps. 2 and 4) had on capturing information from text, the ability to represent knowledge graphs in a dense vector space (Chap. 5) has paved the ground to exploit structured knowledge in neural NLP architectures.

Under this light, consuming structured knowledge graphs in neural NLP architectures emerges as a feasible, possibly even straightforward approach in the mid-term, with tangible benefits. As shown throughout the book, approaches like HolE and Vecsigrafo (Chap. 6) prove that the information explicitly represented in a knowledge graph can be used to obtain improved accuracies across different NLP tasks. Vecsigrafo produces semantic embeddings that, unlike previous knowledge graph embedding algorithms, not only learn from the graph but also from text corpora, increasing domain coverage beyond the actual scope of the graph. Further, based on different strategies (Chap. 8) to process the training set, co-training word, lemma, and concept embeddings improves the quality of the resulting representations beyond what can be learnt individually by state-of-the-art word and knowledge graph embedding algorithms.

Not unlike language models, Vecsigrafo provides embeddings that are linked to the disambiguated sense of each word and are therefore contextual. Beyond Vecsigrafo, approaches like LMMS and extensions like Transigrafo (also discussed in Chap. 6) suggest the advantages of combining language models and existing knowledge graphs. Such approaches have shown clear practical advantages derived from the integration of language models and knowledge graphs in NLP tasks like word-sense disambiguation, including higher accuracy and reduced training time and hardware infrastructure.

We find particularly interesting how the combined use of language models and language graphs opens the door to NLP architectures where the linguistic and knowledge representation aspects can be completely decoupled from each other, hence potentially allowing for parallel development by independent, possibly unrelated teams. While the language model captures the essence of human language and how sentences are constructed, the knowledge graph contains a human-engineered conceptualization of the entities and relations in the target domain. Language model

---

[2]https://www.nytimes.com/2019/09/04/technology/artificial-intelligence-aristo-passed-test.html.

and knowledge graph can therefore be seen as the main modules that machines need in order to understand text in a way that resembles human understanding. The resulting models can in turn be extended with other modules dealing with, e.g. mathematical or symbolic reasoning. We are very excited about the breakthroughs that this direction of research may unroll in the near future of AI and NLP. We foresee a near future where fine-tuning language models using knowledge graphs is possible, infusing a particular vision and semantics over a domain, as captured by the knowledge graph, in the representations of the language model.

For convenience, most of the knowledge graphs we have used in this book are lexico-semantic databases like WordNet or Sensigrafo. However, applying the approaches described herein to other types of graphs like DBpedia or Wikidata, as well as domain-specific or proprietary graphs, is equally feasible and we are looking forward to seeing the results this may entail for different NLP tasks and domains. We are also eager to see future applications based on corporate graphs and to measure their impact in actual NLP tasks.

Our research has demonstrated the benefits of hybrid NLP systems in areas like disinformation analysis (Chap. 10) and multi-modal machine reading comprehension for question answering (Chap. 11), where hybrid approaches have proved to outperform the previous state of the art. Means to evaluate the quality of the resulting representations have also been provided in the book (Chap. 7). Probably more important than performance increase is how the use of structured knowledge can contribute to increase the expressivity of the model. And the other way around: make use of the concepts and relations in a knowledge graph to provide an explicitly represented grounding of the meaning captured in the model. Creating such grounding in ways that can be exploited, e.g. for an enhanced ability to interpret the model will deserve specific research in the coming years.

We expect further impact in areas like result explainability and bias detection, where knowledge graphs shall contribute decisively to interpret the outcomes of NLP models. Capturing commonsense and reasoning with it is another key area in language understanding. In both cases, we have only started to glimpse the challenges that lie ahead. However, based on commonsense knowledge graphs like ConceptNet and ATOMIC, neural models can acquire commonsense capabilities and reason about previously unseen events. On the other hand, the successful adoption of this type of resources may also transform the way in which knowledge graphs are represented nowadays; for example, ATOMIC represents commonsense statements as text sentences and not in some logical form like most knowledge graphs typically do nowadays.

We are living in exciting times that span across different branches of AI, resulting in an increasing number of opportunities for discussion and research in current and future challenges in NLP and many other areas. We hope this book has helped you acquire the necessary knowledge to combine neural networks and knowledge graphs to successfully solve more and more challenging NLP problems.

12.2   What Is Next? Feedback from the Community

Next, we share the feedback obtained from experts about the future of hybrid NLP systems involving the combination of data-driven, neural architectures, and structured knowledge graphs. Let us see, in lexicographic order, what they have to say:

Agnieszka Lawrynowicz (Poznan University of Technology): I strongly support the ideas and solutions presented in the book. Currently, the most popular methods in NLP work on multi-gigabyte raw data and therefore have too much input, which can sometimes be inconsistent, contradictory or incorrect, while knowledge graphs have a very tight representation of the most important facts, which is easier to curate, and therefore a much smaller chance that the knowledge modeled there is incorrect. I think that joint embeddings of text and knowledge graphs is the right way to go.

One of the barriers to realize the scenario envisioned in this book may be human resources due to traditionally separate communities working on symbolic approaches and statistical ones that have grown largely independently, developing their own methodologies, tools, etc. However, this is changing lately with the growing adoption of statistical approaches including deep learning. Another barrier is that neural approaches require large computational resources even in a hybrid setting. Also, much of the work has been done in word embeddings using only one context of the word, and there is a challenge in case of handling multi-sense words, polysemous embeddings. Interestingly, this challenge is also present in open domain knowledge graphs and ontologies, where some concepts may have slightly different meanings depending on the domain—one way to solve it are micro-theories, tackling only sub-domains. Entity linking is also a very big challenge, for example, in cases when we have a domain knowledge graph and we want to use unstructured data from the open domain. Then, wanting to link a resource from the knowledge graph to some mention in the text, one needs to deal with ambiguity.

I see some promising directions in few-shot learning and transfer learning, i.e. in learning from a small amount of training examples and trying to reuse already acquired prior knowledge. Another trend is explainable AI (XAI). XAI approaches are especially important for machine learning from unstructured data such as text where black-box models are produced and when numerical, distributional representations are used. An interesting next step may also be to employ natural language explanations to support both more effective machine learning processes and generating understandable explanations. I also think that combining knowledge graphs and neural-based natural language processing could be better exploited in the future in natural language inference.

Frank van Harmelen (Vrije Universiteit Amsterdam): The integration of symbolic and neural methods is increasingly seen as crucial for the next generation of breakthroughs in AI research and applications. This book is therefore very important and timely, and its hands-on approach in the form of a "practical guide" will make it all the more accessible and useful for researchers and practitioners alike.

Georg Rehm (German Research Centre for Artificial Intelligence, DFKI): For several years, neural technologies have been defining the state of the art in various natural language processing as well as natural language understanding tasks. On the other hand, being symbolic approaches, knowledge graphs and other more traditional and established methods of representing knowledge, e.g. ontologies, taxonomies, and other kinds of hierarchical knowledge structures, share the obvious advantage that they are intuitive and easily understandable. They are not only machine-readable but human-readable, as well as human-editable.

In one of our research projects we are faced with the following challenge: day in and day out, knowledge workers—we can also call them content curators—work with ever increasing amounts of digital content of various different types, lengths, complexity, and languages. This research project is developing several methods to support these content curators in their daily content curation tasks so that they can, ultimately, produce more content in shorter amounts of time, maybe even content of higher quality. Content curators are laypersons when it comes to AI and NLP/NLU, which is why we cannot directly expose them to the task of handling data and training classifiers. What we would like to accomplish is a way for content curators to be able to manipulate a knowledge graph that represents different genres, types, or classes of texts including their defining characteristics, which can also be perceived as descriptive metadata that humans understand. In a second step, such symbolically represented content is to be exploited—most likely including additional datasets—in a classification system that is based on the most recent neural technologies. In this way, we want to combine the ease-of-use of symbolic approaches with the state-of-the-art power of current sub-symbolic approaches.

While it is still open how this challenging setup can be accomplished, we hope that the present book will provide our research team with enough food for thought to tackle at least the initial steps.

Ivan Vulić (University of Cambridge): Combining data-driven, i.e. neural methods and knowledge-based approaches leads to a natural synergy, as the two approaches are often complementary when it comes to knowledge coded, extracted, or used within the two paradigms. However, although their "cooperation" is indeed natural on a high level, there is a multitude of conceptual and practical challenges to overcome in order to make such hybrid approaches work. One practical obstacle is that different research communities often "speak in different tongues," which hinders efficient sharing of ideas, resources, and knowledge. Therefore, I hope that this book will succeed in these main goals: (1) to provide a set of practical guidelines and examples related to such hybrid, i.e., synergistic approaches, as well as (2) to offer a systematic overview of the key practices and challenges so that different research communities start learning from each other.

This book might serve as a bridge which will enable a much smoother sharing of knowledge. As an NLP researcher, I am looking forward to understanding more about the inner workings of ontology and KB creation, and how to leverage such information to boost our data-driven NLP algorithms, and it is great to have this summarized at one place in a concise way. One major area of application where such hybrid approaches can lead to huge breakthroughs in the future is cross-lingual learning and transfer learning. Dealing with a large number of languages, dialects, tasks, and domains, we are bound to be creative and come up with solutions that exploit disparate and complementary data and knowledge sources, and I believe that only through such hybrid approaches we can advance our current methods across a wide spectrum of language varieties and domains. This book will serve as an extremely useful and very pragmatic entry point for anyone interested in tapping into the mysteries of hybrid NLP.

Jacob Eisenstein and Yuval Pinter (Google Research and Georgia Institute of Technology): Recent work has shown that knowledge can be acquired from raw text by training neural networks to "fill in the blanks." A now classic example is BERT, which is a deep self-attention network that is trained to reconstruct texts in which 15% of tokens are masked. Remarkably, BERT and related models are able to learn many things about language and the world, such as:

- Subjects and verbs must agree in English [66].
- Doughnuts are something you can eat.
- Dante was born in Florence [141].
- Tim Cook is the CEO of Apple.

Each of these facts has its own epistemological status: subject-verb agreement is a constant in standard English, but there are dialects with different syntactic constraints [71]; it is possible (though sad) to imagine a world in which doughnuts are used for something other food; there is one particular "Dante" who was born in one particular "Florence," but the statement is incorrect if referring to Dante Smith or Florence, New Jersey; Tim Cook is the CEO of Apple in 2020, but this was not true in the past and will cease to be true at some point in the future. Because neural language models are unaware of these distinctions, they are overconfident, insufficiently adaptable to context, and unable to reason about counterfactuals or historical situations—all potentially critical impediments to sensitive applications.

Future work in natural language processing should therefore develop hybrid representations that enable such metacognitive capabilities. The integration of natural language processing with knowledge graphs seems like a promising approach towards this goal, but there are several challenges towards realizing this vision. From a technical perspective, the arbitrary and dynamic nature of graph structures make them difficult to integrate with state-of-the-art neural methods for natural language processing, which emphasize high throughput computations on static representations. From a modeling perspective, new approaches are needed to incorporate network-level generalizations such as "verbs tend to be derived from more abstract nouns," which have so far only been integrated through hand-engineered features [142]. Most significantly, this research agenda requires benchmarks that accurately measure progress towards systems that not only know what facts are asserted in a collection of texts, but understand how those facts relate to each other and to the external world.

Núria Bel (Universitat Pompeu Fabra): Natural language processing depends on what has been called language resources. Language resources are data of the language that is addressed and data selected for the domain the system is going to address. NLP engines are generic, but they require information to process the particular words and sentences of particular languages. This linguistic information has been provided in the form of dictionaries and rule-based components. These resources are structured knowledge representations. They are meant to feed engines with representations that already capture abstractions to generalize over any comprehensive sample of a language.

The most striking fact in the recent success of deep neural approaches is that they mostly work with language resources that are just raw text. They seem not to require of an intermediate representation that generalizes over the data. However, to achieve the awesome accuracy that leaderboards of most NLP benchmarks consistently show, they depend on very large amounts of raw texts. For instance, BERT has been trained with three billion words, GPT-2 has been trained on 40GB of Internet text (eight million web pages), and the latest neural conversational model to the moment of writing this paragraph has been trained with 341GB of text (40B words).

This dependency of very large amounts of data can make very difficult to apply these deep learning engines to particular scenarios. Current deep systems are not beating statistical or knowledge-based systems when only small datasets are available, which is the case for many specific domains and languages. Therefore, the hybridization of deep learning and knowledge-based approaches is a necessary step to exploit the enormous success of deep learning for a large variety of applications for which it would not be possible to gather enough data otherwise. Knowledge-based techniques provide the generalization capability required to alleviate data dependency in deep learning methods.

Oscar Corcho (Universidad Politécnica de Madrid): The world of natural language processing has been rapidly changing in recent years, offering an enormous set of possibilities to industry, governments, and academia to deal with the large corpora of texts that they have all collectively accumulated or that are available for free on the Web and at specialized document repositories. An important part of the most recent advances is related to the usage of neural-based approaches, which have demonstrated their capacity to perform better than more traditional approaches, and most of the work of research groups and companies that are trying to make research and apply NLP for a range of problems is moving towards that direction.

This is the case of our own work to fight corruption together with associations of journalists and governmental agencies, where we are focusing on named entity recognition over all sorts of documents, to understand better the roles that entitles play in documents such as contracts, so as to apply automatic anonymization techniques for documents, as well as on our work focused on organizing large multi-lingual corpora of texts (e.g., patent databases, scientific literature, project proposals), detecting similarity among documents based on topics that are shared among them. In all these cases, a smart combination of traditional and neural-based approaches, together with the use of existing knowledge graphs, is key to obtain the best results.

Paul Groth (Universiteit van Amsterdam): The combination of neural-based deep learning techniques and massive knowledge graphs have become a central component of modern systems that need to use and understand text. Knowledge graphs both provide additional background information that cannot be easily found in text (e.g., common sense knowledge, statistical information). Additionally, knowledge graphs act, in some sense, as communication mechanism between stakeholders whether they be human or machine. What do agree on as an organization as important entities? What are the important properties that we agree upon?

A critical question going forward is what the representation of our knowledge should be? The advent of large-scale language models as described in this book is an important impetus for this question. Can a language model be our knowledge graph? Can the knowledge graph just be represented in text? What should be text and what should be represented as structured graph form? The view posited in this book that a hybrid approach is needed seems natural but we need to continue to probe what combination of textual, logical, or embedded representation can best serve these important applications.

Marco Rospocher (University of Verona): Despite the growing amount of machine-processable data being released nowadays, the web still abounds of unstructured content (text, images, audio/video materials) mainly foreseen for human consumption. The same web page may contain knowledge about an event or some entities of the world, presented in different forms: consider, for instance, a news item, which may consist of a textual description integrated with images and videos.

While these different signals are all about the same content, each of them may contain some complementary, unique information that cannot be found in the others (e.g., it is unlikely that a text describes, in natural language, visual aspects that are better shown in the accompanying image), which thus makes their joint interpretation and processing—possibly in light of some already available background knowledge—fundamental in order to provide some software agent with full access to the actual knowledge content of the page.

Tackling such a challenging problem requires thus the development of new, hybrid, interdisciplinary, knowledge-based techniques that have to combine research works from different areas, such as knowledge representation and reasoning, natural languages processing, image processing, audio processing, and video processing.

Marco Varone (Expert System President and CTO): After working more than 25 years in the NLP space, designing cutting edge technology and solving real business problems with a measurable ROI, I can affirm that a magic technique to solve all NLP problems does not exist and will never exist. We need to continue improving existing techniques and search for new ones but it is very clear that the future belongs to hybrid approaches that combine different techniques in a pragmatic and cost-effective way: the target is to solve real-world problems and not to improve by 0.5% the result in toy benchmarks.

Philipp Cimiano (Bielefeld University and Cognitive Interaction Technology Excellence Cluster, CITEC): As we attempt to solve natural language processing tasks of increasing complexity, it is becoming clear that the performance of systems and models that are purely data-induced will soon reach a plateau. For practical applications, it is not viable to collect and label large amounts of training data, thus limiting the applicability and generalization ability of deep learning approaches which typically are extremely data-hungry.

If we want machines to generalize faster, be adaptable to new domains, avoid doing mistakes that seem obvious to a human expert as well as explain and justify their decisions at a rational level that a human can understand, the incorporation of domain knowledge is fundamental. Along these lines, the book by Jose Manuel Gomez-Perez and colleagues is addressing a very timely and important challenge, the one of how to design hybrid systems that benefit from the robustness and pattern learning ability of learning approaches combined with the ability to represent and model domain knowledge in the form of knowledge graphs. The ability to combine these methods will ultimately decide about the applicability of artificial intelligence systems in real-world tasks in which machines are required to become competent partners supporting decision-making rather than pre-rational machines solving tasks they do not understand and the solutions to which they cannot really explain because they lack a corresponding conceptualization.

Richard Benjamins (Telefonica Data and AI Ambassador): This book is an excellent example of the type of research we need more of: the combination of data-driven AI with knowledge-driven AI to advance the state of the art. Current success of AI is mostly due to progress in data-driven AI (deep learning), but there is a limit to what this technology can achieve and new breakthroughs are required to make the next step towards artificial general intelligence. Such breakthroughs could come from a hybrid approach where both technologies mutually bootstrap each other.

Rudi Studer (Karlsruhe Institute of Technology): The tremendous boost of AI in recent years is to a large extent based on the success of machine learning, especially deep learning, in various application scenarios, like, e.g. classification tasks or machine translation, where a huge amount of training data is available. As a result, many people equate AI with (sub-symbolic) machine learning, thus ignoring the field of symbolic knowledge modeling, nowadays most prominently represented by the notion of knowledge graphs. Vice versa, people from the knowledge modeling area are often not familiar with the recent developments in the field of (sub-symbolic) machine learning.

Therefore, the book at hand is an urgently needed book to provide a bridge between these still partially separate communities and to show the benefits of integrating symbolic and sub-symbolic methods, here illustrated in the area of NLP. Furthermore, being a more practically oriented text book, these integration aspects are made accessible for practitioners and thus for a broad audience. I also appreciate that approaches that still need a lot of progress, i.e. multi-linguality and multi-modality, are being discussed as well.

I am absolutely convinced that hybrid approaches are very promising and are needed not only in the area of NLP but also in other areas where pure sub-symbolic machine learning approaches lack of explainability, when you, e.g. think of medical applications, or where pure KG approaches lack of methods to make them more complete or more up-to-date by machine learning.

Vinay Chaudhri (Stanford University): An important goal for knowledge acquisition is to create explicit knowledge representations of a domain that matches human understanding and enables precise reasoning with it. While in some domains such as search, recommendation, translation, etc., human understanding and precision are not hard requirements, there are numerous domains where these requirements are essential. Some examples include knowledge of law for income tax calculations, knowledge of a subject domain for teaching it to a student, knowledge of a contract so that a computer can automatically execute it, etc. The creation of an explicit representation of knowledge that is both human understandable and enables accurate reasoning remains a primarily manual exercise. That is because the current generation of natural language processing methods achieve scale by either sacrificing precision or by sacrificing human understanding. As a result, they work well for those problems where an explicit human understandable knowledge representation is not required and/or there is no hard precision requirement on the result of reasoning. There is a need for research that can leverage the automation and scaling properties of natural language processing, and yet, does not sacrifice the goal of precision and explicit human understandable knowledge representation.

We need to conduct experiments in multiple domains with the goal of producing explicit human understandable knowledge representation that support precise reasoning and yet leverage automation. There are situations where the output of natural language processing is so noisy that the cost of correcting its output is greater than the cost of manual knowledge engineering. In other cases, the desired representation is not externalized in the natural language text, and no amount of natural language processing will yield the knowledge representation that one is seeking. We need to better characterize tasks and situations where automation offered by natural language processing leads to net reduction in the cost of creating the representation. We need benchmarks and tasks that can give us quantitative data on tasks such as: extracting key terms, extracting relations between key terms, and algorithms for assembling the relations into a global whole. As the end goal is for the representation to be human understandable, we need to develop new models for getting human input. Such methods may involve dedicated domain experts, crowd workers, or automatic quality checking algorithms.

A major barrier to achieving this vision is to address the narrative in the research community that the knowledge engineering does not scale, and that the natural language processing scales. Such claims are based on false characterization of the tasks addressed by natural language processing and fail to consider that some of the most widely used resources such as the WordNet were manually engineered. The success of web-scale methods is crucially dependent on the human input in the form of hyperlinks, click data, or explicit user feedback. On the technological front, there are three major challenges: advance the semantic parsing technology to produce better quality output from natural language processing; to develop high quality knowledge engineered resources that can serve as training data for NLP; and to develop integrated development environments that incorporate automation, human validation, and knowledge integration capabilities.

References

1. Agirre, E., Alfonseca, E., Hall, K., Kravalova, J., Pas, M., Soroa, A.: A study on similarity and relatedness using distributional and WordNet-based approaches. Human Language Technologies: The 2009 Annual Conference of the North American Chapter of the ACL (June), 19–27 (2009). https://doi.org/10.3115/1620754.1620758
2. Aker, A., Derczynski, L., Bontcheva, K.: Simple Open Stance Classification for Rumour Analysis (2017). https://doi.org/10.26615/978-954-452-049-6_005
3. Ammar, W., Groeneveld, D., Bhagavatula, C., Beltagy, I., Crawford, M., Downey, D., Dunkelberger, J., Elgohary, A., Feldman, S., Ha, V., Kinney, R., Kohlmeier, S., Lo, K., Murray, T., Ooi, H., Peters, M., Power, J., Skjonsberg, S., Wang, L., Wilhelm, C., Yuan, Z., van Zuylen, M., Etzioni, O.: Construction of the literature graph in semantic scholar. In: NAACL-HTL (2018)
4. Antol, S., Agrawal, A., Lu, J., Mitchell, M., Batra, D., Zitnick, C., Parikh, D.: Vqa: Visual question answering. 2015 IEEE International Conference on Computer Vision (ICCV) pp. 2425–2433 (2015)
5. Arandjelovic, R., Zisserman, A.: Look, listen and learn. 2017 IEEE International Conference on Computer Vision (ICCV) pp. 609–617 (2017)
6. Asher, N., Lascarides, A.: Strategic conversation. Semantics and Pragmatics 6(2), 1–62 (2013). https://doi.org/10.3765/sp.6.2
7. Auer, S., Bizer, C., Kobilarov, G., Lehmann, J., Cyganiak, R., Ives, Z.G.: Dbpedia: A nucleus for a web of open data. In: ISWC/ASWC (2007)
8. Augenstein, I., Rocktäschel, T., Vlachos, A., Bontcheva, K.: Stance Detection with Bidirectional Conditional Encoding. In: EMNLP (2016)
9. Babakar, M., Moy, W.: The State of Automated Factchecking -. Tech. rep. (2016). URL https://fullfact.org/blog/2016/aug/automated-factchecking/
10. Bader, S., Hitzler, P.: Dimensions of neural-symbolic integration — a structured survey. In: S. Artemov, H. Barringer, A.S.d. Garcez, L.C. Lamb, J. Woods (eds.) We Will Show Them: Essays in Honour of Dov Gabbay, vol. 1, pp. 167–194. King's College Publications (2005)
11. Bahdanau, D., Cho, K., Bengio, Y.: Neural machine translation by jointly learning to align and translate. arXiv e-prints **abs/1409.0473** (2014). URL https://arxiv.org/abs/1409.0473. Presented at the 7th International Conference on Learning Representations, 2015
12. Baker, C.F., Fillmore, C.J., Lowe, J.B.: The Berkeley Framenet project. In: Proceedings of the 17th International Conference on Computational Linguistics - Volume 1, COLING '98, pp. 86–90. Association for Computational Linguistics, Stroudsburg, PA, USA (1998). https://doi.org/10.3115/980451.980860.

13. Baker, S., Reichart, R., Korhonen, A.: An unsupervised model for instance level subcategorization acquisition pp. 278–289 (2014). https://doi.org/10.3115/v1/D14-1034. URL https://www.aclweb.org/anthology/D14-1034

14. Balažević, I., Allen, C., Hospedales, T.M.: Tucker: Tensor factorization for knowledge graph completion. arXiv preprint arXiv:1901.09590 (2019)

15. Baroni, M., Dinu, G., Kruszewski, G.: Don't count, predict! a systematic comparison of context-counting vs. context-predicting semantic vectors. In: Proceedings of the 52nd Annual Meeting of the Association for Computational Linguistics (Volume 1: Long Papers), pp. 238–247. Association for Computational Linguistics, Baltimore, Maryland (2014). https://doi.org/10.3115/v1/P14-1023. URL https://www.aclweb.org/anthology/P14-1023

16. Baroni, M., Lenci, A.: Distributional memory: A general framework for corpus-based Semantics. Computational Linguistics **36**(4), 673–721 (2010)

17. Barriere, C.: Natural language understanding in a semantic web context, 1st edn. Springer International Publishing (2016)

18. Belinkov, Y., Durrani, N., Dalvi, F., Sajjad, H., Glass, J.: What do neural machine translation models learn about morphology? In: Proceedings of the 55th Annual Meeting of the Association for Computational Linguistics (Volume 1: Long Papers), pp. 861–872. Association for Computational Linguistics, Vancouver, Canada (2017). https://doi.org/10.18653/v1/P17-1080. URL https://www.aclweb.org/anthology/P17-1080

19. Beltagy, I., Cohan, A., Lo, K.: Scibert: Pretrained contextualized embeddings for scientific text (2019)

20. Bender, E.M.: 100 things you always wanted to know about semantics & pragmatics but were afraid to ask. Tech. rep., Melbourne, Australia (2018). URL https://www.aclweb.org/anthology/P18-5001

21. Bengio, Y., Ducharme, R., Vincent, P., Janvin, C.: A neural probabilistic language model. J. Mach. Learn. Res. **3**, 1137–1155 (2003). URL http://dl.acm.org/citation.cfm?id=944919.944966

22. Blum, A., Mitchell, T.: Combining labeled and unlabeled data with co-training. In: COLT (1998)

23. Bojanowski, P., Grave, E., Joulin, A., Mikolov, T.: Enriching word vectors with subword information. Transactions of the Association for Computational Linguistics **5**, 135–146 (2016)

24. Bordes, A., Glorot, X., Weston, J., Bengio, Y.: A semantic matching energy function for learning with multi-relational data. Machine Learning **94**(2), 233–259 (2014)

25. Bordes, A., Usunier, N., Weston, J., Yakhnenko, O.: Translating embeddings for modeling multi-relational data. Advances in NIPS **26**, 2787–2795 (2013). https://doi.org/10.1007/s13398-014-0173-7.2

26. Bruni, E., Boleda, G., Baroni, M., Tran, N.K.: Distributional semantics in technicolor. Proceedings of the 50th Annual Meeting of the Association for Computational Linguistics **1**(July), 136–145 (2012). https://doi.org/10.1109/ICRA.2016.7487801

27. Burns, G., Shi, X., Wu, Y., Cao, H., Natarajan, P.: Towards evidence extraction: Analysis of sci. figures from studies of molecular interactions. In: SemSci@ISWC (2018)

28. Camacho-Collados, J., Pilehvar, M.T., Collier, N., Navigli, R.: Semeval-2017 task 2: Multilingual and cross-lingual semantic word similarity. In: SemEval@ACL (2017)

29. Camacho-Collados, J., Pilehvar, M.T., Navigli, R.: NASARI: Integrating explicit knowledge and corpus statistics for a multilingual representation of concepts and entities. Artificial Intelligence **240**, 36–64 (2016). https://doi.org/10.1016/j.artint.2016.07.005

30. Chang, L., Zhu, M., Gu, T., Bin, C., Qian, J., Zhang, J.: Knowledge graph embedding by dynamic translation. IEEE Access **5**, 20898–20907 (2017)

31. Chen, X., Liu, Z., Sun, M.: A unified model for word sense representation and disambiguation. In: the 2014 Conference on Empirical Methods in Natural Language Processing, pp. 1025–1035 (2014)

32. Cho, K., van Merrienboer, B., Bahdanau, D., Bengio, Y.: On the properties of neural machine translation: encoder–decoder approaches. In: Proceedings of SSST-8, Eighth Workshop on Syntax, Semantics and Structure in Statistical Translation, pp. 103–111. Association for Computational Linguistics, Doha, Qatar (2014). https://doi.org/10.3115/v1/W14-4012. URL https://www.aclweb.org/anthology/W14-4012

33. Cimiano, P., Unger, C., McCrae, J.: Ontology-Based Interpretation of Natural Language. Morgan and Claypool (2014). URL https://ieeexplore.ieee.org/document/6813475

34. Clark, C., Divvala, S.: Pdffigures 2.0: Mining figures from research papers. 2016 IEEE/ACM Joint Conference on Digital Libraries (JCDL) pp. 143–152 (2016)

35. Clark, K., Khandelwal, U., Levy, O., Manning, C.D.: What does BERT look at? An analysis of BERT's attention. ArXiv **abs/1906.04341** (2019)

36. Collobert, R., Weston, J.: A unified architecture for natural language processing: Deep neural networks with multitask learning. In: Proceedings of the 25th International Conference on Machine Learning, ICML '08, pp. 160–167. ACM, New York, NY, USA (2008). https://doi.org/10.1145/1390156.1390177. URL http://doi.acm.org/10.1145/1390156.1390177

37. Conneau, A., Lample, G., Ranzato, M., Denoyer, L., Jégou, H.: Word Translation Without Parallel Data. arXiv preprint (2017). http://dx.doi.org/10.1111/j.1540-4560.2007.00543.x. URL https://arxiv.org/pdf/1710.04087.pdf http://arxiv.org/abs/1710.04087

38. Delobelle, P., Winters, T., Berendt, B.: Robbert: a Dutch RoBERTa-based language model (2020)

39. Denaux, R., Gomez-Perez, J.: Vecsigrafo: Corpus-based word-concept embeddings. Semantic Web pp. 1–28 (2019). https://doi.org/10.3233/SW-190361

40. Denaux, R., Gomez-Perez, J.M.: Towards a Vecsigrafo: Portable semantics in knowledge-based text analytics. In: International Workshop on Hybrid Statistical Semantic Understanding and Emerging Semantics @ISWC17, CEUR Workshop Proceedings. CEUR-WS.org (2017). URL http://ceur-ws.org/Vol-1923/article-04.pdf

41. Denaux, R., Gomez-Perez, J.M.: Assessing the Lexico-semantic relational knowledge captured by word and concept embeddings. In: Proceedings of the 10th International Conference on Knowledge Capture, pp. 29–36. ACM (2019)

42. Deng, J., Dong, W., Socher, R., Li, L.J., Li, K., Fei-Fei, L.: ImageNet: A Large-Scale Hierarchical Image Database. In: CVPR09 (2009)

43. Dettmers, T., Minervini, P., Stenetorp, P., Riedel, S.: Convolutional 2d knowledge graph embeddings. In: Thirty-Second AAAI Conference on Artificial Intelligence (2018)

44. Devlin, J., Chang, M., Lee, K., Toutanova, K.: BERT: pre-training of deep bidirectional transformers for language understanding. CoRR **abs/1810.04805** (2018). URL http://arxiv.org/abs/1810.04805

45. Dinu, G., Lazaridou, A., Baroni, M.: Improving zero-shot learning by mitigating the hubness problem. arXiv preprint arXiv:1412.6568 (2014)

46. Domingos, P.: A few useful things to know about machine learning. Commun. ACM **55**(10), 78–87 (2012). https://doi.org/10.1145/2347736.2347755

47. Duong, L., Kanayama, H., Ma, T., Bird, S., Cohn, T.: Learning crosslingual word embeddings without bilingual corpora. In: Proceedings of the 2016 Conference on Empirical Methods in Natural Language Processing, pp. 1285–1295. Association for Computational Linguistics, Austin, Texas (2016). https://doi.org/10.18653/v1/D16-1136. URL https://www.aclweb.org/anthology/D16-1136

48. Ebisu, T., Ichise, R.: Toruse: Knowledge graph embedding on a lie group. In: Thirty-Second AAAI Conference on Artificial Intelligence (2018)

49. Ebisu, T., Ichise, R.: Graph pattern entity ranking model for knowledge graph completion. arXiv preprint arXiv:1904.02856 (2019)

50. Eisenschtat, A., Wolf, L.: Linking image and text with 2-way nets. 2017 IEEE Conf. on Computer Vision and Pattern Recognition (CVPR) (2017)

51. Eisenstein, J.: Introduction to natural language processing, 1st edn. Adaptive Computation and Machine Learning series, The MIT Press (2019)

52. Emmert-Streib, F., Dehmer, M., Shi, Y.: Fifty years of graph matching, network alignment and network comparison. Information Sciences **346**, 180–197 (2016)
53. Engilberge, M., Chevallier, L., Pérez, P., Cord, M.: Finding beans in burgers: Deep semantic-visual embedding with localization. 2018 IEEE/CVF Conference on Computer Vision and Pattern Recognition (2018)
54. Fader, A., Zettlemoyer, L., Etzioni, O.: Open question answering over curated and extracted knowledge bases. In: Proceedings of the 20th ACM SIGKDD international conference on Knowledge discovery and data mining, pp. 1156–1165. ACM (2014)
55. Faghri, F., Fleet, D., Kiros, J., Fidler, S.: Vse++: Improving visual-semantic embeddings with hard negatives. In: BMVC (2017)
56. Fallis, D.: A Conceptual Analysis of Disinformation. iConference pp. 30–31 (2009). https://doi.org/10.1111/j.1468-5914.1984.tb00498.x
57. Fan, M., Zhou, Q., Chang, E., Zheng, T.F.: Transition-based knowledge graph embedding with relational mapping properties. In: Proceedings of the 28th Pacific Asia Conference on Language, Information and Computing, pp. 328–337 (2014)
58. Feigenbaum, E.A.: The art of artificial intelligence: Themes and case studies of knowledge engineering. Tech. rep., Stanford, CA, USA (1977)
59. Fellbaum, C.: Wordnet : an electronic lexical database (2000)
60. Finkelstein, L., Gabrilovich, E., Matias, Y., Rivlin, E., Solan, Z., Wolfman, G., Ruppin, E.: Placing search in context: the concept revisited. ACM Transactions on Information Systems **20**(1), 116–131 (2002). https://doi.org/10.1145/503104.503110
61. Gábor, D.: Associative holographic memories. IBM Journal of Research and Development **13**(2), 156–159 (1969)
62. Garcia, A., Gomez-Perez, J.: Not just about size - A study on the role of distributed word representations in the analysis of scientific publications. In: 1st ws. on Deep Learning for Knowledge Graphs (DL4KGS) co-located with ESWC (2018)
63. Garcia-Silva, A., Berrio, C., Gómez-Pérez, J.M.: An empirical study on pre-trained embeddings and language models for bot detection. In: Proceedings of the 4th Workshop on Representation Learning for NLP (RepL4NLP-2019), pp. 148–155. Association for Computational Linguistics, Florence, Italy (2019). https://doi.org/10.18653/v1/W19-4317. URL https://www.aclweb.org/anthology/W19-4317
64. Gerz, D., Vulić, I., Hill, F., Reichart, R., Korhonen, A.: SimVerb-3500: A large-scale evaluation set of verb similarity. In: Proceedings of the 2016 Conference on Empirical Methods in Natural Language Processing, pp. 2173–2182. Association for Computational Linguistics, Austin, Texas (2016). https://doi.org/10.18653/v1/D16-1235. URL https://www.aclweb.org/anthology/D16-1235
65. Gilani, Z., Kochmar, E., Crowcroft, J.: Classification of twitter accounts into automated agents and human users. In: Proceedings of the 2017 IEEE/ACM International Conference on Advances in Social Networks Analysis and Mining 2017, ASONAM '17, pp. 489–496. ACM, New York, NY, USA (2017). https://doi.org/10.1145/3110025.3110091. URL http://doi.acm.org/10.1145/3110025.3110091
66. Goldberg, Y.: Assessing bert's syntactic abilities. CoRR **abs/1901.05287** (2019). URL http://arxiv.org/abs/1901.05287
67. Goldberg, Y., Hirst, G.: Neural Network Methods in Natural Language Processing. Morgan and Claypool Publishers (2017)
68. Gómez-Pérez, A., Fernández-López, M., Corcho, Ó.: Ontological engineering: With examples from the areas of knowledge management, e-commerce and the semantic web. In: Advanced Information and Knowledge Processing (2004)
69. Gomez-Perez, J.M., Ortega, R.: Look, read and enrich - learning from scientific figures and their captions. In: Proceedings of the 10th International Conference on Knowledge Capture, K-CAP '19, p. 101–108. Association for Computing Machinery, New York, NY, USA (2019). URL https://doi.org/10.1145/3360901.3364420

70. Grave, E., Joulin, A., Berthet, Q.: Unsupervised alignment of embeddings with Wasserstein procrustes. arXiv preprint arXiv:1805.11222 (2018)

71. Green, L.J.: African American English: A linguistic introduction (2002)

72. Gunning, D., Chaudhri, V.K., Clark, P., Barker, K., Chaw, S.Y., Greaves, M., Grosof, B.N., Leung, A., McDonald, D.D., Mishra, S., Pacheco, J., Porter, B.W., Spaulding, A., Tecuci, D., Tien, J.: Project halo update - progress toward digital Aristotle. AI Magazine **31**, 33–58 (2010)

73. Hammond, T., Pasin, M., Theodoridis, E.: Data integration and disintegration: Managing springer nature SciGraph with SHACL and OWL. In: N. Nikitina, D. Song, A. Fokoue, P. Haase (eds.) International Semantic Web Conference (Posters, Demos and Industry Tracks), *CEUR Workshop Proceedings*, vol. 1963. CEUR-WS.org (2017). URL http://dblp.uni-trier.de/db/conf/semweb/iswc2017p.html#HammondPT17

74. Han, L., L. Kashyap, A., Finin, T., Mayfield, J., Weese, J.: UMBC_EBIQUITY-CORE: Semantic textual similarity systems. In: Second Joint Conference on Lexical and Computational Semantics (*SEM), Volume 1: Proceedings of the Main Conference and the Shared Task: Semantic Textual Similarity, pp. 44–52. Association for Computational Linguistics, Atlanta, Georgia, USA (2013). URL https://www.aclweb.org/anthology/S13-1005

75. Hancock, J.T., Curry, L.E., Goorha, S., Woodworth, M.: On lying and being lied to: A linguistic analysis of deception in computer-mediated communication. Discourse Processes **45**(1), 1–23 (2007). URL https://doi.org/10.1080/01638530701739181

76. Heinzerling, B., Strube, M.: BPEmb: Tokenization-free pre-trained subword embeddings in 275 languages. In: Proceedings of the Eleventh International Conference on Language Resources and Evaluation (LREC 2018). European Language Resources Association (ELRA), Miyazaki, Japan (2018). URL https://www.aclweb.org/anthology/L18-1473

77. Hill, F., Reichart, R., Korhonen, A.: Simlex-999: Evaluating semantic models with (genuine) similarity estimation. Computational Linguistics **41**, 665–695 (2015)

78. Hitzler, P., Bianchi, F., Ebrahimi, M., Sarker, M.K.: Neural-symbolic integration and the semantic web a position paper (2019)

79. Hochreiter, S., Schmidhuber, J.: Long short-term memory. Neural Comput. **9**(8), 1735–1780 (1997). URL http://dx.doi.org/10.1162/neco.1997.9.8.1735

80. Hodosh, M., Young, P., Hockenmaier, J.: Framing image description as a ranking task: Data, models and evaluation metrics. In: J.AI Res. (2013)

81. Howard, J., Ruder, S.: Fine-tuned language models for text classification. CoRR **abs/1801.06146** (2018). URL http://arxiv.org/abs/1801.06146

82. Iacobacci, I., Pilehvar, M.T., Navigli, R.: SENSEMBED: Learning sense embeddings for word and relational similarity. In: 53rd Annual Meeting of the ACL, pp. 95–105 (2015). https://doi.org/10.3115/v1/P15-1010

83. Ioffe, S., Szegedy, C.: Batch normalization: Accelerating deep network training by reducing internal covariate shift. In: ICML 2015 (2015)

84. Jawahar, G., Sagot, B., Seddah, D.: What does BERT learn about the structure of language? In: Proceedings of the 57th Annual Meeting of the Association for Computational Linguistics, pp. 3651–3657. Association for Computational Linguistics, Florence, Italy (2019). https://doi.org/10.18653/v1/P19-1356. URL https://www.aclweb.org/anthology/P19-1356

85. Ji, G., Liu, K., He, S., Zhao, J.: Knowledge graph completion with adaptive sparse transfer matrix. In: Thirtieth AAAI Conference on Artificial Intelligence (2016)

86. Jiang, W., Wang, G., Bhuiyan, M.Z.A., Wu, J.: Understanding graph-based trust evaluation in online social networks: Methodologies and challenges. ACM Computing Surveys (CSUR) **49**(1), 10 (2016)

87. Jozefowicz, R., Vinyals, O., Schuster, M., Shazeer, N., Wu, Y.: Exploring the limits of language modeling. arXiv preprint arXiv:1602.02410 (2016)

88. Jurafsky, D., Martin, J.H.: Speech and Language Processing (2Nd Edition). Prentice-Hall, Inc., Upper Saddle River, NJ, USA (2009)

89. Kalchbrenner, N., Blunsom, P.: Recurrent continuous translation models. In: Proceedings of the 2013 Conference on Empirical Methods in Natural Language Processing, pp. 1700–1709. Association for Computational Linguistics, Seattle, Washington, USA (2013). URL https://www.aclweb.org/anthology/D13-1176

90. Kazemi, S.M., Poole, D.: Simple embedding for link prediction in knowledge graphs. In: Advances in Neural Information Processing Systems, pp. 4284–4295 (2018)

91. Kejriwal, M.: Domain-specific knowledge graph construction. In: SpringerBriefs in Computer Science (2019)

92. Kembhavi, A., Salvato, M., Kolve, E., Seo, M., Hajishirzi, H., Farhadi, A.: A diagram is worth a dozen images. In: ECCV (2016)

93. Kembhavi, A., Seo, M., Schwenk, D., Choi, J., Farhadi, A., Hajishirzi, H.: Are you smarter than a sixth grader? textbook question answering for multimodal machine comprehension. 2017 IEEE Conference on Computer Vision and Pattern Recognition (CVPR) pp. 5376–5384 (2017)

94. Keskar, N.S., McCann, B., Varshney, L.R., Xiong, C., Socher, R.: Ctrl: A conditional transformer language model for controllable generation. ArXiv **abs/1909.05858** (2019)

95. Khot, T., Sabharwal, A., Clark, P.: Scitail: A textual entailment dataset from science question answering. In: Proceedings of the 32nd AAAI Conference on Artificial Intelligence (2018)

96. Kim, Y.: Convolutional neural networks for sentence classification. In: Proceedings of the 2014 Conference on Empirical Methods in Natural Language Processing (EMNLP), pp. 1746–1751. Association for Computational Linguistics, Stroudsburg, PA, USA (2014). https://doi.org/10.3115/v1/D14-1181

97. Kingma, D., Ba, J.: Adam: A method for stochastic optimization. CoRR **abs/1412.6980** (2014)

98. Koehn, P.: Europarl : A parallel corpus for statistical machine translation. MT Summit **11**, 79–86 (2005). https://doi.org/10.3115/1626355.1626380

99. Lacroix, T., Usunier, N., Obozinski, G.: Canonical tensor decomposition for knowledge base completion. arXiv preprint arXiv:1806.07297 (2018)

100. LeCun, Y., Bottou, L., Bengio, Y., Haffner, P.: Gradient-based learning applied to document recognition. Proceedings of the IEEE **86**(11), 2278–2324 (1998)

101. Lenat, D.B.: Cyc: A large-scale investment in knowledge infrastructure. Commun. ACM **38**, 32–38 (1995)

102. Levy, O., Goldberg, Y.: Linguistic regularities in sparse and explicit word representations. In: Proceedings of the Eighteenth Conference on Computational Natural Language Learning, pp. 171–180. Association for Computational Linguistics, Ann Arbor, Michigan (2014). https://doi.org/10.3115/v1/W14-1618. URL https://www.aclweb.org/anthology/W14-1618

103. Levy, O., Goldberg, Y., Dagan, I.: Improving distributional similarity with lessons learned from word embeddings. Transactions of the Association for Computational Linguistics 3(0), 211–225 (2015)

104. Lin, T., Maire, M., Belongie, S., Bourdev, L., Girshick, R., Hays, J., Perona, P., Ramanan, D., Dollár, P., Zitnick, C.: Microsoft coco: Common objects in context. In: ECCV (2014)

105. Lin, Y., Liu, Z., Luan, H., Sun, M., Rao, S., Liu, S.: Modeling relation paths for representation learning of knowledge bases. arXiv preprint arXiv:1506.00379 (2015)

106. Lin, Y., Liu, Z., Sun, M., Liu, Y., Zhu, X.: Learning entity and relation embeddings for knowledge graph completion. In: Twenty-ninth AAAI conference on artificial intelligence (2015)

107. Liu, P.J., Saleh, M., Pot, E., Goodrich, B., Sepassi, R., Kaiser, L., Shazeer, N.: Generating wikipedia by summarizing long sequences. CoRR **abs/1801.10198** (2018). URL http://arxiv.org/abs/1801.10198

108. Liu, V., Curran, J.R.: Web text corpus for natural language processing. In: 11th Conference of the European Chapter of the Association for Computational Linguistics (2006). URL https://www.aclweb.org/anthology/E06-1030

109. Loureiro, D., Jorge, A.: Language modelling makes sense: Propagating representations through WordNet for full-coverage word sense disambiguation. In: Proceedings of the 57th Annual Meeting of the Association for Computational Linguistics, pp. 5682–5691. Association for Computational Linguistics, Florence, Italy (2019). https://doi.org/10.18653/v1/P19-1569. URL https://www.aclweb.org/anthology/P19-1569

110. Luo, Y., Wang, Q., Wang, B., Guo, L.: Context-dependent knowledge graph embedding. In: Proceedings of the 2015 Conference on Empirical Methods in Natural Language Processing, pp. 1656–1661. Association for Computational Linguistics, Lisbon, Portugal (2015). https://doi.org/10.18653/v1/D15-1191. URL https://www.aclweb.org/anthology/D15-1191

111. Luong, T., Socher, R., Manning, C.: Better word representations with recursive neural networks for morphology. In: Proceedings of the Seventeenth Conference on Computational Natural Language Learning, pp. 104–113. Association for Computational Linguistics, Sofia, Bulgaria (2013). URL https://www.aclweb.org/anthology/W13-3512

112. Mancini, M., Camacho-Collados, J., Iacobacci, I., Navigli, R.: Embedding words and senses together via joint knowledge-enhanced training. In: Proceedings of the 21st Conference on Computational Natural Language Learning (CoNLL 2017), pp. 100–111. Association for Computational Linguistics, Vancouver, Canada (2017). https://doi.org/10.18653/v1/K17-1012. URL https://www.aclweb.org/anthology/K17-1012

113. Manning, C.D., Raghavan, P., Schütze, H.: Introduction to Information Retrieval. Cambridge University Press, New York, NY, USA (2008)

114. Manning, C.D., Schütze, H.: Foundations of Statistical Natural Language Processing. MIT Press, Cambridge, MA, USA (1999)

115. Martin, L., Muller, B., Ortiz Suárez, P.J., Dupont, Y., Romary, L., Villemonte de la Clergerie, É., Seddah, D., Sagot, B.: CamemBERT: a Tasty French Language Model. arXiv e-prints arXiv:1911.03894 (2019)

116. Melamud, O., Goldberger, J., Dagan, I.: Context2vec: Learning generic context embedding with bidirectional LSTM. In: Proceedings of The 20th SIGNLL Conference on Computational Natural Language Learning, pp. 51–61. Association for Computational Linguistics, Berlin, Germany (2016). https://doi.org/10.18653/v1/K16-1006. URL https://www.aclweb.org/anthology/K16-1006

117. Mikolov, T., Chen, K., Corrado, G., Dean, J.: Efficient estimation of word representations in vector space. CoRR **abs/1301.3781** (2013). URL http://arxiv.org/abs/1301.3781

118. Mikolov, T., Grave, E., Bojanowski, P., Puhrsch, C., Joulin, A.: Advances in pre-training distributed word representations. In: Proceedings of the 11th Language Resources and Evaluation Conference. European Language Resource Association, Miyazaki, Japan (2018). URL https://www.aclweb.org/anthology/L18-1008

119. Mikolov, T., Karafiát, M., Burget, L., Černockỳ, J., Khudanpur, S.: Recurrent neural network based language model. In: Eleventh annual conference of the international speech communication association (2010)

120. Mikolov, T., Le, Q.V., Sutskever, I.: Exploiting Similarities among Languages for Machine Translation. Tech. rep., Google Inc. (2013). https://doi.org/10.1162/153244303322533223

121. Mikolov, T., Sutskever, I., Chen, K., Corrado, G., Dean, J.: Distributed representations of words and phrases and their compositionality. In: Advances in Neural Information Processing Systems, vol. cs.CL, pp. 3111–3119 (2013). https://doi.org/10.1162/jmlr.2003.3.4-5.951

122. Miller, G.A., Charles, W.G.: Contextual correlates of semantic similarity. Language and Cognitive Processes **6**(1), 1–28 (1991). https://doi.org/10.1080/01690969108406936

123. Navigli, R.: Word Sense Disambiguation: A Survey. ACM Comput. Surv **41**(10) (2009). https://doi.org/10.1145/1459352.1459355

124. Newell, A.: The knowledge level. Artificial Intelligence **18**(1), 87–127 (1982). https://doi.org/10.1016/0004-3702(82)90012-1

125. Nguyen, D.Q.: An overview of embedding models of entities and relationships for knowledge base completion. arXiv preprint arXiv:1703.08098 (2017)

126. Nguyen, D.Q., Nguyen, T.D., Nguyen, D.Q., Phung, D.: A novel embedding model for knowledge base completion based on convolutional neural network. arXiv preprint arXiv:1712.02121 (2017)
127. Nguyen, D.Q., Sirts, K., Qu, L., Johnson, M.: Neighborhood mixture model for knowledge base completion. arXiv preprint arXiv:1606.06461 (2016)
128. Nguyen, D.Q., Vu, T., Nguyen, T.D., Nguyen, D.Q., Phung, D.: A capsule network-based embedding model for knowledge graph completion and search personalization. arXiv preprint arXiv:1808.04122 (2018)
129. Nickel, M., Murphy, K., Tresp, V., Gabrilovich, E.: A review of relational machine learning for knowledge graphs. Proceedings of the IEEE **104**(1), 11–33 (2016)
130. Nickel, M., Rosasco, L., Poggio, T.: Holographic embeddings of knowledge graphs. In: Proceedings of the Thirtieth AAAI Conference on Artificial Intelligence, AAAI'16, pp. 1955–1961. AAAI Press (2016). URL http://dl.acm.org/citation.cfm?id=3016100.3016172
131. Nickel, M., Tresp, V., Kriegel, H.P.: A three-way model for collective learning on multi-relational data. In: ICML, vol. 11, pp. 809–816 (2011)
132. Olah, C., Mordvintsev, A., Schubert, L.: Feature visualization. Distill (2017). https://doi.org/10.23915/distill.00007. Https://distill.pub/2017/feature-visualization
133. Ott, M., Cardie, C., Hancock, J.T.: Negative deceptive opinion spam. In: Proceedings of the 2013 conference of the north american chapter of the association for computational linguistics: human language technologies, pp. 497–501 (2013)
134. Ott, M., Choi, Y., Cardie, C., Hancock, J.T.: Finding Deceptive Opinion Spam by Any Stretch of the Imagination. In: 49th ACL, pp. 309–319 (2011). https://doi.org/10.1145/2567948.2577293. URL https://arxiv.org/pdf/1107.4557.pdf
135. Pan, J.Z., Vetere, G., Gomez-Perez, J.M., Wu, H.: Exploiting Linked Data and Knowledge Graphs in Large Organisations, 1st edn. Springer International Publishing (2017)
136. Pan, S.J., Yang, Q.: A survey on transfer learning. IEEE Trans. on Knowl. and Data Eng. **22**(10), 1345–1359 (2010). URL http://dx.doi.org/10.1109/TKDE.2009.191
137. Parikh, A., Täckström, O., Das, D., Uszkoreit, J.: A decomposable attention model for natural language inference. In: Proceedings of the 2016 Conference on Empirical Methods in Natural Language Processing, pp. 2249–2255. Association for Computational Linguistics, Austin, Texas (2016). https://doi.org/10.18653/v1/D16-1244. URL https://www.aclweb.org/anthology/D16-1244
138. Pennington, J., Socher, R., Manning, C.: Glove: Global vectors for word representation. In: Proceedings of the 2014 Conference on Empirical Methods in Natural Language Processing (EMNLP), pp. 1532–1543. Association for Computational Linguistics, Doha, Qatar (2014). https://doi.org/10.3115/v1/D14-1162. URL https://www.aclweb.org/anthology/D14-1162
139. Peters, M., Neumann, M., Iyyer, M., Gardner, M., Clark, C., Lee, K., Zettlemoyer, L.: Deep contextualized word representations. In: Proceedings of the 2018 Conference of the North American Chapter of the Association for Computational Linguistics: Human Language Technologies, Volume 1 (Long Papers), pp. 2227–2237. Association for Computational Linguistics, New Orleans, Louisiana (2018). https://doi.org/10.18653/v1/N18-1202. URL https://www.aclweb.org/anthology/N18-1202
140. Peters, M.E., Neumann, M., IV, R.L.L., Schwartz, R., Joshi, V., Singh, S., Smith, N.A.: Knowledge enhanced contextual word representations (2019)
141. Petroni, F., Rocktäschel, T., Riedel, S., Lewis, P., Bakhtin, A., Wu, Y., Miller, A.: Language models as knowledge bases? In: Proceedings of the 2019 Conference on Empirical Methods in Natural Language Processing and the 9th International Joint Conference on Natural Language Processing (EMNLP-IJCNLP), pp. 2463–2473. Association for Computational Linguistics, Hong Kong, China (2019). https://doi.org/10.18653/v1/D19-1250. URL https://www.aclweb.org/anthology/D19-1250
142. Pinter, Y., Eisenstein, J.: Predicting semantic relations using global graph properties. In: Proceedings of the 2018 Conference on Empirical Methods in Natural Language Processing, pp. 1741–1751. Association for Computational Linguistics, Brussels, Belgium (2018). https://doi.org/10.18653/v1/D18-1201. URL https://www.aclweb.org/anthology/D18-1201

143. Pires, T., Schlinger, E., Garrette, D.: How multilingual is multilingual bert? In: ACL (2019)
144. Polignano, M., Basile, P., de Gemmis, M., Semeraro, G., Basile, V.: AlBERTo: Italian BERT language understanding model for NLP challenging tasks based on tweets (2019)
145. Porter, S., Ten Brinke, L.: The truth about lies: What works in detecting high-stakes deception? Legal and Criminological Psychology **15**(1), 57–75 (2010). https://doi.org/10.1348/135532509X433151
146. Radford, A., Narasimhan, K., Salimans, T., Sutskever, I.: Improving language understanding by generative pre-training. URL https://s3-us-west-2.amazonaws.com/openai-assets/research-covers/languageunsupervised/languageunderstandingpaper.pdf (2018)
147. Radford, A., Wu, J., Child, R., Luan, D., Amodei, D., Sutskever, I.: Language models are unsupervised multitask learners. OpenAI Blog **1**(8) (2019)
148. Radinsky, K., Agichtein, E., Gabrilovich, E., Markovitch, S.: A word at a time. In: Proceedings of the 20th international conference on World wide web - WWW '11, p. 337. ACM Press, New York, New York, USA (2011). https://doi.org/10.1145/1963405.1963455
149. Raffel, C., Shazeer, N., Roberts, A., Lee, K., Narang, S., Matena, M., Zhou, Y., Li, W., Liu, P.J.: Exploring the limits of transfer learning with a unified text-to-text transformer (2019)
150. Resnik, P.: Using information content to evaluate semantic similarity in a taxonomy. In: Proceedings of the 14th International Joint Conference on Artificial Intelligence - Volume 1, IJCAI'95, pp. 448–453. Morgan Kaufmann Publishers Inc., San Francisco, CA, USA (1995). URL http://dl.acm.org/citation.cfm?id=1625855.1625914
151. Riedel, S., Yao, L., McCallum, A., Marlin, B.M.: Relation extraction with matrix factorization and universal schemas. In: HLT-NAACL (2013)
152. Ristoski, P., Paulheim, H.: RDF2Vec: RDF graph embeddings for data mining. In: International Semantic Web Conference, vol. 9981 LNCS, pp. 498–514 (2016)
153. Rothe, S., Schütze, H.: AutoExtend: Extending word embeddings to embeddings for synsets and lexemes. In: Proceedings of the 53rd Annual Meeting of the Association for Computational Linguistics and the 7th International Joint Conference on Natural Language Processing (Volume 1: Long Papers), pp. 1793–1803. Association for Computational Linguistics, Beijing, China (2015). https://doi.org/10.3115/v1/P15-1173. URL https://www.aclweb.org/anthology/P15-1173
154. Rubenstein, H., Goodenough, J.B.: Contextual correlates of synonymy. Commun. ACM **8**(10), 627–633 (1965). https://doi.org/10.1145/365628.365657
155. dos Santos, C., Gatti, M.: Deep convolutional neural networks for sentiment analysis of short texts. In: Proceedings of COLING 2014, the 25th International Conference on Computational Linguistics: Technical Papers, pp. 69–78 (2014)
156. Sap, M., Bras, R.L., Allaway, E., Bhagavatula, C., Lourie, N., Rashkin, H., Roof, B., Smith, N.A., Choi, Y.: ATOMIC: an atlas of machine commonsense for if-then reasoning. In: The Thirty-Third AAAI Conference on Artificial Intelligence, AAAI 2019, The Thirty-First Innovative Applications of Artificial Intelligence Conference, IAAI 2019, The Ninth AAAI Symposium on Educational Advances in Artificial Intelligence, EAAI 2019, Honolulu, Hawaii, USA, January 27 - February 1, 2019., pp. 3027–3035 (2019). URL https://doi.org/10.1609/aaai.v33i01.33013027
157. Schlichtkrull, M.S., Kipf, T.N., Bloem, P., van den Berg, R., Titov, I., Welling, M.: Modeling relational data with graph convolutional networks (2018). URL https://doi.org/10.1007/978-3-319-93417-4_38
158. Schnabel, T., Labutov, I., Mimno, D., Joachims, T.: Evaluation methods for unsupervised word embeddings. In: Proceedings of the 2015 Conference on Empirical Methods in Natural Language Processing, pp. 298–307. Association for Computational Linguistics, Lisbon, Portugal (2015). https://doi.org/10.18653/v1/D15-1036. URL https://www.aclweb.org/anthology/D15-1036
159. Schuster, M., Nakajima, K.: Japanese and Korean voice search. In: 2012 IEEE International Conference on Acoustics, Speech and Signal Processing (ICASSP), pp. 5149–5152. IEEE (2012)

160. Sennrich, R., Haddow, B., Birch, A.: Neural machine translation of rare words with subword units. arXiv preprint arXiv:1508.07909 (2015)
161. Seo, M., Hajishirzi, H., Farhadi, A., Etzioni, O.: Diagram understanding in geometry questions. In: AAAI (2014)
162. Seo, M.J., Kembhavi, A., Farhadi, A., Hajishirzi, H.: Bidirectional attention flow for machine comprehension. In: 5th International Conference on Learning Representations, ICLR 2017, Toulon, France, April 24-26, 2017, Conference Track Proceedings. OpenReview.net (2017). URL https://openreview.net/forum?id=HJ0UKP9ge
163. Shang, C., Tang, Y., Huang, J., Bi, J., He, X., Zhou, B.: End-to-end structure-aware convolutional networks for knowledge base completion. In: Proceedings of the AAAI Conference on Artificial Intelligence, vol. 33, pp. 3060–3067 (2019)
164. Shazeer, N., Doherty, R., Evans, C., Waterson, C.: Swivel: Improving embeddings by noticing what's missing. CoRR abs/1602.02215 (2016). URL http://arxiv.org/abs/1602.02215
165. Shen, Y., Huang, P.S., Chang, M.W., Gao, J.: Link prediction using embedded knowledge graphs. arXiv preprint arXiv:1611.04642 (2016)
166. Sheth, A., Perera, S., Wijeratne, S., Thirunarayan, K.: Knowledge will propel machine understanding of content: extrapolating from current examples. In: Proceedings of the International Conference on Web Intelligence, WI '17, pp. 1–9. ACM, New York, NY, USA (2017). https://doi.org/10.1145/3106426.3109448
167. Shi, B., Weninger, T.: Proje: Embedding projection for knowledge graph completion. Proceedings of the 32nd AAAI Conference on Artificial Intelligence (2018). URL http://par.nsf.gov/biblio/10054090
168. Shoham, Y.: Why knowledge representation matters. Commun. ACM 59(1), 47–49 (2015). https://doi.org/10.1145/2803170
169. Shortliffe, E.H.: Mycin: A knowledge-based computer program applied to infectious diseases. In: Proceedings of the Annual Symposium on Computer Application in Medical Care, pp. 66–74. PubMed Central (1977)
170. Simonyan, K., Zisserman, A.: Very deep convolutional networks for large-scale image recognition. CoRR abs/1409.1556 (2014)
171. Socher, R., Chen, D., Manning, C.D., Ng, A.: Reasoning with neural tensor networks for knowledge base completion. In: Advances in neural information processing systems, pp. 926–934 (2013)
172. Socher, R., Ganjoo, M., Sridhar, H., Bastani, O., Manning, C., Ng, A.: Zero-shot learning through cross-modal transfer. In: NIPS (2013)
173. Speer, R., Chin, J., Havasi, C.: Conceptnet 5.5: An open multilingual graph of general knowledge. In: Proceedings of the Thirty-First AAAI Conference on Artificial Intelligence, AAAI'17, pp. 4444–4451. AAAI Press (2017). URL http://dl.acm.org/citation.cfm?id=3298023.3298212
174. Sun, Z., Deng, Z.H., Nie, J.Y., Tang, J.: Rotate: Knowledge graph embedding by relational rotation in complex space. arXiv preprint arXiv:1902.10197 (2019)
175. Sutskever, I., Vinyals, O., Le, Q.V.: Sequence to sequence learning with neural networks. In: Proceedings of the 28th Conference on Neural Information Processing Systems (2014)
176. Szegedy, C., Vanhoucke, V., Ioffe, S., Shlens, J., Wojna, Z.: Rethinking the inception architecture for computer vision. 2016 IEEE Conference on Computer Vision and Pattern Recognition (CVPR) pp. 2818–2826 (2015)
177. Tchechmedjiev, A., Fafalios, P., Boland, K., Gasquet, M., Zloch, M., Zapilko, B., Dietze, S., Todorov, K.: Claimskg: A knowledge graph of fact-checked claims. In: International Semantic Web Conference, pp. 309–324. Springer (2019)
178. Tenney, I., Das, D., Pavlick, E.: BERT rediscovers the classical NLP pipeline. In: Proceedings of the 57th Annual Meeting of the Association for Computational Linguistics, pp. 4593–4601. Association for Computational Linguistics, Florence, Italy (2019). https://doi.org/10.18653/v1/P19-1452. URL https://www.aclweb.org/anthology/P19-1452

179. Thoma, S., Rettinger, A., Both, F.: Towards holistic concept representations: Embedding relational knowledge, visual attributes, and distributional word semantics. In: International Semantic Web Conference (2017)
180. Toutanova, K., Chen, D., Pantel, P., Poon, H., Choudhury, P., Gamon, M.: Representing text for joint embedding of text and knowledge bases pp. 1499–1509 (2015). https://doi.org/10. 18653/v1/D15-1174. URL https://www.aclweb.org/anthology/D15-1174
181. Trouillon, T.P., Bouchard, G.M.: Complex embeddings for simple link prediction (2017). US Patent App. 15/156,849
182. Vaswani, A., Shazeer, N., Parmar, N., Uszkoreit, J., Jones, L., Gomez, A.N., Kaiser, L., Polosukhin, I.: Attention is all you need. CoRR **abs/1706.03762** (2017). URL http://arxiv. org/abs/1706.03762
183. Vrandecic, D., Krötzsch, M.: Wikidata: a free collaborative knowledgebase. Commun. ACM **57**, 78–85 (2014)
184. de Vries, W., van Cranenburgh, A., Bisazza, A., Caselli, T., van Noord, G., Nissim, M.: Bertje: A dutch bert model (2019)
185. Wang, A., Pruksachatkun, Y., Nangia, N., Singh, A., Michael, J., Hill, F., Levy, O., Bowman, S.R.: Superglue: A stickier benchmark for general-purpose language understanding systems. arXiv preprint arXiv:1905.00537 (2019)
186. Wang, A., Singh, A., Michael, J., Hill, F., Levy, O., Bowman, S.R.: Glue: A multi-task benchmark and analysis platform for natural language understanding. arXiv preprint arXiv:1804.07461 (2018)
187. Wang, L., Li, Y., Huang, J., Lazebnik, S.: Learning two-branch neural networks for image-text matching tasks. IEEE Transactions on Pattern Analysis and Machine Intelligence **41**, 394–407 (2018)
188. Wang, Q., Mao, Z., Wang, B., Guo, L.: Knowledge graph embedding: A survey of approaches and applications. IEEE Transactions on Knowledge and Data Engineering **29**(12), 2724–2743 (2017)
189. Wang, S., Manning, C.D.: Baselines and bigrams: Simple, good sentiment and topic classification. In: Proceedings of the 50th Annual Meeting of the Association for Computational Linguistics: Short Papers - Volume 2, ACL '12, pp. 90–94. Association for Computational Linguistics, Stroudsburg, PA, USA (2012). URL http://dl.acm.org/citation.cfm?id=2390665. 2390688
190. Wang, Z., Zhang, J., Feng, J., Chen, Z.: Knowledge graph embedding by translating on hyperplanes. In: Twenty-Eighth AAAI conference on artificial intelligence (2014)
191. Weston, J., Bordes, A., Yakhnenko, O., Usunier, N.: Connecting language and knowledge bases with embedding models for relation extraction. CoRR **abs/1307.7973** (2013). URL http://dblp.uni-trier.de/db/journals/corr/corr1307.html#WestonBYU13
192. Weston, J., Chopra, S., Bordes, A.: Memory networks. CoRR **abs/1410.3916** (2014)
193. Yang, B., Yih, W.t., He, X., Gao, J., Deng, L.: Embedding entities and relations for learning and inference in knowledge bases. arXiv preprint arXiv:1412.6575 (2014)
194. Yang, D., Powers, D.M.W.: Verb similarity on the taxonomy of WordNet. 3rd International WordNet Conference pp. 121–128 (2006)
195. Yang, Z., Dai, Z., Yang, Y., Carbonell, J., Salakhutdinov, R., Le, Q.V.: XLNet: Generalized Autoregressive Pretraining for Language Understanding (2019). URL http://arxiv.org/abs/ 1906.08237
196. Yao, L., Mao, C., Luo, Y.: Kg-bert: Bert for knowledge graph completion (2019)
197. Yin, W., Kann, K., Yu, M., Schütze, H.: Comparative study of CNN and RNN for natural language processing (2017)
198. Young, P., Lai, A., Hodosh, M., Hockenmaier, J.: From image descriptions to visual denotations: New similarity metrics for semantic inference over event descriptions. Trans. of the Assoc. for Computational Linguistics **2**, 67–78 (2014)
199. Zhang, W., Paudel, B., Zhang, W., Bernstein, A., Chen, H.: Interaction embeddings for prediction and explanation in knowledge graphs. In: Proceedings of the Twelfth ACM International Conference on Web Search and Data Mining, pp. 96–104. ACM (2019)

200. Zhang, X., Zhao, J., LeCun, Y.: Character-level convolutional networks for text classification. In: Proceedings of the 28th International Conference on Neural Information Processing Systems - Volume 1, NIPS'15, pp. 649–657. MIT Press, Cambridge, MA, USA (2015). URL http://dl.acm.org/citation.cfm?id=2969239.2969312
201. Ziegler, C.N., Lausen, G.: Spreading activation models for trust propagation. In: Proceedings - 2004 IEEE International Conference on e-Technology, e-Commerce and e-Service, EEE 2004, pp. 83–97 (2004). https://doi.org/10.1109/EEE.2004.1287293
202. Ziemski, M., Junczys-Dowmunt, M., Pouliquen, B.: The united nations parallel corpus v1.0. In: N.C.C. Chair), K. Choukri, T. Declerck, S. Goggi, M. Grobelnik, B. Maegaard, J. Mariani, H. Mazo, A. Moreno, J. Odijk, S. Piperidis (eds.) Proceedings of the Tenth International Conference on Language Resources and Evaluation (LREC 2016). European Language Resources Association (ELRA), Paris, France (2016)

Printed in the United States
by Baker & Taylor Publisher Services